Lectures
in
Systematic Theology

LECTURES
IN
SYSTEMATIC THEOLOGY

by
HENRY CLARENCE THIESSEN

Revised by
VERNON D. DOERKSEN

WILLIAM B. EERDMANS PUBLISHING COMPANY
Grand Rapids, Michigan

ISBN 0-8028-3529-5

Library of Congress Cataloging in Publication Data

Thiessen, Henry Clarence.
  Lectures in systematic theology.

  Bibliography: p. 405.
  Includes indexes.
  1. Theology, Doctrinal.   I.   Doerksen, Vernon D.
II.   Title.
BT75.T39   1979   230   79-17723

Contents

PART VI. SOTERIOLOGY

PART VII. ECCLESIOLOGY

PART VIII. ESCHATOLOGY

Preface to the First Edition

Those who are acquainted with Dr. H. C. Thiessen's *An Outline of Lectures in Systematic Theology* in syllabus form will welcome the appearance of the more complete work in book form. Dr. Thiessen was called from his labors while engaged upon the task of writing the book. The actual completion and editing of it since his departure has fallen to my lot at the request of Mrs. H. C. Thiessen.

The first one-third of the book is exactly as he wrote it. Those familiar with the syllabus will notice that it has been completely rewritten and differently arranged. No doubt he would have done the same with the rest of the book had he lived to complete it. He had made a complete outline of chapters and the best I could do was to follow the outline and draw upon the material of the syllabus. Quotations from sources other than those in the syllabus are mostly those which he had written on the blank pages of his own desk copy of the syllabus. In the main I have used only those which in my judgment strengthened the argument, or helped to make the meaning clear. If they were merely interesting sidelights they were rejected.

Due credit has been given in the footnotes to all the authors quoted. I am deeply indebted to all of them, but especially to Augustus Hopkins Strong, *Systematic Theology* (Philadelphia: The Griffith and Rowland Press, 1906) for the section on Problems Connected with the Fall, which Dr. Thiessen followed quite closely in his syllabus.

Mainly it was my task to edit the material, check quotations, round out statements, write a paragraph or a short section here and there, arrange in chapters according to the outline in hand and thus prepare these pages for the publisher.

No work of man is ever perfect, but extreme care has been taken to make this work as accurate as possible. Every Scripture reference, unless it was as familiar as John 3:16, has been checked. But there was not sufficient time to check all the quotations from various authors. Since the syllabus had gone through three editions I took for granted that they were correct, for the instances chosen at random and examined proved to be so.

Deep gratitude is expressed to Dr. Milford L. Baker, president of the California Baptist Theological Seminary, and Dr. H. Vernon Ritter, librarian in the same seminary, for their kindness and cooperation. This seminary had

Preface to the Revised Edition

For thirty years Dr. Thiessen's *Lectures in Systematic Theology* has been used as a standard reference work in Bible institutes, colleges, and seminaries across the nation and throughout the English-speaking world. The broad acceptance enjoyed by this text has come in part, no doubt, because of Dr. Thiessen's careful and extensive use of Scripture and his dispensational approach to theology. In light of current theological trends and emphases and more recent studies in the various divisions of biblical doctrine, an update of his material seems warranted.

In order to retain his basic style and arrangement, the overall organization and the chapter divisions remain essentially intact, except for the addition of a chapter on the Holy Spirit and a section on personal eschatology. Several of the portions, such as those on inspiration, election, foreknowledge, creation, demons, imputation of sin, and pretribulationalism, have been rather extensively revised. The remaining sections have been carefully reviewed with appropriate changes, deletions, and or additions. Citations from many of the older authorities have been deleted in favor of more recent source material, and a selected bibliography has been added. The reader will note the inclusion of many additional Scripture references. Whereas the original work employed the *American Standard Version*, this revision uses the *New American Standard Bible*.

A revision of this nature could not be done without the help of many parties. I gratefully acknowledge my indebtedness to my colleagues on the faculty of Talbot Theological Seminary for their encouragement and helpful suggestions; to my family for their prayerful support; to my wife, Josephine, and my mother, Mrs. Ruth Doerksen, for their labor of love in typing and proof-reading the manuscript in its various stages; to the Lockman Foundation for permission to quote extensively from the *New American Standard Bible*; and to my father, Rev. David Doerksen, for instilling in me from childhood a love for biblical theology.

May our Heavenly Father be pleased to use this book for His glory.

VERNON D. DOERKSEN

La Mirada, California, 1979

acquired Dr. Thiessen's library upon his decease, but with Christian courtesy and generosity they allowed us to take these or any other books out of their library and use them as long as we needed them. Dr. Ritter personally took time to locate a great many of the books for us so that full literary credit could be given for the quotations used. Thanks are also extended to Dr. Richard W. Cramer, chairman of the Division of Biblical Studies and Philosophy at Westmont College, Santa Barbara, Calif., who prepared the Index of Subjects, Index of Authors and Index of Greek Words; to Miss Goldie Wiens, teacher at Shafter, Calif., for the preparation of the Index of Scriptures. My sister, Miss Kate I. Thiessen, a high school teacher in Oklahoma, typed the entire manuscript.

I quote from Dr. Thiessen's *Preface* in the mimeographed syllabus as follows:

"It is hoped that the present edition will set forth the truth more clearly and logically, and that the Triune God, Father, Son, and Holy Spirit will be glorified through its perusal."

As in previous editions, the *American Standard Version* of the Bible has been used throughout, as the better translation of the Hebrew and Greek idiom, except as otherwise noted.

The book is sent forth with the prayer that it will be blessed of God and useful in the training of men for the effective ministry of the Gospel.

JOHN CALDWELL THIESSEN

Detroit, Michigan, 1949

CHAPTER I

The Nature and Necessity of Theology

For generations theology has been considered the queen of the sciences and systematic theology the crown of the queen. Theology itself is the science of God and his works and systematic theology is the systematizing of the findings of that science. Some deny that theology is a science, doubting whether we can reach any conclusions in this field that can be regarded as certain and final. Influenced by the current philosophy of pragmatism, the modern theologian begins with the dictum that in theology, as in all other fields of inquiry, belief must never go beyond the mere setting up of a working hypothesis; it must never be expressed as something that is regarded as fixed and final. Having rejected the Bible as the infallible and inerrant Word of God and having accepted the view that everything is in a flux, the liberal theologian holds that it is unsafe to formulate any fixed views about God and theological truth. Evangelical scholarship, however, believes that there are some things in the world that are stable and fixed. It points to the regularity of the heavenly bodies, of the laws of nature, and of the science of mathematics as the basic proofs for this belief. Science may question the regularity even of the laws of nature, but the experienced believer in God sees in these apparent irregularities the intervention of God and the manifestation of his miraculous power. He maintains that while the apprehension of the divine revelation is progressive, the revelation itself is as stable as the righteousness and truth of God themselves. He, therefore, believes in the possibility of theology and of systematic theology, and he regards them with the same favor as did the ancients. Even the modern student who does not formulate his theological beliefs has fairly definite views with regard to the major questions in the field. The reason for this is found in his own mental and moral constitution. But what is the nature of theology?

I. THE NATURE OF THEOLOGY

The term "theology" is today used in a narrow and also in a broad sense. It is derived from two Greek words, *theos* and *logos*, the former meaning "God" and the latter "word," "discourse," and "doctrine." In the narrow sense,

1

therefore, theology may be defined as the doctrine of God. But in the broad and more usual sense, the term has come to mean all Christian doctrines, not only the specific doctrine of God, but also all the doctrines that deal with the relations God sustains to the universe. In this broad sense, we may define theology as the science of God and his relations to the universe. For the sake of a further clarification of the idea, the differences between theology and ethics, theology and religion, and theology and philosophy must be noted.

A. THEOLOGY AND ETHICS

Psychology deals with behavior; ethics, with conduct. This is true of both philosophical and Christian ethics. Psychology inquires after the how and why of behavior; ethics, after the moral quality of conduct. Ethics may be either descriptive or practical. Descriptive ethics examines human conduct in the light of some standard of right or wrong; practical ethics lays the foundation in descriptive ethics, but more particularly stresses motives for seeking to live up to such a standard. In any case, philosophical ethics is developed on a purely naturalistic basis and has no doctrine of sin, no Savior, redemption, regeneration, and divine indwelling and enabling for the attainment of its goals.

Christian ethics differs greatly from philosophical ethics. It is more comprehensive in that while philosophical ethics is confined to duties between man and man, Christian ethics also includes duties toward God. Furthermore, it is different in its motivation. In philosophical ethics the motive is either that of hedonism, utilitarianism, perfectionism, or a combination of all these, as in humanism; but in Christian ethics the motive is that of affection for and willing submission to God. Even so, theology contains vastly more than belongs to Christian ethics. It includes also the doctrines of the trinity, creation, providence, the fall, the incarnation, redemption, and eschatology. None of these belongs properly to ethics.

B. THEOLOGY AND RELIGION

The term "religion" is used in the greatest number of ways imaginable. It can be used in a very general sense of any adoration or service of God, a god, or gods. It can be expressed in certain forms of worship to God or a god. It can be devotion or faithfulness to anyone or anything. More specifically, it can refer to some particular system of faith and worship. To be religious is to be aware, or conscious, of the existence of a supreme being and to live in light of the demands of that supreme being. The Christian religion is restricted to biblical Christianity, the true religion which is set forth in the Holy Scriptures. It is the awareness of the true God and our responsibility to him. But what is the relation between theology and religion?

The relation between theology and religion is that of effects, in different spheres, produced by the same causes. In the realm of systematic thought, the facts concerning God and his relations to the universe lead to theology; in the sphere of individual and collective life, they lead to religion. In other words, in theology a man organizes his thoughts concerning God and the universe, and in religion he expresses in attitudes and actions the effects these thoughts have produced in him.

C. THEOLOGY AND PHILOSOPHY

Theology and philosophy have practically the same objectives, but they differ very much in their approach to and method of attaining the objectives. They both seek for a comprehensive world and life view. But while theology begins with the belief in the existence of God and the idea that he is the cause of all things, excepting sin, philosophy begins with some other given thing and the idea that it is sufficient to explain the existence of all other things. For some ancients this thing was water, air, or fire; for others it has been mind or ideas; for still others it has been nature, personality, life, or some other thing. Theology does not merely begin with the belief in the existence of God, but also holds that he has graciously revealed himself. Philosophy denies both these ideas. From the idea of God and the study of the divine revelation, the theologian develops his world and life view; from the thing given and the supposed powers inherent in it, the philosopher develops his world and life view.

It is thus clear that theology rests upon a solid objective basis, while philosophy rests merely upon the assumptions and speculations of the philosopher. Yet philosophy has definite value for the theologian. In the first place, it furnishes him some support for the Christian position. On the basis of conscience, a philosopher can argue for the existence of God, freedom, and immortality. Further, it reveals to him the inadequacy of reason to solve the basic questions of existence. While the theologian appreciates all real help that he gets from philosophy, he quickly discovers that philosophy has no real theory of origins and no doctrines of providence, sin, salvation, or a final consummation. Since all these conceptions are vital to an adequate world and life view, the theologian is irresistibly driven to God and the revelation he has made of himself for a treatment of these doctrines. And, finally, it acquaints him with the views of the educated unbeliever. Philosophy is to the unbeliever what the Christian faith is to the believer, and the unbeliever adheres to it with the same tenacity with which the believer adheres to his faith. To know a man's philosophy is, therefore, to get possession of the key to understanding him and also to dealing with him (Acts 14:17; 17:22-31). But the Christian must recognize that philosophy will never bring a person to Christ. Paul writes, "The world through its wisdom did not come to know God" (1 Cor. 1:21), and again, "We do speak wisdom among those who are mature; a wisdom, however, not of this age, nor of the rulers of this age, who are passing away; but we speak God's wisdom . . . the wisdom which none of the rulers of this age understood; for if they had understood it, they would not have crucified the Lord of glory" (1 Cor. 2:6–8).

II. THE NECESSITY OF THEOLOGY

Even those who refuse to formulate their theological beliefs have fairly definite views with regard to the major subjects of theology. That is, some sort of theological belief is necessary. This is due to the nature of the human intellect and the practical concerns of life. Let us, therefore, briefly consider the reasons for this necessity, thinking particularly of its necessity for the Christian.

A. The Organizing Instinct of the Intellect

The human intellect is not content with a mere accumulation of facts; it invariably seeks for a unification and systematization of its knowledge. The mind is not satisfied simply to discover certain facts about God, man, and the universe; it wants to know the relations between these persons and things and to organize its discoveries into a system. The mind is not content with fragmentary knowledge; it wants to organize this knowledge and draw inferences and conclusions.

B. The Pervasive Character of the Unbelief of This Age

The dangers that threaten the church come not from science, but from philosophy. This age, for the most part, is saturated with atheism, agnosticism, pantheism, and unitarianism. All levels of life are permeated with unbelief, be they political, commercial, educational, or social. It is necessary for the Christian to be always "ready to make a defense to every one who asks" him, "to give an account for the hope" which he has (1 Pet. 3:15). Unless the child of God is firmly grounded, he will be as a child, "tossed here and there by waves, and carried about by every wind of doctrine" (Eph. 4:14). We need to have an organized system of thought so as to make a consistent defense of our faith. If we do not, we will be at the mercy of those who have such a system. The Bible gives a consistent world-view and provides answers to the great problems which have faced the philosophers for generations.

C. THE CHARACTER OF SCRIPTURE

The Bible is to the theologian what nature is to the scientist, a body of unorganized or only partly organized facts. God has not seen fit to write the Bible in the form of a systematic theology; it remains for us, therefore, to gather together the scattered facts and to build them up into a logical system. There are, indeed, some doctrines that are treated with a certain fullness in a single context; but there are none that are exhaustively treated in it. Take as an example of a somewhat full treatment of a doctrine or theme in one passage: the meaning of the death of Christ in the five offerings of Lev. 1–7; the qualities of the Word of God in Ps. 19, 119; the teachings of the omnipresence and omniscience of God in Ps. 139; the sufferings, death, and exaltation of the Servant of the Lord in Isa. 53; the restoration to Israel of its temple worship and land in Ezek. 40–48; the predictions concerning the times of the Gentiles in Dan. 2, 7; the return of Christ to this earth and the events immediately connected with it in Zech. 14; Rev. 19:11–22:6; the doctrine of the person of Christ in John 1:1–18; Phil. 2:5–11; Col. 1:15–20; Heb. 1:1–4; Jesus' teaching concerning the Holy Spirit in John 14–16; the status of Gentile Christians with reference to the law of Moses in Acts 15:1–29; Gal. 2:1–10; the doctrine of justification by faith in Rom. 1:17–5:21; the present and future status of Israel as a nation in Rom. 9–11; the question of the gifts of the Spirit in 1 Cor. 12, 14; the character of love in 1 Cor. 13; the doctrine of the resurrection in 1 Cor. 15; the nature of the church in Eph. 2, 3; the accomplishments of faith in Heb. 11; and the problem of suffering in the book of Job and in 1 Peter. Although there is a certain fullness of treatment of the themes in these passages, in none of them are the themes treated exhaustively. It is necessary, therefore, if we are to know all the facts on any given subject, that we gather together the scattered teachings and to construct them into a logical and harmonious system.

D. THE DEVELOPMENT OF AN INTELLIGENT CHRISTIAN CHARACTER

There are two erroneous views on this subject: (1) that there is little or no connection between a man's belief and his character, and (2) that theology has a deadening effect on the spiritual life. The liberal sometimes charges the orthodox believer with the absurdity of contending for the traditional beliefs of the church while living like an infidel. His creed, he insists, has no effect upon his character and conduct. The liberal, on the other hand, sets out to produce the good life without the orthodox creed. How do we reply to this charge? Merely intellectual acceptance of a set of doctrines is insufficient to produce spiritual results, and unfortunately, many people have nothing but an intellectual loyalty to the truth. But true belief, involving the intellect, the sensibilities, and the will, does have an effect on character and conduct.

Men act according to what they really believe, but not according to what they merely pretend to believe.

That theology has a deadening effect upon the spiritual life is true only if the subject is treated as mere theory. If it is related to life, theology will not have a deadening effect upon the spiritual life; it will, instead, be the guide to intelligent thinking about religious problems and a stimulus to holy living. How could correct and full views concerning God, man, sin, Christ, heaven, and hell do otherwise? Theology does not merely teach us what kind of life we should live, but it also inspires us to live such a life. It is worthy of note that often the great doctrinal truths are couched in a practical section of Scripture (cf. the incarnation, 2 Cor. 8:9; Phil. 2:5–11). Theology does not merely indicate the norms of conduct, but it also furnishes the motives for seeking to live up to these norms.

E. The Conditions for Effective Christian Service

Christians need to know Christian doctrine. Christ and his apostles were preachers of doctrine (Mark 4:2; Acts 2:42; 2 Tim. 3:10), and we are exhorted to preach doctrine (2 Tim. 4:2; Titus 1:9). Believers who are thoroughly indoctrinated with the Word of God will be able to be effective Christian workers and staunch defenders of the faith. Only as we know what we believe will we be able to withstand the attacks of the evil one and move forward in the victory provided for us in Christ.

CHAPTER II

The Possibility and Divisions of Theology

Having established the necessity of theology, we shall now present the proof for the possibility of theology and then indicate the usual divisions of theology.

I. THE POSSIBILITY OF THEOLOGY

The possibility of theology grows out of two things: the revelation of God and the endowments of man. The revelation of God takes on two forms: general and special. The endowments of man are of two kinds: mental and spiritual.

A. THE REVELATION OF GOD

Pascal spoke of God as a *Deus Absconditus* (a hidden God), but he also held that this hidden God has revealed himself, and therefore can be known. This is true. Certainly one could never know God if he had not revealed himself. But what is meant by "revelation"? Revelation is that act of God whereby he discloses himself or communicates truth to the mind, whereby he makes manifest to his creatures that which could not be known in any other way. The revelation may occur in a single, instantaneous act, or it may extend over a long period of time; and this communication of himself and his truth may be perceived by the human mind in varying degrees of fullness.

The formal arguments for the existence of God are set forth in the next chapter, but the discussion of the revelation of God is fundamental to the proofs for his existence. In order to prove the possibility of theology, revelation, both general and special, must be dealt with first.

1. The general revelation of God. This is found in nature, history, and conscience. It is communicated through the media of natural phenomena occurring in nature or the course of history; it is addressed to all intelligent creatures generally and is accessible to all; it has for its object the supplying of the natural need of the man and the persuasion of the soul to seek after the true God. Each of these three forms of revelation deserves a brief consideration. First, there is the revelation of God in nature. All naturalists who reject

7

the very idea of God and hold that nature is self-sufficient and self-explaining see no revelation of God in nature. Neither do the pantheists see any true revelation of God in nature. Some of them identify God with the "all," the "universum," or "nature"; others speak of him as the eternal power of energy effecting all the changes in the phenomenal world, and still others, as reason externalizing itself in the universe. Since they all hold the necessitarian view of the world, they find no revelation of an extra-mundane God in the universe. Nor do the present-day theologians of crisis allow for much of a revelation of God in nature. Barth, for example, holds that man has so completely lost the original image of God that without a supernatural act in each individual case, he can have no knowledge of God whatsoever. God must create the capacity for a revelation and also communicate it to man. Brunner holds that while man has lost the content of this image, he has not lost the form of it. He, therefore, believes that man perceives something of God in nature.

The deists, on the other hand, held that nature is the all-sufficient revelation of God. They said that it furnishes us with a few simple, unchanging truths about God, virtue, immortality, and future recompense in so clear a manner that no special revelation is necessary. But sceptical and critical philosophy has shown that there never was such a revelation in nature as the deists maintain. What the deists held were nothing but abstract truths derived, not from nature, but from the other religions, especially from Christianity. The deistic view has been largely superseded by the belief that we have no revelation of God in nature.

But men in general have always seen in nature a revelation of God. The more gifted of them have often expressed their convictions in language similar to that of psalmists, prophets, and apostles (Job 12:7-9; Ps. 8:1-3; 19:1f.; Isa. 40:12-14, 26; Acts 14:15-17; Rom. 1:19f.). The revelation of God in nature reveals that there is a God and that he has such attributes as power, glory, divinity, and goodness. But there are limitations of the revelation of God in nature. Although leaving man without excuse, this revelation alone is insufficient for salvation; it is intended, however, to incite man to search for a fuller revelation of God and his plan of salvation, and it constitutes a general call of God to man to turn to him. Further, this revelation is obscured by the problem of physical evil in the world.

In addition to the revelation of God in nature, there is also the revelation of God in history. The Psalmist makes the bold claim that the fortunes of kings and empires are in God's hands when he writes, "For not from the east, nor from the west, nor from the desert comes exaltation; but God is the Judge; He puts down one, and exalts another" (Ps. 75:6f.; cf. Rom. 13:1). And Paul declares that God has "made from one, every nation of mankind to live on all the face of the earth, having determined their appointed times, and the boundaries of their habitation, that they should seek God, if perhaps they might grope for Him and find Him" (Acts 17:26f.). In line with this declaration, the Christian system finds in history a revelation of the power and providence of God.

The Bible, in like manner, speaks of God's dealings with Egypt (Exod. 9:13–17; Jer. 46:14–26; Rom. 9:17), Assyria (Isa. 10:5–19; Ezek. 31:1–14; Nah. 3:1–7), Babylon (Jer. 50:1–16; 51:1–4), Medo-Persia (Isa. 44:24–45:7), Medo-Persia and Greece together (Dan. 8:1–21), the four kingdoms that followed the break-up of Alexander's kingdom (Dan. 11:5–35), and the Roman Empire (Dan. 7:7f., 23f.). Scripture shows throughout that "righteousness exalts a nation, but sin is a disgrace to any people" (Prov. 14:34). It shows also that although God may, for his own wise and holy purposes, allow a more wicked nation to triumph over a less wicked, he will in the end deal more severely with the more wicked than with the less wicked (Hab. 1:1–2:20).

More particularly, God has revealed himself in the history of Israel—in Israel's conception of God and in God's dealings with Israel. As for the former, it is surely remarkable that at a time when the whole world had sunk into the despondency of polytheism and pantheism, Abraham, Isaac, and Jacob, and their descendants should come to know God as a personal, infinite, holy, and self-revealing God, as the creator, preserver, and governor of the universe (Josh. 24:2). Not only so, but that they should conceive of man as originally created in the image of God, as having fallen from this high position and as having brought sin, condemnation, and death upon himself and his posterity. And even more than this, that they should apprehend God's purpose of redemption through sacrifice, of deliverance through the death of a Messiah, of salvation for all nations, and of a final reign in righteousness and peace. These are truly wonderful conceptions! They are, however, not due to Israel's genius for religion, but to the revelation of God to this people. God is represented as personally appearing to the patriarchs; as making himself and his will known in dreams, visions, and ecstasies; as communicating his message directly to them; and as revealing his holy character in the Mosaic legislation, the sacrificial system, and the service of the tabernacle and the temple.

God's revelation is also seen in the history of the nation. Although Israel was small, lived in an obscure little country, and had little commerce with the rest of the world, it was yet a spectacle to the whole world (Deut. 28:10). When God threatened to destroy the nation in the wilderness because of its grievous sin, Moses appealed to him to spare the people because of the way in which his honor would be involved in the destruction (Exod. 32:12; Deut. 9:28). When Israel obeyed God, they dispossessed seven nations greater than they (Deut. 7:1; 9:1; Josh. 6–12); but when they walked in their own ways, God gave them over to oppressing nations and to captivity in distant lands. When they repented and cried to God, he sent them a deliverer and gave them victory over their enemies. This cycle of sin, repentance, and deliverance is repeated many times in the Book of Judges. David triumphed over all his enemies because he walked in the ways of God (2 Sam. 7:9–11), and all the godly kings met with prosperity at home and triumph in war. But whenever the nation departed from God, it had drought, plagues of locusts, and reverses in war. It can, therefore, be truly said that in all of Israel's experiences God revealed himself, not only to the nation, but through the nation also to the whole world.

And finally, God is revealed in conscience. A fuller definition of conscience will be given in connection with the study of the moral constitution of man (Chapter XVI), but suffice it to say that conscience is not inventive, but rather discriminative and impulsive. It judges whether a proposed course of action or an attitude is in harmony with our moral standard or not and urges us to do that which is in harmony with it and to refrain from that which is contrary to it. It is the presence in man of this sense of right and wrong, of this discriminative and impulsive something, that constitutes the revelation of God. It is not self-imposed, as is evident from the fact that man would often rid himself of its deliverance if he could; it is the reflection of God in the soul. Just as the mirror and the smooth surface of the lake reflect the sun and reveal not only its existence, but also to some extent its nature, so conscience in man reveals both the existence of God and to some extent the nature of God. That is, it reveals to us not only that he is, but also that he sharply distinguishes between right and wrong (Rom. 2:14–16), that he always does that which is right, and that he also holds the rational creature responsible for always doing the right and abstaining from the wrong. It also implies that every transgression will be punished.

We conclude, therefore, that in conscience we have another revelation of God. Its prohibitions and commands, its decisions and urges, would not have any real authority over us if we did not feel that in conscience we somehow have reality, something in our nature that is yet above that nature. In other words, it reveals that there is an absolute law of right and wrong in the universe, and that there is a supreme lawgiver who embodies this law in his own person and conduct.

2. The special revelation of God.   By special revelation we mean those acts of God whereby he makes himself and his truth known at special times and to specific peoples. Although given at special times and to specific peoples, the revelation is not necessarily intended for that time and people only. Indeed, men are asked to proclaim God's doings and marvelous works among all the peoples of the earth (Ps. 105:1f.). The special revelation is, as it were, a treasure that is to be shared with the whole world (Matt. 28:19f.; Luke 2:10; Acts 1:8). It is given to man in various ways: in the form of miracles and prophecy, in the person and work of Jesus Christ, in the Scriptures, and in personal experience. Each of these will be considered briefly.

First, God revealed himself in miracles. A genuine miracle is an unusual event, accomplishing some useful work, and revealing the presence and power of God (Exod. 4:2–5; 1 Kings 18:24; John 5:36; 20:30f.; Acts 2:22). A spurious miracle, if not a mere deception, is a freak exhibition of power, wrought for show and ostentation, and inferior to the genuine miracle. It may also be effected by Satanic or demonic means (Exod. 7:11f., 22; Matt. 24:24; Acts 8:9–11; 13:6–8; 2 Thess. 2:9; Rev. 13:13). A genuine miracle is an unusual event in that it is not a mere product of so-called natural laws. In relation to nature, miracles are of two kinds: (1) those in which the natural laws are intensified or augmented, as in the deluge, in some of the plagues in Egypt, in the strength of Samson, etc., and (2) those in which all participation of nature is excluded, as in the budding of Aaron's rod, the bringing of water from the rock, the multiplication of the loaves and the fishes, the healing of the sick, the raising of the dead, etc. Often the timing itself is miraculous, as in the case of the separation of the Red Sea. A genuine miracle accomplishes some practical and benevolent work. The miracles of Christ were for the benefit of those to whom he ministered.

Genuine miracles are a special revelation of the presence and power of God. They prove his existence, presence, concern, and power. They are occasions on which God, as it were, comes forth from his hiding place and shows to man that he is a living God, that he is still on the throne of the universe, and that he is sufficient for all of man's problems. If a miracle does not create this conviction concerning God, then it is probably not a genuine miracle.

The naturalistic, pantheistic, and deistic systems all reject miracles *a priori*. The universe is for them a great self-sustaining machine. Miracles for them are impossible, for they are violations of the laws of nature, and further, they are incredible, for they contradict human experience. This position can be answered in the following manner. The first proposition assumes incorrectly that the laws of nature are self-sufficient and without outside influence, direction, and maintenance. But the truth is that they are not completely independent, for mere power cannot maintain itself nor operate purposefully; an infinite and intelligent power is needed to do that; and that power concurs in all the operations, both of matter and of mind, without doing violence to them. With the evil acts, however, God concurs only as they are natural acts, and not as they are evil. And if he does that in the usual operation of the laws of nature, why should we deem it a violation of them if in his unusual administrations he intensifies or augments them, counteracts them, or acts independently of them?

The second proposition that miracles are incredible because they contradict human experience, wrongly assumes that one must base all his beliefs on present human experience. Geologists tell of great glacial activities in the past and of the formation of seas and bays by these activities; we did not see this in our experience, but we do accept it. God's revelation of himself in nature, history, and conscience should lead us to expect miracles at various times. Miracles do not contradict human experience unless they contradict all human experience, that in the past as well as that in the present. This fact leaves the door wide open for well-supported evidence as to what did happen.

Furthermore, geologists frankly admit that life has not existed from eternity on this planet. They have no conclusive evidence as to how life has originated. But surely life cannot have come from inanimate substance; it can only have come from life. The introduction of life on this planet is, therefore, itself a testimony to the reality of miracles.

And now, positively, we would say that the proof of miracles rests on testimony. Belief is based upon what we consider true testimony. How little history we would know if we believed only the things which we personally observe and experience! The miracles of the Bible rest on valid testimony. It is not possible here to examine the evidence for all of them, nor is it necessary; if we can prove one of the most important of the biblical miracles, we shall have opened the way for the acceptance of the others also.

The physical resurrection of Christ is one of the best-attested facts of history.[1] Nearly all the accounts that tell of it were written within 20–30 years after the event; they assure us that Christ actually died and was buried; that though his followers did not expect him to rise, many of them saw him alive a few days after the crucifixion; that they were so sure of his resurrection that they boldly and publicly declared the fact in Jerusalem a month and a half after it occurred; that neither at that time nor at any other time when the subject is mentioned in apostolic times was it questioned; that no disproof of the fact has come down to us from any source; that the disciples sacrificed their social standing, earthly possessions, and even their lives for this testimony; that Paul does not argue for the resurrection of Christ, but uses it as proof that all believers will likewise arise; and that in the church, the New Testament, and the Lord's Day we have corroborative testimony of the historicity of this great event. And if the resurrection of Christ is a historical fact, then the way is opened for the acceptance of the other miracles also.

And finally, we believe that miracles still do happen. They are not contrary even to present-day experience. All true Christians testify to the fact that God answers prayer. Indeed, they are convinced that God has wrought miracles on their behalf, or on behalf of some of their friends. They are

---

[1]For a detailed study of the evidence see McDowell, *Evidence That Demands a Verdict*, pp. 185–273.

certain that the laws of nature alone cannot account for the things which they have seen with their own eyes and experienced in their own lives. No amount of opposition on the part of unbelievers will ever persuade them to think otherwise. More specifically, we have the ever-recurring miracle of regeneration. We cannot change the color of our skin, nor can the leopard change his spots, but the Lord can and does change the heart and remove the stains from the sinner. More will be said about this miracle under the revelation of God in Christian experience. Suffice it to say that answers to prayer and the experience of regeneration prove that miracles still do happen.

Further, God revealed himself in prophecy. Prophecy here means the foretelling of events, not through mere human insight or prescience, but through direct communication from God. But inasmuch as we cannot tell whether an utterance has been thus communicated to a man until the time when it is fulfilled (Deut. 18:21f.), the immediate value of prophecy as a proof of the presence and wisdom of God becomes dependent on the question whether the one who utters it is in living touch with God This can be determined only on the basis of his other teachings and godly life (Deut. 13:1-3; Isa. 8:20; Jer. 23:13f.). In the Old Testament "false prophets were featured as drunkards (Isa. 28:7), adulterous (Jer. 23:14), treacherous (Zeph. 3:4), liars (Micah 2:11), and opportunists (Micah 3:11)."[2] The true prophet would not have these characteristics.

As for the seeming fulfillment of prophecy, certain tests must be applied before it is accepted as genuine prophecy. We must determine, for instance, whether the prophecy was far enough from the event which it predicted to preclude the possibility of mere human insight or prescience. The Jews, in Jesus' day, could not discern the signs of the times, namely, that the Romans would come and destroy their city and nation, but many statesmen can foresee and forecast the future with much accuracy. Such a forecast could not, however, be called true prophecy. We must also examine the language of the prediction to note whether it is ambiguous and capable of more than one explanation. An utterance must be unambiguous before we can consider it a true prophecy. Isaiah's clear prophecy of Cyrus was given 150 years before he came to power (Isa. 43:28–45:7; cf. Ezra 1:1–4). Young writes, "Of himself Isaiah of course could not have known his name, but as a true prophet, inspired by the Holy Spirit, he could have spoken the name of Cyrus in this definite manner."[3]

The objections to prophecy may be met in much the same way as the objections to miracles. Christ is in a very real sense the light that lights every man (John 1:9). Because God is the creator and sustainer of the human mind, nothing in human consciousness is independent of God. God concurs with

---

[2]Tan, *The Interpretation of Prophecy*, p. 79.
[3]Young, *The Book of Isaiah*, III, p. 192.

the thoughts of man as he concurs with the laws of nature, without destroying either of them or becoming a partner in sin. And if he operates thus in the usual mental processes, we must not think it strange if he occasionally transcends them and operates independently of them. To this possibility of prophecy may be added direct proof of the fulfillment of prophecy. There is no need to prove the fulfillment of all biblical prophecy; some, indeed, is yet to be fulfilled, but we wish to point out one clear line of prophecy that has already been fulfilled. If this list of passages can be shown to be true prophecy, then no one can say that such direct communications from God are impossible and do not occur.

This line of prophecy is the numerous predictions concerning the first coming of Christ. To suggest that they are due to mere human prescience or to fortuitous coincidence, is to suggest a vastly greater improbability than that they are due to the direct revelation of God. Note some of the predictions concerning him that have been fulfilled. Christ was to be (1) born of a virgin (Isa. 7:14; Matt. 1:23), (2) of the seed of Abraham (Gen. 12:3; Gal. 3:8), (3) of the tribe of Judah (Gen. 49:10; Heb. 7:14), (4) of the line of David (Ps. 110:1; Rom. 1:3); (5) born at Bethlehem (Micah 5:2; Matt. 2:6), (6) anointed of the Spirit (Isa. 61:1f.; Luke 4:18f.). He was to (7) ride into Jerusalem on a donkey (Zech. 9:9; Matt. 21:5), (8) be betrayed by a friend (Ps. 41:9; John 13:18), (9) be sold for thirty pieces of silver (Zech. 11:12f.; Matt. 26:15; 27:9f.), (10) be forsaken by his disciples (Zech. 13:7; Matt. 26:31, 56), (11) be pierced in his hands and in his feet, but not have a bone broken (Ps. 22:16; 34:20; John 19:36; 20:20, 25). Men were (12) to give him gall and vinegar to drink (Ps. 69:21; Matt. 27:34), (13) to part his garments and cast lots for his vesture (Ps. 22:18; Matt. 27:35). He was to be (14) forsaken of God (Ps. 22:1; Matt. 27:46) and (15) buried with the rich (Isa. 53:9; Matt. 27:57–60). He was to (16) rise from the dead (Ps. 16:8–11), (17) ascend on high (Ps. 68:18; Eph. 4:8), and (18) sit at the Father's right hand (Ps. 110:1; Matt. 22:43–45). Have we not in these predictions which have been fulfilled a strong proof that God has revealed himself in prophecy? If he has done this in these predictions, we can expect he has done so in others as well.

In addition, God has revealed himself in his Son, Jesus Christ. The general revelation of God did not lead the Gentile world to any clear apprehension of the existence of God, the nature of God, or the will of God (Rom. 1:20–23); even philosophy did not give men a true conception of God. Paul writes, "In the wisdom of God the world through its wisdom did not come to know God" (1 Cor. 1:21). He further declared that the true wisdom "none of the rulers of this age has understood; for if they had understood it, they would not have crucified the Lord of glory" (1 Cor. 2:8). In spite of the general revelation of God in nature, history, and conscience, the Gentile world turned to mythology, polytheism, and idolatry. They "worshiped and served the creature rather than the Creator" (Rom. 1:25). A fuller revelation of God was greatly needed. This is not to say that natural revelation did not give to man some insight into the greatness and goodness of God, but man in his fallen state did not respond.

Neither did the additional special revelation of God in miracle, prophecy, and theophany lead Israel to a true knowledge of the nature and will of God. Israel believed in the existence of the true and living God, but they had imperfect and rather perverted notions of him. They regarded him chiefly as the great lawgiver and judge who insisted on scrupulous observances of the letter of the law, but cared little for the inner state of the heart and the practice of justice, mercy, and faith (Matt. 23:23–28); as the one who must be placated with sacrifices and persuaded with burnt offerings, but did not need an infinite sacrifice and had no real abhorrence of sin (Isa. 1:11–15; Matt. 9:13; 12:7; 15:7–9); as one who made physical descent from Abraham the one condition to his favor and blessing and looked upon the Gentiles as inferior to Abraham's descendants (Matt. 3:8–12; 12:17–21; Mark 11:17). The Old Testament is full of the love, mercy, and faithfulness of God, but Israel quickly turned to legalism. Israel, too, needed a fuller revelation of God. This we have in the person and mission of Jesus Christ.

Christ is the center of history and of revelation. The writer to the Hebrews says, "God, after He spoke long ago to the fathers in the prophets in many portions and in many ways, in these last days has spoken to us in His Son" (Heb. 1:1f.); and he represents him as "the radiance of His glory and the exact representation of His nature" (v. 3). Paul calls him "the image of the invisible God" (Col. 1:15), and says that "in Him all the fulness of Deity dwells in bodily form" (Col. 2:9). John says, "No man has seen God at any time; the only begotten God, who is in the bosom of the Father, He has explained Him" (John 1:18). And Jesus himself said, "No one knows the Son, except the Father; nor does anyone know the Father, except the Son, and anyone to whom the Son wills to reveal Him" (Matt. 11:27), and "He who has seen Me has seen the Father" (John 14:9). Consequently, the church has from the beginning seen in Christ the supreme revelation of the Father.

We have in Christ a threefold revelation of God: a revelation of his existence, his nature, and his will. He is the best proof for the existence of God, for he lived the life of God among men. He was not merely supremely conscious of the presence of the Father in his life and constantly in communion with him (John 8:18, 28f.; 11:41; 12:28), but showed by his claims (John 8:58; 17:5), sinless life (John 8:46), teaching (Matt. 7:28f.; John 6:46), works (John 5:36; 10:37f.; 15:24), offices and prerogatives (Matt. 9:2, 6; John 5:22, 25, 28), and relations to the Father (Matt. 28:19; John 10:38) that he himself was God. He revealed the absolute holiness of God (John 17:11, 25), the profound love of God (John 3:14–16), the Fatherhood of God, not, indeed, of all men, but of true believers (Matt. 6:32; 7:11; John 8:41–44; 16:27), and the spiritual nature of God (John 4:19–26). He revealed also the will of God that all should repent (Luke 13:1–5), believe on him (John 6:28f.), become perfect as the Father is perfect (Matt. 5:48), and that the believers should carry the gospel to all the world (Matt. 28:19f.).

The revelation of God in Christ is the most profound fact in history and deserves the most careful consideration. But since we shall devote several chapters to a study of the person and work of Christ, it will not be pursued further at this point.

There is also the revelation of God in the Scriptures. The true believer has always maintained that in the Bible we have a revelation of God, in fact, the clearest and only inerrant revelation. The Bible should, however, not be regarded as a revelation that is coordinate with the ones already mentioned, but rather as an embodiment of them. It records, for instance, the knowledge of God and his dealings with the creature which men of old gathered from nature, history, and conscience, and also from miracles, prophecy, the Lord Jesus Christ, and inner experience and divine instruction. The Christian, therefore, turns to the Scriptures as the supreme and only infallible source for the construction of his theology. But since we shall consider this subject more fully in the study of the nature of the Bible, we shall not go into it further at this point.

Finally, God is revealed in personal experience. Men of all ages have professed to have direct fellowship with God. They declare that they know him, not simply by means of nature, history, and conscience, not only by way of miracle and prophecy, but also by direct personal experience. Thus it was in Old Testament times. Enoch and Noah walked with God (Gen. 5:24; 6:9); God spoke to Noah (Gen. 6:13; 7:1; 9:1), to Abraham (Gen. 12:1), to Isaac (Gen. 26:24), to Jacob (Gen. 28:13; 35:1), to Moses (Exod. 3:4), to Joshua (Josh. 1:1), to Gideon (Judg. 6:25), to Samuel (1 Sam. 3:4), to David (1 Sam. 23:9–12), to Elijah (1 Kings 17:2–4), and to Isaiah (Isa. 6:8). Likewise in the New Testament God spoke to Jesus (Matt. 3:16f.; John 12:27f.), to Peter, James, and John (Mark 9:7), to Philip (Acts 8:29), to Paul (Acts 9:4–6), and to Ananias (Acts 9:10).

This experience of communion with God had a transforming power in the lives of those who had it (Ps. 34:5; cf. Exod. 34:29–35). They became more and more like the Lord with whom they had communion (Acts 6:15; cf. 2 Cor. 3:18). Fellowship with God brought with it also a revelation of the deeper truths of God. The revelation of God in personal experience is the main source from which inspiration drew its materials (John 16:13f.; 2 Tim. 3:16; 2 Pet. 1:21; cf. 1 Cor. 2:10–13). But in a fuller sense we may say that from the various revelations of God, still experienced by man, the Holy Spirit made a selection and had them infallibly recorded by divine inspiration in the Holy Scripture. Thus we have in the revelations of God, particularly in those recorded in the Bible, the materials for and possibility of theology.

B. The Endowments of Man

Assuming, then, that God has revealed himself, we ask next, how does man come into possession of this revelation? To this we reply that neither the outer nor the inner world would disclose anything of God without the unique endowments of man. The endowments of man are of two kinds: mental and spiritual.

1. His mental endowments. The man who rejects the idea of a revelation of and from God turns to reason for the solution of all his problems. During the course of history there have appeared three types of rationalism: atheistic, pantheistic, and theistic. Atheistic rationalism appeared first in the early Greek philosophers: Thales, Anaximander, Anaximenes, Empedocles, Heraclitus, Leucippus, and Democritus. Pantheistic rationalism is represented in Anaxagoras and the Stoics, and theistic rationalism appeared first in the form of English and German Deism in the eighteenth century. But while all forms of rationalism assign undue authority to reason in matters of religion, the true believer is apt to assign too little place to it. By "reason," we here mean not simply man's logical powers or his ability to reason, but his cognitive powers, his ability to perceive, compare, judge, and organize. God has endowed man with reason, and the thing that is wrong is not the use of it, but the abuse. It is not possible here to discuss all the abuses of reason, even among professed theists, but four proper uses of reason with which God has endowed man will be mentioned at this point. First, reason is the organ or capacity for knowing truth. Intuitive reason furnishes us with the primary ideas of space, time, cause, substance, design, right, and God, which are the conditions of all subsequent knowledge. Apprehensive reason takes in the facts presented to it for cognition. But it must be remembered that there is a difference between knowing and understanding a thing. We know that a plant grows, that the will controls the voluntary muscles, that Jesus Christ is the God-man, but we do not understand much about how these things can be.

In the second place, reason must judge the credibility of a representation. By "credible," we mean believable. There are things that are manifestly incredible, as a cow jumping over the moon or other such fairy tales, and it is the office of reason to declare whether a representation is credible. Nothing is incredible but the impossible. A thing may be strange, unaccountable, unintelligible, and yet perfectly credible. Unless one is willing to believe the incomprehensible, he can believe nothing. That is impossible which involves a contradiction; which is inconsistent with the known character of God; which is contradictory to the laws of belief with which God has endowed us; and which contradicts some other well-authenticated truth. Further, reason must judge the evidence of a representation. Since faith involves assent, and assent is conviction produced by evidence, it follows that faith without evidence is irrational or impossible. Thus reason must examine the credentials of communications professing to be, and of documents professing to record, such a revelation. It must ask, are the records genuine or spurious; are they pure or mixed; are they complete or incomplete? This evidence must be appropriate to the nature of the truth considered. Historical truth requires historical evidence; empirical truth, the testimony of experience; mathematical truth, mathematical evidence; moral truth, moral evidence; and the things of the Spirit, the demonstration of the Spirit (1 Cor. 2:14-16). In many cases, different kinds of evidence concur in the support of the same truth, as the belief in the deity of Christ. Furthermore, the evidence must not only be appropriate, but also adequate, that is, such as to command assent in every well-constituted mind to which it is presented.

Finally, reason must also organize the facts presented into a system. Just as truly as a pile of bricks does not make a house, so also do the simple facts of revelation not make a usable system. Reason must discover the integrating factor and assemble all the relevant facts around it, assigning to each part its proper place in a coordinated and subordinated system. This is the systematizing ability of reason, which is its instinctive urge. Thus it is clear that reason occupies a most important place in theology.

2. His spiritual endowments.   We reject the view of the philosophical mystic who holds that all men can, by rigorous discipline and contemplation, come into direct contact with ultimate reality, which is their name for God, apart from repentance and faith in Jesus Christ. This is a pagan belief and a part of an extreme pantheistic world-view. Whatever religious experience such a mystic may have, it is not a Christian experience of fellowship with the true God through the mediation of Jesus Christ and the Holy Spirit. The extreme forms of Pietism, Quakerism, and Quietism that arose in Europe during the last part of the seventeenth century must also be rejected. The extreme types of Pietism believed in the possibility of an absolute union with God, a congeniality with him that went beyond the teaching of Scripture. The extreme forms of Quakerism held that all men have an inner light which, quite apart from the Bible, could lead them into a pious and godly life. The extreme forms of Quietism held that we should seek for such a fellowship with God, for such a state of perfect quietude in which all thought, all activity, are suspended and the soul is lost in God. Unfortunately, that which is a precious privilege of the believer was in many instances carried to extremes, and, as in some types of Quakerism, even affirmed to be the possession of the unsaved.

But after making due allowance for the unscriptural views just mentioned, it must be insisted that man has an intuitive knowledge of God. The Scriptures teach that "that which is known about God is evident within them; for God made it evident to them. For since the creation of the world His invisible attributes, His eternal power and divine nature, have been clearly seen, being understood through what has been made, so that they are without excuse" (Rom. 1:19f.).

More particularly, there is a spiritual endowment for the believer by means of which he enters into very real and very precious fellowship with God (Rom. 8:15f.; 1 Cor. 1:9; Gal. 4:6; 1 John 1:3). There is a Christian mysticism, a direct fellowship of the soul with God, which no one who has had a vital Christian experience is likely to deny. But there is, in addition to this, the illumination of the Holy Spirit which is vouchsafed to every believer. Jesus said, "I have many more things to say to you, but you cannot bear them now. But when He, the Spirit of truth, comes, He will guide you into all the truth; for He will not speak on His own initiative, but whatever He hears, He will speak; and He will disclose to you what is to come" (John 16:12f.). And Paul wrote, "We have received, not the spirit of the world, but the Spirit who is from God, that we might know the things freely given to us by God" (1 Cor. 2:12). That is, the Spirit will enable us to understand the revelation God has already made of himself, especially that revelation of himself in the Scriptures. There is then available for the seeker after truth, not only his own reason, but also the aid of the Holy Spirit. The latter, of course, is available only to the true child of God. John writes, "As for you, the anointing which you received from Him abides in you, and you have no need for any one to teach you; but as His anointing teaches you about all things, and is true and is not a lie, and just as it has taught you, you abide in Him" (1 John 2:27; cf. 2:20).

II. THE DIVISIONS OF THEOLOGY

The broad field of theology is commonly divided into four parts: exegetical, historical, systematic, and practical theology.

A. EXEGETICAL THEOLOGY

Exegetical theology occupies itself directly with the study of the biblical text and such related subjects as help in the restoration, orientation, illustration, and interpretation of that text. It includes the study of biblical languages, biblical archaeology, biblical introduction, biblical hermeneutics, and biblical theology.

B. HISTORICAL THEOLOGY

Historical theology traces the history of God's people in the Bible and of the church since the time of Christ. It deals with the origin, development, and spread of the true religion, and also with its doctrines, organizations, and practices. It embraces biblical history, church history, history of missions, history of doctrine, and the history of creeds and confessions.

C. SYSTEMATIC THEOLOGY

Systematic theology takes the materials furnished by exegetical and historical theology and arranges them in logical order under the great heads of theological study. But the contributions of exegetical and historical theology must be carefully distinguished. The former is the only real and infallible source of the science; but the latter, in its exhibition of the progressive apprehension by the church of the great doctrines of the faith, often contributes to an understanding of the biblical revelation. Dogmatic theology is, strictly speaking, the systematization and defense of the doctrines expressed in the symbols of the church, though dogmatic theology is often used synonymously with systematic theology. Under systematic theology are included apologetics, polemics, and biblical ethics.

D. PRACTICAL THEOLOGY

This area of theology treats the application of theology in the regeneration, sanctification, edification, education, and service of men. It seeks to apply to practical life the things contributed by the other three departments of theology. Practical theology embraces areas such as homiletics, church organization and administration, worship, Christian education, and missions.

PART I

THEISM

The term "theism" is used in four different senses. Although only the last of these is really satisfactory, we do well to note briefly each of them.

1. The belief in a supernatural power or supernatural powers, in a spiritual agent or spiritual agents, in one or many gods. This view includes all the various beliefs in a god or gods, whatever their kind or number, and is opposed only to atheism.

2. The belief in the existence of but one God, whether personal or impersonal, whether at present active in the universe or not. This view includes monotheism, pantheism, and deism, and is opposed to atheism, polytheism, and henotheism.

3. The belief in a personal God who is both transcendent and immanent and exists in only one person. This is the Jewish, Mohammedan, and Unitarian conception of God, and is opposed to atheism, polytheism, pantheism, and deism.

4. The belief in one personal God, both immanent and transcendent, who exists in three personal distinctions, known respectively as Father, Son, and Holy Spirit. This is the position of Christian theism, and it is opposed to all the other conceptions named. It is a form of monotheism, yet not of the unitarian, but of the trinitarian type. The Christian holds that since all the other beliefs mentioned have a false conception of God, this view is the only true theistic view. This interpretation of the term is the one adopted in this book.

We have shown in the preceding chapter that God has revealed himself and that man is capable of apprehending this revelation. These two facts provide the foundations for theological study. The next two chapters are further clarification and establishment of the theistic world-view.

CHAPTER III

The Definition and Existence of God

In this chapter we shall seek to formulate the definition of God and to advance the significant arguments for the existence of God. Both these subjects are worthy of exhaustive consideration because they are fundamental to all other theological study, but we can only briefly touch on the more important conceptions of God and the more significant aspects of the proofs of his existence.

I. THE DEFINITION OF GOD

Language, too, has its rights, and terms that have been long used to convey a certain specific meaning cannot rightly be appropriated to express an entirely different meaning. Nevertheless, this has very often been done in theological discussion. The term "God" has in recent times been so misused that we need to restore to it its original meaning in the Christian system. Let us look at a few of these misuses, list the biblical names for God, and set forth the theological formulation of the Christian conception of God.

A. The Erroneous Uses of the Term

Both philosophical and theological writers are guilty at this point. For Plato, God is the eternal mind, the cause of good in nature. Aristotle considered him to be "the first ground of all being." Spinoza defined God as "the absolute, universal Substance, the real Cause of all and every existence; and not only the Cause of all being, but itself all being, of which every special existence is only a modification." Leibniz says that the final reason of things is called God. Kant defined God as a being who, by his understanding and will, is the cause of nature; a being who has all rights and no duties; the moral author of the world. For Fichte, God was the moral order of the universe, actually operative in life. Hegel considered God the absolute spirit, yet a spirit without consciousness until it becomes conscious in the reason and thoughts of man. Strauss identified God with the *Universum*; Comte, with humanity; and Matthew Arnold, with the "Stream of Tendency that Makes for Righteousness."

Let us note also a few more recent abuses of the term. Kirtly F. Mather, a geologist, says God is a spiritual power, immanent in the universe, who is involved in the hazard of his creation. Henry Sloane Coffin says, "God is to me that creative Force, behind and in the universe, who manifests himself as energy, as life, as order, as beauty, as thought, as conscience, as love." He prefers to say that God has personal relations with us to saying that he is personal. For Edward Ames, God is "the idea of the personalized, idealized whole of reality." He thinks of God as growing and as finite. So much for non-biblical conceptions of God; we must now turn to the true concept of God.

B. The Biblical Names for God

The biblical names of persons and places often carry great significance. This is true of the names for deity. One of the most widely used terms for deity is *El*, with its derivations *Elim*, *Elohim*, and *Eloah*. It is similar to the Greek *theos*, the Latin *Deus*, and the English *God*. It is a general word to indicate deity, and is used to include all members of the class of deity. The plural *Elohim* is used regularly by the Old Testament writers with singular verbs and adjectives to denote a singular idea. Though it usually refers to God, it can also be used of pagan deities or gods. The compound *El-Elyon* designates him as the highest, the most high (Ps. 78:35), and *El-Shaddai* as the Almighty God (Gen. 17:1).

Jehovah or *Yahweh* is the personal name *par excellence* of Israel's God. The term is connected with the Hebrew verb "to be," and means the "self-existent one," or the "one who causes to be" (Exod. 6:2f.; cf. 3:13–16). This name is often translated into the English versions by the word "Lord," often using upper case letters. This name occurs in a number of significant combinations: Jehovah-Jireh, the Lord will provide (Gen. 22:14); Jehovah-Rapha, the Lord that heals (Exod. 15:26); Jehovah-Nissi, the Lord our banner (Exod. 17:15); Jehovah-Shalom, the Lord our peace (Judg. 6:24); Jehovah-Raah, the Lord my shepherd (Ps. 23:1); Jehovah-Tsidkenu, the Lord our righteousness (Jer. 23:6); and Jehovah-Shammah, the Lord is present (Ezek. 48:35).

Adonai, my Lord, is a title that appears frequently in the prophets, expressing dependence and submission, as of a servant to his master, or of a wife to her husband. The title, Lord of hosts, appears frequently in the prophetical and post-exilic literature (Isa. 1:9; 6:3). Some take the term to refer to God's presence with the armies of Israel in the times of the monarchy (1 Sam. 4:4; 17:45; 2 Sam. 6:2), but a more probable meaning is God's presence with the hosts of heaven, the angels (Ps. 89:6–8; cf. James 5:4).

In the New Testament the term *theos* takes the place of *El*, *Elohim*, and *Elyon*. The names *Shaddai* and *El-Shaddai* are rendered *pantokrator*, the almighty, and *theos pantokrator*, God almighty. Sometimes the Lord is called the Alpha and the Omega (Rev. 1:8), who is and who was and who is to come (Rev. 1:4), the first and the last (Rev. 2:8), and the beginning and the end (Rev. 21:6).

C. The Theological Formulation of the Definition

Because God is infinite, a comprehensive definition giving a complete and exhaustive portrayal of God is impossible. However, we can give a definition of God insofar as we know him and know about him. We certainly can set forth the attributes of God as revealed to man. And further, we can say that God is a being, and then indicate the ways in which he is different from other beings. What are some definitions of God?

Buswell writes, "The best summary of the doctrine of God as taught in the Bible is found in answer to question four of the *Westminster Shorter Cate-chism*, 'What is God? God is spirit, infinite, eternal, and unchangeable, in His being, wisdom, power, holiness, justice, goodness, and truth.' "[1] Hoeksema states, "God is the one, simple, absolute, purely spiritual, personal Being of infinite perfections, wholly immanent in all the world, yet essentially tran-scendent in relation to all things!"[2] Berkhof defines him in this manner, "God is one, absolute, unchangeable and infinite in His knowledge and wisdom, His goodness and love, His grace and mercy, His righteousness and holiness."[3] For a short and comprehensive definition of God, Strong's is probably the best: "God is the infinite and perfect Spirit in whom all things have their source, support, and end."[4]

II. THE EXISTENCE OF GOD

It has been shown that God has revealed himself and that man has the ability to apprehend this revelation. We move now to the arguments for the exis-tence of God. They fall into three broad groups.

A. The Belief in the Existence of God is Intuitive

It is a first truth, being logically prior to the belief in the Bible. A belief is intuitive if it is universal and necessary. Paul writes, "That which is known about God is evident within them; for God made it evident to them" (Rom.

[1]Buswell, *A Systematic Theology of the Christian Religion*, I, p. 30.
[2]Hoeksema, *Reformed Dogmatics*, p. 60.
[3]Berkhof, *Systematic Theology*, p. 56.
[4]Strong, *Systematic Theology*, p. 52.

1:19). He goes on to say, "Since the creation of the world His invisible attributes, His eternal power and divine nature, have been clearly seen" (v. 20). This information leaves unbelievers "without excuse" (v. 20). Even the most depraved know that those who live in sin are "worthy of death" (Rom. 1:32) and that all men have "the work of the Law written in their hearts" (Rom. 2:15).

History shows that the religious element of our nature is just as universal as the rational or social one. Religion or a belief system is categorized as one of the universals in culture.[5] There are in man's belief everywhere, various forms of religious phenomena and awareness of the supernatural. It may be an abstract form of supernatural power called "mana," or the true belief in a personal God. Often man's religion has degenerated because of unbelief. Paul writes that when men rejected God, "they became futile in their speculations, and their foolish heart was darkened. Professing to be wise, they became fools, and exchanged the glory of the incorruptible God for an image in the form of corruptible man and of birds and four-footed animals and crawling creatures" (Rom. 1:21–23).

The belief in the existence of God is also necessary. It is necessary in the sense that we cannot deny his existence without doing violence to the very laws of our nature. If we do deny it, the denial is forced and can only be temporary. Just as the pendulum of a clock can be pushed off center by an internal or external force, so a man can be pushed off his normal belief in the existence of God. But just as the pendulum returns to its original position when the pressure is removed, so a man returns to his normal belief in God when he is not consciously under the influence of a false philosophy. Hodge says:

> Under the control of a metaphysical theory, a man may deny the existence of the external world, or the obligation of the moral law; and his disbelief may be sincere, and for a time persistent; but the moment the speculative reasons for his disbelief are absent from his mind, it of necessity reverts to its original and normal convictions. It is also possible that a man's hand may be so hardened or cauterized as to lose the sense of touch. But that would not prove that the hand in man is not normally the great organ of touch.[6]

This universal and necessary belief is intuitive. It cannot be explained as the necessary deduction of reason on the ground that the evidence for his existence is so obvious that the mind is constrained to accept it; for only the educated person is capable of this type of generalization, and both agnosticism and atheism are found more frequently among the so-called educated

---

[5]Herskovits, *Cultural Anthropology*, p. 117.
[6]Hodge, *Systematic Theology*, I, pp. 197, 198.

than among the uneducated, who have no training in the art of reasoning. Nor can it be explained as due to tradition simply. We admit that the earlier revelations of God have been handed down from generation to generation, but we do not believe that this is the whole explanation of the belief, for the Bible declares that the law of God is written on the heart of man (Rom. 2:14–16). We also feel that the theory does not account for the strength of the belief in man.

B. The Existence of God is Assumed by the Scriptures

We have already shown several times that the Bible regards all men as believing in the existence of God. Because of this, it does not attempt to prove his existence. Throughout the Bible, the existence of God is taken for granted. The Scriptures begin with the majestic statement, "In the beginning God" (Gen. 1:1), and they continue throughout to take his existence for granted. Such texts as Ps. 94:9f. and Isa. 40:12–31 are not proofs of God's existence, but rather analytical accounts of all that is involved in the idea of God, and admonitions to recognize him in his character of deity.

Not only so, but the Scriptures also do not argue nor prove that God may be known, nor yet do they speculate how the knowledge of God has arisen in man's mind. Man's consciousness is aware of the existence of God, and the writers of Scripture had minds filled and aglow with the thoughts and knowledge of him. They wrote with certitude concerning the existence of God to readers who were likewise assured of his existence.

C. The Belief in the Existence of God is Corroborated by Arguments

In approaching the study of the arguments used for the existence of God, the following must be borne in mind: (1) that they are not independent proofs of the existence of God, but rather corroborations and expositions of our innate conviction of his existence; (2) that, since God is a spirit, we must not insist on the same type of proof that we demand for the existence of material things, but only on such evidence as is suitable to the object of proof; and (3) that the evidence is cumulative, a single argument for the existence of God being inadequate, but a number of them together being sufficient to bind the conscience and compel belief. We, therefore, now turn to a brief study of these arguments.

1. The cosmological argument. This argument may be stated thus: "Everything begun must have an adequate cause. The universe was begun; therefore, the universe must have an adequate cause for its production." The argument is implied in Heb. 3:4: "For every house is built by someone, but the builder of all things is God." This argument can also be stated as Buswell states it: "If something now exists, (1) something must be eternal unless (2) something comes from nothing."[7]

That the universe is eternal or that it has been eternally created is held by some. But astronomy shows that there have been great changes in the heavens, and geology that there have been great changes in the earth. All this shows that the present order is not eternal. Furthermore, the existence of the world is contingent, or dependent. Every part of it is dependent upon the other parts and stands in a definite relation to them. Can the whole be self-existent when the several parts that make up the whole are dependent? There is also a succession in the effects. Causes produce effects, but the causes are themselves the effects of something else. There must, therefore, be a first cause, or an eternal series of causes. But the latter is unthinkable. The second law of thermodynamics, or the law of entropy, indicates that the universe is running down. Energy is becoming less available, and order is giving way to randomness. If the universe is running down, then it is not self-sustaining; and if it is not self-sustaining, then it must have had a beginning.

Just what does this argument prove? Not merely that there is a necessary being, whether personal or impersonal, but that this being is extra-mundane, for everything contingent must have the cause of its existence out of itself, and this being must be intelligent because the world of finite minds is a part of the universe. We, therefore, conclude that the argument proves that the universe was brought into being by an adequate cause. There is a weakness to the argument in that "if every existing thing has an adequate cause, this also applies to God."[8] Thus we are led to an endless chain. But this argument does suggest that the first cause was outside the universe and intelligent. These two ideas are, however, more clearly established by the further arguments to be presented.

2. The teleological argument.   The teleological argument may be stated thus: "Order and useful arrangement in a system imply intelligence and purpose in the organizing cause. The universe is characterized by order and useful arrangement; therefore, the universe has an intelligent and free cause." The major premise is intimated in several Psalms: "When I consider Thy heavens, the work of Thy fingers, the moon and the stars, which Thou hast ordained; what is man, that Thou dost take thought of him? And the son of man, that Thou dost care for him?" (Ps. 8:3f.); "The heavens are telling the glory of God; and their expanse is declaring the works of His hands. Day to day pours forth speech, and night to night reveals knowledge" (Ps. 19:1f.); and "He who planted the ear, does He not hear? He who formed

---

[7]Buswell, *A Systematic Theology of the Christian Religion*, I, p. 82.
[8]Berkhof, *Systematic Theology*, p. 26.

the eye, does He not see?" (Ps. 94:9). It has, indeed, been objected that there may be order and useful arrangement without design, that things may be due to the operation of law or chance. But the dependent character of the laws of nature rules out the former idea. These laws are neither self-originating nor self-sustaining; they presuppose a lawgiver and a law-sustainer. Who formed the snowflake or made the seasons? Surely, these speak of an intelligent being. Paul uses this argument and concept in establishing the guilt of the infidel (Rom. 1:18-23).

The minor premise is seldom disputed today. The structures and adaptations in the plant and animal world, including man, indicate order and design. Plants, animals, and man are so constructed that they can appropriate the necessary food, grow, and reproduce after their kind. The planets, asteroids, satellites, comets, meteors, and constellations of stars are all kept in their courses by the great centrifugal and centripetal forces in the universe. The atom displays an orderly arrangement of protons, neutrons, deutrons, mesotrons, electrons, etc. We can see a relation between the animate and the inanimate world. Light, air, heat, water, and soil are provided for the maintenance of plant and animal life. We can also see the general uniformity of the laws of nature, which allows man to plant and raise his crops and use his scientific discoveries in the advancement of human welfare. Paul declares, "He did not leave Himself without witness, in that He did good and gave you rains from heaven and fruitful seasons, satisfying your hearts with food and gladness" (Acts 14:17).

What does this argument prove? It has been objected that both men and animals have useless organs, or vestigial structures, and that therefore the teleological argument is invalid. But science is again and again discovering that the so-called useless organs are after all not useless; and we can assume that those whose uses have not yet been discovered may also have their uses. The teleological argument suggests not only that the first cause is intelligent and free, but that it is outside the universe, for design is seen to emanate not simply from within, but also and chiefly from without, by the adaptation of things external to the organisms and by the disposition and orderly arrangement of vast bodies of matter, separated by millions and billions of miles. We conclude, therefore, that the argument proves that the first cause is intelligent, free, extra-mundane, and incomprehensibly great.

But again, this argument has limitations; it proves that a great and intelligent architect fashioned the world, but it does not prove that he was God. Further, the existence of physical evil and disorder limit the value of this argument. With the other arguments for the existence of God, it has value, but standing alone, it is of reduced value.

3. *The ontological argument.*   As commonly stated, this argument finds in the very idea of God the proof of his existence. It holds that all men have

intuitively the idea of God, and then tries to find proof of his existence in the idea itself. Or, as Hoeksema writes, this argument "argues that we have an idea of God. This idea of God is infinitely greater than man himself. Hence, it cannot have its origin in man. It can only have its origin in God Himself."[9]

Care must be used with this argument because we cannot deduce real existence from mere abstract thought; the idea of God does not have within itself the proof of his existence. But although the ontological argument does not prove the existence of God, it shows what God must be if he exists. Since the cosmological and teleological arguments have already proved the existence of a personal cause and designer external to the universe, the present argument proves that this being is infinite and perfect, not because these qualities are demonstrably his, but because our mental constitution will not allow us to think otherwise. It is self-evident that every idea in our human culture has some cause. The idea of the God of the Bible must have some cause, and this cause must be God himself.

4. The moral argument. Kant points out that the theoretic proofs can give us no knowledge of God as a moral being. For this, we are dependent upon the practical reason. Kant holds that the fact of obligation and duty is at least as certain as the fact of existence. On the basis of conscience, he argues for freedom, immortality, and God. This is his categorical imperative. The Bible also appeals to the moral argument in proof of the existence of God (Rom. 1:19–32; 2:14–16).

Hoeksema presents the argument thus: "Every man has a sense of obligation, of what is right and wrong, together with an undeniable feeling of responsibility to do what is right and a sense of self-condemnation when he commits what is evil." He goes on to say, "There is in him, as it were, a voice that will not be silenced, ever saying to his inner consciousness, '*Du sollst.*' This presupposes that there is a speaker, and moreover, one that is Lord and Sovereign."[10] Man's knowledge of good and evil is from God, as is his sense of obligation. Herskovits observes that "concepts of right and wrong can be found in the systems of belief of all groups."[11] Thus, we conclude that there is a permanent moral law and it has supreme and abiding authority over us. Evolutionists do not like to admit this. They like to think of everything as constantly changing. But that conscience is not self-imposed nor developed from our primitive instincts by our life in society, is evident from the fact that the sense of duty has no regard to our inclinations, pleasures, or fortunes, nor to the practices of society, but is often in conflict with them. Yet conscience does not tell us what to do; it merely insists that

[9]Hoeksema, *Reformed Dogmatics*, p. 45.
[10]Hoeksema, *Reformed Dogmatics*, p. 46.
[11]Herskovits, *Cultural Anthropology*, p. 230.

there is a fundamental moral law in the universe and that it is our duty to observe it. Further, known violations of this moral law are followed by feelings of ill-desert and fears of judgment. In the Bible David is a good example of this (Ps. 32:3f.; 38:1-4).

We must conclude that since this moral law is not self-imposed and these fears of judgment are not self-executing, there is a holy will that imposes this law and a punitive power that will execute the threats of our moral nature. Our consciences cry out, "He has told you, O man, what is good; and what does the Lord require of you . . . ?" (Mic. 6:8), and "God will bring every act to judgment, everything which is hidden, whether it is good or evil" (Eccl. 12:14). In other words, conscience recognizes the existence of a great lawgiver and the certainty of the punishment of all violations of his law.

5. The argument from congruity. This argument is based on the belief that the postulate which best explains the related facts is probably true. As related to the present discussion, it runs as follows: the belief in the existence of God best explains the facts of our moral, mental, and religious nature, as well as the facts of the material universe; therefore, God exists. It holds that without this postulate the related facts are really inexplicable. This principle may be illustrated from microscopic and telescopic studies. The particles that make up an atom are not discoverable by direct observation; they are inferred from the effects they produce and the combinations they enter into. Thus in science we assume that a postulate which explains and harmonizes the related facts is true. Should we not on this same principle conclude that there is a God, since the theistic postulate is in harmony with all the facts of our mental, moral, and religious nature, as well as with the facts of the material universe?

To believe in a personal, self-sufficient, and self-revealing God is in harmony with our moral and mental nature; history and natural law have an explanation; and the universal belief in a supreme being with its accompanying religious experiences can be accounted for. Atheism, pantheism, and agnosticism do not provide an adequate answer to satisfy the human heart. We may conclude from these arguments that there is a personal, extramundane, self-existent, ethical, and self-revealing God. He is the incomprehensible (Job 11:7; Isa. 40:18; Rom. 11:33), yet knowable one (John 17:3; 1 John 5:20).

CHAPTER IV

The Non-Christian World-Views

To anyone who gives thoughtful consideration to the proofs for God's existence already advanced, the evidence appears conclusive. He can only exclaim, "Surely, there is a God!" God himself regards the evidence as conclusive. If he did not so regard it, he would have given us more evidence, but the evidence is sufficient (Acts 14:17; 17:23–29; Rom. 1:18–20). The Bible simply assumes the existence of God. To believe in the existence of God is, therefore, the normal and natural thing to do, and agnosticism and atheism are the abnormal and unnatural positions. Indeed, the latter are tantamount to saying that God has not furnished us with sufficient evidence of his existence. Such attitudes are a reflection on a benevolent and holy God and are sinful.

Nevertheless, men as a whole have refused to have God in their knowledge (Rom. 1:28). Sin has so distorted their vision and corrupted their hearts as to make them reject the evidence and go on without a God or set up gods of their own creation. We shall, therefore, briefly examine the leading non-Christian world-views and reply to them. They fall into six great classes.

I. THE ATHEISTIC VIEW

In a general sense, the term "atheism" refers to a failure to recognize the only true God. As such, it applies to all non-Christian religions. But in a more restricted sense, the term "atheism" applies to three distinct types: practical atheism, dogmatic atheism, and virtual atheism.

Practical atheism is found among many people. Many have rashly decided that all religion is fake. People like this are usually not confirmed atheists; they merely are indifferent to God. While perhaps acknowledging a God somewhere, they live and act as if there is no God to whom they are responsible. They are practical atheists as far as their religious interests are concerned.

Dogmatic atheism is the type that openly professes atheism. Most people do not boldly flaunt their atheism before men, for the term is one of reproach; but there are some who do not shrink from declaring themselves atheists. In recent years there has been a revival of this kind of atheism.

Communism openly professes itself to be atheistic and religion to be the opiate of the people.

Virtual atheism is the kind that holds principles that are inconsistent with belief in God or that define him in terms that do violence to the common usage of language. Most naturalists belong to the first of these varieties. Those who define God in such abstractions as "an active principle in nature," "the social consciousness," "the unknowable," "personified reality," or "energy" are atheists of the second of these varieties. They are, in reality, doing violence to the established meaning of the term "God." Theism, too, has its well-established nomenclature, and it cannot be juggled at will to suit the fancy of modern belief.

The atheistic position is a very unsatisfactory, unstable, and arrogant one. It is unsatisfactory because all atheists lack the assurance of the forgiveness of their sins; they all have a cold and empty life; and they know nothing of peace and fellowship with God. It is unstable because it is contrary to man's deepest convictions. Both Scripture and history show that man necessarily and universally believes in the existence of God. The virtual atheist testifies to this fact in that he adopts abstraction to account for the world and its life. It is arrogant because it really pretends to be omniscient. Limited knowledge can infer the existence of God, but exhaustive knowledge of all things, intelligences, and times is needed to state dogmatically that there is no God. The dogmatic atheist can be explained as being in an abnormal condition. Just as the pendulum of a clock can be pushed off the center by an internal or external force, so the mind of man can be pushed off its normal position by a false philosophy. When the force is removed, both the pendulum and the human mind return to their normal position.

II. THE AGNOSTIC VIEW

The term "agnostic" is sometimes applied to any doctrine that affirms the impossibility of any true knowledge, holding that all knowledge is relative and therefore uncertain. In this sense the Greek Sophists and Sceptics as well as all the empiricists from Aristotle down to Hume were agnostics. In theology, however, the term is limited to those views which affirm that neither the existence nor the nature of God, nor yet the ultimate nature of the universe, is known or knowable.

Positivism in science and pragmatism in philosophy and theology are the outstanding types of agnosticism. Auguste Comte (1798–1859), the founder of positivism, decided to accept nothing as true beyond the details of observed facts; and since the idea of God could not thus be subjected to examination, he omitted it and devoted himself entirely to the study of phenomena. But Einstein's theory of relativity has shown that we have to reckon with the intangibles, for instance of time and space, even in the study of the physical world. His theory has dealt a death blow to positivism.

Pragmatism in philosophy and theology, like positivism in science, rejects a special revelation and the competence of reason in the study of ultimate reality. It argues, however, that since suspension of judgment is not only painful, but often even costly and impossible, we should adopt the view that yields the best results. Accordingly, Albrecht Ritschl and William James adopt a *fiat* God, a pragmatic postulation of his existence in order to secure certain desirable results. John Dewey contents himself with postulating vague abstractions.

The agnostic position, too, is highly unsatisfactory and unstable, and often displays a false humility. It is unsatisfactory in that it suffers the same spiritual impoverishment as does the atheistic, but it is unsatisfactory also from the intellectual standpoint. Agnosticism proves this in its adoption of tentative views as working hypotheses. It is unstable because it admits that it has not attained to absolute certainty. Ritschl and James claimed to have reached a fair measure of stability in their beliefs, but Dewey held that his beliefs were very temporary. And agnosticism often displays a false humility in that it claims to know so little. Others, some agnostics charge, haughtily pretend to have a superior understanding, but we frankly recognize man's true limitations in knowledge. Now, from the Christian standpoint, this is a false humility, for Christians regard the evidence for the existence of a personal, extra-mundane, almighty, and holy God as ample and conclusive.

III. THE PANTHEISTIC VIEW

Pantheism is that theory which holds that all finite things are merely aspects, modifications, or parts of one eternal and self-existent being. It regards God as one with the natural universe. God is all; all is God. It appears in a variety of forms today, some of them having in them also atheistic, polytheistic, or theistic elements. The devotees of pantheism usually look upon their beliefs as a religion, bringing to them a kind of reverential submission. For that reason, the inadequacy of pantheism needs to be all the more clearly apprehended. We shall set forth in the briefest manner possible the character of the leading types of pantheism and then present the Christian refutation of them.

A. THE LEADING TYPES OF PANTHEISM

The following are the leading types of pantheism.

1. Materialistic pantheism. This form of pantheism holds that matter is the cause of all life and mind. David Strauss believed in the eternity of matter and in the spontaneous generation of life. He held that the universe, the totality of existence that we call nature, is the only God which the modern man enlightened by science can consent to worship. But surely the belief in the eternity of matter is an illogical assumption, and the doctrine of spontaneous generation has been discarded by reputable scientists.

2. Hylozoism and Panpsychism.   These are names for the same theory. There are, however, two types of this theory. The first holds that every particle of matter has, besides its physical properties, a principle of life. The earliest form emphasized the physical properties and was practically a type of materialism. The modern form goes back to G. W. Leibniz, who emphasized the psychical properties. He held that ultimate units are not atoms, but monads, little souls, having the power of perception and appetite. The second holds that mind and matter are distinct, but intimately and inseparably united. God, in this view, is the soul of the world. The Stoics held this form of hylozoism.

3. Neutralism.   Neutralism is a form of monism which holds that ultimate reality is neither mind nor matter, but a neutral stuff of which mind and matter are but appearances or aspects. Baruch Spinoza is the best representative of this type. He held that there is but one substance with two attributes, thought and extension, or mind and matter, the totality of which is God.

4. Idealism.   This form of pantheism holds that ultimate reality is of the nature of mind and that the world is the product of mind, either of the individual mind or of the infinite mind. George Berkeley held that objects which one perceives are but one's perceptions and not the things themselves. That is, everything exists only in the mind. But we reply that if everything exists only in the mind, then other people and God also exist only in the mind. Indeed, logically one must conclude that oneself alone exists, which reduces the theory to an absurdity. Subjective idealism says the world is *my* idea; objective idealism says it is idea.

There are two main types of absolute idealism or objective idealism. Impersonal absolutism holds that ultimate reality is one single mind or one single unified system; it denies that this mind or system is personal. Personalistic absolutism holds that the absolute is a person. He includes within himself all finite selves and shares the experiences of these selves because they are numerically a part of him, while he also has thoughts other than their thoughts.

5. Philosophical mysticism.   Philosophical mysticism is the most absolute type of monism in existence. The idealist still distinguishes between the outside world and himself, the great self and all finite selves; but for the mystic, the sense of otherness drops out altogether and the knower realizes that he is identical with the inner being of his subject. Ultimate reality is a unit, it is indescribable; the human self is not merely like it in kind, but identical with it; and union with this absolute is realized by moral effort rather than theoretical abstractions.

In concluding this survey of the pantheistic views, we reiterate the statement made at the beginning of this section, that some pantheists also have atheistic, polytheistic, or theistic elements in their theories. The above five types have been treated as pantheistic simply because that is their real or principal character. Their errors and destructive character must now be briefly pointed out.

B. The Refutation of the Pantheistic Theories

The human mind is peculiarly fond of monistic world-views. It likes to think of all existence as having some common originating cause or principle. The philosophers hold that this cause or principle is entirely within the world. Christians also believe that there is a common originating cause, but they hold that it is outside the world as well as inside it. The former view is known as monism, the latter, as monotheism. Because of the profound religious significance associated with pantheistic beliefs, we deem it necessary to offer a detailed refutation of them. Pantheistic theories must be rejected for the following reasons:

1. *They are necessitarian.*   All freedom of second causes is denied; everything exists and acts of necessity. Materialistic pantheism thinks in terms of dynamic necessity, while absolute idealism thinks in terms of logical necessity. Against this we affirm that we have the consciousness that we are free agents and that we are accountable for our conduct. It is because of this conviction that we institute government and punish criminals for their misdeeds.

2. *They destroy the foundations of morals.*   If all things are necessitated, then error and sin are also necessitated. But if that is true, then three other things follow: (1) Sin is not that which absolutely ought not to be, that which deserves condemnation. Consequently, pantheism speaks of sin as an unavoidable weakness, a stage in our development. But we have the conviction that we are under condemnation and the wrath of a holy God. (2) We have no standard by which to distinguish between right and wrong. If we do all things of necessity, then how can we tell when we do wrong and when right? Pantheists make expediency the moral test. And (3) God himself is sinful, for if all things are necessitated by him, then he must be ignorant or evil at heart. If ignorant, then how can he be unclouded light and perfect truth? If wicked, then how can he punish sin? In pagan societies, where

pantheism has received more of a religious significance, this idea has led men to deify evil and to honor and worship the deities who best represent evil. Thus pantheism destroys the foundations of morals.

3. They make all rational religion impossible.   Some would not regard this as an objection to pantheism, but from the standpoint of the philosophy of religion this is very important. In stressing the metaphysical union of the human with the divine, pantheistic views tend to destroy human personality. This is done especially in absolute idealism and mysticism. But true religion is possible only between persons who retain their distinct individualities, for true religion is the worship and service offered by a human being to the divine being. When these distinctions disappear or to the extent that they disappear, true religion becomes impossible. What some men would still call religion can, in that case, be only the worship of self.

4. They deny personal and conscious immortality.   If man is but a part of the infinite, he is also but a moment in the life of God, a wave on the surface of the sea; when the body perishes, the personality ceases and the sea becomes a smooth surface again. Thus, there is no conscious existence for man after death. The only kind of immortality pantheists hope for is survival in the memory of others and absorption into the great ultimate reality. But we are conscious that we stand in the relation of personal responsibility to God and that we shall be asked to give an account of the deeds done in the body, whether they be good or bad (2 Cor. 5:10). We know that after death, as in this life, there will be a difference between the good and the bad, that is, that our identity and individuality will be preserved.

5. They deify man by making him a part of God.   Pantheism flatters man and encourages human pride. If everything that exists is but a manifestation of God, and if God does not come to consciousness except in man, then man is the highest manifestation of God in the world. Indeed, we may measure the religious greatness of a man by the extent to which he realizes his identity with God. Pantheists claim that Jesus Christ was the first man who came to a perfect realization of this great truth when he said, "I and the Father are one" (John 10:30). And the Hindu thinks that when he can say, "I am Brahman!" then the moment of his absorption into the infinite has arrived. But we have no right to say of ourselves what Jesus could say of himself, for we are but sinful creatures, while he is the eternal Son of God. Christianity gives to man the highest position under God but does not make him a part of God.

6. These cannot account for concrete reality.   Materialistic pantheism dismisses the subject by saying that matter in motion has always existed, but that is assertion and not proof. The universe is not self-sustaining; and if it is not self-sustaining, then it must have had a beginning. Nor can materialistic pantheism account for the mind, for inanimate matter cannot conceivably generate either life or mind. And idealistic pantheism forgets that thought without a thinker is a mere abstraction. Reality is always substantive, is an agent. Without an agent there is no activity, either mental or physical. Nor can individual existences be produced by abstract universals. Thus pantheism cannot account for concrete reality.

IV. THE POLYTHEISTIC VIEW

We assert that monotheism was the original religion of mankind. The first departure from monotheism seems to have been in the direction of nature worship. Sun, moon, and stars, the great representatives of nature, and fire, air, and water, the great representatives of earth, became objects of popular worship. At first they were merely personified; then men came to believe that personal beings presided over them. Polytheism has a strong affinity for fallen human nature. Men join themselves to idols (Hos. 4:17) and find it most difficult to break away. Idolatry not only leaves the heart empty, but also debases the mind. Paul speaks of how men "professing to be wise, . . . became fools, and exchanged the glory of the incorruptible God for an image in the form of corruptible man and of birds and fourfooted animals and crawling creatures" (Rom. 1:22f.). The Thessalonian believers are represented as having "turned to God from idols to serve a living and true God" (1 Thess. 1:9). John exhorts, "Guard yourselves from idols" (1 John 5:21).

In the Bible the gods of the heathen are sometimes declared to be of no account and futile (Isa. 41:24; 44:9–20), and at other times, the representatives, if not the embodiment, of demons (1 Cor. 10:20). This seems to mean that the worship of idols is the worship of demons.

V. THE DUALISTIC VIEW

This theory assumes that there are two distinct and irreducible substances or principles. In epistemology these are idea and object; in metaphysics, mind and matter; in ethics, good and evil; in religion, good or God, and evil or Satan. The Christian, however, does not believe that Satan is co-eternal with God, but rather a creature of God and subject to him.

Kant, Sidgwick, the modern personalistic philosophers, Christians, and the common man hold to epistemological dualism. For them, thought and thing are two distinct entities. The early Greek philosophers, such as Thales, Empedocles, Anaxagoras, and Pythagoras, are usually classed as monists, but they were in reality metaphysical dualists. They distinguished between the two principles of mind and matter. Even Plato, in making a sharp distinction between ideas and the real world, was after all a dualist. Kant and all the British moralists who held that there is an absolute right and wrong in the universe were ethical dualists. They, therefore, held up standards of absolute right. More important from the Christian standpoint are the religious dualists.

Originating in the main from Persian Zoroastrianism, Gnosticism and Manicheanism arose to torment the early church. The Gnostics seem to have arisen during the last half of the first century. They tried to solve the problem of evil by postulating two gods—a supreme God and a demiurge. The God of the Old Testament is not the supreme God, for the supreme God is entirely good; he is the demiurge, who created the universe. There is a constant conflict between these two gods, a conflict between good and evil. Mani, having apparently been brought up with an old Babylonian sect, became the founder of Manicheanism. When brought into contact with Christianity, he conceived the idea of blending Oriental dualism and Christianity into a harmonious whole. He regarded himself as an apostle of Christ and as the promised Paraclete. He set to work to eliminate all Judaistic elements from Christianity and to substitute Zoroastrianism in its place.

In the last century, the problem of the origin and presence of evil in the world has again forced itself to the front. It has led some to return to an ancient form of dualism. God and matter, some might say God and Satan, are both eternal. God is limited in power and perhaps in knowledge, but not in quality of character. God is doing the best he can with the recalcitrant world and will ultimately triumph completely over it. Man ought to assist God in this struggle and hasten the complete overthrow of evil. God is considered as growing and as finite.

The problem of evil is admittedly a difficult one on any theory, but a doctrine of dualism is not the solution. Surely, a finite God cannot satisfy the human heart, for what guarantee does such a God offer for the final triumph of good? Something unforeseen may come up at any time to frustrate all his good intentions; and how shall the believer keep up faith in prayer on such a theory? Further, finiteness does not any more absolve God of responsibility for evil than does the traditional view. Most adherents of this theory would teach that God somehow creates, although they make it an eternal process. Believing that to create involves the necessity of evil, they cannot clear God of the act of creating such a world. Furthermore, the doctrine involves the belief in a developing, growing God; he succeeds more and more, and perhaps becomes better and better. But this is a clear disregard of the many biblical indications that he is perfect and unchangeable in his wisdom, power, justice, goodness, and truth, and it does not satisfy our idea of God. And finally, it ignores or denies the existence of Satan, the archenemy, who in Scripture is represented as having much to do with present-day evil.

VI. THE DEISTIC VIEW

As pantheism holds to the immanence of God to the exclusion of his transcendence, so deism holds to his transcendence to the exclusion of his immanence. For deism, God is present in creation only by his power, not in his very nature and being. He has endowed creation with invariable laws over which he exercises a mere general oversight; he has imparted to his creatures certain properties, placed them under his invariable laws, and left them to work out their destiny by their own powers. Deism denies a special revelation, miracles, and providence. It claims that all truths about God are discoverable by reason and that the Bible is merely a book on the principles of natural religion, which are ascertainable by the light of nature.

The Christian rejects deism because he believes that we have a special revelation of God in the Bible; that God is present in the universe in his being as well as in his power; that God exercises a constant providential control over all his creation; that he sometimes uses miracles in the accomplishment of his purposes; that God answers prayer; and that the deists obtain much of their religious dogma from the Bible, and not from nature and reason alone. He holds that a deistic, absentee God is not much better than no God at all.

PART II
BIBLIOLOGY

Having now shown that God has revealed himself and having proved his existence by many proofs, we next desire to know where we can find out more about him. In other words, we inquire after the sources of theology, after accurate and infallible information concerning him and his relations to the universe. There are four directions in which men look for such sources: reason, mystical insight, the church, and the Scriptures. We have already shown the proper place and also the limitations of reason and mystical insight. It remains to inquire whether God has given any such authority to the church or whether the Scriptures are the only real source of authority.

Roman Catholicism has long claimed that God has made the church the authoritative and infallible teacher. It claims that God has communicated all his revelations to it, written and unwritten, and the church has the constant presence and guidance of the Holy Spirit, preserving it from all error in instructions. This infallibility extends to matters of faith and morals and to all things which the church pronounces to be a part of the revelation of God. On this view, the Roman Catholic Church is the only true church. When the bishops meet, they are, in their collective capacity, infallible; and when the pope, the bishop of Rome, speaks *ex cathedra*, he is the organ of the Holy Spirit and he expresses the infallible judgment of the church.

But God has committed no such authority to any visible organization. There is value in deciding a disputed point of doctrine in consulting the opinion of the true people of God, for the church is the "pillar and support of the truth" (1 Tim. 3:15); but this relates to the invisible body of Christ, not to an external organization. God is not present in the visible organization as such, but in the hearts of his true followers; and the progressive guidance into truth promised in John 16:12f. does not extend beyond the men to whom it was promised, except in the sense of enabling them to understand the things freely given to them of God (1 Cor. 2:12), that is, the things recorded in the Scriptures. Each child of God has the illuminating ministry of the Holy Spirit to enable him to understand the Word; this is not a gift given to an external organization (1 John 2:20, 27).

The Bible is to be received as the final authority. The true church has believed all through its history that the Bible is the embodiment of a divine revelation and that the records which contain that revelation are genuine, credible, canonical, and supernaturally inspired. Bibliology examines the Scriptures to see if these beliefs concerning the Bible are true.

41

CHAPTER V

The Scriptures: The Embodiment of a Divine Revelation

The possibility of theology arises from the revelation of God and the endowments of man. The second of these ideas has received sufficient treatment for the present, but the first needs to be dealt with more fully here. The Christian view has always maintained that the revelation of God has had written embodiment, and that in the Scriptures there is such an embodiment. The Scriptures are, therefore, the supreme source of Christian theology. What are the proofs for this belief?

I. THE *A PRIORI* ARGUMENT

This is, strictly speaking, an argument from something prior to something posterior. As related to the present discussion, it may be stated thus: man being what he is and God being what he is, we may possibly expect a revelation from God and also an embodiment of such parts of that revelation as are needed to supply a reliable and infallible source of theological truth. The parts of this argument must be examined more closely.

Man is not only a sinner and under condemnation of eternal death, but he is also inclined away from God, ignorant of God's purposes and methods of salvation, and incapable of returning to God in his own strength. He is, in other words, in a most desperate condition, of which he is only partially aware, and he does not know whether he can be saved from it, or if he can, how he can be saved. The unwritten general and special revelations of God furnish no real answers to this question. Very clearly, therefore, man needs infallible instruction concerning his most important problem in life, his eternal welfare.

Over against this profound need of man, we have the unique attributes and character of God that make possible, if not probable, the supply of this need. The Christian God is omniscient, holy, loving and kind, and omnipotent. Since he is omniscient, he knows all about man's need; since he is holy, he cannot excuse sin and take man in his fallen condition into fellowship with himself; since he is loving and kind, he may be moved to search for and put into operation a plan of salvation; and since he is omnipotent, he can not only reveal himself, but can also set forth in writing such revelations of himself as are needful for the experience of salvation.

We grant that this argument does not take us beyond the point of possibility, or, at the most, of probability. For although God is love and he exercises this attribute in the Godhead, apart from a clear revelation to that effect we cannot be sure that he loves the sinner. We must not make his love a necessary attitude toward the sinner, or else love is no longer love, mercy no longer mercy, and grace no longer grace. The element of voluntariness must be retained in all of them, since man has lost all claims to love, mercy, and grace. But even so, the argument has some value in inspiring hope that God will provide for the profoundest needs of man.

II. THE ARGUMENT FROM ANALOGY

This is an argument from the correspondence between ratios or relations between things. It strengthens the preceding argument in the direction of the probability of an embodiment of the divine revelation. The argument may be stated in two parts. First, as soon as we pass into that region of our world where there is need for communication between individuals possessed of intelligence of any kind, we meet with direct utterance, or "revelation." Even the animals reveal by their voices their various feelings. And everywhere in society there is speech of some sort. There is direct communication from one to the other, a constant immediate revelation of inward thoughts and feelings, delivered in such a way as to be clearly understood, Consequently, there can be no *prima facie* opposition to the fact of a direct, clear, and truthful revelation drawn from the analogy of nature. Although this argument may not prove that the revelation of God will be embodied in a book, it yet contributes to that view.

Secondly, in nature there are signs of reparative goodness, and in the life of individuals and nations evidences of forbearance in providential dealings, which afford ground for hope. There is the healing of limbs, the cure of diseases, and the delay of judgment. These furnish some ground for thinking that the God of nature is a God of forbearance and mercy (Acts 14:15-17).

This argument takes us a little further than the argument *a priori*. The former merely holds out the hope that God may come to the help of a fallen being; the latter, by showing that God has made provision for the healing of many ills in the plant and animal world and by showing that he deals patiently and benevolently with mankind in general, proves that he does come to the help of his needy creatures. But again, we can only in a very general way derive from this argument the assurance that he will embody his plans and promises in a written record.

III. THE ARGUMENT FROM THE INDESTRUCTIBILITY OF THE BIBLE

When we recall that only a very small percentage of books survive more than a quarter of a century, that a much smaller percentage last for a century, and that only a very small number live a thousand years, we at once realize that the Bible is a unique book. And when in addition to this we remember the circumstances under which the Bible has survived, this fact becomes very startling. Further, "Not only has the Bible received more veneration and adoration than any other book, but it has also been the object of more persecution and opposition."[1]

Mention can be made of only a few of the efforts that have been put forth to suppress or exterminate the Bible, or, when that did not succeed, to rob it of its divine authority. The Roman emperors soon discovered that the Christians grounded their beliefs on the Scriptures. Consequently, they sought to suppress or exterminate them. Diocletian, by a royal edict in 303 A.D., demanded that every copy of the Bible be destroyed by fire. He killed so many Christians and destroyed so many Bibles that when the Christians remained silent for a season and stayed in hiding, he thought that he had actually put an end to the Scriptures. He caused a medal to be struck with the inscription, "The Christian religion is destroyed and the worship of the gods restored." But it was only a few years later that Constantine came to the throne and made Christianity the state religion.

During the Middle Ages, schoolmen put the creed above the Bible. While most of them still sought to support the creed with the Scriptures, tradition became increasingly important. The state church assumed the authority of interpreting Scripture, and the study of Scripture by laymen was restricted and regarded with suspicion, if not absolutely forbidden.

During the time of the Reformation, when the Bible was translated into the tongue of the common people, the established church put severe restrictions on the reading of the Bible on the ground that laymen were incapable of interpreting it. The reader was not to seek to interpret for himself. Many laid down their lives for the simple reason that they were the followers of Christ and put their trust in the Scriptures. Laws were even made to prohibit the publishing of the Bible.

It is interesting to note in this connection that Voltaire, the noted French infidel, who died in 1778, predicted that in 100 years from his time Christianity would be extinct.

Neither imperial edict nor ecclesiastical restraints have succeeded in exterminating the Bible. The greater the efforts put forth to accomplish such a destruction the greater has been the circulation of the Bible. The latest

---

[1]Bancroft, *Christian Theology*, p. 360.

attempt to rob the Bible of its authority is the effort to degrade it to the level of all the other ancient religious books. If the Bible must be in circulation, then it has to be shown that it does not possess supernatural authority. But the Bible continues to have supernatural power, and it is being read by millions of believers around the world and being translated into hundreds of languages. The fact of the indestructibility of the Bible strongly suggests that it is the embodiment of a divine revelation.

IV. THE ARGUMENT FROM THE CHARACTER OF THE BIBLE

When we consider the character of the Bible, we are forced to come to but one conclusion: it is the embodiment of a divine revelation. Consider first the contents of the Bible. This book recognizes the personality, unity, and trinity of God; it magnifies the holiness and love of God; it accounts for the creature as a direct creation of God, made in the likeness of God; it represents man's fall as a free revolt against the revealed will of God; it pictures sin as inexcusable and under the judgment of eternal punishment; it teaches the sovereign rule of God in the universe; it sets forth in great detail God's provision of salvation and the conditions on which it may be experienced; it delineates the purposes of God concerning Israel and the church; it forecasts the developments of the world, socially, economically, politically, and religiously; it portrays the culmination of all things in the second coming of Christ, the resurrections, the judgments, the millennium, and the eternal state. Surely, this book comes from the hand of an infinite God.

Consider, in the second place, the unity of the Bible. Although written by some forty different authors over a period of about 1600 years, the Bible is one book. It has one doctrinal system, one moral standard, one plan of salvation, one program of the ages. Its several accounts of the same incidents or teachings are not contradictory, but supplementary. For example, the superscription on the cross was no doubt as follows, "This is Jesus the Nazarene, the King of the Jews." Matthew says, "This is Jesus the King of the Jews" (27:37); Mark, "The King of the Jews" (15:26); Luke, "This is the King of the Jews" (23:38); and John, "Jesus the Nazarene, the King of the Jews" (19:19). Law and grace are seen to harmonize when one understands the exact nature and purpose of each. The accounts of wicked men and nations are inoffensive and even helpful if one notices that they are recorded to be condemned. The doctrine of the Holy Spirit finds its harmonization in the progressive character of the revelation of this truth. In contrast to the Mohammedan, Zoroastrian, and Buddhist scriptures, which are for the most part collections of heterogeneous materials without beginning, middle, or end, the Bible is an amazingly unified whole.

In view of the contents and unity of the Bible we are obliged to conclude that it is the embodiment of a divine revelation. What men could have originated such a world and life view? What authors could have set it forth in such a harmonious and self-consistent form? Paché declares, "Only the Lord, for whom time has no meaning, can take in with a glance the destiny of all the universe. From eternity to eternity He is God (Ps. 90:2). He envisions at once the eternity behind us and that before us, so to speak. He alone, the One who inspired all of Scripture, could have given to it the singleness of perspective which it has."[2]

V. THE ARGUMENT FROM THE INFLUENCE OF THE BIBLE

The Koran, the Book of Mormon, Science and Health, the Zend Avesta, and the Classics of Confucius have all had a tremendous influence in the world. But there is a vast difference in the kind of influence they have exerted when compared with that of the Bible. The former have led to a low view of God and sin, even to the ignoring of it. They have produced a Stoical indifference toward life and have merely resulted in a view of morals and conduct. The Bible, on the contrary, has produced the highest results in all walks of life. It has led to the highest type of creations in the fields of art, architecture, literature, and music. The fundamental laws of the nations have been influenced; great social reforms have been made. Where is there a book in all the world that even remotely compares with it in its beneficent influence upon mankind? Surely, this is proof of its being the revelation of God to needy humanity. And in addition to this, there is the impact of the regenerating effect on millions of individual lives.

VI. THE ARGUMENT FROM THE FULFILLED PROPHECY

This might seem to belong to the argument from the character of the Bible, but because of its uniqueness it is here treated separately. The fact of predictive prophecy was established in Chapter II; here we look at it to establish that the Bible is the embodiment of a divine revelation. Only God can reveal the future, and prophecy as it relates to prediction is a miracle of knowledge. Fulfilled prophecy indicates that the writers of prophecy possessed in some manner supernatural intelligence. Peter speaks of this when he declares of the Old Testament prophets, "Men moved by the Holy Spirit spoke from God" (2 Pet. 1:21). If we can demonstrate that Old Testament prophecies have been fulfilled in every particular, then we can prove divine revelation. Let us consider certain prophecies.

[2]Paché, *The Inspiration and Authority of Scripture*, p. 112.

The prophecies concerning Israel's dispersion have been minutely fulfilled (Deut. 28:15–68; Jer. 15:4; 16:13; Hos. 3:4). In the fulfillment Samaria was to be overthrown, but Judah to be preserved (1 Kings 14:15; Isa. 7:6–8; Hos. 1:6f.); Judah and Jerusalem, though rescued from the Assyrians, were to fall into the hands of the Babylonians (Isa. 39:6; Jer. 25:9–12); the destruction of Samaria was to be final (Mic. 1:6–9), but that of Jerusalem was to be followed by a restoration (Jer. 29:10–14); the very restorer of Judah was foretold by name (Isa. 44:28; 45:1); the Medes and the Persians were to overthrow Babylon (Isa. 21:2; Dan. 5:28); the city of Jerusalem and the temple were to be rebuilt (Isa. 44:28).

So also the prophecies concerning the Gentile nations were fulfilled. Prophecies concerning Babylon, Tyre, Egypt, Ammon, Moab, Edom, and Philistia were fulfilled (Isa. 13–23; Jer. 46–51). Particularly, the prophecies concerning the four great world empires in Dan. 2 and 7 have been fulfilled. Certain parts connected with the fourth of these are manifestly still future and lead us to the return of Christ, but the rest have been fulfilled. So also the prophecy of the detailed struggle between Syria and Egypt, following the break-up of Alexander's empire, has been fulfilled. So minute are the correspondences of the predictions in Dan. 11 with the facts of history that the anti-supernaturalists are dogmatic in their assertion that this is history and not prediction. On the basis of this assumption they date the book of Daniel 168–65 B.C. But those who believe in the supernatural revelation of God continue to hold that we have in this chapter one of the strongest proofs that in the Bible we have the embodiment of the divine prescience and not the record of events already past, made for the purpose of pious fraud.

There are many other predictions in the Bible that could be mentioned as proof of the same thing. Some are the increase of knowledge and of travel in the latter days (Dan. 12:4), the continuation of wars and rumors of wars (Matt. 24:6f.), the increase of wickedness (2 Tim. 3:1–13), the preservation of a remnant of Israel (Rom. 11:1–5, 25–32), and the stirring of these dry bones and their return to national and spiritual life (Ezek. 37:1–28). What man could foresee and predict any of these things! This, again, proves we have in the Bible the embodiment of a divine revelation.

VII. THE CLAIMS OF THE SCRIPTURES THEMSELVES

The Bible claims to be not only a revelation from God, but an infallible record of that revelation. The infallibility of Scripture will be considered later. Here we are concerned with its own claims to be the revelation of God. But at the onset we meet with the objection that it is begging the question to appeal to the testimony of Scripture for proof of its being a divine revelation. Would not the testimony have to be suspected? But if we can prove the genuineness of the books of the Bible and the truthfulness of the things which they report on other subjects, then we are justified in also accepting their testimony in their own behalf. If we have verified the credentials of an ambassador and have satisfied ourselves as to his truthfulness in regard to his authorization, then we may also accept his personal statements respecting the nature of his powers and the source of his information.

Often we have statements like this in the Pentateuch, "Now the Lord spoke to Moses, saying" (Exod. 14:1; Lev. 4:1; Num. 4:1; Deut. 32:48). He was commanded to write in a book what God told him (Exod. 17:14; 34:27), and he did this (Exod. 24:4; 34:28; Num. 33:2; Deut. 31:9, 22, 24). Likewise the prophets say: "For the Lord speaks" (Isa. 1:2); "The Lord said to Isaiah" (Isa. 7:3); "Thus says the Lord" (Isa. 43:1); "The word which came to Jeremiah from the Lord, saying" (Jer. 11:1); "The word of the Lord came expressly to Ezekiel" (Ezek. 1:3); "The word of the Lord which came to Hosea" (Hos. 1:1); "The word of the Lord that came to Joel" (Joel 1:1). It is claimed that statements like these occur more than 3,800 times in the Old Testament. Thus the Old Testament claims to be a revelation from God.

The New Testament writers likewise claim that they declare the message of God. Paul claims that the things he wrote were the commandments of God (1 Cor. 14:37); that what he preached, men were to receive as the very word of God (1 Thess. 2:13); that the salvation of men depends upon faith in the doctrines which he taught (Gal. 1:8). John teaches that his testimony was God's testimony (1 John 5:10). Peter wanted his readers to remember "the words spoken beforehand by the holy prophets and the commandment of the Lord and Savior spoken by your apostles" (2 Pet. 3:2). And the writer to the Hebrews predicts a severer punishment for those who reject the message that was confirmed to him by those who heard Christ, than that which fell upon the violators of the law of Moses (Heb. 2:1-4).

The force of the evidence is cumulative. If we weigh separately the arguments presented in this chapter we may not find any of them conclusive; but if we permit each argument to contribute its modicum of truth, we shall be forced to the conclusion that the Bible is the embodiment of a divine revelation. Accepting this idea as established, we have a background for the study of the other subjects of Bibliology.

CHAPTER VI

The Genuineness, Credibility, and Canonicity of the Books of the Bible

When we accept the fact that in the Bible we have the embodiment of a divine revelation, we at once become interested in the character of the documents that convey that revelation. We forthwith wish to know whether the several books of the Bible are genuine, credible, and canonical. To this we now turn.

I. THE GENUINENESS OF THE BOOKS OF THE BIBLE

By genuineness we mean that a book is written by the person or persons whose name it bears or, if anonymous, by the person or persons to whom ancient tradition has assigned it, or if not assigned to some definite author or authors, to the time to which tradition has assigned it. A book is said to be forged or spurious if it is not written at the time to which it has been assigned, or by the author professed by it. A book is considered to be authentic when it relates facts as they really occurred. It is corrupt when the text has been in any manner changed.

That the books of both the Old and the New Testament are authentic and genuine can be shown in the following manner.

A. THE GENUINENESS OF THE BOOKS OF THE OLD TESTAMENT

For a complete survey of the evidence the student is referred to the scholarly works on Old Testament Introduction. We can at this point only deal with the subject in a general way. The Old Testament Scriptures will be approached in their threefold division: the Law, the Prophets, and the Kethubhim.

1. The genuineness of the books of the Law. Much modern criticism denies the Mosaic authorship of the Pentateuch. The documentary hypothesis divides the authorship of these books up into the Jehovistic, Elohistic, Deuteronomistic, and Priestly codes, with many redactors.[1] For our purpose

---

[1]For a summary statement, evaluation, and refutation of this position, see Allis, *The Five Books of Moses;* Archer, *A Survey of Old Testament Introduction,* pp. 73–154; nd Harrison, *Introduction to the Old Testament,* pp. 495–541.

we can only briefly indicate the proofs of the Mosaic authorship of the Pentateuch. First, it is known generally that a considerable portion of the people could read and write as far back as the time of Hammurabi; that genealogical tablets and lists were known in Babylonia centuries before Abraham; that it is possible that Abraham carried cuneiform tablets containing such records with him from Haran to Canaan; and that in this manner Moses may have come into possession of them. Whether because he had access to such records, or because he had only oral tradition, or because he had only a direct revelation from God, or because of a combination of these, conservative scholarship has always held that Moses wrote Genesis.

Furthermore, in the rest of the Pentateuch, Moses is repeatedly represented as the author of that which is written. He was to write it (Exod. 17:14; 34:27), and it is said that he did write (Exod. 24:4; 34:28; Num. 33:2; Deut. 31:9, 24). What he wrote is described as "the words of this law" (Deut. 28:58), "the book of this law" (Deut. 28:61), "this book" (Deut. 29:20, 27), "this book of the law" (Deut. 29:21; 30:10; 31:26), and "the words of this law" (Deut. 31:24). In addition, thirteen times outside the Pentateuch in the Old Testament Moses is represented as the author of a written work. It is called "the book of the law of Moses" (Josh. 8:31; 23:6; 2 Kings 14:6), "the law of Moses" (1 Kings 2:3; 2 Chron. 23:18; Dan. 9:11), and "the book of Moses" (Neh. 13:1).

In the New Testament our Lord frequently speaks of "Moses" as a written work (Luke 16:29; 24:27; cf. John 7:19). He also ascribes various teachings in the Pentateuch to Moses (Matt. 8:4; 19:7f.; Mark 7:10; 12:26; John 7:22f.). Once he speaks of the "writings" of Moses (John 5:47). Various writers of the New Testament speak of "Moses" as a book (Acts 15:21; 2 Cor. 3:15) and of "the law of Moses" (Acts 13:39; 1 Cor. 9:9; Heb. 10:28; cf. John 1:45). They also ascribe certain teachings found in the Pentateuch to Moses (Acts 3:22; Rom. 9:15; Heb. 8:5; 9:19).

Certain other internal evidence may also be mentioned which attests to the Mosaic authorship of the Pentateuch. The author is obviously an eyewitness to the account of the exodus; he shows an acquaintance with the land of Egypt, its geography, flora, and fauna; he uses several Egyptian words; and he makes reference to customs which go back to the second millennium B.C. Harrison concludes:

> The Pentateuch is a homogeneous composition of five volumes, and not an agglomeration of separate and perhaps only rather casually related works. It described, against an accredited historical background, the manner in which God revealed Himself to men and chose the Israelites for special service and witness in the world and in the course of human history. The role of Moses in the formulation of this literary corpus appears pre-eminent, and it is not without good reason that he should be accorded a place of high honor in the growth of the epic of

Israelite nationhood, and be venerated by Jews and Christians alike as the great mediator of the ancient law.[2]

2. The genuineness of the books of the Prophets.   The Hebrew speaks of the former and the latter prophets. To the former prophets belong Joshua, Judges, 1 and 2 Samuel, 1 and 2 Kings; to the latter belong Isaiah, Jeremiah, Ezekiel, and the so-called Minor Prophets. First, looking at the former prophets, there is no reason for rejecting the traditional view that Joshua wrote the book that bears his name, nor that Samuel wrote Judges. Judges was written after the commencement of the monarchy (19:1; 21:25) and before the accession of David (1:21; cf. 2 Sam. 5:6–8). In 1 Chron. 29:29 we read of the things "written in the chronicles of Samuel the seer, in the chronicles of Nathan the prophet, and in the chronicles of Gad the seer." Tradition has, accordingly, felt justified in assigning 1 Sam. 1–24 to Samuel, and 1 Sam. 25–2 Sam. 24 to Nathan and Gad. Jeremiah has been commonly considered the author of the books of Kings; at least the author was a contemporary of his. Kings speaks of the book of the acts of Solomon (1 Kings 11:41), the book of the chronicles of the kings of Israel (1 Kings 14:19), and the book of the chronicles of the kings of Judah (1 Kings 14:29); and it has frequent insertions of the records of eyewitnesses in the portions about Elijah, Elisha, and Micaiah, in which older material is used.

Second, the latter prophets are also genuine.[3] The acts and deeds of Hezekiah are said to have been written "in the vision of Isaiah the prophet" (2 Chron. 32:32); Isaiah is also said to have written "the acts of Uzziah" (2 Chron. 26:22). The prophecy of Isaiah is assigned to him (1:1). Jesus and his apostles speak of the writing of Isaiah, assigning even the disputed parts to him (Matt. 8:17, cf. Isa. 53:4; Luke 4:17f., cf. Isa. 61:1; John 12:38–41, cf. Isa. 53:1 and 6:10). Jeremiah was instructed, "Write all the words which I have spoken to you in a book" (Jer. 30:2), and we are told that he "wrote in a single scroll all the calamity which would come upon Babylon" (Jer. 51:60). No doubt Baruch was his amanuensis for a large part of his work (Jer. 36; cf. 45:1). Ezekiel also was asked to write (Ezek. 24:2; 43:11), as was Habakkuk (Hab. 2:2). It is commonly assumed by conservative scholars that the names which appear in the opening verses of a prophetic book are intended to give us faithfully the name of the author of that book. Even Malachi is probably intended as the name of the author as well as of the book, and not as a reference to 3:1.

3. The genuineness of the Kethubhim.   The remaining books were divided into three groups: the poetic books, which consist of the Psalms, Proverbs,

---

[2]Harrison, *Introduction to the Old Testament*, p. 541.
[3]For a valuable introduction to the Old Testament prophets, see Freeman, *An Introduction to the Old Testament Prophets*.

and Job; the Megilloth, which consists of Song of Solomon, Ruth, Lamentations, Ecclesiastes, and Esther; and the non-prophetical historical books, which include Daniel, Ezra, Nehemiah, and the Chronicles. Several things can be noted. As for the Psalms and the works of Solomon, we read of "the writing of David" and "the writing of his son Solomon" (2 Chron. 35:4). Although the inscriptions to the Psalms are not a part of the original text, they are generally accepted as accurate. Of the 150 Psalms, 100 are assigned to authors: 73 to David, 11 to the sons of Korah, 12 to Asaph, two to Solomon, and one each to Ethan and to Moses. The remainder are anonymous. According to the headings in Proverbs, Solomon was the author of chapters 1 to 24. He was also the author of chapters 25 to 29, although these chapters were copied from his writings by the men of Hezekiah. Chapter 30 is ascribed to Agur the son of Jakeh, and chapter 31 to King Lemuel. The Book of Job does not give us the name of the author, but it is not unlikely that Job himself wrote the book. We regard the book as narrating faithfully the experiences of the man Job in the days of the patriarchs, and as not being mere poetic fiction. Who but Job himself could narrate faithfully his own experiences and sayings and also the speeches of Eliphaz, Bildad, Zophar, Elihu, and God?

The Song of Solomon is also inscribed to Solomon (1:1), and there is no reason for questioning the truthfulness of the inscription. Archer writes, "It has been the uniform tradition of the Christian church until modern times that Canticles is a genuine Solomonic production."[4] Ruth has frequently been associated with Judges and was probably written by the same man who wrote the book of Judges, probably Samuel. Though as Davis observes, "This cannot be verified."[5] That David's name is mentioned (Ruth 4:22) and not Solomon's is an argument favoring the dating of the book as not later than David.

Lamentations is ascribed to Jeremiah by the heading in our Bibles, and tradition has always attributed the book to this prophet. In form of expression and in general argument it has much in common with the book of Jeremiah, and we may confidently ascribe the book to this writer. Ecclesiastes is said to be by "the Preacher, the son of David, king in Jerusalem" (1:1), and this expression has usually been taken by conservatives to be none other than Solomon. There is reference to the author's incomparable wisdom (1:16), and the great works which he made (2:4–11). Until the Reformation period, the book was assigned to Solomon by uniform consent of all Jewish and Christian scholars, and most conservative scholars still assign it to him, though there is some linguistic evidence that it may have been written by someone other than Solomon.

Esther may have been written by Mordecai the Jew, who best knew the

[4]Archer, *A Survey of Old Testament Introduction*, pp. 472, 473.
[5]Davis, *Conquest and Crisis*, p. 156.

facts related in the book, but 10:2f. seem to argue against this position. Whitcomb concludes, "The author must have been a Jew who lived in Persia at the time of the events narrated and who had access to the official chronicles of the kings of Media and Persia (2:23; 9:20; 10:2)."[6] Critics tend to agree that it was written by a Persian Jew, because of the absence of marks of its being written in Palestine. The diction is admittedly late, being comparable to that of Ezra, Nehemiah, and Chronicles.

Daniel was undoubtedly written by the statesman who bore that name. The author identifies himself as Daniel and writes in the first person (7:2; 8:1, 15; 9:2; 10:2). Further, Daniel was commanded to preserve the book (12:4). There is a noticeable unity in the book, with the name Daniel appearing throughout. Jesus attributed the book to Daniel (Matt. 24:15). Conservative scholarship dates the book to the 6th century B.C., though because of their rejection of predictive prophecy, modern critics generally place the book into the Maccabean period and assign it to a date between 168–165 B.C.

Ezra was undoubtedly written by Ezra the scribe. Since some of the book is written in the first person singular by a man identified as Ezra (7:28; cf. 7:1), and because the book bears the marks of unity, "it would seem to follow that the remainder is his also."[7]

Nehemiah was no doubt written by Nehemiah, the Persian king's cupbearer. This is made clear by the opening words, "The words of Nehemiah the son of Hacaliah" (1:1), and the fact that the author speaks in the first person many times. It was written in the time of Malachi, somewhere between 424–395 B.C. The Chronicles are placed by the critics on a much lower plane than the books of Kings. The reason seems to be that while Kings deals with the prophetic aspects of the history, Chronicles deals more with the priestly aspects. Tradition has assigned these books to Ezra. The position of the books in the canon, the closing of the history at the very point where that of Ezra begins, and the style make this possible if not probable. They must have been written about 450–425 B.C., before Ezra.

B. The Genuineness of the Books of the New Testament

Here again the student must be referred to the works on New Testament Introduction for a complete statement,[8] but a few facts can be noted. Criticism is more and more returning to the traditional view as to the date and authorship of the several books. There is reason for believing that the Synoptic Gospels were written in the order: Matthew, Luke, and Mark. Origen

[6]Whitcomb, "Esther," *The Wycliffe Bible Commentary*, p. 447.
[7]Young, *An Introduction to the Old Testament*, p. 370.
[8]See Hiebert, *An Introduction to the New Testament*, 3 vols., and Guthrie, *New Testament Introduction*.

frequently cites them in that order, and Clement of Alexandria before him puts the Gospels that contain the genealogies first on the basis of the tradition which he received from the elders before him.[9] This view is supported by the consideration that the Gospels grew out of the circumstances and occasions of the time. Tradition declares that for fifteen years Matthew preached in Palestine, and that after that he went to minister to foreign nations. On the basis of the famous statement in Papias that "Matthew composed the Logia in the Hebrew (i.e., Aramaic) tongue," we must hold that it is most natural to suppose that when he left Palestine he left behind him this Aramaic Gospel, about A.D. 45, and that a little later he also wrote the Greek Gospel that has come down to us, for his new hearers, about A.D. 50. There is also very general agreement that the second Gospel was written by John Mark. From the circumstances of the times and internal evidence, we assign it to the years A.D. 67 or 68. There is also very general agreement that the third Gospel was written by Luke, the beloved physician. It was probably written about the year A.D. 58.

The Gospel of John is rejected by some because of its emphasis on the deity of Christ. It is said that the Synoptics do not reveal any such belief concerning him during the first century. But this is not true, for in the Synoptics he is no less deity than in John. The discovery of Papyrus 52, containing five verses of John 18 and dated in the first half of the second century, has done much to confirm the traditional date of the Gospel of John. Metzger writes, "Had this little fragment been known during the middle of the past century, that school of New Testament criticism which was inspired by the brilliant Tübingen professor, Ferdinand Christian Baur, could not have argued that the Fourth Gospel was not composed until about the year 160."[10]

The book of Acts is today quite generally ascribed to Luke, the same man who wrote the third Gospel. Ten of the so-called Pauline Epistles are today for the most part attributed to Paul, doubt being cast only upon the Pastoral Epistles, on the basis of style. But style changes can be due to change in subject matter and the age of the author.

The Epistle to the Hebrews is anonymous and no one knows who wrote it. It was undoubtedly written by a learned Christian somewhere between A.D. 67 and 69. James and Jude were undoubtedly written by two of the brothers of Jesus. 1 and 2 Peter were written by the Apostle Peter. Some cast doubt upon 2 Peter on the ground of style. But Peter may have had Silvanus as his amanuensis in the first Epistle (1 Pet. 5:12), and so have had some help with his diction, and may have written the second Epistle without his help.

The three Epistles of John and the Revelation were written by the Apostle John. The difference in style in the book of Revelation as compared with the

[9]Eusebius, *Ecclesiastical History*, VI:xiv.
[10]Metzger, *The Text of the New Testament*, p. 39.

Epistles may be accounted for in the same way as the differences in 1 and 2 Peter. That is, he may have had help in the writing of the Epistles, but have written the Revelation all by himself, and further, the subject matter would itself account for the difference of style. This does not affect the question of inspiration in the least, for we argue for the inspiration of the final result that was produced and not for the inspiration of the man as such.

II. THE CREDIBILITY OF THE BOOKS OF THE BIBLE

A book is credible if it relates truthfully the matters which it treats. It is said to be corrupt when its present text varies from the original. Credibility then embraces both the ideas of truthfulness of the records and purity of the text. A brief word must be said on this subject concerning both the Old and New Testament.

A. THE CREDIBILITY OF THE BOOKS OF THE OLD TESTAMENT

This is established by two great facts:

1. *The proof from Christ's recognition of the Old Testament.* Christ received the Old Testament as relating truthfully the events and doctrines which it treats (Matt. 5:17f.; Luke 24:27, 44f.; John 10:34–36). He definitely endorsed a number of the main teachings of the Old Testament as true, as, for example, the creation of the universe by God (Mark 13:19), the direct creation of man (Matt. 19:4f.), the personality of Satan and his malignant character (John 8:44), the destruction of the world by a flood in the days of Noah (Luke 17:26f.), the destruction of Sodom and Gomorrah and the rescue of Lot (Luke 17:28–30), the revelation of God to Moses at the burning bush (Mark 12:26), the Mosaic authorship of the Pentateuch (Luke 24:27), the giving of the manna in the wilderness (John 6:32), the existence of the tabernacle (Luke 6:3f.), the experience of Jonah in the big fish (Matt. 12:39f.), and the unity of Isaiah (Matt. 8:17; Luke 4:17f.). If Jesus was God manifest in the flesh, he knew what were the facts, and if he knew them, he could not accommodate himself to any erroneous views of his day regarding matters of such fundamental importance, and be honest. His testimony must, therefore, be accepted as true, or he must be rejected as a religious teacher.

2. *The proof derived from history and archaeology.* History furnishes many proofs of the correctness of the biblical representations of life in Egypt, Assyria, Babylonia, Medo-Persia, and so forth. A number of the rulers of

these countries are mentioned by name in Scripture, and none of them is represented in a manner contradictory to what is known of him in history. Shalmaneser IV is said to have besieged the city of Samaria, but the king of Assyria, whom we now know to have been Sargon II, is said to have carried the people away into Assyria (2 Kings 17:3–6). History shows that he reigned from 722–705 B.C. He is mentioned by name only once in the Bible (Isa. 20:1). Neither Belshazzar (Dan. 5:1–30) nor Darius the Mede (Dan. 5:31–6:28) is any longer regarded as a fictitious character.

Archaeology likewise supplies many confirmations of the biblical accounts. The Babylonian "Epic of Creation," while hardly a confirmation of the Genesis account, shows, nevertheless, that the idea of a special creation was widespread in early times. The same can be said about the Babylonian legends of the fall. More important is a tablet that has been found in Babylon containing an account of the flood which has marked similarities to the biblical account. The so-called battle of the kings (Gen. 14) can no longer be regarded with suspicion, since the inscriptions in the Valley of the Euphrates show that the four kings mentioned in the Bible as joining in this expedition are historical persons. The Nuzi tablets throw light on the action of Sarah and Rachel in giving their handmaids to their husbands. The Egyptian hieroglyphics indicate that writing was known more than a thousand years before Abraham. Archaeology also confirms that Israel lived in Egypt, that the people were in bondage in that land, and that they finally left the country. The Hittites, whose very existence was questioned, have been shown to be a powerful people in Asia Minor and Palestine at the very time indicated in the Bible. The Tel el-Amarna tables give evidence of the trustworthiness of the book of Judges. As the science of archaeology progresses, no doubt more and more information will come to light confirming the accuracy of the biblical record.

B. The Credibility of the Books of the New Testament

This can be established by four great facts:

1. The writers of the New Testament were competent. They were qualified to bear testimony and to teach divine truth. Matthew, John, and Peter were disciples of Christ and eyewitnesses of his works and teachings (2 Pet. 1:18; 1 John 1:1–3). Mark, according to Papias, was the interpreter of Peter and wrote down accurately what he remembered of the teaching of Peter. Luke was a companion of Paul and, according to Irenaeus, recorded in a book the gospel preached by him. Paul was definitely called and appointed by Christ and claimed that he received his gospel directly from God (Gal. 1:11–17). James and Jude were brothers of Christ, and their messages come to us with this background. All of them had received the enduement of the Holy Spirit and so wrote not merely from memory, the deliverances of oral and written testimony, and spiritual insight, but as qualified by the Spirit for their tasks.

2. The writers of the New Testament were honest.   The moral tone of their writings, their evident regard for the truth, and the circumstantiality of their accounts indicate that they were not deliberate deceivers, but honest men. The same thing is also apparent from the fact that their testimony endangered all their worldly interests, such as their social standing, their material prosperity, and even their lives. What could be their motive in inventing a story that condemns all hypocrisy and is contrary to all their inherited beliefs, if they had to pay such a price for it?

3. Their writings harmonize with each other.   The Synoptics do not contradict but supplement each other. The details in the Gospel of John can be fitted together with the first three Gospels into a harmonious whole. The Acts furnishes an historical background for ten of Paul's Epistles. The Pastoral Epistles do not have to be fitted into the Acts, for in none of them is it intimated that they belong to the period of the Acts. Hebrews and the General Epistles, as well as the Revelation, can without any violence to the contents be fitted into the first century. Doctrinally, also, the writings of the New Testament harmonize. Christ is deity in the Synoptics as well as in John's Gospel. Paul and James do not contradict each other, but present faith and works from different viewpoints. There is a difference of emphasis, but not of fundamental conception. There is progress in the unfolding of doctrine from the Gospels to the Epistles, but not contradiction. The twenty-seven books of the New Testament present an harmonious picture of Jesus Christ and his work. This argues for the truthfulness of the record.

4. Their accounts agree with history and experience.   There are many references to contemporary history in the New Testament, such as the enrollment when Quirinius was governor of Syria (Luke 2:2), the acts of Herod the Great (Matt. 2:16–18), of Herod Antipas (Matt. 14:1–12), of Herod Agrippa I (Acts 12:1), of Gallio (Acts 18:12–17), of Herod Agrippa II (Acts 25:13–26:32), etc., but thus far no one has been able to show that the biblical account is contradicted by a single fact derived from other trustworthy sources. And as for experience, we have already said that if we grant the existence of a personal, omnipotent, and loving God, miracles are not only possible but probable. Physical miracles do not occur often now because they are not needed in the sense in which they were needed then. They were intended to attest God's revelation when first made, but now that Christianity has been introduced they are no longer needed for this purpose. Spiritual miracles still occur in abundance. We may, therefore, say that there is nothing in experience or history that contradicts the narratives of the Gospels and the Epistles.

III. THE CANONICITY OF THE BOOKS OF THE BIBLE

Again this study must be very general. The word "canon" comes from the Greek *kanon*. It means, in the first place, a reed or rod; then a measuring-rod; hence a rule or standard. In the second place, it means an authoritative decision of a church council; and in the third place, as applied to the Bible, it means those books which have been measured, found satisfactory, and approved as inspired of God.

A. THE CANONICITY OF THE BOOKS OF THE OLD TESTAMENT

Again the consideration of the separate books must be left to Biblical Introduction, but a few general observations must be made here. The threefold division of the books of the Old Testament in the Hebrew Bible into the Law, the Prophets, and the Kethubhim does not imply three periods of canonization. The books of the Pentateuch were put together at the beginning of the Old Testament because they were believed to have been written by Moses. With the Prophets were put such books as were believed to have been written by a prophet in office. Daniel, having the prophetic gift but not being a prophet in office, was put into the third group. The Kethubhim were subdivided according to their contents or the purpose for which they were used. Psalms, Proverbs, and Job were classified as Poetical Books, because of their literary character. The Song of Solomon, Ruth, Lamentations, Ecclesiastes, and Esther were called the Megilloth because they were read at the Jewish feasts of the Passover and of Pentecost, at the fast on the ninth of Ab, at the Feast of Tabernacles, and at that of Purim, respectively. Daniel, Ezra, Nehemiah, and Chronicles were classed as the Non-prophetical Historical Books because they were written by men who were not prophets in office. Amos was not a prophet at first, but God took him from following the flock and sent him to prophesy to his people (Amos 7:14f.); that is, he became a prophet in office and was rightly classed with the latter prophets.

Because the canonicity of Ecclesiastes and the Song of Solomon was not settled until the Council of Jamnia (A.D. 90),[11] some maintain that the canon of the Old Testament was not closed until that time, or, since the discussion concerning them continued even after that date, not until about A.D. 200. But if the character and number of the books that should constitute our Bible cannot be settled until all are agreed on this point, then we can

[11]Archer, *A Survey of Old Testament Introduction*, p. 65.

never have an authoritative canon, which is just what some would want, for there are always those who would add to the canon or challenge those books which are included. With regard to the Old Testament as we have it today, we may accept the view of David Kimchi (1160–1232) and Elias Levita (1465–1549), two Jewish scholars, who held that the final collection of the Old Testament canon was completed by Ezra and the members of the Great Synagogue in the fifth century before Christ. Several things can be said which make this view possible. Josephus, who wrote near the end of the first century A.D., included the same threefold division as did the Masoretic Canon.[12] He further indicated that the canon was completed in the reign of Artaxerxes, which corresponds to the lifetime of Ezra.[13] It seems likely that Ezra was the one who finally organized the sacred books of the Old Testament, since he is called "the scribe" (Neh. 8:1; 12:36), "a scribe skilled in the law of Moses" (Ezra 7:6), and "the scribe, learned in the words of the commandments of the Lord and His statutes to Israel" (Ezra 7:11). Further, no more canonical writings were composed since the days of Artaxerxes, son of Xerxes, until New Testament times. The Apocrypha, though included in the Septuagint, was never accepted into the Hebrew canon.

B. THE CANONICITY OF THE BOOKS OF THE NEW TESTAMENT

The formation of the canon of the New Testament did not come about as a result of an organized effort to produce such, but rather it seemed to have shaped itself as a result of the obviously genuine character of the books. Several broad principles aided in the determination of which books should be accepted as canonical. Apostolicity was of primary importance. The author of a book had either to be an apostle of Christ or to sustain such a relation to an apostle as to raise his book to the level of the apostolic books. Another factor in determining the choice of a book was its suitability to public reading. A third factor was its universality. Was the book universally received throughout the Christian community? The contents of the book, further, had to be of such a spiritual character as to entitle them to this rank. And finally, the book had to give evidence of having been inspired by the Holy Spirit.

By the end of the second century all but seven books, Hebrews, 2 and 3 John, 2 Peter, Jude, James, and Revelation, the so-called antilegomena, were recognized as apostolic, and by the end of the fourth century all the twenty-seven books in our present canon were recognized by all the churches in the West. After the Damasine Council of Rome (382) and the third Council of

---

[12]Josephus spoke of twenty-two books in the canon, since 1 and 2 Sam. were considered as one, as were 1 and 2 Kings, Ezra and Nehemiah, Ruth and Judges, Jeremiah and Lamentations, and the twelve minor prophets.
[13]Josephus, *Against Apion*, I:8.

Carthage (397), the question of the canon was closed in the West. By the year 500, the whole Greek-speaking church seems also to have accepted all the books in our present New Testament. From that time on, the question was closed in the East also. But, as stated earlier, there has perhaps never been a time when all have accepted this general verdict of the church. There have always been individuals and smaller bodies of men who have questioned the right of some books or books to a place in the canon.

CHAPTER VII

The Inspiration of the Scriptures

We have been encouraged in our quest for certainty by the evidence that in the Bible we have the embodiment of a divine revelation. The records that give us that revelation have been shown to be genuine, credible, and the only ones qualified to convey that revelation. But if we had to stop here, we would still have merely an honest ancient work on religious subjects. Can we affirm anything further of the Scriptures? Are they also verbally inspired and infallible in all that they say? We believe they are, and we turn now to a study of the question of inspiration.

I. THE DEFINITION OF INSPIRATION

In order to give an adequate and precise definition of inspiration, several related theological concepts must be considered, and the false theories refuted.

A. RELATED TERMS

The related terms are revelation, inspiration, authority, inerrancy, and illumination.

1. Revelation. We have noted that God has revealed himself in nature, history, and conscience. He has also revealed himself in his Son and in his Word. We are primarily concerned at this point with direct revelation as distinct from indirect, immediate as distinct from mediate. Revelation has to do with the communication of truth that cannot be otherwise discovered; inspiration has to do with the recording of revealed truth. We can have revelation without inspiration, as has been the case with many of the godly people in the past. This is clear from the fact that John heard the seven thunders utter their voices, but was not permitted to write what they said (Rev. 10:3f.). We may also have inspiration without direct revelation, as when the writers set down what they had seen with their own eyes or discovered by research (Luke 1:1–4; 1 John 1:1–4). Luke, as a historian, searched out written records and verified oral tradition in the penning of his gospel, and was an eyewitness to much of the Acts; John, on the other hand, received much of the Revelation by direct revelation from God. Both men were inspired in the penning of their material, but the material was received in different manners. Of course, in the broader sense we speak of the entirety of Scripture as God's self-revelation; some of the revelation came directly, and some of it came indirectly through God's saving operations in human history.

2. Inspiration.   Inspiration has to do with the recording of the truth. The Spirit of God moved upon men to write the sixty-six books of the Bible (Acts 1:16; Heb. 10:15–17; 2 Pet. 1:21). Scripture is fully and verbally inspired; it is God-breathed (2 Tim. 3:16). A fuller definition of inspiration will follow later in this chapter.

3. Authority.   The Bible carries with it the divine authority of God. It is binding upon man—on his mind, conscience, will, and heart. Man, creed, and church are all subject to the authority of Scripture. God has spoken; we must submit. The eternal "thus saith the Lord" is our standard.

4. Inerrancy.   Not only is Scripture inspired and authoritative, it is also inerrant and infallible. By this we mean that it is without error in the original manuscripts. It is inerrant in all that it affirms, whether in historical, scientific, moral, or doctrinal matters. Inerrancy extends to all of Scripture and is not limited to certain teachings of Scripture.

5. Illumination.   The one who inspired men in the writing of Scripture, illumines the minds of those who read it. Because of sin and the darkened understanding brought about because of sin, no one can understand Scripture properly (Rom. 1:21; Eph. 4:18). But the Spirit can enlighten the mind of the believer to understand the Scriptures. This is the burden of 1 Cor. 2:6–16 (cf. Eph. 1:18); John speaks of this as well in 1 John 2:20, 27.

B. Inadequate Theories of Inspiration

Various theories of inspiration have been suggested down through the ages which often contain some truth, but remain inadequate definitions.

1. Natural inspiration or the intuition theory.   This theory holds that inspiration is merely a superior insight on the part of natural man. It is merely the intensifying and elevating of the religious perceptions of the writer. This view puts some of the church's great hymns on a level with the Bible. In reality it confuses the Spirit's work of illumination with his special work of inspiration. Illumination does not deal with the transmission of the truth, but with the understanding of truth already revealed.

2. The dynamic or partial-inspiration theory.   This theory holds that God supplied the ability needed for the trustworthy transmission of the truth which the writers of Scripture were commissioned to deliver. This made them infallible in matters of faith and practice, but not in things which are not of an immediately religious character. Thus the writer could be in error in things which relate to history or science. The problems with this view are obvious. How can we accept one sentence of Scripture and not another? Who can tell us which part is right and which part is not? And further, who can tell us how to distinguish between things that are essential to faith and practice and those that are not? Nowhere does the Bible tell us that inspiration covers only things which relate to faith and practice. It declares all Scripture to be God-breathed (2 Tim. 3:16).

3. The theory that the thoughts, not the words, are inspired.   According to this theory, God suggested the thoughts of the revelation, but left it up to man to put the revelation into words. But Scripture indicates that the words themselves are inspired. Paul records that he spoke, "not in words taught by human wisdom, but in those taught by the Spirit" (1 Cor. 2:13). He further declared that all Scripture is inspired (2 Tim. 3:16); this means the very words used. Additionally, it is difficult to think of thought apart from words. As Paché states, "Ideas can be conceived of and transmitted only by means of words."[1] It is inconceivable to dissociate them from each other. Saucy concludes, "There cannot be an inspiration of thoughts, therefore, which at the same time does not encompass the words through which the thoughts are expressed."[2] Surely, the words themselves must be inspired, and not just the thoughts and ideas.

4. The theory that the Bible contains the Word of God.   On this theory the Bible is a human book which God can make his Word at the moment of personal encounter. The writers of Scripture wrote of their encounters with God in thought patterns of their day. These authors incorporated into their writings various supernatural myths and miraculous tales to convey spiritual truths. The interpreter's job is to strip away all the mythical embellishments and seek to arrive at the spiritual truth God has for us. Thus, Scripture must be demythologized. Scripture becomes the Word of God to us at that existential moment when God breaks through to us and reveals himself in his Word. Against this view, several things can be said. In the first place, it is a

[1]Paché, *The Inspiration and Authority of Scripture*, p. 58.
[2]Saucy, *The Bible: Breathed from God*, p. 48.

very subjective approach to Scripture. The Bible could be made to say one thing to one person and something else to another. This position takes away the objective approach to the interpretation of Scripture. It virtually discards propositional truth. Paché questions, "If a great many of the pages of the Bible are unauthentic and mythical, what remains that is sure?"[3] Since man, down through history, has adequately demonstrated his fallibility and untrustworthiness as it relates to theories of interpretation, should we not rather accept Scripture as the revelation of God to man, inspired by the Spirit of God, and completely trustworthy and inerrant at every point?

5. The dictation theory. The dictation theory holds that the authors of Scripture were mere pens, amanuenses, not beings whose individualities were preserved and somehow pressed into service in the act of inspiration. On this view the style is that of the Holy Spirit. Some have even argued that the grammar must be everywhere perfect because it is the Holy Spirit's grammar. But this theory ignores the manifest differences in the style of Moses, David, Peter, James, John, and Paul, for example. Some have tried to meet this difficulty by supposing that the Holy Spirit in each case adopted the style of the writer, but there is a better way of accounting for and defending verbal inspiration. We must acknowledge the twofold nature of Scripture: on the one hand it is a God-breathed book, but on the other hand it has a human character. God used living men, not dead tools. He did not set aside human personality, but rather used the very personality of the human authors in the penning of his revelation.

C. The Biblical Doctrine of Inspiration

The Holy Spirit so guided and superintended the writers of the sacred text, making use of their own unique personalities, that they wrote all that he wanted them to write, without excess or error. Several things must be noted. (1) Inspiration is inexplicable. It is the operation of the Holy Spirit, but we do not know exactly how that power of the Spirit operates. (2) Inspiration, in this restricted sense, is limited to the authors of Scripture. Other books are not inspired in the same sense. (3) Inspiration is essentially guidance. That is, the Holy Spirit supervised the selection of the materials to be used and the words to be employed in writing. (4) The Holy Spirit preserved the authors from all error and from all omission. (5) Inspiration extends to the words, not merely to the thoughts and concepts. Thus, we speak of the plenary and verbal inspiration of the Scriptures; plenary, because the inspiration is entire and without restriction, that is, it includes all and every Scripture (2 Tim. 3:16); verbal, because it includes every word (1 Cor. 2:13). And (6) inspira-

---

[3]Paché, *The Inspiration and Authority of Scripture*, p. 65.

tion is affirmed only of the autographs of the Scriptures, not of any of the versions, whether ancient or modern, nor of any Hebrew or Greek manuscripts in existence, nor of any critical texts known. All these are either known to be faulty in some particulars, or are not certainly known to be free from all error. While there are no original autographs available, the number of words which are still in doubt is very small, and no doctrine is affected by this situation.

A word should be said about the distinction between inspiration and authority. Usually the two are identical, so that what is inspired is also authoritative for teaching and conduct; but occasionally that is not the case. For example, Satan's statement to Eve is recorded by inspiration, but it is not true (Gen. 3:4f.). The same thing can be said about Peter's advice to Christ (Matt. 16:22) and the declaration of Gamaliel to the council (Acts 5:38f.). Since none of these represents the mind of God, they are not authoritative, although they are found in the Bible. The same thing can be said about texts that are taken out of their contexts and given a very different meaning from the one they have in their contexts. The words still are inspired, but the new meaning is not authoritative. We should regard every statement as both inspired and authoritative, unless there is some hint in the context that the latter is not the case in a given instance.

II. THE PROOFS OF INSPIRATION

There are two fundamental things on which we may base the theory of verbal, plenary inspiration: the character of God and the character and claims of the Bible itself.

A. The Character of God

The existence of God is evident from the fact that he has revealed himself, and it has been established by means of various proofs for his existence. In the study of that revelation and those proofs, we have already discovered some of his distinctive characteristics. We have yet to study various things about his nature, but have already seen that he is a personal, almighty, holy, and loving God.

If God is all this, we would expect him to have a loving concern for his creatures and come to their aid. That he has such a concern and does come to man's aid is evident from his provision for man's material and temporal needs. He has stored the earth with minerals and fuel; he has provided an atmosphere in which man can live; he has given fertility to the soil, has supplied the sunshine and rain, the cold and the snow; and he has given man an understanding as to the ways of making these things fulfill needs. But man also has spiritual and eternal needs. He has a sin problem. Nothing in nature or conscience tells him what is the true ethical standard of life, nor does anything indicate how to become right with God. Man feels that he is immortal and wonders what he can do to prepare for eternity. Will not God, who has provided so abundantly for man's lower needs, provide also for his higher? It seems that the answer must be an emphatic "yes." God being such a God as that, and man having such a need as that, God may be expected to make his standards and plan of salvation known. And if he makes them known, will he leave them to uncertain and fallible expression? It is true that God uses redeemed, but fallible, men as his ministers of reconciliation (2 Cor. 5:18-20). But we, saved though sinful men, need an infallible Word to declare. The God of all truth has given to us an authoritative, inerrant Word to believe and proclaim. Shedd writes:

> It is improbable that God would reveal a fact or doctrine to the human mind, and do nothing towards securing an accurate statement of it. This is particularly the case, when the doctrine is one of the mysteries of religion. Such profound truths as the trinity, the incarnation, vicarious atonement, etc., require the superintendence and guidance of an infallible Spirit to secure an enunciation that shall not be misleading. Hence it is more natural to suppose that a prophet or an apostle who has received directly from God a profound and mysterious truth inaccessible to the human intellect, will not be left to his own unassisted powers in imparting what he has received. Especially is it improbable that communication from the deity would be veiled in extravagant and legendary costume.[4]

B. THE CHARACTER AND CLAIMS OF THE BIBLE

The Bible is superior to all other religious books in content. It sets up the highest ethical standards, enjoins the most absolute obedience, denounces every form of sin, and yet informs the sinner how he can become right with God. How could uninspired men write a book like that? The Bible displays a remarkable unity. Although it took some forty men a period of approximately 1600 years to produce the sixty-six books that compose the Bible, the Bible is in reality but one book. It has one doctrinal viewpoint, one moral standard, one plan of salvation, one program of the ages, one world-view. The peculiarities of the Mosaic system are clear in the light of a progressive revelation. Law and grace and the doctrine of the Holy Spirit are bound up with the dispensational purpose of God. The arrangement for the close alliance of the political and the religious elements in the Jewish polity was intended to be temporary, and was not intended for the present. In all this

[4]Shedd, *Dogmatic Theology*, I, p. 76.

there is a plan and a purpose. No other sacred books display any such organic unity as that found in Scripture.

It claims to be the Word of God. If a man or a book speaks truthfully on all other matters, we should allow them also to speak for themselves. The Bible speaks truthfully on other matters, and it makes certain claims about itself. These claims appear in various ways. (1) More than 3,800 times the Old Testament writers use the terms, "thus says the Lord," "the word of the Lord came to" such and such a person, "the Lord said," or some such equivalent. (2) The New Testament writers use such expressions as, "declaring to you the whole purpose of God," "in words . . . taught by the Spirit," "what it really is, the word of God," and "the Lord's commandment." (3) Various writers claim absolute perfection and authority for the law and the testimony (Deut. 27:26; 2 Kings 17:13; Ps. 19:7; 33:4; 119:89; Isa. 8:20; Gal. 3:10; 1 Pet. 2:23). (4) One book recognizes another book as speaking with absolute finality (Josh. 1:7f.; 8:31f.; Ezra 3:2; Neh. 8:1; Dan. 9:2, 11, 13; Zech. 7:12; Mal. 4:4; Acts 1:16; 28:25; 1 Pet. 1:10f.). (5) Peter puts the Epistles of Paul on a par with "the rest of Scripture" (2 Pet. 3:15f.). And (6) Paul declares the whole Old Testament to be inspired (2 Tim. 3:16). Peter writes, "But know this first of all, that no prophecy of Scripture is a matter of one's own interpretation, for no prophecy was ever made by an act of human will, but men moved by the Holy Spirit spoke from God" (2 Pet. 1:20f.).

Note also the Lord's views on inspiration. He said that "Scripture cannot be broken" (John 10:35). In all the three parts of the Old Testament, "the Law of Moses and the Prophets and the Psalms," he found teachings concerning himself (Luke 24:44; cf. v. 27). He also said that he came not to abolish the law, but to fulfill it (Matt. 5:17); and he indicated his conception of inspiration by saying, "Until heaven and earth pass away, not the smallest letter or stroke shall pass away from the Law, until all is accomplished" (Matt. 5:18; cf. Luke 16:17). That is, he believed in the verbal inspiration of the law. "Law" in this setting no doubt included the entire Old Testament.

Further, Jesus made some significant predictions concerning the preservation and interpretation of the facts that are connected with him and his mission. Before he went away, he told the disciples that the Holy Spirit would make them competent teachers of the truth. This, Jesus said, the Spirit would do by coming to them, by teaching them all things, by bringing to their remembrance all that he had said to them, by guiding them into all the truth, and by showing them things to come (John 14:26; 16:13). These promises embrace the facts concerning the earthly life of Christ, the experiences of the early disciples, the doctrines set forth in the Epistles, and the predictions in the Revelation. The apostles claimed to have received this Spirit (Acts 2:4; 9:17; 1 Cor. 2:10–12; 7:40; James 4:5; 1 John 3:24; Jude 19) and to speak under his influence and authority (Acts 2:4; 4:8, 31; 13:9;

1 Cor. 2:13; 14:37; Gal. 1:1, 12; 1 Thess. 2:13; 4:2, 8; 1 Pet. 1:12; 1 John 5:10f.; Rev. 21:5; 22:6, 18f.). Thus our Lord may be understood as guaranteeing the inspiration of the New Testament also.

III. THE OBJECTIONS TO THIS VIEW OF INSPIRATION

In the light of the facts above, men ought to believe in the verbal inspiration of the Scriptures; but there are problems with this view which need to be addressed.

A. QUOTATIONS OF IGNORANCE OR ERROR

Paul said before Ananias, "I was not aware, brethren, that he was high priest" (Acts 23:5). Here Paul merely admits his ignorance and does not deal with the question of inspiration. The record of this statement is fully inspired. The speeches of Job's comforters contain error. Inspiration guarantees the accurate recording of these speeches, not the truthfulness of the contents of the speech. There is a difference between what is recited and what is asserted, between the fact that something was said and the truthfulness of what was said. Whatsoever Scripture "asserts as true and free from error is to be received as such."[5]

But what does the following mean: "But to the rest I say, not the Lord" 1 Cor. 7:12? The Lord has given commands concerning divorce (Matt. 5:31f.; 19:3-9); now Paul speaks with the authority given him. He is not drawing a line between the authoritative commands of Christ and his own. Rather, he himself is claiming inspiration and the authority to set forth doctrine and practice (cf. 1 Cor. 7:12, 25). He has "the Spirit of God" (1 Cor. 7:40).

B. IN SCIENCE AND HISTORY

The Bible is not a textbook on either science or history; but if it is verbally inspired, then we expect it to speak truthfully whenever it touches on either of these subjects. But just as scientists still speak of the rising and setting of the sun, the four corners of the earth, etc., so the Bible often uses the language of appearance. The seeming imperfections, errors, and contradictions usually disappear when we take into account the nontechnical style of the writers, the fragmentary character of many of the accounts, the supplementary nature of many of the things that are recorded by the several authors, the historical situations that gave rise to a line of conduct, and the fallibility of the scribes.

[5]Pinnock, *Biblical Revelation*, p. 79.

Archaeological discoveries have done much to confirm the historical accuracy of the Old Testament. Hammurabi, Sargon II, the Hittites, and Belshazzar no longer present problems to the historian. This is likewise true of the New Testament. Quirinius (Luke 2:2), Lysanias (Luke 3:1), Paulus (Acts 13:7), and Gallio (Acts 18:12) have all been identified, thus proving the historicity of the accounts.

The differences in the number that fell in the plague (Num. 25:9; 1 Cor. 10:8) disappear on a careful reading of the two texts. The "level place" (Luke 6:17) was probably a level place on the mountain (Matt. 5:1). There was an old Jericho and a new Jericho, and the blind men were probably healed between the two Jerichos (Matt. 20:29; Mark 10:46; Luke 18:35). Mark and Luke probably meant to mention only the more conspicuous one, as also in the healing in Decapolis (Matt. 8:28; Mark 5:2; Luke 8:27).

C. In Miracle and Prophecy

The proof for miracles and prophecy has already been given, but we may add that the record of the miracles of Christ is so organically interwoven with the record of the rest of his life that it is impossible to eliminate the former without at the same time destroying the latter. If one believes in the physical resurrection of Christ, then there remains no insuperable hindrance to the acceptance of all the other miracles of Scripture as well. Or as Saucy notes, "When the fact of God is accepted . . . there can be no legitimate reason for denying His supernatural intervention where and when He wills."[6]

In the light of the fulfillments of prophecies concerning Babylon, Medo-Persia, Greece, and Rome, concerning Israel, concerning Christ, and concerning the character of the present age, we ought not to be sceptical concerning the possibility of predictive prophecy. What are regarded as errors in prophecy are usually but false interpretations of it. Parts of Dan. 2, 7, 9, 11, 12, parts of Zech. 12–14, and most of the Revelation are still awaiting fulfillment.

C. In Quoting and Interpreting the Old Testament

Most of our difficulties here will vanish if we observe several items. (1) Sometimes the New Testament writers merely express their ideas in words borrowed from an Old Testament passage, without pretending to interpret the passage (Rom. 10:6–8; cf. Deut. 30:12–14). (2) Sometimes they point out a typical element in a passage that has not been generally recognized as typical (Matt. 2:15; cf. Hos. 11:1). (3) Sometimes they give credit to an earlier prophecy when they really quote from a later form of it (Matt. 27:9;

[6]Saucy, *The Bible: Breathed from God*, p. 89.

cf. Zech. 11:13). (4) Sometimes they quote an apparently false translation in the Septuagint on the ground that the mistranslation conveys at least one of the meanings contained in the Hebrew text (Eph. 4:26; cf. Ps. 4:4 in the LXX). And (5) sometimes they combine two quotations into one and assign the whole to the more prominent author (Mark 1:2f.; cf. Isa. 40:3; Mal. 3:1).

Furthermore, if we believe in the possibility of a supernatural work of the Holy Spirit in the heart of man, then we ought not to find it difficult to believe in the possibility of a supernatural operation of the Spirit in the production of the Scriptures. And if we recognize the Spirit as the true author of the Scriptures, then we cannot deny to him the right to use the Old Testament in any of the ways cited above.

D. In Morals and Religion

Practically all of the so-called errors in morals and religion are in the Old Testament. But all difficulties along these lines will disappear if we bear in mind the following facts. (1) The sinful acts of men may be recorded, but they are never sanctioned; as, for example, Noah's drunkenness (Gen. 9:20-27), Lot's incest (Gen. 19:30-38), Jacob's falsehood (Gen. 27:18-24), David's adultery (2 Sam. 11:1-4), Solomon's polygamy (1 Kings 11:1-3; cf. Deut. 17:17), Esther's severity (Esth. 9:12-14), and Peter's denials (Matt. 26:69-75). (2) Some evil acts appear to be sanctioned, but it is really the good intention or accompanying virtue that is recognized and not the evil act itself; as, for example, Rahab's faith, not her duplicity (Josh. 2:1-21; Heb. 11:31; James 2:25), Jael's patriotism, not her treachery (Judg. 4:17-22; cf. 5:24), and Samson's faith, not his vagabondage (Judg. 14-16; cf. Heb. 11:32). (3) Some things were permitted as relatively, not absolutely, right; for example, divorce (Deut. 24:1; cf. Matt. 5:31f.; 19:7-9) and retaliation (Exod. 21:23-25; cf. Matt. 5:38f.; Rom. 12:19-21). (4) Some prayers and divine commands express but the purpose of a sovereign God, who frequently uses men to carry out his designs; for example, the imprecatory Psalms (35, 69, 109, 137), and the command to destroy the Canaanites (Deut. 7:1-5, 16; 20:16-18).

Some have charged that certain books are unworthy of a place in the sacred canon. Esther, Job, Song of Solomon, Ecclesiastes, Jonah, James, and Revelation have been singled out for such criticism. In reply, we would say that this opinion rests upon a misapprehension of the aim and method of these books and ignores the testimony of many as to their values. When the true design of these books is perceived, they do not justify themselves as merely useful, but even as indispensable to a rounded-out scheme of doctrine.

PART III
THEOLOGY

Assuming, then, that we have in the Scriptures the supreme and only infallible source of theology, we proceed now to base our further study on them. In speaking this highly of the Bible, we do not forget the importance of reason, intuition, the creeds and confessions of the church, and so forth; but, as we have already stated, they are not really sources for theology, but aids in the understanding of the revelation of God, particularly as contained in the Scriptures. In the development of a biblical system of theology, we shall, in the first place, study the person and work of God. For the sake of convenience this subject is divided into four parts: the nature of God, the unity and trinity of God, the decrees of God, and the works of God.

CHAPTER VIII

The Nature of God: Essence and Attributes

Many of the characteristics of God have already been expressed in connection with the previous study of the revelation of God and the proofs for his existence. But they were mentioned rather indirectly and unsystematically, and some of the facts were scarcely noted. The subject will now be examined more fully and the materials developed into an orderly system. This chapter concerns the nature of God, with special reference to his essence and attributes.

I. THE ESSENCE OF GOD

The terms "essence" and "substance" are practically synonymous when used of God. They may be defined as that which underlies all outward manifestation; the reality itself, whether material or immaterial; the substratum of anything; that in which the qualities or attributes inhere. Both of these terms refer to the basic aspect of the nature of God; if there were no essence or substance, there could be no attributes. To speak of God, is to speak of an essence, a substance, not of a mere idea or the personification of an idea.

Since there is a difference between the essence and the attributes of God, one is faced with the question of how to distinguish between them. We recognize that perhaps some of the so-called attributes are, strictly speaking, not attributes at all, but different aspects of the divine substance. Spirituality, self-existence, immensity, and eternity are such.

A. SPIRITUALITY

God is a substance. He is, however, not a material substance, but a spiritual substance. Jesus said, "God is spirit" (John 4:24). Having no article in the Greek, this statement defines God's nature as spiritual.

1. He is immaterial and incorporeal. Jesus said, "A spirit does not have flesh and bones as you see that I have" (Luke 24:39). If God is spirit, he is immaterial and incorporeal. The second commandment of the Decalogue, which forbids the making of any graven image or likeness of anything (Exod. 20:4), is based on the incorporeal nature of God. So also are the numerous commands against idolatry (Lev. 26:1; Deut. 16:22).

But what about the expressions that represent God as having bodily parts: hands (Isa. 65:2; Heb. 1:10), feet (Gen. 3:8; Ps. 8:6), eyes (1 Kings 8:29; 2 Chron. 16:9), ears (Neh. 1:6; Ps. 34:15)? They are anthropomorphic and symbolic representations which serve to make God real and to express his various interests, powers, and activities.

Man differs in that he has finite spirit, which is able to dwell in a material body (1 Cor. 2:11; 1 Thess. 5:23). God is infinite spirit and as such is non-corporeal (Acts 7:48f.).

2. He is invisible. The Israelites "did not see any form" when the Lord appeared to them in Horeb, and, therefore, they were prohibited from making any image of him (Deut. 4:15–19). God told Moses that no man could see him and live (Exod. 33:20). John says, "No man has seen God at any time" (John 1:18). Paul calls him "the invisible God" (Col. 1:15; cf. Rom 1:20; 1 Tim. 1:17) and declares that no man has seen him or can see him (1 Tim. 6:16). Certain Scriptures, however, indicate that the redeemed will some day see him (Ps. 17:15; Matt. 5:8; Heb. 12:14; Rev. 22:4).

But how about the Scriptures that say men saw God, such as Gen. 32:30; Exod. 3:6; 24:9f.; Num. 12:6–8; Deut. 34:10; and Isa. 6:1? When one sees his face in a mirror, he in a sense sees himself; yet, in another sense, he does not literally see himself. So men saw the reflection of God's glory, but they did not see his essence (Heb. 1:3). Then, too, spirit can be manifested in visible form (John 1:32; Heb. 1:7).

When Moses saw the "back" of God (Exod. 33:23), it was in response to his request to see the glory of the Lord (v. 18). Rather than interpreting this as literally and visibly seeing God, which in the context is said to be impossible (v. 20), it is better to understand this as seeing the aftereffects, or as Driver says, "the afterglow" of God.[1]

Theophanies are manifestations of deity in visible form. Jacob said, after he had wrestled with the man, "I have seen God face to face" (Gen. 32:30). "The angel of the Lord" was a visible manifestation of deity (Gen. 16:7–14; 18:13–33; 22:11–18; Exod. 3:2–5; Judg. 6:11–23; 1 Kings 19:5–7; 2 Kings 19:35). It is to be noted that in certain of these passages "the angel of the Lord" is identified as "the Lord" (cf. Gen. 16:11 with v. 13; Exod. 3:2 with v. 4; Judg. 6:12 with v. 16).

3. He is alive. The idea of *spirit* excludes not only the idea of material substance, but also that of inanimate substance. It implies that God is alive.

[1]Driver, *The Book of Exodus*, p. 363.

He is, therefore, called the "living" God (Josh. 3:10; 1 Sam. 17:26; Ps. 84:2; Matt. 16:16; 1 Tim. 3:15; Rev. 7:2). Life implies feeling, power, and activity. God has all these (Ps. 115:3). He is also the source and support of all life: plant, animal, human, spiritual, and eternal (Ps. 36:9; John 5:26). The living God is often contrasted with dead idols (Ps. 115:3-9; Acts 14:15; 1 Thess. 1:9). Our God is alive; he sees, hears, and loves. The idols of the heathen are dead, incapable of seeing, hearing, and loving.

4. He is a person.   Hegel and the idealistic philosophers are wrong in representing God as an impersonal spirit, for the very idea of spirit implies personality. The only way of determining what spirit is like, apart from the Scriptures, is by analogy with the human spirit. Since the human spirit is personal, the Divine Spirit must be personal as well, for otherwise he is of a lower order of being than man. In man, personality and corporeity are united in one individual for the period of this life. At death this relationship is severed; the body goes over into corruption, but the personality survives. At the resurrection the personality is again embodied and the normal constitution of man is restored. But in God there is personality without corporeity. What then is the essence of personality? Self-consciousness and self-determination.

Self-consciousness is more than consciousness. As a conscious being, man at times has feelings and appetites which he does not relate to himself. He thinks spontaneously, but does not think of what he thinks. The brute probably has some degree of consciousness. But as a self-conscious being, man relates his feelings, appetites, and thoughts to himself. Likewise, self-determination is more than determination. The beast has determination, but it is mechanical. Man has the feeling of freedom and makes his choices from within, in view of motives and ends. The Scripture writers ascribe both self-consciousness (Exod. 3:14; Isa. 45:5; 1 Cor. 2:10) and self-determination (Job 23:13; Rom. 9:11; Eph. 1:9, 11; Heb. 6:17) to God. He is a being who can say "I" and "me" (Exod. 20:2f.) and can respond when addressed as "you" (Ps. 90:1ff.).

Scripture also represents God as possessing the psychological characteristics of personality: intellect (Gen. 18:19; Exod. 3:7; Acts 15:18), sensibility (Gen. 6:6; Ps. 103:8-14; John 3:16), and volition (Gen. 3:15; Ps. 115:3; John 6:38). Furthermore, it ascribes qualities and relations of personality to God. He is represented as speaking (Gen. 1:3), seeing (Gen. 11:5), hearing (Ps. 94:9), grieving (Gen. 6:6), repenting (Gen. 6:6), and being angry (Deut. 1:37), jealous (Exod. 20:5), and compassionate (Ps. 111:4). He is said to be the creator (Acts 14:15), upholder (Neh. 9:6), ruler (Ps. 75:7; Dan. 4:32), and sustainer (Ps. 104:27-30; Matt. 6:26-30) of all things.

One must, however, distinguish between the personality of the essence and that of the several distinctions that make up the essence. Clearly, the essence cannot be at the same time three persons and one person if the term "person" is used in the same sense both times; but the essence can be, and is, at once three persons and one personal being. The existence of three distinct persons in the Godhead results in the self-consciousness and self-determination of the one God; but there is also the self-consciousness and self-determination of each of the three persons.

B. Self-Existence

While man's ground of existence is outside of himself, God's existence is not dependent upon anything outside of himself. As Thomas Aquinas said, "He is the first cause; himself uncaused." His self-existence is implied in his affirmation, "I am who I am" (Exod. 3:14; cf. the "I am" of Christ's teaching concerning himself, John 8:58, and Isa. 41:4; Rev. 1:8), and as is usually held, in the name "Jehovah" (Exod. 6:3). Yet God's self-existence is not grounded in his will, but in his nature. He exists by the necessity of his nature as the uncaused being. It is not correct to say that God is his own cause, for then he would have the power to annihilate himself.

C. Immensity

God is infinite in relation to space. He is not limited or circumscribed by space; on the contrary, all finite space is dependent upon him. He is, in fact, above space. Scripture clearly teaches God's immensity (1 Kings 8:27; 2 Chron. 2:6; Ps. 113:4–6; 139:7f.; Isa. 66:1; Jer. 23:24; Acts 17:24–28). Due to the spirituality of his nature and our inability to think in spaceless terms, this is a difficult doctrine to apprehend. However, this much is clear: God is both immanent and transcendent, and he is everywhere present in essence as well as in knowledge and power. Whenever and wherever it is present, spiritual substance, like the soul, is a complete whole at every point.

D. Eternity

God is also infinite in relation to time. He is without beginning or end, he is free from all succession of time, and he is the cause of time. That he is without beginning or end may be inferred from the doctrine of his self-existence; he who exists by reason of his nature rather than his volition, must always have existed and must continue to exist forever. That God is eternal is abundantly taught in Scripture. He is called "the Everlasting God" (Gen. 21:33). The Psalmists say, "From everlasting to everlasting, Thou art God" (Ps. 90:2) and "Thou art the same, and Thy years will not come to an end" (Ps. 102:27). Isaiah represents God as "the high and exalted One Who lives forever" (Isa. 57:15). Paul says that God "alone possesses immortality" (1 Tim. 6:16; cf. Hab. 1:12).

Time is, as commonly understood, duration measured by succession, but God is free from all succession of time. God, writes Shedd, "has a *simultaneous* possession of his total duration. . . . The whole of the Divine knowledge and experience is ever before the Divine being, so that there are not parts succeeding parts."[2] Eternity for God is one now, one eternal present. "He possesses the whole of His existence in one indivisible present."[3] In Scripture this is referred to as "the day of eternity" (2 Pet. 3:18) and "today" (Ps. 2:7; cf. 2 Pet. 3:8). But one must not suppose that time has no objective reality for God, but rather that he sees the past and the future as vividly as he sees the present. A person may view a procession from the top of a high tower, where he can see the whole procession at one glance, or he may view it from the street corner, where only one part can be seen at a time. God sees the whole as one unit, although he is aware of the sequence in the procession.

He is also the cause of time (Heb. 1:2; 11:3). The reference to God in Isaiah 9:6 may be translated "Father of Eternity."[4] Both time and space are among "all things" which "came into being through Him" (John 1:3). Strong says:

> Yet time and space are not *substances*; neither are they *attributes* (qualities of substance); they are rather *relations* of finite existence. . . . With finite existence they come into being; they are not mere regulative conceptions of our minds; they exist objectively, whether we perceive them or not.[5]

Time will some day merge into eternity (1 Cor. 15:28). Shedd thinks, however, that for the creature eternity will not be successionless existence, for "every finite mind must think, feel, and act in time."[6]

II. THE ATTRIBUTES OF GOD

The attributes of God, in distinction from the substance or essence of God, are the qualities that inhere in the substance and constitute an analytical and closer description of it. They are to be thought of as objectively real, not merely as man's subjective mode of conceiving God, and as descriptions of

---

[2]Shedd, *Dogmatic Theology*, I, p. 343.
[3]Berkhof, *Systematic Theology*, p. 60.
[4]Young, *The Book of Isaiah*, I, p. 338.
[5]Strong, *Systematic Theology*, p. 275.
[6]Shedd, *Dogmatic Theology*, I, p. 349.

the particular ways in which the divine essence exists and operates, not as denoting distinct parts of God. Various classifications of the attributes have been made. One of the best known is the division into natural attributes, God's attributes in reference to and in contrast with nature, and moral attributes, his attributes as a moral governor. Another is into immanent attributes, those which relate to God as he is in himself, and transitive ones, those by which he is revealed outwardly in his relations to his creation. A third is into positive attributes, by which certain perfections are expressed, and negative, by which certain limitations are denied. A fourth is derived from the constitution of our own nature. As in man there is the substance of the soul, the intellect, and the will, so, it is said, the attributes of God may be arranged under three heads: those pertaining to his essence, those referring to his intellect, and those relating to his will. Here they will be discussed under two headings: the non-moral and the moral attributes.

A. The Non-Moral Attributes

The non-moral attributes are those necessary predicates of the divine essence that do not involve moral qualities. These are omnipresence, omniscience, omnipotence, and immutability.

1. Omnipresence.   These first three attributes are compound words using the Latin prefix *omni,* meaning "all." Thus *omnipresent* means "present everywhere at once." God is present in all his creation, but in no manner limited by it. Whereas immensity emphasizes the transcendence of God in that he transcends all space and is not subject to the limitations of space, omnipresence has special reference to his presence within the universe (1 Kings 8:27; Ps. 139:7–10; Isa. 66:1; Jer. 23:23f.; Acts 7:48f.; 17:24f.; Rom. 10:6–8). It must be remembered that the omnipresence of God is not a necessary part of his being, but is a free act of his will. If God should will to destroy the universe, his omnipresence would cease, but he himself would not cease to be. Pantheism binds God to the universe, but God is transcendent and not subject to it. The doctrine of the omnipresence of God is both comforting and subduing. It is a source of comfort to the believer, for God, the ever-present one, is always available to help us (Deut. 4:7; Ps. 46:1; 145:18; Matt. 28:20). It is a source of warning and restraint to the believer. No matter how much he may try, the sinner cannot escape from God. Neither distance nor darkness hides from him (Ps. 139:7–10). "There is no creature hidden from His sight, but all things are open and laid bare to the eyes of Him with whom we have to do" (Heb. 4:13). This consciousness often checks the sinner in his evil ways and leads him to seek God. "Thou art a God who sees" (Gen. 16:13) becomes both a warning and a comfort to the child of God (Ps. 139:17f.).

2. Omniscience. God is infinite in knowledge. He knows himself and all other things perfectly from all eternity, whether they be actual or merely possible, whether they be past, present, or future. He knows things immediately, simultaneously, exhaustively, and truly.

Evidences of design in creation and of intelligence in man prove God's omniscience. These evidences are found in the animate world, the inanimate world, and in the relation between these two worlds. They find their highest expression in the intelligence of man. The omnipresence of God further proves his omniscience (Ps. 139:1–10; Prov. 15:3; Jer. 23:23–25). Scripture declares that God's understanding is infinite (Isa. 46:10), that nothing is hidden from him (Ps. 147:5; Heb. 4:13), and that even the hairs on our head are numbered (Matt. 10:30).

The scope of God's knowledge is infinite. *a.* He knows himself perfectly. No created being has complete and perfect knowledge of himself.

b. The Father, the Son, and the Spirit know each other perfectly. They alone have such knowledge of each other. Jesus said, "No one knows the Son, except the Father; nor does anyone know the Father, except the Son, and anyone to whom the Son wills to reveal Him" (Matt. 11:27). Paul wrote, "The thoughts of God no one knows except the Spirit of God" (1 Cor. 2:11; cf. Rom. 8:27).

c. God knows things actually existing. This includes inanimate creation (Ps. 147:4), brute creation (Matt. 20:29), men and all their works (Ps. 33:13–15; Prov. 5:21), men's thoughts and hearts (Ps. 139:1–4; Prov. 15:3), and men's burdens and wants (Exod. 3:7; Matt. 6:8, 32).

d. He knows all things possible. He knew that Keilah would betray David to Saul if David remained in that vicinity (1 Sam. 23:11f.). Jesus knew that Tyre and Sidon would have repented had they seen the miracles that were done in Bethsaida and Chorazin (Matt. 11:21). He also knew that Sodom and Gomorrah would have been spared had they seen the works that were done in Capernaum (Matt. 11:23f.; cf. Isa. 48:18). Certain idealists deny a distinction between knowledge and power, holding that knowledge and thought always mean the exertion of creative power. According to them, God creates by thinking and knowing. But the possession of a faculty and the exercise of it are two different things. Thus, God has knowledge of the possible as well as the actual. Omniscience should not be confused with causation. Foreknowledge and foreordination are not necessarily the same.

e. God knows the future. From man's standpoint God's knowledge of the future is foreknowledge, but from God's standpoint it is not, since he knows all things by one simultaneous intuition. He foreknew the future in general (Isa. 46:9f.; Dan. 2, 7; Matt. 24, 25; Acts 15:18), the evil course that Israel would take (Deut. 31:20f.), the rise of Cyrus (Isa. 44:26–45:7), the coming of Christ (Micah 5:2), and his crucifixion at the hands of wicked men (Acts 2:23; 3:18). Two things must be noted at this point: (1) The knowledge of the future is not itself causative. Free actions do not take place because they are foreseen, but they are foreseen because they will take place. (2) Just because something morally evil has been predicted this prediction does not remove human responsibility from the perpetrator (Matt. 18:7; John 13:27; Acts 2:23; cf. the hardening of Pharaoh's heart, Exod. 4:21).

Wisdom is the intelligence of God displayed in the choice of the highest ends and of the fittest means for the accomplishment of those ends. Though God sincerely seeks to promote the happiness of his creatures and to perfect the saints in holiness, neither of these is the highest possible end. The end is his own glory. All his works in creation (Ps. 19:1–6; Prov. 3:19), preservation (Neh. 9:6; Rev. 4:11), providence (Ps. 33:10f.; Dan. 4:35; Eph. 1:11), and redemption (1 Cor. 2:7; Eph. 3:10f.) have this end in view.

3. *Omnipotence.*   God is all-powerful and able to do whatever he wills. Since his will is limited by his nature, God can do everything that is in harmony with his perfections. There are some things which God cannot do because they are contrary to his nature as God. He cannot look with favor on iniquity (Hab. 1:13), deny himself (2 Tim. 2:13), lie (Titus 1:2; Heb. 6:18), or tempt or be tempted to sin (James 1:13). Further, he cannot do things which are absurd or self-contradictory, such as make a material spirit, a sensitive stone, a square circle, or a wrong to be right. These are not objects of power and so denote no limitation of God's omnipotence.

The possession of omnipotence does not demand the exercise of his power, certainly not the exercise of all his power. God can do what he wills to do, but he does not necessarily will to do anything. That is, God has power over his power; otherwise, he would act of necessity and cease to be free. Omnipotence includes the power of self-limitation. God has limited himself to some extent by giving free will to his rational creatures. That is why he did not keep sin out of the universe by a display of his power and why he does not save anyone by force.

The Bible clearly teaches the omnipotence of God. The Lord, who is called "Almighty" (Gen. 17:1; Rev. 4:8), is said to be able to do all things he purposes (Job 42:2), for with him all things are possible (Matt. 19:26) and nothing is too difficult (Jer. 32:17). He, indeed, reigns (Rev. 19:6).

A distinction may be drawn between God's absolute power and his ordinate power. Absolute power means that God may work directly without secondary causes. Creation, miracles, immediate revelation, inspiration, and regeneration are manifestations of his absolute power. The works of providence would be illustrations of ordinate power whereby God uses second causes. In either case, God is exercising his divine efficiency.

Repeatedly the believer is urged to trust God in every walk of life on the ground of his creative, preserving, and providential power (Isa. 45:11–13; 46:4; Jer. 32:16–44; Acts 4:24–31). To the Christian the omnipotence of

God is a source of great comfort and hope, but to the unbeliever so mighty a God is ever a warning and a source of fear (1 Pet. 4:17; 2 Pet. 3:10f.; Rev. 19:15). Even the demons shudder (James 2:19), for they know that God has power over them (Matt. 8:29). Some day even the strongest and greatest will seek to hide from him (Rev. 6:15-17; cf. Isa. 2:10-21), and every knee will bow at the name of Jesus (Phil. 2:10).

4. Immutability.   God is unchangeable in his essence, attributes, consciousness, and will. All change must be to the better or the worse, but God cannot change to the better, since he is absolutely perfect; neither can he change to the worse, for the same reason. He is exalted above all causes and above even the possibility of change. He can never be wiser, more holy, more just, more merciful, more truthful, nor less so. Nor do his plans and purposes change.

The immutability of God is due to the simplicity of his essence. Man has a soul and a body, two substances, immaterial and material. God is *one*; he does not change. God's immutability is due also to his necessary being and self-existence. That which exists uncaused, by the necessity of its nature, must exist as it does. It is due also to his absolute perfection. Neither improvement nor deterioration is possible. Any change in his attributes would make him less than God; any change in his purposes and plans would make him less wise, good, and holy.

Scripture declares that there is no variation with God (James 1:17). He does not change with regard to his character (Ps. 102:26f.; Mal. 3:6; Heb. 1:12), his power (Rom. 4:20f.), his plans and purposes (Ps. 33:11; Isa. 46:10), his promises (1 Kings 8:56; 2 Cor. 1:20), his love and mercy (Ps. 103:17), or his justice (Gen. 18:25; Isa. 28:17).

Immutability is not to be confused with immobility. God is active and enters into relationships with changing men. In these relationships it is necessary for an unchangeable God to change in his dealings with changing men in order to remain unchangeable in his character and purposes. God deals differently with men before salvation than after (Prov. 11:20; 12:12; 1 Pet. 3:12). The God who cannot repent (Num. 23:19), repents (i.e., his dealings with man change) when man changes from evil to good, or good to evil (Gen. 6:6; Exod. 32:14; Jer. 18:7-11; Joel 2:13; Jonah 3:10).

God's immutability consists in his always doing the right and in adapting the treatment of his creatures to the variations in their character and conduct. His threats are sometimes conditional in nature, as when he threatened to destroy Israel (Exod. 32:9-14) and Nineveh (Jonah 1:2; 3:4, 10).

B. The Moral Attributes

The moral attributes are those necessary predicates of the divine essence that involve moral qualities.

1. Holiness. God is absolutely separate from and exalted above all his creatures, and he is equally separate from all moral evil and sin. In the first sense, his holiness is not really an attribute that is coordinate with the other attributes, but is rather coextensive with them all. It denotes the perfection of God in all that he is. In the second sense, it is viewed as the eternal conformity of his being and his will. In God purity of being is before purity of willing or doing. God does not will the good because it is good, nor is the good good because God wills it; if such were the case, there would be a good above God or the good would be arbitrary and changeable. Instead, God's will is the expression of his nature, which is holy.

Holiness occupies the foremost rank among the attributes of God. It is the attribute by which God wanted to be especially known in Old Testament times (Lev. 11:44f.; Josh. 24:19; 1 Sam. 6:20; Ps. 22:3; Isa. 40:25; Ezek. 39:7; Hab. 1:12). It is emphasized by the bounds set about Mt. Sinai when God came down upon it (Exod. 19:12-25), the division of the tabernacle and temple into the holy and most holy places (Exod. 26:33; 1 Kings 6:16, 19), the prescribed offerings that must be brought if an Israelite would approach God (Lev. 1-7), the special priesthood to mediate between God and the people (Lev. 8-10), the many laws about impurity (Lev. 11-15), the feasts of Israel (Lev. 23), and the special position of Israel in Palestine (Num. 23:9; Deut. 33:28f.). The Lord is called "the Holy One" some thirty times in Isaiah alone (cf. the use of "holy" with regard to the Son, Acts 3:14, and the Spirit, Eph. 4:30).

In the New Testament, holiness is ascribed to God with less frequency than in the Old, but it is not wanting (John 17:11; Heb. 12:10; 1 Pet. 1:15f.). John declares, "God is light, and in Him there is no darkness at all" (1 John 1:5). The angels round about the throne call out antiphonally, "Holy, Holy, Holy" (Isa. 6:3; Rev. 4:8). Because of the fundamental character of this attribute, the holiness of God, rather than the love, the power, or the will of God, should be given first place. Holiness is the regulative principle of all three of them, for his throne is established on the basis of his holiness.

Three important things should be learned from the fact that God is holy.

a. There is a chasm between God and the sinner (Isa. 59:1f.; Hab. 1:13). Not only is the sinner estranged from God, but God is estranged from the sinner. Before sin came, man and God had fellowship with each other; now that fellowship is broken and impossible.

b. Man must approach God through the merits of another if he is to approach him at all. Man neither possesses nor is able to acquire the sinlessness which is necessary for access to God. But Christ has made such access possible (Rom. 5:2; Eph. 2:18; Heb. 10:19f.). In God's holiness lies the reason for the atonement; what his holiness demanded, his love provided (Rom. 5:6-8; Eph. 2:1-9; 1 Pet. 3:18).

c. We should approach God "with reverence and awe" (Heb. 12:28). A correct view of the holiness of God leads to a proper view of the sinful self (Ps. 66:18; 1 John 1:5-7). Job (40:3-5), Isaiah (6:5-7), and Peter (Luke 5:8) are striking examples of the relation between the two. Humiliation, contrition, and confession flow from a scriptural view of God's holiness.

2. Righteousness and justice. The righteousness and justice of God is that aspect of God's holiness which is seen in his treatment of the creature. Repeatedly, these qualities are ascribed to God (2 Chron. 12:6; Ezra 9:15; Neh. 9:33; Isa. 45:21; Dan. 9:14; John 17:25; 2 Tim. 4:8; Rev. 16:5). Abraham ponders, "Shall not the Judge of all the earth deal justly?" (Gen. 18:25). The Psalmist declares that "Righteousness and Justice are the foundation of Thy throne" (Ps. 89:14; 97:2). God has instituted a moral government in the world, imposed just laws upon the creatures, and attached sanctions thereto. Because of the latter, he executes his laws through the bestowal of rewards and punishments. The distribution of rewards is called remunerative justice (Deut. 7:9-13; 2 Chron. 6:15; Ps. 58:11; Matt. 25:21; Rom. 2:7; Heb. 11:26). Remunerative justice is based on divine love, not strict merit. The infliction of punishment is called punitive justice. It is the expression of divine wrath (Gen. 2:17; Exod. 34:7; Ezek. 18:4; Rom. 1:32; 2:8f.; 2 Thess. 1:8). God cannot make a law, establish a penalty, and then not follow through if the law is disobeyed. When the law is violated, punishment must be meted out, either personally or vicariously. In other words, justice demands punishment of the sinner, but it may also accept the vicarious sacrifice of another, as in the case of Christ (Isa. 53:6; Mark 10:45; Rom. 5:8; 1 Pet. 2:24). The righteousness of God is revealed in his punishing the wicked (Rev. 16:5-7), vindicating his people from evildoers (Ps. 129:1ff.), forgiving the penitent of their sin (1 John 1:9), keeping promises made to his children (Neh. 9:7ff.), and rewarding the faithful (Heb. 6:10).

Some may suggest that the infliction of punishment is primarily for reformation or rehabilitation, but the chief end of punishment is the maintenance of justice. Punishment may serve a secondary purpose of reformation or deterrence (1 Tim. 5:20).

God's righteousness is an encouragement to the believer in that he knows that God judges righteously (Acts 17:31), that he is secure in the righteousness of Christ (John 17:24; 1 Cor. 1:30; 2 Cor. 5:21), and that the righteous things he has done will not go unnoticed (Prov. 19:17; Heb. 6:10; Rev. 19:8).

3. Goodness. In the larger sense of the term, the goodness of God includes all the qualities that answer to the conception of an ideal personage; that is, it includes such qualities as God's holiness, righteousness, and truth, as well as his love, benevolence, mercy, and grace. It is probably in this broad sense that Jesus said to the young ruler, "Why do you call Me good? No one is good except God alone" (Mark 10:18). In the narrower sense, however, the term is limited to the last four qualities named.

a. The love of God. God's love is that perfection of the divine nature by which God is eternally moved to communicate himself. It is not a mere emotional impulse, but a rational and voluntary affection, having its ground in truth and holiness and its exercise in free choice. This is not to deny feeling, for true love necessarily involves feeling. If there is no feeling in God, then there is no love in God. The fact that God grieves over the sins of his people implies that he loves his people (Isa. 63:9f.; Eph. 4:30). God's love finds its primary objects in the several persons of the trinity. Thus, the universe and man are not necessary to the exercise of God's love.

The Scriptures frequently testify to the love of God. They speak of him as "the God of love" (2 Cor. 13:11) and declare him to be "love" (1 John 4:8, 16). It is his nature to love. He initiates love (1 John 4:10). He is unlike the gods of the heathen, who hate and are angry, and the god of the philosopher, who is cold and indifferent. The Father loves the Son (Matt. 3:17), and the Son loves the Father (John 14:31). God loves the world (John 3:16; Eph. 2:4), his ancient people Israel (Deut. 7:6–8, 13; Jer. 31:3), and his true children (John 14:23). He loves righteousness (Ps. 11:7) and justice (Isa. 61:8). The assurance of God's love is a source of comfort to the believer (Rom. 8:35–39). A loving God is not unfeeling toward his own.

b. The benevolence of God. Because of his goodness, God deals bountifully, tenderly, and kindly with all his creatures. "The Lord is good to all, and His mercies are over all His works. . . . The eyes of all look to Thee, and Thou dost give them their food in due time. Thou dost open Thy hand, and dost satisfy the desire of every living thing" (Ps. 145:9, 15f.). Creation is God's handiwork and declared to be very good (Gen. 1:31). God cannot hate what he has made (Job 10:3; 14:15). The benevolence of God is manifested in his concern for the welfare of the creature and is suited to the creature's needs and capacities (Job 38:41; Ps. 104:21; 145:15; Matt. 6:26). His benevolence is not restricted to believers, "for He causes His sun to rise on the evil and the good, and sends rain on the righteous and the unrighteous" (Matt. 5:45; cf. Acts 14:17).

c. The mercy of God. God's mercy is his goodness manifested towards those who are in misery or distress. Compassion, pity, and lovingkindness are other terms in Scripture that denote practically the same thing. Mercy is an eternal, necessary quality in God as an all-perfect being, but the exercise of it in a given case is optional. To deny the freeness of mercy is to annihilate it, for if it is a matter of debt, then it is no longer mercy. God is "rich in mercy" (Eph. 2:4), "is full of compassion and is merciful" (James 5:11), and has "great mercy" (1 Pet. 1:3). He is said to be merciful toward Israel (Ps. 102:13), the Gentiles (Rom 11:30f.), and all that fear him (Ps. 103:17; Luke

1:50) and seek his salvation (Isa. 55:7). The term is often used in salutations and benedictions (Gal. 6:16; 1 Tim. 1:2; 2 Tim. 1:2; 2 John 3; Jude 2).

d. The grace of God. The grace of God is God's goodness manifested toward the ill-deserving. Grace has respect to sinful man as guilty, while mercy has respect to him as miserable and pitiful. Scripture speaks of the "glory of His grace" (Eph. 1:6), "surpassing riches of His grace" (Eph. 2:7; cf. 1:7), "manifold grace" (1 Pet. 4:10), and "true grace" (1 Pet. 5:12).

The exercise of grace, like that of mercy, is optional with God. He must be holy in all his actions. He may or may not show grace to a guilty sinner. The Scriptures show that the grace of God is manifested toward the natural man in his forbearance and long-suffering delay of the punishment of sin (Exod. 34:6; Rom. 2:4; 3:25; 9:22; 1 Pet. 3:20; 2 Pet. 3:9, 15), distribution of gifts and talents among men, showering men with blessings instead of immediate judgment (Heb. 6:7), provision of salvation (1 John 2:2), the Word of God (Hos. 8:12), the convicting work of the Spirit (John 16:8–11), the influence of God's people (Matt. 5:13f.), and prevenient grace, that is, common grace (Titus 2:11).

Scripture also shows that his grace is uniquely manifested towards those who are his chosen ones in their election and foreordination (Eph. 1:4–6), redemption (Eph. 1:7f.), salvation (Acts 18:27; Eph. 2:7f.), sanctification (Rom. 5:21; Titus 2:11f.), perseverance (2 Cor. 12:9), service (Rom. 12:6; 1 Pet. 4:10f.), and glorification (1 Pet. 1:13). This is God's special grace. Like mercy, this term is also often used in salutations and benedictions (1 Cor. 1:3; 16:23; Eph. 1:2; Philem. 25; Rev. 1:4; 22:21).

4. Truth. God is truth. His knowledge, declarations, and representations eternally conform to reality. The truth of God is not only the foundation of all religion, but also of all knowledge. God is true God in that he is genuine God as well as truthful God. He is the source of all truth. The conviction that the senses do not deceive, that consciousness is trustworthy, that things are what they appear to be, and that existence is not merely a dream, rests ultimately upon the truth of God. In other words, we live in a world that is true. Many ask with Pilate, "What is truth?" (John 18:38). Ultimate truth or reality is God.

Both man's nature and the Scriptures teach that God is true. One is forced to believe that natural law has a personal lawmaker. Both the regularity of the laws of nature and their evident purposefulness testify to an intelligent author. Jesus affirmed that God is "the only true God" (John 17:3). John wrote, "We are in Him who is true" (1 John 5:20; cf. Jer. 10:10; John 3:33; Rom. 3:4; 1 Thess. 1:9; Rev. 3:7; 6:10). In his relationship to the creature, the truth of God is known as his veracity and faithfulness. His veracity relates to what he reveals of himself and to what he says. His revelations of himself in nature, consciousness, and Scripture are true and trustworthy (Ps.

31:5; Heb. 6:17f.). His faithfulness leads him to fulfill all his promises, whether expressed in words or implied in the constitution he has given us (Deut. 7:9; Isa. 25:1). That God is faithful to himself (2 Tim. 2:13), to his Word (Heb. 11:11), and to his people (1 Cor. 1:9; 10:13; 1 Thess. 5:24; 2 Thess. 3:3) is an abiding source of encouragement and strength for the believer. In Joshua we read these amazing words, "Not one of the good promises which the Lord had made to the house of Israel failed; all came to pass" (21:45).

But how is the veracity of God to be reconciled with the apparent non-performance of some of his threats? The promises and threats of God are always literally fulfilled if they are absolute; but if conditional, their fulfillment is dependent upon the obedience or repentance of the persons involved. The condition may be expressed or implied, and there is no breach in God's faithfulness if, because of disobedience and impenitence or obedience and penitence on the part of man, God does not carry out his promises (Jonah 3, 4). Further, are the invitations and exhortations to sinners, who will ultimately be lost, sincere? Since the invitations are made on practical conditions and there is no obstacle to their acceptance, except man's unwillingness, one cannot question God's sincerity in extending them. God knew beforehand that Israel would refuse to enter Canaan from Kadesh-barnea, but that did not keep him from sincerely urging his people to do so (Deut. 1:19–33). Thus, the veracity and faithfulness of God remain unimpeached.

Truly, our God is incomprehensible! Paul cries out, "Oh, the depth of the riches both of the wisdom and knowledge of God! How unsearchable are His judgments and unfathomable His ways! . . . For from Him and through Him and to Him are all things. To Him be the glory forever. Amen" (Rom. 11:33, 36). In the presence of deity, the child of God falls down and worships. Omniscience is not ignorant; God knows. Love is not indifferent; he cares. Omnipotence is not powerless; he acts.

CHAPTER IX

The Nature of God: Unity and Trinity

The unity and trinity of God also pertain to the nature of God and call for special treatment.

I. THE UNITY OF GOD

The unity of God means that there is but one God and that the divine nature is undivided and indivisible. That there is one God is the great truth of the Old Testament (Deut. 4:35, 39; I Kings 8:60; Isa. 45:5f.). The same truth is frequently taught in the New Testament (Mark 12:29–32; John 17:3; 1 Cor. 8:4–6; 1 Tim. 2:5). But God is not merely one, he is the only God; as such, he is unique (Exod. 15:11; Zech. 14:9). There can be only one infinite and perfect being. To postulate two or more infinite beings is illogical and inconceivable.

That the divine nature is undivided and indivisible, is intimated in Deut. 6:4, "Hear, O Israel! The Lord is our God, the Lord is one!" (cf. Mark 12:29; James 2:19). God does not consist of parts nor can he be divided into parts. His being is simple, numerically one, free from composition; man's is compound, having both a material and an immaterial part. But God is spirit and is not susceptible of any such division. This unity is, however, not inconsistent with the conception of the trinity, for a unity is not the same as a unit. A unit is marked by mere singleness. The unity of God allows for the existence of personal distinctions in the divine nature, while at the same time recognizing that the divine nature is numerically and eternally one. Unity does imply that the three persons of the trinity are not separate essences within the divine essence. Many sects and cults have broken with the historical Christian faith at this point by failing to accept the doctrine of three persons but one essence.

II. THE TRINITY OF GOD

The doctrine of the trinity is not a truth of natural theology, but of revelation. Reason may show us the unity of God, but the doctrine of the trinity comes from direct revelation. Though the term "trinity" does not occur in the Bible, it had very early usage in the church. Its Greek form, *trias*, seems to have been first used by Theophilus of Antioch (d. A.D. 181), and its Latin form, *trinitas*, by Tertullian (d. ca. A.D. 220). In Christian theology, the term "trinity" means that there are three eternal distinctions in the one divine essence, known respectively as Father, Son, and Holy Spirit. These three distinctions are three persons, and one may speak of the tripersonality of God. We worship the triune God. The Athanasian Creed expresses the trinitarian belief thus, "We worship one God in the Trinity, and the Trinity in unity; we distinguish among the persons, but we do not divide the substance." It goes on to say, "The entire three persons are coeternal and coequal with one another, so that . . . we worship complete unity in Trinity and Trinity in unity."

The doctrine of the trinity must be distinguished from both Tritheism and Sabellianism. Tritheism denies the unity of the essence of God and holds to three distinct Gods. The only unity that it recognizes is the unity of purpose and endeavor. God is a unity of essence as well as of purpose and endeavor. The three persons are consubstantial. Sabellianism held to a trinity of revelation, but not of nature. It taught that God, as Father, is the creator and lawgiver; as Son, is the same God incarnate who fulfills the office of redeemer; and as Holy Spirit, is the same God in the work of regeneration and sanctification. In other words, Sabellianism taught a modal trinity as distinguished from an ontological trinity. Modalism speaks of a threefold nature of God, in the same sense in which a man may be an artist, a teacher, and a friend, or as one may be a father, a son, and a brother. But this is in reality a denial of the doctrine of the trinity, for these are not three distinctions in the essence, but three qualities or relationships in one and the same person.

To be sure, the doctrine of the trinity is a great mystery. It may appear to some as an intellectual puzzle or a contradiction. The Christian doctrine of the trinity, mysterious as it may seem, is not an outgrowth of speculation, but of revelation. What has God revealed about this doctrine in his Word?

A. Intimations in the Old Testament

Although the great emphasis of the Old Testament is the unity of God, hints of plurality in the Godhead are not lacking, nor are suggestions that this plurality is a trinity.

It is interesting that God used plural pronouns (Gen. 1:26; 3:22; 11:7; Isa. 6:8) and plural verbs (Gen. 1:26; 11:7) to refer to himself. The name for God (*Elohim*) is plural and may imply plurality, though this is dubious. The plural form is probably used for intensity, rather than for expressing plurality.

More definite indications that this plurality is a trinity are found in the following facts: (1) The Lord is distinguished from the Lord. Gen. 19:24 states, "Then the Lord rained on Sodom and Gomorrah brimstone and fire from the Lord out of heaven," and Hosea 1:7 declares, "I will have compassion on the house of Judah and deliver them by the Lord their God" (cf. Zech. 3:2; 2 Tim. 1:18). (2) The Son is distinguished from the Father. The Son speaking through Isaiah the prophet said, "The Lord God has sent Me, and His Spirit" (Isa. 48:16; cf. Ps. 45:6f.; Isa. 63:9f.). Ps. 2:7 reads, "Thou art My Son, today I have begotten Thee." Jesus is not only called the Son of God (Rom. 1:4), but also the only begotten Son (John 3:16, 18) and his first-born Son (Heb. 1:6). Christ did not become the eternal Son of God at the incarnation; he was the Son before he was given (Isa. 9:6). "His goings forth are from long ago, from the days of eternity" (Mic. 5:2). (3) The Spirit is also distinguished from God. Gen. 1:1 reads, "In the beginning God created the heavens and the earth." Then v. 2 states, "The Spirit of God was moving over the surface of the waters." Note also the quotation, "The Lord said, 'My Spirit shall not strive with man forever'" (Gen. 6:3; cf. Num. 27:18; Ps. 51:11; Isa. 40:13; Hag. 2:4f.). (4) Other such matters as the triple use of "holy" in Isa. 6:3 may imply a trinity (cf. Rev. 4:8), as well as the triple benediction of Num. 6:24–26.

The oft-recurring phrase "the angel of the Lord," as found in the Old Testament, has special reference to the preincarnate second person of the trinity. His appearances in the Old Testament foreshadowed his coming in the flesh. The angel of the Lord is identified with the Lord and yet distinguished from him. He appeared to Hagar (Gen. 16:7–14), Abraham (Gen. 22:11–18), Jacob (Gen. 31:11–13), Moses (Exod. 3:2–5), Israel (Exod. 14:19), Balaam (Num. 22:22–35), Gideon (Judg. 6:11–23), Manoah (Judg. 13:2–25), Elijah (1 Kings 19:5–7), and David (1 Chron. 21:15–17). The angel of the Lord slew 185,000 Assyrians (2 Kings 19:35), stood among the myrtle trees in Zechariah's vision (Zech. 1:11), defended Joshua the high priest against Satan (Zech. 3:1f.), and was one of the three men who appeared to Abraham (Gen. 18).

In light of the above intimations of the trinity in the Old Testament, we conclude with Berkhof, "The Old Testament contains a clear anticipation of the fuller revelation of the Trinity in the New Testament."[1]

B. The Teaching of the New Testament

The doctrine of the trinity is more clearly set forth in the New Testament than in the Old Testament. It can be proven along two lines: by means of general statements and allusions and by demonstrating that there are three that are recognized as God.

[1]Berkhof, *Systematic Theology*, p. 86.

1. General statements and allusions. Several times the three persons of the trinity are shown together and seemingly are on par with one another. At the baptism of Jesus, the Spirit descended on him and a voice from God out of heaven identified Jesus as his beloved Son (Matt. 3:16f.). Jesus prayed that the Father would send another Comforter (John 14:16). The disciples were told to baptize in the name (sing.) of the Father, the Son, and the Holy Spirit (Matt. 28:19). The three persons of the trinity are associated together in their work (1 Cor. 12:4–6; Eph. 1:3–14; 1 Pet. 1:2; 3:18; Rev. 1:4f.). In addition, the apostolic benediction unites the three together (2 Cor. 13:14).

2. The Father is recognized as God. A brief scanning of the New Testament reveals numerous times that the Father is identified as God (John 6:27; Rom. 1:7; Gal. 1:1).

3. The Son is recognized as God. The doctrine of the deity of Christ is crucial to the Christian faith. "What think you of Christ?" is the paramount question of life (cf. Matt. 16:15; 22:42). Surely Jesus Christ is the greatest of all men, but he is infinitely more than mere man. It can be demonstrated that he is God in several ways.

　　a. The attributes of deity. Christ possesses the five attributes which are uniquely and distinctly divine: eternity, omnipresence, omniscience, omnipotence, and immutability. (1) He is eternal. He was not only before John (John 1:15), before Abraham (John 8:58), and before the world came into being (John 17:5, 24), but he is "the firstborn of all creation" (Col. 1:15), being in existence "in the beginning" (John 1:1; cf. 1 John 1:1), and, in fact, "from the days of eternity" (Mic. 5:2). And as to the future, he continues forever (Isa. 9:6f.; Heb. 1:11f.; 13:8). The Father's communication of life to him is an eternal process (John 5:26; cf. 1:4). (2) He is omnipresent. He was in heaven while on earth (John 3:13) and is on earth while he is in heaven (Matt. 18:20; 28:20). He fills all (Eph. 1:23). (3) He is omniscient. Jesus knows all things (John 16:30; 21:17). In fact, in him "are hidden all the treasures of wisdom and knowledge" (Col. 2:3). Several examples of his omniscience are given in the Gospels. He knew what was in man (John 2:24f.), and he knew the history of the Samaritan woman (John 4:29), the thoughts of men (Luke 6:8; 11:17), the time and manner of his exit out of this world (Matt. 16:21; John 12:33; 13:1), the one who would betray him (John 6:70f.), and the character and termination of the present age (Matt. 24, 25). He knew the Father as no mortal could (Matt. 11:27).

　　Now it is true that there are certain statements which seem to indicate something less than omniscience. Jesus was ignorant of the date of his return (Mark 13:32), marveled at the people's unbelief (Mark 6:6), and went to the fig tree expecting perhaps to find figs (Mark 11:13). However, it must be recognized that in the days of his humiliation, Jesus surrendered the independent exercise of his divine attributes. The Father did not permit the use of his omniscience in these cases. Without doubt, Jesus now knows the time of his second coming.

(4) He is omnipotent (John 5:19). He is the mighty God (Isa. 9:6; cf. Rev. 1:8), he "upholds all things by the word of His power" (Heb. 1:3), and all authority is given to him (Matt. 28:18). He has power over demons (Mark 5:11-15), disease (Luke 4:38-41), death (Matt. 9:11-25; Luke 7:12-16; John 11:38-44), the elements of nature (Matt. 21:19; John 2:3-11), indeed all things (Matt. 28:18). During Christ's ministry on earth, he subjected himself to the will of God, and, though done in the power of the Spirit, his miracles are cited as proofs of his deity (John 5:36; 10:25, 38; 20:30f.). Jesus himself declared, "The Son can do nothing of Himself, unless it is something He sees the Father doing; for whatever the Father does, these things the Son also does in like manner" (John 5:19). (5) He is immutable (Heb. 1:12; 13:8). This is true of his plans, promises, and person. But this does not preclude the possibility of a variety of manifestations on his part, nor of a restriction of some of his instructions and purposes to particular ages and persons.

b. The offices of deity. He is the creator (John 1:3; Col. 1:16; Heb. 1:10) and the upholder of all things (Col. 1:17; Heb. 1:3). Neither accident nor mere natural law caused the universe to come into existence or keeps the universe in existence and everything in its proper place. This is the work of deity (2 Pet. 3:5-7).

c. The prerogatives of deity. Christ forgave sins (Matt. 9:2, 6; Luke 7:47f.). None of the disciples claimed to have this authority (cf. Matt. 16:19; 18:18; and John 20:23 with Acts 8:20-22 and 1 John 1:9). He will raise the dead in the resurrection (John 5:25-29; 6:39f., 54; 11:25). This resurrection will be different from the raising of the three when he was on earth (the widow's son, Luke 7:12-16; Jairus' daughter, Mark 5:35-43; Lazarus, John 11:38-44). In the future, all his saints will be raised; they will be raised from decomposition as well as from death; they will be raised never more to die; and they will be raised by Christ's inherent power rather than by the Spirit's power. And, finally, he will execute judgment (John 5:22), that of believers (Rom. 14:10; 2 Cor. 5:10), of the beast and his followers (Rev. 19:15), of the nations (Matt. 25:31f.; Acts 17:31), of Satan (Gen. 3:15), and of the wicked dead (Acts 10:42; 2 Tim. 4:1; 1 Pet. 4:5).

d. His identification with the Old Testament Jehovah. Things that are in the Old Testament said of Jehovah are in the New Testament said of Christ. He was the creator (Ps. 102:24-27; Heb. 1:10-12), was seen by Isaiah (Isa. 6:1-4; John 12:41), was to be preceded by a forerunner (Isa. 40:3; Matt. 3:3), disciplines his people (Num. 21:6f.; 1 Cor. 10:9), is to be regarded as holy (Isa. 8:13; 1 Pet. 3:15), is to lead captivity captive (Ps. 68:18; Eph. 4:8), and is to be the object of faith (Joel 2:32; Rom. 10:9, 13).

e. Names that imply deity. (1) Jesus used certain metaphors of himself that imply supernatural character. For example, Jesus said, "I am the bread that came down out of heaven" (John 6:41; cf. v. 50); "I am the door; if anyone enters through Me, he shall be saved" (John 10:9); "I am the way, and the truth, and the life; no one comes to the Father, but through Me" (John 14:6); "I am the vine, you are the branches; he who abides in Me, and I in him, he bears much fruit; for apart from Me you can do nothing" (John 15:5). He also used certain designations of himself that imply deity, such as, "the Alpha and the Omega, the first and the last, the beginning and the end" (Rev. 22:13), "the resurrection and the life" (John 11:25), and "the Amen, the faithful and true Witness, the Beginning of the creation of God" (Rev. 3:14). Further, he said, "Before Abraham was born, I AM" (John 8:58; cf. Exod. 3:14).

(2) He was called Immanuel. Matthew explicitly applies Isa. 7:14 to Jesus (Matt. 1:22f.). He was born of a virgin and given the name Immanuel, meaning God with us. This name in the New Testament occurs only here in Matthew, though the concept occurs elsewhere (John 1:14; Rev. 21:3). (3) The term "Word" (*Logos*) is used to emphasize his deity (John 1:1–14; Rev. 19:13). Although the term seems first to have been used by Heraclitus to mean reason, then to have been taken over from him by Plato and the Stoics, and finally to have been taken into Jewish theology by Philo, it seems clear that John derived it from none of these sources. He most definitely took it over from the Old Testament personification of Wisdom and the Hebrew term *memra*, but filled it with the Christian concept of deity.[2]

(4) Jesus' favorite name for himself was Son of Man. In all but one instance (Acts 7:56), it is he who uses this term of himself in the New Testament. The term does not always clearly denote deity, as in Matt. 8:20; 11:18f.; 17:12; and Luke 9:44, but it very often does. For instance, it is as Son of Man that he has authority on earth to forgive sins (Matt. 9:6), to interpret the sabbath law (Matt. 12:8), and to execute judgment (John 5:27). It is as Son of Man that he gives his life a ransom for many (Matt. 20:28), will send his angels to gather out the tares (Matt. 13:41), will sit upon the throne of his glory (Matt. 19:28; 25:31), and will come again (Matt. 24:44; 26:64). When Jesus declared he was the Son of Man spoken of in Daniel, who was to come in great power, the high priest accused him of blasphemy (Matt. 26:63f.; cf. Dan. 7:13).[3]

(5) Christ is called Lord. In the New Testament the Greek term is used in four ways. It is used of God the Father (Matt. 4:7; 11:25; Luke 2:29; Acts

[2]For a fuller discussion, see Kittel, "Lego, Logos, etc." in *Theological Dictionary of the New Testament*, IV, pp. 130–36.
[3]For further discussion of "Son of Man," see Ridderbos, *The Coming of the Kingdom*, pp. 31–36.

17:24; Rom. 4:8; 2 Cor. 6:17f.; Rev. 4:8), as a title of courtesy (Matt. 13:27; 21:29; 27:63; Luke 13:8; John 12:21), as a name for a master or owner (Matt. 20:8; Luke 12:46; John 15:15; Col. 4:1), and as a title of address to, or as a name for, Christ (Matt. 7:22; 8:2; 14:28; Mark 7:28). It is doubtful whether all who called Jesus "Lord" thought of him as deity, but on numerous occasions there can be no question that they did (Matt. 7:21f.; Luke 1:43; 2:11; John 20:28; Acts 16:31; 1 Cor. 12:3; Phil. 2:11). The title "Lord," as it is often used of Jesus, is the translation of the Hebrew name Jehovah. Thus, Christ is identified with the Jehovah of the Old Testament (cf. John 12:40f.; Rom. 10:9, 13; and 1 Pet. 3:15 with Isa. 6:1ff.; Joel 2:32; and Isa. 8:13 respectively).

(6) Christ is called Son of God. The full title is never applied by Jesus to himself in the Synoptics, but in John he once uses it of himself (John 10:36; cf. v. 33). It is, however, applied to him by others, and he accepts it in such a way as to assert his claims to it. Though the term is also applied to the angels (Job 2:1), Adam (Luke 3:38), the Hebrew nation (Exod. 4:22; Hos. 11:1), the king of Israel (2 Sam. 7:14), and all saints (Gal. 4:6), in John 5:18, 10:33 and 36 Jesus' claim to divine sonship is clearly intended to denote deity. This is implied in the designation of the phrase "only begotten Son" (John 3:16, 18). When he acknowledged himself to be the Son of God, he was accused of blasphemy (Matt. 26:63–65; cf. John 5:18; 10:36). As the Son of God, he is said to execute all judgment (John 5:22), to have life in himself and to quicken whom he will (John 5:21, 26), and to give eternal life (John 10:10). It is the Father's will that all should honor the Son, even as they do the Father (John 5:23). Jesus is also called Son in the sense of being the Messiah, the anointed of God (John 1:49; 11:27). Through the experience of the incarnation, he is also called Son (Luke 1:32, 35; John 1:14).

(7) Jesus is called God several times in the New Testament. John 1:1 is very emphatic in the original. It reads as follows, "And the Word was God." The absence of the article before *theos* indicates that "God" is in the predicate position. It is not a question as to who God is, but as to who the *Logos* is. He is not only the only begotten Son, but also the only begotten God (John 1:18). Thomas addressed Christ, "My Lord and my God" (John 20:28). Titus 2:13 refers to "our great God and Savior, Christ Jesus." God said to the Son, "Thy throne, O God, is forever and ever, and the righteous scepter is the scepter of His kingdom" (Heb. 1:8). Peter writes of "our God and Savior, Jesus Christ" (2 Pet. 1:1). 1 John 5:20 reads, "in His Son Jesus Christ. This is the true God, and eternal life" (cf. also Rom. 9:5).

f. Certain relations proving his deity. The Father and he are put side by side with each other and with the Holy Spirit in the baptismal formula (Matt. 28:19; cf. Acts 2:38; Rom. 6:3) and in the apostolic benediction (2 Cor. 13:14; cf. 1 Cor. 1:3). He is the radiance (Heb. 1:3) and image of God (Col. 1:15; cf. 2:9). He and the Father are one (John 10:31; "one" is neuter, not masculine; one substance, not one person; cf. John 14:9; 17:11). He and the Father act together (John 14:23; 1 Thess. 3:11; 2 Thess. 2:16f.). Whatever the Father has, belongs also to Christ (John 16:15; 17:10). The Christian sustains the same relationship to the Father as he does to the Son (Eph. 5:5; Rev. 20:6).

g. Divine worship rendered to and accepted by him (Matt. 14:33; 28:9; Luke 5:8; 1 Cor. 1:2). Since the Old Testament (Exod. 34:14) and Christ himself (Matt. 4:10) declare that God only is to be worshipped, and both ordinary men and angels refused the worship which was offered them (Acts 10:25f.; Rev. 19:10; 22:8f.), for Christ to accept it, if he were not God, would be blasphemy. And what is still more, the Scriptures not only inform us that Christ was worshipped, but they ask us to worship him (John 5:23; Heb. 1:6). If he is not God, he is a deceiver or is self-deceived, and, in either case, if he is not God he is not good (*Christus, si non Deus, non bonus*).

h. Christ's own consciousness and claims as proofs of his deity. At the age of twelve he recognized the peculiar claims of his Father (Luke 2:49), at his baptism he was assured of his special sonship (Matt. 3:17), in the Sermon on the Mount he set himself over against the ancients (Matt. 5:21f., 27f., 33–36), when he sent forth the disciples he gave them power to perform miracles (Matt. 10:1, 8; Luke 10:9, 19), he asserted his pre-existence (John 8:58; 17:5), he requested that prayer be offered in his name (John 16:23f.), he claimed that he and the Father were one (John 10:30; 14:9; 17:11), and he claimed that he was the Son of God (John 10:36). Logic seems to demand that he either is what he knew himself to be and what he claimed to be, or that he is unfit to be recognized at all.

4. *The Holy Spirit is recognized as God.* a. He is a person. Before it can be demonstrated that the Holy Spirit is God, it must first be established that he is a person, not a mere influence or divine power. This is done along the following lines: (1) Personal pronouns are used of him. Though the Greek term for spirit is neuter, Jesus in John 14:26 and 16:13f. used the masculine demonstrative pronoun "he" (that one) of the Holy Spirit. (2) He is called Helper (Comforter). This designation is applied both to the Holy Spirit (John 14:16, 26; 15:26; 16:7) and to Christ (John 14:16; 1 John 2:1), and since it expressed personality when applied to Christ, it must do so also when applied to the Spirit. (3) Personal characteristics are ascribed to him. He has the three essential elements of personality: intellect (1 Cor. 2:11), sensibilities (Rom. 8:27; 15:30), and will (1 Cor. 12:11).

(4) Personal acts are performed by him. He regenerates (John 3:5), teaches (John 14:26), bears witness (John 15:26), convicts (John 16:8–11), guides into truth (John 16:13), glorifies Christ (John 16:14), calls man into service (Acts 13:2), speaks (Acts 13:2; Rev. 2:7), directs men in service (Acts

16:6f.), intercedes (Rom. 8:26), searches out (1 Cor. 2:10), and works (1 Cor. 12:11). (5) He relates to the Father and the Son as a person. This is the case in the baptismal formula (Matt. 28:19), in the apostolic benediction (2 Cor. 13:14), and in his office as administrator of the church (1 Cor. 12:4–6; cf. also 1 Pet. 1:1f.; Jude 20f.).

(6) He is susceptible of personal treatment. He can be tempted (Acts 5:9), lied to (Acts 5:3), grieved (Eph. 4:30; Isa. 63:10), resisted (Acts 7:51), insulted (Heb. 10:29), and blasphemed (Matt. 12:31f.). (7) He is distinguished from his own power (Acts 10:38; Rom. 15:13; 1 Cor. 2:4). All these things prove that the Holy Spirit is a person, not a mere influence.

b. He is deity. He is not, however, merely a person. He is a divine person. This can be shown in several ways: (1) Attributes of deity are affirmed of him. He is eternal (Heb. 9:14), omniscient (1 Cor. 2:10f.; John 14:26; 16:12f.), omnipotent (Luke 1:35), and omnipresent (Ps. 139:7–10). (2) Works of deity are ascribed to him, such as creation (Gen. 1:2; Job 33:4; Ps. 104:30), regeneration (John 3:5), inspiration of the Scriptures (2 Pet. 1:21; cf. Acts 1:16; 28:25), and raising of the dead (Rom. 8:11). (3) The way in which he is associated with the Father and the Son proves not only his personality, but also his deity, as in the baptismal formula (Matt. 28:19), the apostolic benediction (2 Cor. 13:14), and the administration of the church (1 Cor. 12:4–6).

(4) The words and works of the Holy Spirit are considered as the words and works of God (cf. Isa. 6:9f. with John 12:39–41 and Acts 28:25–27; Exod. 16:7 with Ps. 95:8–11; Isa. 63:9f. with Heb. 3:7–9; Gen. 1:27 with Job 33:4. (5) Finally, he is expressly called God (Acts 5:3f.; 2 Cor. 3:17f.). Other divine names are also given to him (cf. Exod. 17:7 with Heb. 3:7–9; and 2 Tim. 3:16 with 2 Pet. 1:21). All these references prove that the Holy Spirit, equally with the Father and the Son, is God. In church history some opposition to the doctrine of the deity of the Holy Spirit has arisen. Arius and his followers held that the Holy Spirit was created by the Son; Macedonius, Bishop of Constantinople from A.D. 341–360, and his followers held that the Holy Spirit was a creature subordinate to the Son; and later, Socinus propounded that he was the eternal manifestation of God's power.

Orthodox Christianity has always held to the deity of the Holy Spirit. The Council of Constantinople (381) affirmed this doctrine, just as the Council of Nicaea (325) clarified the doctrine of the deity of Christ. These are considered the first two general councils of the church.

As Jesus Christ is the Son of God, so the Spirit is the Spirit of God. An early controversy (Filioque Controversy) in the church concerned the procession of the Holy Spirit. Did the Spirit proceed from the Father or from the Father and the Son? The Council of Toledo (589) acknowledged the Spirit's procession from both the Father and the Son. This doctrine is established in two ways: Jesus declared that he would send the Spirit (John 15:26), and the Spirit is called the Spirit of Christ (Rom. 8:9), of Jesus (Acts 16:7), and of his Son (Gal. 4:6).

C. Some Observations and Deductions Based on the Study of the Trinity

1. This doctrine is not in conflict with the unity of God.   There are three persons in the one essence. Though there is no perfect analogy in human experience to explain or illustrate the doctrine of the trinity, the analogy of the human mind does provide a suggestion. The human mind is able to dialogue with itself and at the same time is able to pass verdicts on its deliberations. The trinity is faintly analogous to this.

2. These distinctions are eternal.   This is evident from the passages which imply Christ's existence with the Father from eternity (John 1:1f.; 17:5, 24; Phil. 2:6) and from those which assert or imply the eternity of the Holy Spirit (Gen. 1:2; Heb. 9:14). The nature of the eternal relationship existing between the Father and the Son is commonly spoken of as "generation," while the relationship between the Father and the Son, on the one hand, and the Holy Spirit, on the other, is spoken of as "procession." By "eternal generation" is meant "eternal emanation." God says, "Thou art My Son, today I have begotten Thee" (Ps. 2:7). The word "today" denotes the universal present, the everlasting now. When Jesus said, "For just as the Father has life in Himself, even so He gave to the Son also to have life in Himself" (John 5:26), he spoke of an eternal communication of the life of the Father to the Son. The term "procession," as applied to the Holy Spirit, has very much the same meaning as the term "generation" in connection with the Son, except that the Holy Spirit "proceeds" from both the Father and the Son (John 14:26; 15:26; Acts 2:33: Heb. 9:14).

3. The three are equal.   And yet this does not exclude the arrangement by means of which the Father is first, the Son second, and the Spirit third. This is not a difference in glory, power, or length of existence, but simply of order. The Spirit and the Son are equal, though subordinate to the Father. This subordination is voluntary, not necessary (Phil. 2:5–7).

4. The doctrine has great practical value.   *a.* It allows for eternal love. Love was before creation, yet love needs an object. Love is always flowing among the persons of the trinity.
   b. Only God can reveal God. By God the Father sending God the Son, God could be made manifest.

c. Only God can atone for sin. This is accomplished through the incarnation of God the Son.

d. It is hard to conceive of personality existing without society. The persons of the Godhead relate one to another in perfect harmony, a perfect society. "If there were no trinity, there could be no incarnation, no objective redemption, and therefore no salvation; for there would be no one capable of acting as Mediator between God and man."[4]

[4]Boettner, *Studies in Theology*, p. 135.

CHAPTER X

The Decrees of God

If God works all things after the counsel of his will (Eph. 1:11), it is proper that after a discussion of the person of God, the works of God should be set forth. Before this can be done, however, an analysis of the decrees of God must be made.

I. THE DEFINITION OF THE DECREES

The decrees of God may be defined as God's eternal purpose (in a real sense all things are embraced in one purpose) or purposes, based on his most wise and holy counsel, whereby he freely and unchangeably, for his own glory, ordained either efficaciously or permissively all that comes to pass. This definition includes several items: (1) The decrees are God's eternal purpose. He does not make his plans or alter them as human history develops. He made them in eternity, and because he is immutable, they remain unaltered (Ps. 33:11; James 1:17). (2) The decrees are based on his most wise and holy counsel. He is omniscient and so knows what is best, and he is absolutely holy and so cannot purpose anything that is wrong (Isa. 48:11). (3) The decrees originate in God's freedom (Ps. 135:6; Eph. 1:11). He is not obligated to purpose anything *ad extra*, but purposes unconstrainedly, if he purposes at all. The only necessity laid upon him in this respect is the necessity that comes from his own attributes as a wise and holy God. We, therefore, can know only by a special revelation from God whether or not he has purposed anything *ad extra* and, if he has, what it is that he has purposed. (4) He is omnipotent and able to do all that he desires (Dan. 4:35). (5) The decrees have as their end the glory of God. They do not primarily aim at the happiness of the creature, nor at the perfecting of the saints, although both these things are included in his aims, but at the glory of him who is absolute perfection (Num. 14:21; Isa. 6:3). (6) There are two kinds of decrees: efficacious and permissive. There are things which God purposes that he also determines efficaciously to bring about; there are other things which he merely determines to permit (Rom. 8:28). But even in the case of the permissive decrees, he overrules all for his glory (Matt. 18:7; Acts 2:23). (7) And, finally, the decrees embrace all that comes to pass. They include all

100

the past, the present, and the future; they embrace the things which he efficaciously brings about and the things which he merely permits (Isa. 46:10f.). "In other words, with infinite power and infinite wisdom God has, from all eternity past, decided and chosen and determined the course of all events without exception for all eternity to come."[1]

II. THE PROOF OF THE DECREES

That the events in the universe are neither a surprise nor a disappointment to God, nor the result of his caprice or arbitrary will, but the outworking of a definite purpose and plan of God, is the teaching of Scripture:

> The Lord of hosts has sworn saying, "Surely, just as I have intended so it has happened, and just as I have planned so it will stand, . . . This is the plan devised against the whole earth; and this is the hand that is stretched out against all the nations. For the Lord of hosts has planned, and who can frustrate it? And as for His stretched-out hand, who can turn it back?" (Isa. 14:24, 26f.)
> He made known to us the mystery of His will, according to His kind intention which He purposed in Him. . . . In Him also we have obtained an inheritance, having been predestined according to His purpose who works all things after the counsel of His will. (Eph. 1:9–11)

The decrees are sometimes represented as one decree: "called according to His purpose" (Rom. 8:28; cf. Eph. 1:11). Though the decrees may appear to be many purposes, to the divine mind they are in reality but one great, all-inclusive purpose. Thus, we can speak of a universe, rather than a multiverse.

Further, they are represented as eternal: "in accordance with the eternal purpose which He carried out in Christ Jesus our Lord" (Eph. 3:11); "foreknown before the foundation of the world" (1 Pet. 1:20); "just as He chose us in Him before the foundation of the world" (Eph. 1:4); "according to His own purpose and grace which was granted us in Christ Jesus from all eternity" (2 Tim. 1:9); and "in the hope of eternal life, which God, who cannot lie, promised long ages ago" (Titus 1:2). As Shedd says, "The things decreed come to pass in time, and in successive series; but they constitute one great system which as one *whole*, and a *unity*, was comprehended in one eternal purpose of God."[2]

---

[1]Buswell, *A Systematic Theology of the Christian Religion*, I, p. 163.
[2]Shedd, *Dogmatic Theology*, I, p. 395.

III. THE BASES OF THE DECREES

Much light is shed upon the doctrine of the decrees by a clear understanding of the bases on which they rest. We spontaneously ask, Why was he not content to confine his fellowship and activity to the trinity?

It must be emphasized that the decrees of God did not originate in necessity. God did not have to decree anything, nor was he limited by anything outside of himself in making the decrees. What God decreed, he decreed freely, voluntarily; it was not necessitated. Further, the decrees are not due to mere caprice or arbitrary will. God does not act from mere emotional impulse; he always acts rationally. He may not always disclose his reasons for decreeing one thing instead of another, but we are assured that there are always reasons (Deut. 29:29). "You shall understand hereafter" (John 13:7) is an encouragement in that we shall some day understand the meaning of certain puzzling Scriptures and the mysteries of certain perplexing acts of God. Neither does God exercise an arbitrary will. Certain extreme determinists have held to the absoluteness of the divine will. They have taught that there is no criterion of value that determines God's will. A thing is right because God wills it. If this is true, then the death of Christ was also not necessitated by any inner principle in God, but merely by the will of God, and if God had willed to save man without the death of Christ, he could have justly done so.

Rather, the decrees of God are based on his most wise and holy counsel. Being all-wise, knowing the end from the beginning, knowing that sin would come (since he had decided to permit it to come), knowing what would be the nature of sin and how he would have to deal with it if he was to save anyone, he based his plans on all his knowledge and understanding. Being perfectly holy, and incapable of partiality or unfairness, he made his plans according to that which is absolutely right. He can save the sinner only if in doing so he can remain absolutely just (Rom. 3:25). In this manner God can be both loving and just (Ps. 85:10). It is on the basis of his wisdom and holiness, then, that he has made the decrees, both the efficacious and the permissive decrees.

IV. THE PURPOSE OF THE DECREES

What was God's fundamental reason for purposing and undertaking to do anything *ad extra*? Is there an end, any object, in the universe? If so, what is it?

Surely, it is not primarily the happiness nor the holiness of the creature. God does seek to promote the happiness of his creatures. Paul said at Lystra, "He did not leave Himself without witness, in that He did good and gave you rains from heaven and fruitful seasons, satisfying your hearts with food and gladness" (Acts 14:17). And in his letter to Timothy, he wrote, "God . . . richly supplies us with all things to enjoy" (1 Tim. 6:17). Paul regarded the ascetic principles of the Gnostics, who said, "Do not handle, do not taste, do not touch," as "the commandments and teachings of men" which have "the appearance of wisdom in self-made religion and self-abasement and severe treatment of the body, but are of no value against fleshly indulgence" (Col. 2:21–23). God does seek to promote the happiness of man, even so-called outward happiness, but happiness is a secondary, not the primary, end.

And God is certainly concerned to promote the holiness of his creatures. To prove this we need only note that he created man in "righteousness and holiness of the truth" (Eph. 4:24). He admonishes man to be holy as he is holy (Lev. 11:44; 1 Pet. 1:16), he gave him his holy law as the standard of life (Rom. 7:12), Christ died that he might sanctify the people (Eph. 5:25–27), and the Holy Spirit has come to regenerate and sanctify men (John 3:5; 1 Pet. 1:2). Though God does seek to promote the sanctification of the creature, this is not the highest end of God.

The highest aim of the decrees is the glory of God. Creation glorifies him. David says, "The heavens are telling of the glory of God; and their expanse is declaring the work of His hands" (Ps. 19:1). God declares that he will refine Israel in the furnace of affliction and adds, "For My own sake, for My own sake, I will act; for how can My name be profaned? And My glory I will not give to another" (Isa. 48:11). Paul explains that God delays judgment "in order that He might make known the riches of His glory upon vessels of mercy, which He prepared beforehand for glory" (Rom. 9:23), and that he has foreordained believers "to the praise of the glory of His grace" (Eph. 1:6; cf. 1:12, 14; 2:8–10). And the twenty-four elders cast their crowns before God's throne and say, "Worthy art Thou, our Lord and our God, to receive glory and honor and power; for Thou didst create all things, and because of Thy will they existed, and were created" (Rev. 4:11). Thus, the end of all things is the glory of God; and only as we also adopt this as our real goal in life are we living on the highest plane and in full harmony with the purposes of God.

In man it would be selfishness to seek for his own glory, but that is because man is sinful and imperfect. To seek for his own glory, would be to seek to glorify sinfulness and imperfection. But this is not the case with God. He is absolutely sinless and perfect in holiness. For him to aim at his own glory is, therefore, merely to seek the glory of absolute holiness and sinless perfection. There is no one and nothing higher to glorify. In fact, God does, and we must, aim in everything at the glory of him who is the manifestation of all goodness, purity, wisdom, and truth.

V. THE CONTENT AND ORDER OF THE DECREES

God has decreed all that comes to pass. This can be divided into four broad
categories.

A. IN THE MATERIAL AND PHYSICAL REALM

God decreed to create the universe and man (Gen. 1:26; Ps. 33:6–11; Prov.
8:22–31; Isa. 45:18). God decreed to establish the earth (Ps. 119:90f.) and
the seasons of the year (Gen. 8:22). He also decreed never again to destroy
the population of the earth by means of a flood (Gen. 9:8–17). Furthermore,
God decreed the distribution of the nations (Deut. 32:8), their appointed
seasons, and the bounds of their habitation (Acts 17:26). Paul adds that he
did this "that they should seek God, if perhaps they might grope for Him and
find Him, though He is not far from each one of us" (v. 27). He also decreed
the length of human life (Job 14:5) and the manner of our exit from this life
(John 21:19; 1 Cor. 15:51f.; 2 Tim. 4:6–8). All the other events in the
material and physical realm have likewise been decreed and are in his plan
and purpose (Ps. 104:3f., 14–23; 107:25, 29; Isa. 14:26f.).

B. IN THE MORAL AND SPIRITUAL REALM

As we relate the decrees of God to this realm, we are faced with two basic
problems: the existence of evil in the world, and the freedom of man. How
can a holy God allow moral evil, and how can a sovereign God permit man to
be free? Certain assumptions or presuppositions must be made: (1) God is
not the author of sin, (2) God must take the initiative in salvation, (3) man is
responsible for his actions, and (4) God's actions are based upon his holy and
wise counsel.

As to the logical order of the decrees and how sin fits into the permissive
will of God, theologians differ. Some say the logical order is as follows: God
decreed (1) to save certain men and reprobate others, (2) to create both, (3) to
permit the fall of both, (4) to send Christ to redeem the elect, and (5) to send
the Holy Spirit to apply this redemption to the elect. This view is called
"supralapsarianism."

Another view called "infralapsarianism" or "sublapsarianism" holds the
decrees to be in the following order: God decreed (1) to create man, (2) to
permit the fall, (3) to elect some of the fallen to be saved and leave others as
they are, (4) to provide a redeemer for the elect, and (5) to send the Spirit to
apply this redemption to the elect. This view teaches limited atonement.

A variation of the above, which allows for unlimited atonement, is the
following: God decreed (1) to create man, (2) to permit the fall, (3) to provide
in Christ redemption sufficient for all, (4) to elect some to salvation and leave

others as they are, and (5) to send the Spirit to secure the acceptance of redemption on the part of the elect. This last order of the decrees seems to be most in harmony with Scripture in that it allows for election and unlimited atonement (1 Tim. 2:6; 4:10; Titus 2:11; 2 Pet. 2:1; 1 John 2:2), while acknowledging its special efficacy for the elect (John 17:9, 20, 24; Acts 13:48; Rom. 8:29f.; Eph. 1:4; 2 Tim. 1:9f.; 1 Pet. 1:1f.).

In endeavoring to understand more fully the place of sin and the provision of salvation to the sinner, four things must be noted.

1. God determined to permit sin. Though God is not the author of sin (James 1:13f.), nor did he necessitate it, he did, on the basis of his wise and holy counsel, decree to permit the fall and sin to come. He did this in the light of what he knew would be the nature of sin, of what he knew sin would do to the creature, and of what he knew he would have to do if he was to save anyone. God could have prevented sin's coming. If he had decided to preserve the will of the angels and of man from lapsing, they would have persevered in holiness. But for wise and holy reasons, which we may not be able entirely to fathom (Rom. 11:33), he decided to permit sin. That sin is thus permitted, though not necessitated, appears (1) from all the threatenings of punishment for sin (Gen. 2:17; Exod. 34:7; Eccl. 11:9; Ezek. 18:20; 2 Thess. 1:7f.), (2) from the Psalmists' declarations, "their desire He gave to them" (Ps. 78:29), and "He gave them their request, but sent a wasting disease among them" (Ps. 106:15), and (3) from Paul's statement, "And in the generations gone by He permitted all the nations to go their own ways" (Acts 14:16; cf. 17:30).

2. God determined to overrule sin for the good. This determination is inseparable from the one to permit sin. He decreed to permit it, but also to overrule it for the good. Several things may be mentioned in proof of this point. Joseph said to his brothers, "You meant evil against me, but God meant it for good in order to bring about this present result, to preserve many people alive" (Gen. 50:20). The Psalmists say, "The Lord nullifies the counsel of the nations; He frustrates the plans of the peoples. The counsel of the Lord stands forever, the plans of His heart from generation to generation" (Ps. 33:10f.) and, "For the wrath of man shall praise Thee; with a remnant of wrath Thou shalt gird Thyself" (Ps. 76:10). Nebuchadnezzar's attempted destruction of the three Hebrew children in the fiery furnace resulted in the royal recognition of the God of the Hebrews and the promotion of the three youths (Dan. 3:19–30). Paul expressed his confidence that the experiences in the Roman prison would result in his deliverance (Phil. 1:19f.). This is due to the fact that God is sovereign, holy, and wise.

It seems evident that he who could have kept sin out of the universe can also regulate and control its manifestation. He has the right and the power to rule in his own creation. Furthermore, he has a resentment against sin (Jer. 44:4; Amos 5:21-24; Zech. 8:17; Rev. 2:6); he cannot permit it to thwart his purposes of holiness; it must be overruled for the good. Paul resented the slander that taught, "Let us do evil that good may come" (Rom. 3:8; cf. 6:1). God did not permit sin in order to bring about good; rather, God has permitted sin to come for other reasons, and he has decreed to overrule it for the good. Finally, he has the knowledge and the understanding to overrule for good. He knows just how far to allow it to go, how much of it to prevent, and how to make it all work out for his own holy purposes.

3. God determined to save from sin.   Here is the heart of the problem. All Christians are agreed that God has decreed to save men, but not all are agreed as to how he does this. We must, in this connection, particularly remember (1) that God must take the initiative in salvation, (2) that man, even in his present helpless state, is really responsible, and (3) that God's decrees are not based on caprice or arbitrary will, but on his wise and holy counsel.

Acknowledging these three presuppositions, evangelicals interpret this matter in one of two primary ways: some see election as dependent upon divine foreknowledge, others see election and foreknowledge, as they relate to saving faith, as essentially inseparable. These two approaches deserve analysis. *a.* Election is seen, in the former approach, as that sovereign gracious act of God whereby he chose in Christ for salvation all those whom he foreknew would respond positively to prevenient grace. This can be analyzed in the following manner. Originally man had freedom in two senses of the term: freedom to carry out the dictates of his nature and freedom to act contrary to his nature. Man had the ability to sin and the ability not to sin. In the fall he lost his ability not to sin; his ability to sin became inability not to sin (Gen. 6:5; Job 14:14; Jer. 13:23; 17:9; Rom. 3:10-18; 8:5-8). Now he is free only in the sense that he is able to do as his fallen nature suggests. Because man is without any ability or desire to change, God responded by prevenient grace. This grace (sometimes considered a part of common or universal grace) restores to the sinner the ability to make a favorable response to God (Rom. 2:4; Titus 2:11). This fact is implied in God's dealing with Adam and Eve after the fall (Gen. 3:8f.) and in the many exhortations to sinners to turn to God (Prov. 1:23; Isa. 31:6; Ezek. 14:6; 18:32; Joel 2:13f.; Matt. 18:3; Acts 3:19), to repent (1 Kings 8:47; Matt. 3:2; Luke 13:3, 5; Acts 2:38; 17:30), and to believe (2 Chron. 20:20; Isa. 43:10; John 6:29; 14:1; Acts 16:31; Phil. 1:29; 1 John 3:23).

Because of prevenient grace man is able to make an initial response to God, and God will then give to him repentance and faith (Jer. 31:18; Acts 5:31; 11:18; Rom. 12:3; 2 Tim. 2:25; 2 Pet. 1:1). God in his foreknowledge knows what men will do in response to his prevenient grace, whether or not they will "receive the grace of God in vain" (2 Cor. 6:1). Thus, foreknowledge is not itself causative. There are things which God foreknows because he has purposed to permit them to come to pass, and still other things which he foreknows because he foresees what men will do without causing them to do so. God foreknew what men would do in response to his prevenient grace, and he elected those whom he foresaw would respond positively. In this way election follows foreknowledge. In election God determines (a) to save those whom he has foreknown would respond (1 Pet. 1:1f.), (b) to give them life (Acts 13:48), (c) to place them in the position of sons (Gal. 4:5f.; Eph. 1:5), and (d) to conform them to the image of Christ (Rom. 8:29f.). Briefly, in this approach toward a solution, God, through prevenient grace, provides everyone with the ability to respond to him if they so choose. God, foreknowing those who will respond, elects them to salvation.

b. Election and foreknowledge are inseparable and essentially the same. In this approach, election is interpreted differently than in the one just considered. Here election may be interpreted as that act of God by which he graciously and on account of no foreseen merit chooses out from among sinful men certain ones to be the recipients of his special saving grace. This position does not consider prevenient grace to be a part of common grace, nor foreknowledge to be merely prescience. Granted, common grace comes to all (Acts 14:17), God is not wishing for any to perish (2 Pet. 3:9), the atonement is unlimited (1 John 2:2), and the call for salvation is universal (Rom. 10:13); nonetheless, the Scriptures are abundantly clear that only those who are the elect shall be saved. The reasonableness of this can be shown in several ways. God can show grace on whom he wills (Matt. 20:12–15; John 15:16; Rom. 9:20f.). He does elect some to salvation (Acts 13:48; Eph. 1:4; 2 Thess. 2:13). Foreknowledge is not mere prescience, but includes also a kindly selection and relationship (Rom. 8:27–30; 1 Pet. 1:1f.; cf. the use of "know" in Scripture: Exod. 2:25; Ps. 1:6; Matt. 7:23; Rom. 11:2; Gal. 4:9; 1 Thess. 5:12; 1 Pet. 1:20; 1 John 2:3, 13). Further, election was done in eternity past (Eph. 1:4; 2 Tim. 1:9); God gave the elect to his Son (John 6:37; 17:2, 6, 9; 1 Pet. 2:9); salvation is because of God's will, not man's (John 1:13; 1 John 4:10); and, finally, repentance, faith, and holiness are all gifts of God (John 6:65; Acts 5:31; 1 Cor. 12:3; Eph. 2:8f.; 2 Tim. 2:25).

Arguments against this approach to election must be examined. It could be argued that this is unjust to the non-elect. But there is no injustice with God in condemning; salvation is a matter of pure grace. God is to be praised for saving the few, rather than accused of condemning the masses (Ps. 44:3; Luke 4:25–27; 1 Cor. 4:7). It is also charged that this presents God as arbitrary. But God's choice is not arbitrary; it is the free choice of a wise, holy, and loving God. Does this imply reprobation? No, God simply permits the sinner to pursue his self-chosen rebellion, resulting in eternal punishment (Hos. 4:17; Rom. 9:22f.; 1 Pet. 2:8).

The doctrine of election, properly understood, drives the believer to admiration (Deut. 32:4), reverence (Jer. 10:7), humility (Rom. 11:33), submissiveness (Dan. 4:35), and worship (Rom. 11:33–36).

4. God determined to reward his servants and to punish the disobedient.   In his goodness God has not merely decreed to save some, but also to reward those who serve him (Isa. 62:11; Matt. 6:4, 19f.; 10:41f.; 1 Cor. 3:8; 1 Tim. 5:18). Fundamentally, this decree originates in his grace. Man can do no more than his duty. Jesus said, "So you too, when you do all the things which are commanded you, say, 'We are unworthy slaves; we have done only that which we ought to have done' " (Luke 17:10). In other words, God is entitled to absolute obedience in all things and at all times, and is under no obligation to reward even the most perfect and constant observance of His commandments. But in his great goodness, he has decreed to reward those of his children who serve him. Some have spoken of this as his remunerative justice, in contrast to his retributive justice, but fundamentally the decree of rewards is due to his goodness and not to his justice.

By contrast, because of his absolute holiness and justice, God has decreed to punish the wicked and disobedient. This applies to Satan and his hosts (Gen. 3:15; Matt. 25:41; Rom. 16:20; Rev. 20:1–3, 10) and to men (Ps. 37:20; Ezek. 18:4; Nah. 1:3). To some extent this punishment is meted out to wicked men during their lifetime (Num. 16:26; Ps. 11:6; 37:28; Isa. 5:20f.; Jer. 25:31), but the real punishment is postponed until the day of judgment (Ps. 9:17; Isa. 3:11; Matt. 13:49f.; 25:46; 2 Thess. 1:8f.; Rev. 20:11–15).

C. In the Social and Political Realm

1. The family and human government.   The fundamental decree, in this area, is that of the family and the home. In the very beginning God said: "It is not good for the man to be alone; I will make him a helper suitable for him" (Gen. 2:18). By the fact that he made but one man and one woman, he indicated that marriage was to be monogamous and indissoluble (Matt. 19:3–9). All through the Scriptures the sanctity of marriage is recognized (2 Sam. 12:1–15; Matt. 14:3f.; John 2:1f.; Eph. 5:22–33; Heb. 13:4). The decree of marriage implies the decree to have children (Gen. 1:27f.; 9:1, 7; Ps. 127:3–5) and to establish a home (Deut. 24:5; John 19:27; 1 Tim. 5:4; Titus 2:5).

Closely connected with this is the decree of human government (Gen. 9:5f.). God has by decree determined the location, seasons, and boundaries of the nations (Deut. 32:8; Acts 17:26). He has likewise ordained the rulers of nations (Dan. 4:34f.; Rom. 13:1f.). All rulers are to recognize the sovereign rule of God and to seek and carry out his will (Ps. 2:10–12). If a ruler fails to do so, and the requirements of his government conflict with the commandments of God, the subjects are to obey God rather than man (Acts 4:19f.; 5:29).

2. *The call and mission of Israel.* God chose Abraham to be the head of a special people (Gen. 12:1–3). He limited the line after him to Isaac (Gen. 17:21), Jacob (Gen. 25:23; 27:27–29), and the twelve sons of Jacob (Gen. 49). He chose Israel for himself, to make them a kingdom of priests, and a holy nation (Exod. 19:4–6). It was not a decree to salvation in the first place, but to outward standing and privilege. This outward standing and privilege was, however, by means of his holy law and divine institutions to lead them to salvation and acceptable service. Included in the latter was the solemn responsibility to be a spiritual blessing to the surrounding nations (Gen. 12:2).

But Israel miserably failed God. God sought for grapes, but the nation yielded only wild grapes (Isa. 5:1–7). Indeed, they mistreated and killed God's representatives that demanded spiritual fruit of the nation. As a result, the kingdom was temporarily withdrawn from them as a nation (Matt. 21:33–43). The natural branches have been broken off and the Gentiles, the branches of a wild olive tree, have been grafted into the stem (Rom. 11:11–22). Some day God will graft in again the natural branches (Rom. 11:23–27; cf. Ezek. 37:1–23; Hos. 2:14–23). In the meantime, there is even today a remnant according to the election of grace (Rom. 11:1–10). All these details are embraced in the original decree of God.

3. *The founding and mission of the church.* From all eternity God has decreed the founding and building of the church, although this fact was not fully revealed until the time of Jesus and the apostles. The fact that Jesus declared that he would build his church (Matt. 16:18) indicates that it was not yet in existence at that time. Paul declared that while the church was included in God's eternal purpose, the nature of it was not fully revealed until his day (Eph. 3:1–13). The church is, thus, not an improved Judaism (Matt. 9:14–17), but a perfectly new creation. In the church, God made of the two, Jew and Gentile, one new man (Eph. 2:11–15). God's present purpose is to call out a people from the Gentiles and the remnant of Israel, according to the election of grace, for his name (Acts 15:13–18; Rom. 11:1, 30f.). The Holy Spirit and the church are the media through which he seeks to accomplish this purpose (Matt. 28:19f.; Acts 1:8). When this purpose has been accomplished, Christ will return, take his people to himself (John 14:3; Rom. 11:25; 1 Thess. 4:16–18), present the church to himself (Eph. 5:25–27), and return to bless and save Israel (Zech. 12:10–13:1; Rom. 11:25–27).

4. *The final triumph of God.* God has decreed to give all the kingdoms of the world to Christ (Ps. 2:6–9; Dan. 7:13f.; Luke 1:31–33; Rev. 11:15–17;

19:11–20:6). In connection with his taking over these kingdoms, there will be the "regeneration" of nature (Matt. 19:27–30; Rom. 8:19–22; cf. Isa. 35:1–10). His rule will be characterized by peace and righteousness (Ps. 2:8f.; 72:1–19; Isa. 9:6f.). This first phase of God's triumph on the earth will last for a period of a thousand years (Rev. 20:1–6). After Satan's final revolt and the great white throne judgment (Rev. 20:7–15), there will come the new heavens, the new earth, and the new Jerusalem (Rev. 21:1–22:5). Then Christ will deliver up the kingdom to God, even the Father; and the triune God, Father, Son, and Holy Spirit, will reign forever and ever (1 Cor. 15:23–28). All of these things were decreed by God and they will most surely come to pass.

CHAPTER XI

The Works of God: Creation

I. THE DEFINITION OF CREATION

The term "create" is used in two senses in Scripture: in the sense of immediate creation and in the sense of mediate creation. Immediate creation is that free act of the triune God whereby in the beginning and for his own glory, without the use of pre-existing materials or secondary causes, he brought into being, immediately and instantaneously, the whole visible and invisible universe. Immediate creation was thus the free act of God, in contrast to all pantheistic notions of necessary creation; it was an act in which the whole trinity had a part, involving the equality of Father, Son, and Holy Spirit; it was the first act of God *ad extra*; it was effected for the glory of God; it was not a reshaping of pre-existing materials or the work of secondary causes; it was an immediate act of God that had immediate results; and it was all-embracing in its scope, including not only all material existences, but also all immaterial existences.

Mediate creation, on the other hand, is those acts of God which are also denominated "creation," but which do not originate things *ex nihilo;* they, instead, shape, adapt, combine, or transform existing materials. God may himself directly shape, adapt, combine, or transform the existing materials, or he may indirectly do this through the operation of secondary causes. Hodge says, comparing immediate and mediate creation, "The one was instantaneous, the other gradual; the one precludes the idea of any preexisting substance, and of cooperation, the other admits and implies both. There is evident ground for this distinction in the Mosaic account of the creation."[1] The term "immediate creation" should probably be restricted to the statement in Gen. 1:1 and to other similar statements referring to the same events.

II. THE PROOF OF THE DOCTRINE OF CREATION

From ancient times man has been trying to solve the "riddle" of the universe. He has been asking, "Did it always exist or has it had a beginning? If it

[1]Hodge, *Systematic Theology*, I, p. 556.

has had a beginning, how and when did it come into being?" Mere science or reason cannot solve the problem. Science may seek to find an answer to the problem of origins, but because it must work in the area of empirical knowledge, the study of origins and first causes is necessarily outside its domain. And philosophy has given no adequate solution to the problem. It either denies creation altogether, or it explains it in such a way as virtually to deny it. A solution to the issues of origins must come from Scripture and be accepted by faith (Heb. 11:3). Scripture declares the how and why of physical and spiritual existence.

A. The Mosaic Account of Creation

This is found in Gen. 1 and 2. These Scriptures record the immediate and the mediate creation of the universe and of man.

1. The immediate creation of the universe.   The opening statement of the Bible declares that "in the beginning God created the heavens and earth" (Gen.1:1). According to these words, the universe is neither eternal, nor formed out of pre-existing things, nor sprung from necessity, but due to the immediate creative act of God. It was created *ex nihilo,* that is, out of nothing.

The doctrine of creation *ex nihilo* does not rest on the usage of the Hebrew word *bara* and the Greek word *ktizein;* for they are at times used interchangeably with the words *asah* and *poiein.* Thus, God is said both to have "created" and "made" the world (Gen. 1:1; Neh. 9:6; Col. 1:16f.). But it is clear that in Gen. 1:1 and 2:3f., the word does mean to create out of nothing. Davis explains:

> The verb *bārā'* ("to create") expresses better than any other verb the idea of an absolute creation, or creation *ex nihilo.* The qal stem of this verb is employed exclusively in the Old Testament for God's activity; the subject of the verb is never man. God is said to create "the wind" (Amos 4:13), "a clean heart" (Ps. 51:10), and "new heavens and a new earth" (Isa. 65:17). Genesis 1 emphasizes three great beginnings, each initiated by God (cf. 1:1, 21, 27). . . . The creative act of God reflected in verse 1, therefore, involved no preexisting material; a sovereign, all-powerful God created the heavens and the earth from nothing.[2]

2. The mediate creation of the present universe.   Whether due to deliberate incompleteness in the original act of creation, or to some catastrophe that befell the original creation, we find in Gen. 1:2 that the earth was "formless

---

[2]Davis, *Paradise to Prison,* pp. 40, 41.

and void, and darkness was over the surface of the deep." Then there follows the formation of the present order. Certain problems, therefore, are raised.

a. Was the creation immediate, mediate, or a combination of both? Some limit immediate creation to the act described in v. 1 and regard the rest of the chapter as mediate creation. Others see a combination of immediate and mediate creation throughout the entire chapter. The sun may have been included in the original creation, and the light (vss. 3–5) may have come from the sun. God, however, probably created light apart from the sun. The germs of vegetable life may have survived from a primitive condition, so that God needed merely to command the earth to "sprout vegetation, plants yielding seed, and fruit trees bearing fruit after their kind, with seed in them" (v. 11). It seems more probable, though, that vegetation was directly created by God. In Gen. 2:19, we read, "And out of the ground the Lord God formed every beast of the field and every bird of the sky." This would seem to teach the mediate creation of all animals, fish, fowl, reptiles, etc. (1:20–25), though surely animal life itself was directly created by God. And we are definitely informed that "the Lord God formed man of dust from the ground, and breathed into his nostrils the breath of life" (Gen. 2:7). This would show that he, too, was created mediately, as far as his body is concerned. Though man and animals were made of dust and return to dust, the soul of man was surely immediately created by God.

b. What was included in the immediate creation of God? Certainly not only the heavens, but also the angelic inhabitants of heaven (Job 38:7; Neh. 9:6); and certainly not only the earth, but also all the waters and gases of the earth (Isa. 42:5; Col. 1:16; Rev. 4:11). Some have suggested that possibly some of the angelic beings, under the headship of him who turned out to be Satan, were assigned to this earth (cf. Luke 4:5–8). This is a plausible supposition, but there is no positive Scripture to support it, unless Ezek. 28:12–19 is to be interpreted in that way (cf. also Isa. 14:9–14).

c. Does Gen. 1:2 represent the original condition of the earth or a condition due to some great cataclysm? This is answered in three ways: (1) The restoration theory, or gap theory, proposes that after the original creation (v. 1), Satan fell, resulting in divine judgment upon the earth (v. 2). What follows are six days of recreating the earth. This view holds that "was" (v. 2) should better be translated "became." It further argues that the picture of formlessness, emptiness, and darkness (v. 2) is chiefly a picture of divine judgment, for God could not have created the earth this way (Isa. 34:11; 45:18; Jer. 4:23; 1 John 1:5). Further, this position provides a time framework in which the fall of Satan may have taken place (Isa. 14:9–14; Ezek. 28:12–19.[3]

---

[3]For a scholarly presentation, see Custance, *Without Form and Void.*

(2) Another view sees the gap as occurring before Gen. 1:1, and vss. 1ff. as telling of a recreation. In this view v. 1 is a summary statement of what follows, just as 2:1 summarizes what has gone before. Verse 2 is indicative of the judgment of God, but how or why this judgment came about is shrouded with mystery. It seems probable, however, that Satan's fall may well have been the cause. In this view Moses gives the order of the present creation, and he is not concerned with the original creation or what had caused the judgment from God.[4]

(3) Perhaps the most common view interprets v. 2 as presenting the universe in a state of incompleteness. After stating that the earth was unfinished, Moses continued to tell how it was made into an inhabitable place for man. The picture of formlessness, emptiness, and darkness is not necessarily a description of judgment, but rather of incompleteness; God's created earth was meant to be inhabited (Isa. 45:18). This view does not allow for a gap between vss. 1 and 2, nor for a creation before v. 1. As far as the fall of Satan, the history is not concerned with it; however, it obviously must have occurred before Gen. 3:1.[5]

d. Are the six days of creation to be thought of as six revelatory days, long periods of time, or six literal days? (1) Some hold that Moses received the revelation concerning creation during a span of six days. In this view the six days were days in the life of Moses, not days of creation. "Creation was *revealed* in six days, not *performed* in six days."[6] Against this view would be a verse like Exod. 20:11, "For in six days the Lord made the heavens and the earth, the sea and all that is in them, and rested on the seventh day."

(2) Others hold that the days refer to long eras of time. This is the day-age theory. There are variations within the position, but the primary thrust is that God created the physical universe and life and then guided the evolutionary processes through eons of time. This position, often called theistic evolution, allows for the geological ages, evolutionary processes, and the active involvement of a creator God. Some refine this theory into what is known as threshold evolution, which contends that God stepped in at certain key points in the evolutionary process and created some new thing. This view rejects macro-evolution, but accepts micro-evolution, that is, that there can be "a wide and varied change within the 'kinds' originally created by God."[7] Man himself is considered a special creative act of God.

A similar approach to threshold evolution, though not necessarily in harmony with the day-age concept, is progressive creationism. God created by

---

[4]For a good presentation of this view, see Waltke, *Creation and Chaos.*
[5]See Leupold, *Exposition of Genesis,* I, pp. 42–47, and Morris, *The Genesis Record,* pp. 46–52.
[6]Ramm, *The Christian View of Science and Scripture,* p. 222.
[7]Carnell, *An Introduction to Christian Apologetics,* p. 238.

fiat the unformed matter and then, through the inworking of his Spirit, formed and directed the creation progressively according to his preordained plan. God took the raw material and formed the finished product. This involved several acts of fiat creation as well as the employment of his ordained natural laws.[8]

Finally, (3) many interpret the six days as literal days. But what does the term "day" mean? It is used in various ways in the Bible: daylight as distinguished from darkness (Gen. 1:5, 16, 18), daylight and darkness combined (Gen. 1:5), the six creative days (Gen. 2:4), and indefinite periods such as "the day of their calamity" (Deut. 32:35), "the day of battle" (1 Sam. 13:22), "the day of fury" (Job 21:30), "the day of salvation" (2 Cor. 6:2), and "the day of the Lord" (Amos 5:18). Sometimes it is rendered "time" (Gen. 26:8; 38:12). A casual reading of Gen. 1 would suggest the literal or twenty-four hour day. Several arguments can be advanced: the use of evening and morning, the statement of Exod. 20:11, the appearance of the sun and moon to rule the day and night, the interdependence of the created universe (Can green grass exist over a prolonged period of time without the sun?), and the use of numerals before the word "day." The seemingly long geological ages are a problem with this last position. Several solutions are suggested: the universal flood had major effects on the topography of the earth; there are gaps in the early genealogies of Genesis, and therefore creation should be considered to have occurred much before 4000 B.C.; and since God created man with the appearance of age, he may have created the earth with the appearance of age as well.

e. What is the age of the earth? There are several views. (1) Various theories are propounded by the non-theistic scientists. Some see the origin of the universe as the burst of the primeval atom into the present universe; others hypothesize that the universe is in a continuing state of localized progression and regression. Within this universe the earth took form from an original mass of dust and gas some ten billion years ago. Dating the age of the earth along secular scientific methods is very inexact. One scientist acknowledges, "On the average, the 'age' of the Earth has been doubling every 15 years for the past three centuries; the rate, perhaps, has been somewhat faster during the past century."[9]

The Standard Geological Column, used by geologists for dating the earth's strata, was developed from a study of the fossil content (paleontology) in the various rock formations and strata. It dates according to eras: precambrian (3,500 million or more years of age), paleozoic (270–3,500 million years),

[8]For a fuller explanation of progressive creationism, see Ramm, *The Christian View of Science and Scripture*, pp. 112ff., 271ff.
[9]Whipple, "The History of the Solar System," in *Adventures in Earth History*, p. 101.

mesozoic (135–270 million years), and cenozoic (present–135 million years). The earliest forms of life are found in the precambrian era.

Various kinds of dating methods are used. One method, by measuring the annual increase of sodium in the ocean, determines the ocean to be just under 100 million years old. Another method measures geological time by studying the rate of decay of radioactive elements, such as uranium, potassium, and rubidium. According to this method, some meteorites show an age of 4,700 million years. Certain earth minerals are 3,500 million years. Another method uses radiocarbon dating:

> The theory of radiocarbon dating is as follows: the ratio of the isotopes of carbon in most living matter is virtually identical with their ratio in the carbon dioxide of the air. When an organism dies, it no longer derives radiocarbon from the air so that the ratio of radiocarbon to the stable isotopes, C^{12} and C^{13}, accompanying it in the body cells of the organism begins to decline. A comparison of the ratio of radiocarbon to the stable isotopes of carbon in a dead organism with that ratio in the atmosphere is thus a measure of the time elapsed since the organism died.[10]

These systems of dating are not exact, for they assume a uniformitarian geology, conditions available only in a scientific laboratory. Uniformitarianism either presupposes the absence of or ignores the presence of a personal God who acts in his creation.

(2) Theistic evolution, as stated earlier, postulates that God directs and controls the evolutionary processes from the rudimentary beginnings to the culmination of man. The dating methods are no different than in the nontheistic geological methods mentioned above. The day-age theory or similar approaches also seek to harmonize the geological eras with the Gen. 1 account.[11]

And finally, (3) others hold a recent creation date of approximately 6 thousand to 20 or 30 thousand years. After careful analysis, Ussher (1581–1656) placed the date of creation at 4004 B.C.; others suggest that "the Bible will not support a date for the creation of man earlier than about 10,000 B.C."[12] There seems to be some evidence for primitive cultures before 10,000 B.C.;[13] therefore, the flood should probably be dated earlier than 12,000 B.C. The recent creation theory of 10 to 20 thousand years seems

[10]Gilluly, *et al., Principles of Geology*, p. 116.
[11]A scholarly harmonization is attempted by geologist Davis A. Young, *Creation and the Flood*.
[12]Morris, *The Genesis Record*, p. 45.
[13]Davis, *Paradise to Prison*, p. 31.

more tenable and more in keeping with the grammatical-historical methods of interpretation than does the early dating of millions of years.

Another consideration is the gap theory. If, as has been suggested by many, Gen. 1:2ff. is a recreation, the date of the original creation could be early or late. The period between the creation and recreation is unknown. Some postulate long eons; others a short period of time. If creation (or recreation) is recent, and the literal interpretation of Scripture favors this, the interpretation of long geological ages and the Standard Geological Column must be challenged. What is the answer to the seemingly astronomical expanse of time necessary for the earth's formation? As was suggested earlier, answers can be found in mature creationism, flood geology, and/or omissions in the Genesis genealogies.

The fact that Adam was created full-grown seems obvious from Gen. 2. Therefore, in at least the creation of Adam, we have the appearance of age. Is it not also conceivable that the whole creation of God had the appearance of age, perhaps even including the fossils? Further, the Bible teaches a universal flood, and such a cataclysmic event would have far-reaching effects upon the topography of the land. Also, a study of the various biblical genealogies indicates that they are incomplete and contain omissions. Acknowledging these three items allows one to postulate a creation date earlier than 4,000 B.C., while at the same time not demand the millions of years. The doctrine of creation is a doctrine of faith (Heb. 11:3). Therefore, the biblical record must be accepted as the final authority.

B. Other Biblical Proofs of Creation

There are many other Scriptures that teach the doctrine of creation. A few of them speak of the original creation of heaven and earth (Isa. 40:26; 45:18). A goodly number of them speak of God's creation of all men (Ps. 102:18; 139:13–16; Isa. 43:1, 7; 54:16; Ezek. 21:30). Many represent God as the creator of heaven and earth and of all things in them (Isa. 45:12; Acts 17:24; Rom. 11:36; Eph. 3:9; Rev. 4:11). As in Gen. 1, God is also represented as creating by means of his Spirit (Ps. 104:30), his Son (John 1:3; Col. 1:16), and his Word (Ps. 148:5).

Many philosophies deny the doctrine of creation and postulate other origins for the universe. Atheism, which denies the existence of God, must either make matter eternal or find some other natural cause. Dualism argues for either two eternal principles, one good and one evil, or two eternal beings, God and Satan or God and matter. Pantheism makes creation a part of God. Agnosticism says no one can know about God or his creation. Christianity affirms that creation came through the sovereign will and working of an infinite God, who, though immanent in his creation, also transcends his creation.

III. THE END OF GOD IN CREATION

The same motive that caused God to formulate his purposes and decrees also caused him to carry them out. That is, he created all things for his own glory. First and primarily, he created in order to display his glory. The Scriptures declare, "O Lord, our Lord, how majestic is Thy name in all the earth, who hast displayed Thy splendor above the heavens" (Ps. 8:1); "The heavens are telling of the glory of God" (Ps. 19:1); and "Then the glory of the Lord will be revealed, and all flesh will see it together" (Isa. 40:5; cf. Ezek. 1:28; Luke 2:9; Acts 7:2; 2 Cor. 4:6).

He created, secondly, in order to receive glory. The Bible commands, "Ascribe to the Lord the glory due His name" (1 Chron. 16:29); "Ascribe to the Lord, O sons of the mighty, ascribe to the Lord glory and strength. Ascribe to the Lord the glory due to His name; worship the Lord in holy array" (Ps. 29:1f.); and "Give glory to the Lord your God" (Jer. 13:16). The responsibility of the church is to glorify God (Rom. 15:6, 9; 1 Cor. 6:20; 2 Cor. 1:20; 1 Pet. 4:16).

The universe is God's handiwork, and it is intended to display his glory. It is, therefore, proper to study it in order to behold his glory. And also, it is proper to do what we can to enhance and declare his glory. Answers to our prayers should naturally lead us to give God the glory; so also should an intelligent study of the promises and provisions of God for his people. Indeed, as Paul admonishes us, "Whether, then, you eat or drink or whatever you do, do all to the glory of God" (1 Cor. 10:31).

CHAPTER XII

The Works of God: His Sovereign Rule

Having shown that all things have their origin in the decrees or purposes of God, and that God has created the whole material and immaterial universe, we come next to consider the question of the government of the universe.

God, as creator of all things visible and invisible, and the owner of all, has an absolute right to rule over all (Matt. 20:15; Rom. 9:20f.), and he exercises this authority in the universe (Eph. 1:11). Hodge writes:

> If God be a Spirit, and therefore a person, infinite, eternal, and immutable in his being and perfections, the Creator and Preserver of the universe, He is of right its absolute sovereign. . . . This sovereignty of God is the ground of peace and confidence to all his people. They rejoice that the Lord God omnipotent reigneth; that neither necessity, nor chance, nor the folly of man, nor the malice of Satan controls the sequence of events and all their issues.[1]

The Scriptures abundantly teach that God is sovereign in the universe: "Indeed everything that is in the heavens and the earth; Thine is the dominion, O Lord" (1 Chron. 29:11); "But our God is in the heavens; He does whatever He pleases" (Ps. 115:3); "Woe to the one who quarrels with his Maker—an earthenware vessel among the vessels of earth! Will the clay say to the potter, 'What are you doing?' Or the things you are making say, 'He has no hands'?" (Isa. 45:9); "Behold, all souls are Mine; the soul of the father as well as the soul of the son is Mine. The soul who sins will die" (Ezek. 18:4); "All the inhabitants of the earth are accounted as nothing, but He does according to His will in the host of heaven and among the inhabitants of earth; and no one can ward off His hand or say to Him, 'What hast Thou done?'" (Dan. 4:35); and "Is it not lawful for me to do what I wish with what is my own?" (Matt. 20:15; cf. Rom. 9:14–21; 11:36; Eph. 1:11; 1 Tim. 6:15f.; Rev. 4:11). God's sovereignty involves preservation and providence.

[1]Hodge, *Systematic Theology*, I, pp. 440–441.

I. THE DOCTRINE OF PRESERVATION

A. THE DEFINITION OF PRESERVATION

By preservation we mean that God sovereignly, by a continuous agency, maintains in existence all the things which he has made, together with all their properties and powers. This definition implies that preservation is to be distinguished from the act of creation, for only that which is already in existence can be preserved; that the objective creation is not self-existent and self-sustaining; and that preservation is not merely a refraining from destroying that which has been created, but a continuous agency of God by means of which he maintains in existence that which he has created.

B. THE PROOF OF THE DOCTRINE OF PRESERVATION

The doctrine of preservation can be demonstrated from reason and from Scripture. Matter does not have the cause of its being in itself. It is everywhere contingent, dependent, and changing; it is not self-existent or self-sustaining. No force is self-existent or self-renewing, for everywhere force implies the existence of a will that exerts and sustains it. And again, God would not be absolutely sovereign if anything occurred or existed in the universe apart from his will and power.

The Scriptures teach that although God rested after he had completed the work of creation and had established an order of natural forces, he yet continues his activity in upholding the universe and its powers. Christ is the mediating agent in preservation, as he was the mediating agent in creation. Some Scriptures speak of his preserving activity in a comprehensive way. For example, "Thou alone art the Lord. Thou hast made the heavens, the heaven of heavens with all their host, the earth and all that is on it, the seas and all that is in them. Thou dost give life to all of them" (Neh. 9:6); "He is before all things, and in Him all things hold together" (Col. 1:17); "And He is the radiance of His glory and the exact representation of His nature, and upholds all things by the word of His power" (Heb. 1:3).

Other Scriptures mention definite things that he preserves. He preserves animate and inanimate creation: "O Lord, Thou preservest man and beast" (Ps. 36:6); "Thou dost hide Thy face, they are dismayed; Thou dost take away their spirit, they expire, and return to their dust" (Ps. 104:29); "Who keeps us in life, and does not allow our feet to slip" (Ps. 66:9); and "For in Him we live and move and exist" (Acts 17:28). God also preserves his saints: "Guarding the paths of justice, and He preserves the way of His godly ones" (Prov. 2:8); "For the Lord loves justice, and does not forsake His godly ones; they are preserved forever; but the descendants of the wicked will be cut off"

(Ps. 37:28); "And I give eternal life to them, and they shall never perish; and no one shall snatch them out of My hand" (John 10:28).

C. The Method of Preservation

Although all theists would agree that God in some way or other preserves all that he has created, they would not all agree as to the way in which he does this. Indeed, two of the theories that have been put forward virtually deny the doctrine of preservation.

1. The deistic theory. Deism explains preservation in terms of natural law. It holds that God created the universe and endowed it with powers sufficient to keep itself in existence. The universe is, thus, a great self-sustaining mechanism, and God is a mere spectator of the world and of its operations, exerting no direct efficiency in sustaining it. But this is a false assumption, for where is there a machine that can sustain itself? Furthermore, there is evidence to show that God has not withdrawn from the universe. The Christian believes that we have a special revelation of God in the Bible, that God has become incarnate in Jesus Christ by a miraculous birth, that regeneration is a supernatural work of God in the heart of man, that God answers prayer, and that he sometimes intervenes miraculously in the affairs of the world. From the Christian standpoint, therefore, this theory is very unsatisfactory.

2. The continuous creation theory. This theory confounds creation and preservation. The deistic view holds that all is upheld by natural law; this view holds that from moment to moment God creates the universe with all that is in it. It is based on the conception that all force is divine will in direct exercise. It leaves no room for human will and the indirect exercise of the divine will in the form of natural law. This theory necessarily leads to pantheism. The errors of this theory are: (1) that it makes the regular activity in nature the repetition of creation, rather than the indirect exercise of God's power; (2) that it makes God the author of sin by making all will his will; (3) that it removes man from being a real, self-determining moral agent; and (4) that it does away with moral accountability.

3. The theory of concurrence. This theory is the biblical approach. It holds that God concurs in all the operations of both matter and mind. Though God's will is not the only force in the universe, without his concurrence no force or person can continue to exist or to act (Acts 17:28; 1 Cor. 12:6). His power interpenetrates that of man without destroying or absorbing it. Men retain their natural powers and exercise them. But it is evident that, although God preserves mind and body in their working, he concurs with the evil acts of his creatures only as they are natural acts, and not as they are evil. In other words, in evil actions God gives only the natural power; the evil direction of these powers is caused by man only. God's declared hatred of sin proves that he is not the cause of man's evil acts: "Oh, do not do this abominable thing which I hate" (Jer. 44:4); and "Let no one say when he is tempted, 'I am being tempted by God'; for God cannot be tempted by evil, and He Himself does not tempt any one. But each one is tempted when he is carried away and enticed by his own lust" (James 1:13f.; cf. Hab. 1:13).

II. THE DOCTRINE OF PROVIDENCE

The Christian view affirms that God has not merely created the universe, together with all its properties and powers, and that he is preserving all that he has created, but that as a holy, benevolent, wise, and omnipotent being, he also exercises sovereign control over it. This sovereign control is called providence.

A. The Definition of Providence

Etymologically, the word "providence" means foreseeing. From this basic idea has developed the meaning of providing for the future. But in theology the word has received a more specialized meaning. In this field, "providence" means that continuous activity of God whereby he makes all the events of the physical, mental, and moral realms work out his purpose, and this purpose is nothing short of the original design of God in creation. To be sure, evil has entered the universe, but it is not allowed to thwart God's original, benevolent, wise, and holy purpose.

B. The Proofs of the Doctrine

1. The nature of God and the universe.   Since God is not only a personal being, infinite in wisdom, goodness, and power, but is also the creator and consequent owner of the universe, he may be expected to govern his own possession. As a personal and wise God, he may be expected to act rationally; as a good God, he may be expected to have the interests of his creatures at heart; and as the omnipotent God, he may be relied upon as having the ability to accomplish all his purposes. The Christian bases his confidence in the ultimate triumph of the right partly on his conception of the nature of God.

As a practical proof of the belief that God exercises sovereign rule over his creation, we note that the universe everywhere exhibits evidence of intelligence and control, although this intelligence is not in matter itself. Means are adapted to ends, both in the visible and in the invisible world. We find that one kingdom is adapted to another and the solar system to our world as a whole. This evidence of intelligence and control is seen also in man's constitution. Our sense of dependence involves the idea, not only of our origination by him, but also of our continued existence. He holds our soul in life; when he takes away our breath, we die. The same thing may be argued from our sense of responsibility. It implies that God has a right to lay down the laws of moral conduct, that he knows all about our ways, and that he will reward the righteous and punish the unrighteous. In other words, the universe itself bears evidence of God's sovereign rule over it.

2. The teaching of Scripture.   The Scriptures say more about God's work in providence than about his work in creation. They show that God exercises sovereign rule over all the physical universe, over plant and animal creation, over the nations of the earth, and over all individuals.

   a. Over the physical universe. Scripture indicates that God controls all the physical universe. Sunshine (Matt. 5:45), wind (Ps. 147:18), lightning (Job 38:25, 35), rain (Job 38:26; Matt. 5:45), thunder (1 Sam. 7:10), waters (Ps. 147:18), hail (Ps. 148:8), ice (Job 37:10), snow (Job 37:6; 38:22), and frost (Ps. 147:16) are all subject to his bidding. The heavenly bodies, such as the sun (Matt. 5:45) and the stars (Job 38:31–33), obey his will. The mountains are removed (Job 9:5), the earth quakes (Job 9:6), and the ground yields her increase (Acts 14:17) at his mandate. He uses the beneficent elements as expressions of his goodness and love, the destructive as instruments of discipline and punishment. Men should, therefore, humble themselves in the times of physical visitation and pray to him who has all the elements in his power.

   b. Over the plant and animal creation. Every living creation is in the hand of God (Job 12:10). God provides for and controls all plants (Jonah 4:6; Matt. 6:28–30), fowl (Matt. 6:26; 10:29), beasts (Ps. 104:21, 27f.; 147:9), and fish (Jonah 1:17; Matt. 17:27).

   c. Over the nations of the earth. God "rules over the nations" (Ps. 22:28). He increases and destroys them (Job 12:23), observes and judges them (Ps. 66:7; 75:7), establishes and dethrones rulers (Dan. 2:37–39; 4:25), sets national boundaries (Acts 17:26), and uses nations and their rulers in the exercise of his will (Isa. 7:20; 10:5–15; 45:1–4). "There is no authority except from God, and those which exist are established by God" (Rom. 13:1).

   d. Over all areas of each man's existence. (1) Over the birth, career, and death of men. God is actively involved before one is yet born (Ps. 139:16; Jer. 1:5) and works out his purposes in one's life (1 Sam. 16:1; Gal. 1:15f.). This is the case whether one recognizes it or not (Isa. 45:5; Esth. 4:14). God provides for man's needs (Matt. 5:45; 6:25–32; Acts 14:17) and determines the time and circumstances of man's death (Deut. 32:49f.; John 21:19; 2 Tim. 4:6–8). (2) Over the successes and failures of men. The Lord promotes and demotes people (Ps. 75:7), puts down princes and exalts the lowly (Luke 1:52), makes rich and makes poor (1 Sam. 2:6–8). He is involved in the very thinking process of man (Prov. 21:1). (3) Over the most trivial of circumstances. He is concerned with the sparrow, and more so the hairs of our head (Matt. 10:29f.). He determines the way the lot falls (Prov. 16:33). He even gives and withholds sleep (Esth. 6:1). (4) Over the needs of his people. He cares for his own (1 Pet. 5:7), gives safety (Ps. 4:8), protects (Ps. 121:3), provides good (Ps. 5:12), sustains (Ps. 63:8), supplies needs (Phil. 4:19), and in general makes all things work out for good for those who love him (Rom. 8:28). "For from old they have not heard nor perceived by ear, neither has the eye seen a God besides Thee, Who acts in behalf of the one who waits for Him" (Isa. 64:4). (5) Over the destinies of the saved and the unsaved. He will bring the believer through this life to glory (Ps. 73:24), and, though he fall, the Lord will uphold him (Ps. 37:23f.), but judgment shall come from the Lord upon the unbeliever (Ps. 11:6). (6) Over the free acts of men. He worked in the hearts of the Egyptians to do his bidding (Exod. 12:36), and likewise in the hearts of David (1 Sam. 24:18), Artaxerxes (Ezra 7:27), the believer (Phil. 2:13), the king (Prov. 21:1), even all men (Jer. 10:23). "The plans of the heart belong to man, but the answer of the tongue is from the Lord" (Prov. 16:1).

How then do the sinful acts of men fit into the program of a sovereign God? Does God necessitate sin? Several incidents make it appear that way. God hardened Pharaoh's heart (Exod. 10:27); it was sin for David to number Israel, yet the Lord moved him to do it (2 Sam. 24:1; cf. 1 Chron. 21:1); God gave the sinner up to more sin (Rom. 1:24, 26, 28); he shut up all in disobedience (Rom. 11:32); and, during the tribulation, God will send a deluding influence so that the unbelievers will believe a lie (2 Thess. 2:11). If God is not the author of sin (Hab. 1:13; James 1:13; 1 John 1:5; 2:16), how can these incidents be explained? How is God related to man's sinful acts? This can be answered in four ways. (1) Often God restrains man from the sin which man intends to do. This is called "preventative providence." God said to Abimelech, "I also kept you from sinning against Me; therefore I did not let you touch her" (Gen. 20:6). David prayed, "Also keep back thy servant from presumptuous sins; let them not rule over me" (Ps. 19:13; cf. Matt. 6:13). God has promised not to allow the believer to be tempted above what he can bear (1 Cor. 10:13). (2) God, instead of actively restraining man from doing evil, will sometimes permit sin to take its course. This is called "permissive providence." In Hosea 4:17, God said, "Ephraim is joined to idols; let him alone." God "permitted all the nations to go their own ways" (Acts 14:16; cf. 2 Chron. 32:31; Ps. 81:12; Rom. 1:24, 26, 28). (3) Further, God uses directive providence. He allows evil, but directs the way it goes. Jesus said to Judas, "What you do, do quickly" (John 13:27). Those involved in the crucifixion of Christ did what God predestined to occur (Acts 2:23; 4:27f.). Man's intent was evil, but God used this evil intent to accomplish his will. God uses the wrath of man to praise him (Ps. 76:10; cf. Isa. 10:5–15). (4) Finally, God, through restrictive providence, determines the limits to which evil and its effects may go. He said to Satan, "Behold, all that he has is in your power, only do not put forth your hand on him" (Job 1:12; cf. 2:6; 1 Cor. 10:13; 2 Thess. 2:7; Rev. 20:2f.).

From these considerations it is clear that all the evil acts of the creature are under the complete control of God. They can occur only by his permission, and only insofar as he permits them. Though they are evil in themselves, he overrules them for good. Thus the wicked conduct of Joseph's brethren, the obstinacy of Pharaoh, the lust for conquest of the heathen nations that invaded the Holy Land and finally carried the people into captivity, the rejection and crucifixion of Christ, the persecution of the church, and the wars and revolutions among the nations have all been overruled for God's purpose and glory. The fact that God has turned evil into good ought to induce his children to trust him to do the same with the evil of the present generation.

C. The Ends Towards Which Providence is Directed

God governs the world with a view to the happiness of the creature. Satan implied in his temptation of Eve that God was trying to withhold something good from her and Adam (Gen. 3:4f.), and he has been endeavoring all along to make men believe that God is doing this. In contrast Paul says, "He did not leave Himself without witness, in that He did good and gave you rains from heaven and fruitful seasons, satisfying your hearts with food and gladness" (Acts 14:17). Jesus says, God "causes His sun to rise on the evil and the good, and sends rain on the righteous and the unrighteous" (Matt. 5:45). His goodness has the important purpose of leading people to repentance (Rom. 2:4). God seeks the welfare of his children in particular, for the Psalmist says, "No good thing does He withhold from those who walk uprightly" (Ps. 84:11). And Paul says, "And we know that God causes all things to work together for good to those who love God, to those who are called according to His purpose" (Rom. 8:28).

God also governs the world with a view to the mental and moral development of the race. There is such a thing as an education of the race, but it is not an education that takes the place of salvation. The entire Levitical system was educational, preparing the way for the introduction of the true Lamb of God that takes away the sin of the world (Gal. 3:24). This mental and moral development is seen in various ways during the Christian centuries. It is seen in the elevation of woman, the erection of hospitals, the introduction of educational systems, the abolition of slavery, the granting of religious liberty, the development of technology in such areas as communication and transportation, etc. These are all humanitarian developments, but even so, we must ultimately trace them back to God's providential government of the world. Though in themselves they have but a temporal value, they may be used as aids in the spread of the gospel.

God governs the world with a view to the salvation and preparation of a people for his own possession. He chose Israel that they might be such a possession (Exod. 19:5f.), and he has called the church for the same purpose (Titus 2:14; 1 Pet. 2:9). The incarnation of God in Christ, the atoning death of Christ, the gift and coming of the Holy Spirit, the production and preservation of the Scriptures, and the institution of the church and its ministry are all intended to help save and prepare this people for himself. In a very real sense, God's providence is directed toward the production and preservation of saints (Eph. 3:9f.; 5:25–27). It is clear also that God bestows many blessings upon the unsaved people because of the presence of his people among them (Gen. 18:22–33; 2 Kings 3:13f.; Matt. 5:13–16).

The primary end of God's government is his own glory. He rules for the purpose of manifesting his perfections: his holiness and righteousness, his power, his wisdom, his love, his truth. The providence of God is directed to the exhibition of these qualities of his being. His holiness and righteousness are manifested in his hatred of and opposition to sin; his power is manifested in his work of creation, preservation, providence, and redemption; his wisdom, in his establishing ends and means to these ends; his love, in his provision for his creatures, especially in his provision of salvation through the gift of his Son; and his truth, in the establishing of the laws of nature and of the mind, and in his faithfulness to his promises. Thus the primary object of his sovereign rule is the manifestation of his own glory. As he himself says, "For My own sake, for My own sake, I will act; for how can My name be profaned? And my glory I will not give to another" (Isa. 48:11).

D. The Means Employed in the Exercise of Divine Providence

In outward affairs, God employs the laws of nature. By means of these laws, he has established the seasons and assured us of food for our subsistence (Gen. 8:22). By means of these, he has also given man the instinct of self-preservation and the sense of moral responsibility (Rom. 1:26; 2:15). He sometimes supplements these laws by miracles. Thus, he delivered and prepared Israel by a miracle (Exod. 14:21–31), he provided relief in time of war (2 Kings 3:16f.), he delivered his servant Elisha (2 Kings 6:18), and he freed Peter for further ministry (Acts 12:1–19). He sometimes brings things to pass by uttering his powerful word. When he speaks, it is done; when he commands, it stands fast (Ps. 33:9); when he calls for destructive insects, they come (Ps. 105:31, 34); when he speaks the word of healing, sickness vanishes (Matt. 8:8, 13); and when the lawless one will come and for a time rule the world, Christ will appear and destroy him with his powerful word (2 Thess. 2:8; cf. Rev. 19:20f.).

In the inward affairs of his government, he uses a variety of means. (1) He uses his Word. Men are frequently referred to the Scriptures for guidance and direction (Josh. 1:7f.; Isa. 8:20; Col. 3:16). Kings, as well as subjects, are to be subject to the Word of God (Deut. 17:18–20). (2) God appeals to man's reason in the solution of their problems (Acts 6:2). God's ways cannot be fathomed by reason, but they are not contrary to sound reason. (3) God uses persuasion. He has instituted the ministry to instruct and persuade people of the truth (Jer. 7:13; 44:4; Zech. 7:7; Acts 17:30). Through his servants, God entreats men to be reconciled to himself (2 Cor. 5:20). (4) God uses inner checks and restraints. Paul was very sensitive to such inner indications of God's will (Acts 16:6f.). (5) God uses outward circumstances. He leads by closed doors as well as by open doors (1 Cor. 16:9; Gal. 4:20). It is, of course, always possible that inauspicious circumstances may be a test of our faith rather than a providential hindrance to a certain action. Only prayer and careful study can determine which is the case in any given instance. (6) God inclines the hearts of men in one direction rather than in another (1 Kings 8:58; Ps. 119:36; Prov. 21:1; 2 Cor. 8:16). He even inclines the hearts of evil men to do his will (2 Kings 19:28; Isa. 45:1–6; Rev. 17:17). (7) God sometimes guides men by dreams and visions. Joseph (Matt. 2:13, 19, 22) and Paul (Acts 16:9f.; 22:17f.) were thus guided.

In some of his providential dealings, God employs special agents. These are the angels and the Holy Spirit. It appears as if the angels are used in the outward administration of his government (2 Kings 19:35; Dan. 6:22; 10:5–21; 12:1; Matt. 28:2; Acts 8:26; 12:7–10), and the Holy Spirit in the inward and spiritual part of his rule (Luke 4:1; John 16:7–15; Acts 8:29; 10:19f.; 16:6f.; Rom. 8:14, 26). The former, of course, though great in power, are not omnipotent; the latter, being himself God, is both omniscient and omnipotent.

E. The Theories Opposed to the Doctrine of Providence

Although the doctrine under consideration is one of the most precious to the child of God, it is denied by those who do not believe in the true God. Three theories opposed to it may be briefly noted.

1. Naturalism.   Naturalism holds that nature is the whole of reality. Everything that occurs in the universe is due to the operation of the laws of nature. Man's happiness and chances of success are dependent upon his knowledge of and cooperation with these laws. While the Scriptures recognize the existence of the laws of nature, they do not teach that they operate independently. They represent them as neither self-directing nor self-sustaining. God concurs in all the operations of these laws, both of matter and of mind, and sometimes he acts entirely independent of them. In this way the miracles of the incarnation and resurrection of Christ can be explained.

2. *Fatalism.* Fatalism is to be distinguished from determinism. The former holds that all events are determined by fate, instead of by natural causes, and that nothing man can will or do affects the course of events; determinism holds that events take place of necessity, but that they are made necessary by events immediately preceding, to which they stand in a relation of cause and effect. The fatalist may speak of the decreeing power as God, but it is certainly not the God of the Scriptures. Fatalism recognizes the inadequacy of naturalism to explain all that happens and ascribes the events which take place in spite of natural law to the direct operation of fate. The chief objection to fatalism is that it makes the originating cause arbitrary and non-moral, and usually impersonal.

3. *Pantheism.* Since all pantheistic theories are necessitarian in nature, they have no real doctrine of providence. Since they are obliged to make the governing cause also the author of sin, they destroy all possibility of true morality. Man, being a part of this pantheistic god, cannot help sinning. Further, these theories cannot explain miracles. They may speak of "mutations" and "emergent evolution," but these ideas cannot explain the miracles of the incarnation and the resurrection of Christ, nor, indeed, any of the other biblical miracles. Also, they deny the freedom of man. Being part of this world system, man, too, acts of necessity. Yet man feels that in a very real sense he can initiate action and that he is responsible for his conduct. He will not sacrifice his freedom to a logical process or a great mechanism of which he is supposed to be a part.

F. The Relation of Providence to Some Special Problems

It is difficult to refrain from adopting one or the other of two extremes: that God is the sole actor in the universe or that man is the sole actor. The truth lies somewhere between these two extremes. This fact has to be kept in mind in connection with our conception of the freedom of man and of prayer. Note these relations briefly:

1. *The relation of providence to freedom.* As has been said, God sometimes allows man to do as he pleases; that is, he puts no restraints in the way of man's carrying out his wicked desires. Also, God sometimes keeps a man from doing what, in his freedom, he would otherwise do. He uses circum-

stance, the influence of friends, and inner restraints to accomplish this purpose. Sometimes he controls sin by allowing it to go so far and no further. Finally, God always overrules what man does in order to accomplish his own ends. He makes even the wrath of man to praise him.

2. The relation of providence to prayer.   Some hold that prayer can have no real effect upon God, since he has already decreed just what he will do in every instance. But that is an extreme position. "You do not have because you do not ask" (James 4:2) must not be ignored. God does some things only in answer to prayer; he does some other things without anyone's praying; and he does some things contrary to the prayers made. In his omniscience he has taken all these things into account, and in his providence he sovereignly works them out in accordance with his own purpose and plan. If we do not pray for the things that we might get by prayer, we do not get them. If he wants some things done for which no one prays, he will do them without anyone's praying. If we pray for things contrary to his will, he refuses to grant them. Thus, there is a perfect harmony between his purpose and providence, and man's freedom.

PART IV

ANGELOLOGY

The doctrine of angels follows logically the doctrine of God, for the angels are primarily ministers of God's providence. Although the Scriptures have much to say about angels, there is today a very general disregard, often amounting to a rejection of the doctrine. Various things have contributed to this attitude. There is first the Gnostic worship of angels (Col. 2:18); then there are the often foolish speculations of the Scholasticism of the Middle Ages; then there is the exaggerated belief in witchcraft in more recent times; and then, finally, the rise in demon and Satan worship in our own day. Yet there are many reasons for believing in angels.

(1) The existence and ministry of angels are abundantly taught in the Scriptures. Jesus has very much to say about angels, and we cannot dismiss his teaching with a haughty pretense to superior knowledge. (2) The evidence of demon possession and oppression and of demon worship argues for the existence of angels. Paul regarded idolatry as demon worship (1 Cor. 10:20f.). In the latter days this demon and idol worship is to increase greatly (Rev. 9:20f.). (3) The increase in the practice of spiritualism suggests a need to understand this doctrine. Scripture condemns necromancy, or the consulting of familiar spirits (Deut. 18:10–12; Isa. 8:19f.). This phenomenon is to increase in the latter days (1 Tim. 4:1). And (4) the work of Satan and the evil spirits in hindering the progress of grace in our own hearts and the work of God in the world must be understood so we may know what to expect for the future in this warfare and be assured that Satan will soon be defeated (Gen. 3:15; Rom. 16:20; Rev. 12:7–9; 20:1–10).

The subject of angelology will be divided into two parts: (1) the origin, nature, fall, and classification of the angels, and (2) the work and destiny of the angels.

CHAPTER XIII

The Origin, Nature, Fall, and Classification of the Angels

I. THE ORIGIN OF ANGELS

Scripture everywhere assumes the existence of angels, both good and evil. Psalm 148:2-5 includes angels with the sun, moon, and stars as a part of God's creation. John 1:3 indicates that Jesus created all things. Among "all things" are all things "in the heavens and on earth, visible and invisible, whether thrones or dominions or rulers or authorities" (Col. 1:16; cf. Eph. 6:12). That God alone has immortality (1 Tim. 6:16) implies that angels were created by God and owe their continued existence to God's continual support. The time of their creation is nowhere definitely indicated, but it is most probable that it occurred before the creation of the heavens and the earth (Gen. 1:1), for according to Job 38:4-7, "the sons of God shouted for joy" when God laid the foundations of the earth. Clearly, they were in existence by Gen. 3:1 when Satan, an angelic being, made his appearance. While the Scriptures give no definite figures, we are told that the number of angels is very great (Dan. 7:10; Matt. 26:53; Heb. 12:22; Rev. 5:11).

II. THE NATURE OF ANGELS

A. They are Not Glorified Human Beings

Man and angels are distinguished. Matt. 22:30 says that believers shall be like the angels, but it does not say that they shall be angels. The "myriads of angels" are distinguished from the "spirits of righteous men made perfect" (Heb. 12:22f.). Man was made lower than the angels, and shall be made higher (Ps. 8:5 [LXX]; Heb. 2:7). Believers will in the future actually judge angels (1 Cor. 6:3).

B. They are Incorporeal

They are called "winds" or "spirits" (Heb. 1:7; cf. Ps. 104:4). Heb. 1:14 reads, "Are they not all ministering spirits, sent out to render service for the sake of those who will inherit salvation?" Their incorporeality also seems to

133

be clear from Eph. 6:12, where Paul says that "our struggle is not against flesh and blood, but against the rulers, against the powers, against the world forces of this darkness, against the spiritual forces of wickedness in the heavenly places."

Angels have often revealed themselves in bodily form (Gen. 18, 19; Luke 1:26; John 20:12; Heb. 13:2), but this does not suggest that they have material bodies as part of their necessary existence.

C. They are a Company, Not a Race

Angels are spoken of as hosts, but not as a race (Ps. 148:2). They neither marry nor are they given in marriage, nor do they die (Luke 20:34–36). They are called "sons of God" in the Old Testament (Job 1:6; 2:1; 38:7; cf. Gen. 6:2, 4), but never do we read of the sons of angels. The word "angel" in Scripture occurs in the masculine gender. Though gender does not necessarily signify a given sex, the angels at the tomb of the Lord were identified as men (Luke 24:4). A young man was sitting in the tomb (Mark 16:5). Because the angels are a company and not a race, they sinned individually, and not in some federal head of the race. It may be that because of this, God made no provision of salvation for the fallen angels. Scripture does say, "For assuredly He does not give help to angels, but He gives help to the seed of Abraham" (Heb. 2:16).

D. They are Greater than Man in Knowledge, though Not Omniscient

The wisdom of an angel is considered great wisdom (2 Sam. 14:20). Jesus said, "But of that day and hour no one knows, not even the angels of heaven" (Matt. 24:36). Angels are called upon as witnesses by Paul: "I solemnly charge you in the presence of God and of Christ Jesus and of His chosen angels" (1 Tim. 5:21). Even the fallen angels have wisdom beyond the natural. One said to Christ, "I know who You are—the Holy One of God!" (Luke 4:34). Angels "seek to learn through investigation something of the marvels of salvation (1 Pe. 1:11–12)."[1]

E. They are Stronger than Man, though Not Omnipotent

They are said to be greater in might and power than man (2 Pet. 2:11; cf. "mighty in strength," Ps. 103:20). Paul calls them "mighty angels" (2 Thess. 1:7). Illustrations of the power of angels are found in the freeing of the apostles from prison (Acts 5:19; 12:7) and the rolling away of the stone from the tomb (Matt. 28:2). They are limited in strength as seen in the warfare

[1]Dickason, *Angels Elect and Evil*, p. 27.

between the good and the evil angels (Rev. 12:7). The angel who came to Daniel needed assistance from Michael in his struggle with the prince of Persia (Dan. 10:13). Neither Michael the archangel (Jude 9) nor Satan (Job 1:12; 2:6) has unlimited power.

F. They are More Noble than Man, though Not Omnipresent

They cannot be in more than one place at once. They roam and walk about on the earth (Job 1:7; Zech. 1:11; 1 Pet. 5:8), moving from one place to another (Dan. 9:21–23). This involves time and sometimes delays (Dan. 10:10–14). Even the concept of flying suggests that angels are "ministering spirits, sent out to render service for the sake of those who will inherit salvation" (Heb. 1:14). Fallen angels are Satan's servants (2 Cor. 11:15).

III. THE FALL OF ANGELS

A. The Fact of Their Fall

The problem of the origin of evil must be considered at this point, for evil originated in heaven and not on earth. Except for some Hindu philosophers, who speak of it as "maya" or "illusion," and the Christian Scientists, who call it "error of mortal mind," all men recognize the stern and solemn fact of evil in the universe. Indeed, its presence in the world is one of the most perplexing problems in philosophy and theology. This is due to the difficulty of harmonizing the idea of evil with the conception of a benevolent, holy, and infinite God. Some hold that the two ideas are absolutely incongruous and adopt the position of dualism, holding that the evil as well as the good is eternal. Therefore, there never was a perfect universe and, consequently, there never was a "fall." This is the view of Persian Zoroastrianism, Gnosticism, and Manicheanism. Some modern theologians hold much the same view and teach that God is a finite God and has carried on an eternal conflict with evil. All these theories were invented to absolve God of all responsibility for evil, but they do so by making him less than God.

But there is every reason to believe that the angels were created perfect. In the creation account (Gen. 1), we are told seven times over that all that God made was good. In Gen. 1:31 we read, "And God saw all that He had made, and behold, it was very good." Surely that includes the perfection of the angels in holiness when originally created. If Ezek. 28:15 refers to Satan, as many suggest, then Satan is definitely said to have been created perfect. But various Scriptures represent some of the angels as evil (Ps. 78:49; Matt. 25:41; Rev. 9:11; 12:7–9). This is because they sinned, having left their own principality and proper abode (2 Pet. 2:4; Jude 6). Satan no doubt was the leader in the apostasy. Ezek. 28:15–17 seems to describe his fall. Another possible allusion to his fall is found in Isa. 14:12–15. There can be no question but that there was a definite fall for some of the angels.

B. The Time of Their Fall

Scripture is silent on this point, but it is clear that the fall of the angels occurred before the fall of man, since Satan entered the garden in the form of a serpent and induced Eve to sin (Gen. 3:1ff.). But we cannot say definitely just how long before the incident in Eden the angels fell. Those who consider the creation days long epochs will naturally think of this fall as taking place sometime before or during this long period; those who hold that Gen. 1:2 represents the outcome of some great catastrophe will ordinarily place the fall of the angels sometime before 1:1 or between vss. 1 and 2. That it occurred before Gen. 3:1 is certain.

C. The Cause of Their Fall

This is one of the deep mysteries of theology. The angels were created perfect; every affection of their hearts was directed toward God; their wills were inclined toward God. The question is, how could such a being fall? How could the first unholy affection arise in such a heart and how could the will get its first impulse to turn away from God? Various solutions to the problem have been proposed. A few can be noted.

Some say that everything that is, is due to God; therefore, he must be the author of sin. To this we reply that if God is the author of evil and condemns the creature for committing sin, we have no moral universe. Others say that evil is due to the nature of the world. The existence of the world is the greatest of all evils and the source of all other evils. Nature itself is evil. But the Scriptures repeatedly declare that all that God made is good and they positively reject the idea that nature is inherently evil (1 Tim. 4:4). And finally, some suggest that evil is due to the nature of the creature. They hold that sin is a necessary stage in the development of the spirit. But the Scriptures speak of no such evolutionary development and look upon the universe and the creatures as originally perfect.

It is helpful to remember that the creature originally had what the Latin theologians called the ability *posse peccare et posse non peccare*, that is, to sin and not to sin. He was put into the position where he could do either without being constrained to do the one or the other. In other words, his will was autonomous.

We must, therefore, conclude that the fall of the angels was due to their deliberate, self-determined revolt against God. It was their choice of self and its interests in preference to the choice of God and his interests. If we ask what particular motive may have been behind this revolt, we seem to get several replies from Scripture. Great prosperity and beauty seem to be possible hints in this respect. The Tyrian king seems to symbolize Satan in Ezek. 28:11–19, and he is said to have fallen because of these things (cf. 1 Tim. 3:6). Undue ambition and the desire to surpass God seem to be another hint. The king of Babylon is charged with this ambition, and he, too, may be symbolic of Satan (Isa. 14:13f.). In any case, it was selfishness, discontentment with what he had, and the craving to get what rightfully belonged to someone else. No doubt the cause of the fall of Satan was also the cause of the fall of the other evil angels. The dragon drew one third of the stars by his tail (Rev. 12:4). This may have reference to one third of the angels falling with Satan.

D. The Result of Their Fall

Several results of their fall are noted in Scripture. (1) All of them lost their original holiness and became corrupt in nature and conduct (Matt. 10:1; Eph. 6:11f.; Rev. 12:9). (2) Some of them were cast down to hell (*Tartarus*) and are there held in chains until the day of judgment (2 Pet. 2:4; Jude 6). (3) Some of them are left free and engage in definite opposition to the work of good angels (Dan. 10:12f., 20f.; Jude 9; Rev. 12:7–9). (4) There may also have been an effect upon the original creation. We read that the ground was cursed because of Adam's sin (Gen. 3:17–19) and that creation is groaning because of the fall (Rom. 8:19–22). It is suggested by some that the sin of the angels had something to do with the ruination of the original creation in Gen. 1:2. (5) They will in a future day be cast to the earth (Rev. 12:8f.), and following their judgment (1 Cor. 6:3), they will be cast into the lake of fire (Matt. 25:41; 2 Pet. 2:4; Jude 6). Satan will be assigned to the abyss for a thousand years before he is cast into the lake of fire (Rev. 20:1–3, 10).

IV. THE CLASSIFICATION OF ANGELS

The angels fall into two large classes: the good angels and the evil angels. There are various subdivisions in both of these classes.

A. The Good Angels

Of these there are several kinds.

1. *The angels.*   The word *angel*, both in Hebrew and Greek, means "messenger." The disciples that John sent to Jesus are called *aggeloi* or messengers (Luke 7:24). Only the context can make clear whether the word

denotes human or superhuman messengers. Of the angels there are myriads. Daniel says, "Thousands upon thousands were attending Him, and myriads upon myriads were standing before Him" (7:10; cf. Rev. 5:11). The Psalmist says, "The chariots of God are myriads, thousands upon thousands; the Lord is among them as at Sinai, in holiness" (Ps. 68:17). Our Lord told Peter that his Father would send him more than twelve legions of angels if he asked him (Matt. 26:53). And in Hebrews we read of "myriads of angels" (12:22). They may appear individually (Acts 5:19), in couples (Acts 1:10), or in groups (Luke 2:13).

2. The cherubim.   The cherubim are mentioned in Gen. 3:24; 2 Kings 19:15; Ezek. 10:1–22; 28:14–16. The etymology of the word is not known for certain, though it has been suggested that it means "to cover" or "to guard." A cherub guarded the entrance to the garden (Gen. 3:24). Two cherubim were placed on top of the ark in the tabernacle and temple (Exod. 25:19; 1 Kings 6:23–28). Cherubim were also wrought into the texture of the inner curtains and veil of the tabernacle (Exod. 26:1, 31) and carved on the doors of the temple (1 Kings 6:32, 35). From the fact that they guard the entrance to paradise, that they are represented as somehow supporting the throne of God (Ps. 18:10; 80:1; 99:1), and that figures of them were wrought into the curtains and veil of the tabernacle and the doors of the temple, we gather that they are chiefly the guardians of the throne of God. Satan may have been one of the cherubim before he fell (Ezek. 28:14–16).

3. The seraphim.   The seraphim are mentioned by name only in Isa. 6:2, 6. They seem to be distinct from the cherubim, for God is said to be seated above the cherubim (1 Sam. 4:4; Ps. 80:1; 99:1), but the seraphim stand above him (Isa. 6:2). Their duties are also different from those of the cherubim. They lead heaven in the worship of God Almighty and purify God's servants for acceptable worship and service. That is, they appear to be concerned with worship and holiness, rather than justice and might. In deep humility and profound reverence, they carry on their ministry. The cherubim, on the contrary, are the guardians of the throne of God and God's ambassadors extraordinary. Thus each has its distinct position and ministry.

4. The living creatures.   Some identify the living creatures of Rev. 4:6–9 with the seraphim,[2] and others with the cherubim.[3] There are striking differences between them, so it is probably best to identify them as a different type of angel than either the seraphim or the cherubim. They worship God, direct the judgments of God (Rev. 6:1ff.; 15:7), and witness the worship of

---

[2]Dickason, *Angels Elect and Evil*, p. 67.
[3]Hoyt, *An Exposition of the Book of Revelation*, p. 35.

the one hundred and forty-four thousand (Rev. 14:3). They are active about the throne of God as are the seraphim and the cherubim.

5. *The archangels.* The term "archangel" occurs but twice in Scripture (1 Thess. 4:16; Jude 9), but there are other references to at least one archangel, Michael. He is the only angel called an archangel. He is represented as having his own angels (Rev. 12:7) and is said to be the prince of the nation of Israel (Dan. 10:13, 21; 12:1). The apocryphal book of Enoch (20:1–7) enumerates six angels of power: Uriel, Raphael, Raguel, Michael, Zariel, and Gabriel. The variant reading in the margin adds Remiel as the seventh. Tobit 12:15 reads, "I am Raphael, one of the seven holy angels who offer up the prayers of the saints and enter in before the glory of the Holy One." Though these books are apocryphal, they nevertheless show what the ancients believed in this respect. It would seem that Gabriel might qualify as a second archangel (Dan. 8:16; 9:21; Luke 1:19, 26).

The archangels appear to have the specific responsibility of protecting and prospering Israel (Dan. 10:13, 21; 12:1), of announcing the birth of the Savior (Luke 1:26–38), of defeating Satan and his angels in their attempt to kill the man-child and the woman (Rev. 12:7–12), and of heralding the return of Christ for his own (1 Thess. 4:16–18).

6. *The watchers.* In Dan. 4:13 a holy watcher is mentioned and that in the singular; v. 17 uses the plural "watchers." These are probably angels who are sent by God to observe. The name suggests vigilance. They are also involved in bringing a message from God to man. Whether these are a special class of angels is unknown.

7. *Sons of God.* Another phrase that is used of angels is "sons of God." This phrase is used in Job 1:6; 2:1; and 38:7 to refer to angels, including Satan. They are sons of God in the sense of being created by God. In fact, "gods" (*elohim*) is used of angels (Ps. 8:5; cf. Heb. 2:7). Some hold that the sons of God mentioned in Gen. 6:2 are angels who cohabited with women. It may, however, have reference to the godly line of Seth.

There are indications of organization among the angels. In Col. 1:16 Paul speaks of thrones, dominions, rulers, and authorities, and adds that they were "created through Him and for Him." This seems to indicate that Paul has reference to the good angels. In Eph. 1:21 the reference appears to include both the good and the evil angels. Elsewhere this terminology refers definitely to the evil angels (Rom. 8:38; Eph. 6:12; Col. 2:15).

It is not likely, however, that Paul aims to present in Col. 1:16 a regular hierarchy of angels, and certainly he did not have an elaborate system of *aeons* to serve the purpose of metaphysical theology and ethics. The Testaments of the Twelve Patriarchs (Levi 3), written about the close of the first century, teaches about seven heavens. The first is not populated, but all above that are populated by various spirits or angels. But Paul does not teach any such systematic gradation of the angels. We can only say that the thrones perhaps refer to angelic beings whose place is in the immediate presence of God. These angels are invested with regal power, which they exercise under God. The dominions appear to stand next in dignity to the thrones. The rulers seem to refer to rulers over distinct peoples or nations. Thus Michael is said to be Israel's prince (Dan. 10:21; 12:1); we read also of the prince of Persia and the prince of Greece (Dan. 10:20). That is, each one is a prince in one of these princedoms. This seems to be true also of the church, for mention is made in the Revelation of angels over the seven churches (1:20). The authorities are possibly subordinate authorities, serving under one of the other orders.

The phrase "angel of the Lord" occurs often in the Old Testament, but it has reference not to an ordinary angel, but to the preincarnate Christ; therefore, it is not under discussion at this point.

B. The Evil Angels

As with good angels, there are also differences among the evil angels.

1. The angels that are kept in prison.   These are mentioned specifically in 2 Pet. 2:4 and Jude 6. All seem to agree that Peter and Jude have the same angels in mind. Peter merely says that they sinned and that God cast them down to Tartarus, committing them to pits of darkness and reserving them unto judgment. But Jude represents their sin as consisting of leaving their own principality and their proper habitation. It may be that Jude had the Septuagint reading of Deut. 32:8 in mind. There God is said to have divided the nations "according to the number of the angels of God." It is assumed that God appointed one or more angels over each of the nations. The fact that various nations are thus under one or another of these angelic princes is clear from Daniel (10:13, 20f.; 12:1). To leave their own principality might thus mean that they became unfaithful in the performance of their duties, but more probably it means that they sought to obtain a more coveted principality. To leave their proper habitation might mean that they left their heavenly dwelling and came down to earth.

Another interpretation has also been advanced. In Jude 7, the sin of Sodom and Gomorrah seems to be likened to the sin of the enchained angels. This may mean that the sin of the angels was some type of gross immorality. Some have suggested that the sin of Gen. 6:2 is that of angels being sexually involved with women. As the punishment for their sin, God thrust them down to Tartarus. In the New Testament the term "Tartarus" occurs only in 2 Pet. 2:4, though it appears three times in the Septuagint. In Homer,

Tartarus is a murky place beneath Hades. If wicked men go down to Hades, it does not seem unlikely that Tartarus, the place where wicked angels are confined, is still farther down. Their punishment consists of being confined in pits of darkness and of being bound with everlasting chains, reserved unto the judgment of the great day.

2. *The angels that are free.*   These are often mentioned in connection with Satan, their leader (Matt. 25:41; Rev. 12:7–9). At other times, they are referred to separately (Ps. 78:49; Rom. 8:38; 1 Cor. 6:3; Rev. 9:14). They are included in the "rule and authority and power and dominion" of Eph. 1:21, and are explicitly mentioned in Eph. 6:12 and Col. 2:15. Their chief occupation seems to be that of supporting their leader Satan in his warfare against the good angels and God's people and cause.

3. *The demons.*   Demons are often mentioned in Scripture, particularly in the Gospels. They are spirit beings (Matt. 8:16), often called "unclean spirits" (Mark 9:25). They serve under the authority of Satan (Luke 11:15–19), though they are ultimately subject to God (Matt. 8:29). Demons are able to cause dumbness (Matt. 9:32f.), blindness (Matt. 12:22), personal injury (Mark 9:18), and other physical defects and deformities (Luke 13:11–17). They oppose the work of God by corrupting sound doctrine (1 Tim. 4:1–3), godly wisdom (James 3:15), and Christian fellowship (1 Cor. 10:20f.).

Are the demons distinct from or to be equated with the free fallen angels? Some suggest that demons are disembodied spirits of a pre-Adamic race. It is preferable to identify them with the fallen angels which are yet free. That they possess individuals is part of their continuing effort to frustrate the program of God, rather than merely a desire to be clothed with a human body. They, under Satan, are enemies of God and his kingdom. Unger writes:

> Satan holds sway over the fallen spirits, who concurred in his primal rebellion. His authority is without doubt what he has been permitted to retain from his creation. These spirits, having [made] an irrevocable choice to follow Satan, instead of remaining loyal to their Creator, have become irretrievably confirmed in wickedness, and irreparably abandoned to delusion. Hence, they are in full sympathy with their prince, and render him willing service in their varied ranks and positions of service in his highly organized kingdom of evil (Matt. 12:26).[4]

4. *Satan.*   This superhuman being is mentioned in the Old Testament expressly only in Gen. 3:1–15; 1 Chron. 21:1; Job 1:6–12; 2:1–7; Zech. 3:1f.

[4]Unger, *Biblical Demonology*, p. 73.

Perhaps he is also mentioned in reference to the scapegoat in Lev. 16:8, one of the two goats used on the Day of Atonement. In the New Testament, Satan is mentioned very frequently (Matt. 4:1–11; Luke 10:18f.; John 13:2, 27; 1 Pet. 5:8f.; Rev. 12; 20:1–3, 7–10).

The Scriptures abundantly testify to the personality of Satan. Personal pronouns are applied to him (Job 1:8, 12; Zech. 3:2; Matt. 4:10; John 8:44); personal attributes are ascribed to him (will, Isa. 14:13f.; cf. 1 Tim. 3:6; and knowledge, Job 1:9f.); and personal acts are performed by him (Job 1:9–11; Matt. 4:1–11; John 8:44; 1 John 3:8: Jude 9; Rev. 12:7–10).

In the Scriptures this powerful being is referred to by several different names. (1) Satan (1 Chron. 21:1; Job 1:6; Zech. 3:1; Matt. 4:10; 2 Cor. 2:11; 1 Tim. 1:20). This term means "adversary"; he is the adversary of both God and man (1 Pet. 5:8). (2) Devil (Matt. 13:39; John 13:2; Eph. 6:11; James 4:7). As the devil, a term used only in the New Testament, he is the slanderer and the accuser of the brethren (Rev. 12:10). He slanders God to man (Gen. 3:1–7), and man to God (Job 1:9; 2:4). (3) Dragon (Rev. 12:3, 7; 13:2; 20:2; cf. Isa. 51:9). The word "dragon" seems to mean literally "serpent" or "sea-monster." The dragon is taken as the personification of Satan, as it is of Pharaoh in Ezek. 29:3 and 32:2. The dragon as a sea animal may properly represent Satan's activity in the seas of the world. (4) Serpent (Gen. 3:1; Rev. 12:9; 20:2; cf. Isa. 27:1). By this term, his crookedness and deceitfulness (2 Cor. 11:3) are pointed out. (5) Beelzebub or Beelzebul (Matt. 10:25; 12:24–27; Mark 3:22; Luke 11:15–19). The exact meaning of the term is not known. In Syriac it means "lord of dung." It is also suggested that the term means "lord of the house." (6) Belial or Beliar (2 Cor. 6:15). This term was used in the Old Testament in the sense of "worthlessness" (2 Sam. 23:6). Thus we read of the "worthless fellows" (lit. "sons of Belial," Judg. 20:13; cf. 1 Sam. 10:27; 30:22; 1 Kings 21:13). (7) Lucifer (Isa. 14:12). This term means the morning star, an epithet of the planet Venus. It is literally "light-bearer," and it may have reference to Satan. As Lucifer, Satan is seen as an angel of light (2 Cor. 11:14).

Satan is also given a set of names of a slightly different character. He goes by several descriptive words and phrases. (8) The evil one (Matt. 13:19, 38; Eph. 6:16; 1 John 2:13f.; 5:19). This is a description of his character and work. He is evil, wicked, cruel, and tyrannical over all that he can control, and he is out to do evil wherever possible. (9) The tempter (Matt. 4:3; 1 Thess. 3:5). This name indicates his constant purpose and endeavor to incite man to sin. He presents the most plausible excuses and suggests the most striking advantages for sinning. (10) The god of this world (lit., "age," 2 Cor. 4:4). As such, he has his servants (2 Cor. 11:15), doctrines (1 Tim. 4:1), sacrifices (1 Cor. 10:20), and synagogues (Rev. 2:9). He sponsors the religion of the natural man and is, no doubt, back of the false cults and systems that have cursed the true church through the ages. (11) The prince of the power of the air (Eph. 2:2). As such, he is the leader of the evil angels (Matt. 12:24; 25:41; Rev. 12:7; 16:13f.). He has a vast host of underlings that carry out his desires, and he rules with despotic power. (12) The ruler of this world (John 12:31; 14:30; 16:11). This seems to refer to his influence over the governments of this world. Jesus did not dispute Satan's claim to some sort of right here on this planet (Matt. 4:8f.); God, however, has set definite bounds for him, and when the time comes, he will be superseded by the rule of the Lord Jesus, the one whose right it is to rule.

The hosts of wickedness are organized, and Satan is at the head. The principalities in Rom. 8:38 are princedoms of evil rulers (cf. Dan. 10:13, 20). It appears that both the good and the bad organizations of angels are included in the rule, authority, power, and dominion of Eph. 1:21. In Eph. 6:12, the rulers, powers, world forces of this darkness, and the spiritual forces of wickedness in heavenly places refer to the organization of the forces of evil, as do the rulers and authorities in Col. 2:15. Just how these Satanic forces are related to Satan and to one another is not made clear in Scripture.

CHAPTER XIV

The Work and Destiny of the Angels

I. THE WORK OF THE ANGELS

This can be divided into three sections: the work of the good angels, the work of the evil angels, and the work of Satan.

A. THE WORK OF THE GOOD ANGELS

For the sake of convenience, this subject is divided into two parts: first, the work of the angels in connection with the life and ministry of Christ, and secondly, the work of the good angels in general.

1. The work of the angels in connection with the life and ministry of Christ. It is a striking fact that far from repudiating the belief in angels, the Lord experienced their help in a most remarkable degree. Mary was informed by the angel Gabriel that she would become the mother of the Savior (Luke 1:26–38). Joseph was assured by an angel that "that which has been conceived in her is of the Holy Spirit" (Matt. 1:20). The angels announced to the shepherds the fact of Christ's birth in Bethlehem (Luke 2:8–15). Angels came and ministered to Christ after the temptation in the wilderness (Matt. 4:11). Jesus told Nathanael that he would see the angels of God ascending and descending upon the Son of Man (John 1:51). An angel from heaven came and strengthened him in the garden (Luke 22:43). He said he could ask the Father for twelve legions of angels to come to his aid, if it were necessary or desirable (Matt. 26:53). An angel rolled away the stone from the sepulchre of Jesus and spoke to the women that came to the tomb (Matt. 28:2–7). Angels accompanied Christ at the ascension (Acts 1:10f.). Angels will accompany him when he comes the second time (Matt. 16:27; 25:31). The angels are represented as eager to look into the plan of salvation wrought by Christ (1 Pet. 1:12). Surely, this indicates a very intimate relation between Christ and the angels.

2. The work of the good angels in general. There are, first of all, the more constant and regular ministries. (1) They stand before God and worship him (Ps. 148:2; Matt. 18:10; Heb. 1:6; Rev. 5:11). (2) They protect and deliver

144

God's people (Gen. 19:11; 1 Kings 19:5; Dan. 3:28; 6:22; Acts 5:19; 12:10f.). Scripture promises the believer, "He will give His angels charge concerning you, to guard you in all your ways" (Ps. 91:11; cf. Matt. 4:6). Angels are "ministering spirits, sent out to render service for the sake of those who will inherit salvation" (Heb. 1:14). Michael is the patron angel of Israel (Dan. 10:13, 21; 12:1). It is not unlikely that the seven angels to the seven churches in Asia were patron angels for each church (Rev. 1:20). Jesus warns of despising his little ones, saying, "Their angels in heaven continually behold the face of My Father who is in heaven" (Matt. 18:10). (3) They guide and encourage God's servants (Matt. 28:5-7; Acts 8:26; 27:23f.). (4) They interpret God's will to men (Job 33:23). This is particularly evident in the experience of Daniel (Dan. 7:16; 10:5, 11), Zechariah (Zech. 1:9, 19), and John (Rev. 1:1). (5) They are executors of judgment toward individuals and toward nations such as Sodom and Gomorrah (Gen. 19:12f.), Jerusalem (2 Sam. 24:16; Ezek. 9:1), and Herod (Acts 12:23), and toward the earth (Rev. 16). (6) They carry the saved home after physical death (Luke 16:22).

In addition to their regular ministries, they will be actively involved in the future. (1) The Lord's return in the air will be accompanied "with the voice of the archangel" (1 Thess. 4:16). (2) They will be actively involved as God's agents of judgment during the tribulation period (Rev. 7:2; 16:1). (3) When Jesus comes in judgment, he will be accompanied by "His mighty angels in flaming fire" (2 Thess. 1:7; cf. Jude 14). (4) The angels will gather together elect Israel at Christ's return (Matt. 24:31). (5) In the harvest at the end of the age they will be involved in the separating of the false from the true, the evil from the good (Matt. 13:39, 49f.). (6) They will stand before the gates of the New Jerusalem, apparently to serve as a kind of honorary body of sentinels, as if to guarantee that nothing that is unclean or defiled will ever enter the city (Rev. 21:12).

B. The Work of the Evil Angels

Some distinguish between evil angels and demons, but it seems more likely that they are one and the same. They are actively involved in opposing God and his program. (1) They endeavor to separate the believer from Christ (Rom. 8:38). (2) They oppose the good angels in their work (Dan. 10:12f.). (3) They cooperate with Satan in the carrying out of his purposes and plans (Matt. 25:41; Eph. 6:12; Rev. 12:7-12). (4) They cause physical and mental disorders (Matt. 9:33; 12:22; Mark 5:1-16; Luke 9:37-42). (5) The phrase "unclean spirit" suggests that they lead men into moral impurity (Matt. 10:1; Acts 5:16). (6) They disseminate false doctrine (2 Thess. 2:2; 1 Tim. 4:1). (7) They oppose God's children in their spiritual progress (Eph. 6:12). (8) They sometimes possess human beings and even animals (Matt. 4:24; Mark 5:8-14; Luke 8:2; Acts 8:7; 16:16). A distinction must be made, however, between demon influence and demon possession; the former is a temporary operation of the demons from without, the latter the more permanent operation from within. (9) They are sometimes used by God in the carrying out of his purposes (Judg. 9:23; 1 Kings 22:21–23; Ps. 78:49). It appears that he will especially so use them during the tribulation period (Rev. 9:1–12; 16:13–16). They will apparently be invested with miraculous powers for a time (2 Thess. 2:9; Rev. 16:14).

There are three types of demonology that should be especially mentioned in this connection. The first is fortune-telling. On the lowest plane, this may be mere human foresight, studied deception, or pure superstition. In biblical times there was augury or foretelling of the future by means of natural signs, such as the flight of birds or the disposition of the entrails (Ezek. 21:21), hydromancy or foretelling from the appearance of water poured into a vessel or of objects dropped into the water (Gen. 44:5), and astrology or the determination of the supposed influence of the stars on the destiny of a person (Isa. 47:13). These practices are a form of demonology. Whenever a person attempts to read the future by a kind of divine inspiration (Acts 16:16), he is in reality doing so by the assistance of demons.

The second form is the direct worship of demons. Apostate Israel sacrificed to demons (Deut. 32:17; Ps. 106:37). Food sacrificed to idols in New Testament times was actually sacrificed to demons (1 Cor. 10:19f.). During the tribulation period there will be renewed demon activity and open worship of the dragon (Rev. 13:4; 16:13f.).

The third form is that which is known as spiritualism or spiritism. Spiritism is the belief that the living can communicate with the dead and that the spirits of the dead can manifest their presence to men. Necromancy, as this is called, is supposedly done through the agency of a human being, known as a medium. Though Israel did not always heed, she was strongly warned against consulting those who profess to communicate with the dead (Lev. 19:31; 20:6, 27; Deut. 18:11; 2 Kings 21:6; 23:24; 1 Chron. 10:13; 2 Chron. 33:6; Isa. 8:19; 19:3; 29:4). The witch of Endor (1 Sam. 28:3–14), Simon the magician (Acts 8:9–24), Elymas the magician (Acts 13:6–12), and the girl with the spirit of divination (Acts 16:16–18) are biblical examples of this form of demonism. The Bible often speaks of this practice as sorcery (Exod. 7:11; Jer. 27:9; Dan. 2:2; Mic. 5:12; Nah. 3:4; Rev. 9:21).

With regard to the whole question of demonism, the Scriptures exhort us to try the spirits, to see whether they be of God or not (1 John 4:1; cf. 1 Cor. 12:10), to have no fellowship with such as commune with demons (Lev. 19:31; 1 Cor. 10:20), much less to consult with the evil spirits ourselves (Deut. 18:10–14; Isa. 8:19), to put on the whole armor of God for the conflict with these spirits (Eph. 6:12f.), and to give ourselves to prayer and supplication at all seasons and with all perseverance (Eph. 6:18).

C. THE WORK OF SATAN

There are indications of Satan's work in the various names given to him, for each name expresses a quality of character, or a method of operation, or both. As Satan, he opposes; as the devil, he slanders and accuses; and as the tempter, he seeks to lure men to commit sin.

In addition, the Scriptures reveal the nature of his work directly. Generally speaking, Satan's object is to assume the place of God. Although the Scriptures give no authority for the view that hell is a kingdom in which he rules, the Word of God does represent him as having power, a throne, and great authority (Matt. 4:8f.; Rev. 13:2). In order to achieve his avowed purpose, he sought to kill the child Jesus (Matt. 2:16; Rev. 12:4), and then when that effort failed, to induce him to worship him (Luke 4:6f.). Had Christ failed, Satan would have achieved the first part of his purpose to establish his rule in the earth.

Satan employs various methods for the realization of his purpose. Since he cannot attack God directly, he attacks God's master-creation, man. The Scriptures mention the following methods used by Satan: lying (John 8:44; 2 Cor. 11:3), tempting (Matt. 4:1), robbing (Matt. 13:19), harassing (2 Cor. 12:7), hindering (1 Thess. 2:18), sifting (Luke 22:31), imitating (Matt. 13:25; 2 Cor. 11:14f.), accusing (Rev. 12:10), smiting with disease (Luke 13:16; cf. 1 Cor. 5:5), possessing (John 13:27), and killing and devouring (John 8:44; 1 Pet. 5:8). The believer must not let Satan gain an advantage over him by remaining ignorant of his schemes (2 Cor. 2:11), but should be sober and alert and resist him (Eph. 4:27; James 4:7; 1 Pet. 5:8f.). He should not speak lightly of him (Jude 8f.; cf. 2 Pet. 2:10), but put on the whole armor of God and take his stand against him (Eph. 6:11). Christ did conquer Satan at the cross (Heb. 2:14), and the believer must live by faith in light of that victory. As Pentecost states, "By His death and resurrection Jesus passed sentence upon the adversary of God."[1]

II. THE DESTINY OF THE ANGELS

A. THE DESTINY OF THE GOOD ANGELS

There is every reason to believe that the good angels will continue in the service of God throughout all eternity. In John's vision of the New Jerusalem, which certainly belongs to a future age and is evidently destined to continue forever along with the new heaven and the new earth (Rev. 21:1f.), he saw angels at the twelve gates of the city (Rev. 21:12). If any

[1]Pentecost, *Your Adversary the Devil*, p. 184.

angels at all will be in service, there is no reason why we should not believe that all the good angels will be thus continued in their appointed places.

B. The Destiny of the Evil Angels

The evil angels will have their part in the lake of fire (Matt. 25:41). Presently some are kept in chains and are under darkness unto the day of their final judgment (2 Pet. 2:4; Jude 6), while others are yet free. At the coming of Christ, believers will have a part in judging the evil angels (1 Cor. 6:3), and these angels will, with Satan, be cast into the lake of fire.

C. The Destiny of Satan

The history of Satan may be briefly traced. He is first found in heaven (Ezek. 28:14; Luke 10:18). It is not known how long he lived in the enjoyment of God's favor, but there came a time when he and many other angels with him fell. Next, he was in the Garden of Eden in the form of a serpent (Gen. 3:1; Ezek. 28:13). There he became the agent in the fall of man. Then he was found in the air, with access to both heaven and earth (Job 1:6f.; 2:1f.; Eph. 2:2; 6:12). This seems to have been his headquarters ever since the fall of man. In the future he will be cast down to earth (Rev. 12:9-13). This will apparently take place during the coming tribulation period. When Christ comes back to earth in power and glory to set up his kingdom, Satan will be cast into the abyss (Rev. 20:1-3). He will be bound and confined there for a thousand years. Then he will be loosed for a short time and during this time attempt to frustrate the purposes of God on earth (Rev. 20:3, 7-9). But his plans will be thwarted. Fire will come down out of heaven and destroy the armies which he has marshalled, and he himself will be cast into the lake of fire (Rev. 20:7-10), his final destiny, where he and his followers will be tormented forever and ever.

PART V
ANTHROPOLOGY

Anthropology is the doctrine of man, but today the term has both a theological and a scientific use. Theological anthropology deals with man in relation to God, while scientific anthropology deals with his psycho-physical organism and natural history. There are, however, wide variations in the latter usage when it comes to the range of topics included in the subject by different writers. Naturalists, for example, embrace under this head the natural history of the race, while philosophers broaden the term to include psychology, sociology, and ethics, together with anatomy and physiology. It should be noted that this distinction applies to topics only, not to methods of treatment; for scientific anthropology is no more scientific than theological anthropology, but merely deals with different aspects of the doctrine of man.

The subject of anthropology in this study covers such topics as the origin of man, the unity of the race, the fall of man, and the consequences of his fall.

CHAPTER XV

The Origin and Original Character of Man

I. THE ORIGIN OF MAN

Every thoughtful person is confronted with the question as to the origin of the human race. As he looks back into history, he observes that the men now existing seem to have sprung from other men by the process of natural generation for thousands of years. In analyzing the origin of man, the biblicist is confronted with the basic issue: Did God create man immediately or mediately, was man formed directly by the hand of God or did he evolve through natural processes? The Christian must acknowledge God's involvement, but was it direct or indirect? Theistic evolutionists teach that man evolved from a lower form. Threshold evolutionists and creationists hold that man is a direct and immediate creation of God. Carnell, a threshold evolutionist, writes, "Man was made out of the dust by a special, *ab extra*, divine act, with a body which is structurally similar to the higher Vertebrata, and soul formed after the image and likeness of God."[1] Another threshold evolutionist writes, "May we not hold that . . . God intervened in the past, even in the midst of a long evolutionary process, and created man as an entirely new factor?"[2] Some evolutionists suggest that the human body developed through a long evolutionary process, but that God broke into the process and directly created the soul, bringing man into being. Pope Pius XII in his encyclical *Humani Generis* (1950) notes, "The teaching of the Church leaves the doctrine of evolution an open question, as long as it confines its speculations to the development, from other living matter already in existence, of the human body. (That souls are immediately created by God is a view which the Catholic faith imposes on us.)"[3] Others suggest that Adam was one among many contemporaries and that God conferred his image on Adam's collaterals as well as on Adam; thus Adam's federal headship extended to his contemporaries as well as to his offspring.[4] As can be seen, seeking to harmonize secular science with the biblical record can take several

[1]Carnell, *An Introduction to Christian Apologetics*, p. 238.
[2]Barnhouse, "Adam and Modern Science," *Eternity Magazine*, May 1960, p. 8.
[3]Clarkson, *et al.*, eds., *The Church Teaches*, p. 154.
[4]Kidner, *Genesis*, p. 29.

forms. The arguments for evolution need to be stated and answered, then a biblical solution can be stated.

A. ARGUMENTS FOR THE EVOLUTIONARY HYPOTHESIS

1. Comparative anatomy. There are marked similarities between the anatomy of man and that of the higher vertebrata. This, it is suggested, points to the evolution of man from animal. However, if man and animals partake of the same food, same air, and have the same environment as other creatures, should not the lungs, digestive tract, skin, eyes, and so forth, be similar? Further, similarity in anatomy suggests a common creator, not one creature springing from another. Two symphonies by one composer might be expected to have some marked similarities.

2. Vestigial organs. These are organs, like the tonsils, appendix, and thymus gland, which, according to the evolutionist, were useful to our supposedly more primitive ancestors but now have become functionally useless. Against this view, we note that with an increase in knowledge, science is beginning to learn more about and recognize the usefulness of these allegedly useless organs. As Culp states, "Just because we do not as yet understand fully the use of these various organs, we should not question the wisdom of the Creator who put them there."[5]

3. Embryology. The evolutionists argue that the human fetus develops through various stages which are parallel to the alleged evolutionary process, from a one-celled organism to an adult species. But a close study of the human fetus reveals that there are too many dissimilarities to supposed parallels in the worm, fish, tail, and hair stages. Further, developments are often the reverse of what is alleged. The earthworm has circulation, but no heart, and it is therefore advanced that circulation must have come before the heart. However, in the human fetus, the heart develops first, then the circulation. The so-called gill slits were at one time assumed to be rudimentary gills, but have more recently been found to be simply a groove between two parallel blood vessels.[6]

4. Bio-chemistry. Living organisms are all similar in their bio-chemical makeup. This is to be expected because the various life systems all depend on the same or similar acids, proteins, etc.

5. Paleontology. The study of fossils is used to defend evolution. Evidence for various kinds of life is found in the various rock strata, from the pre-

[5]Culp, *Remember Thy Creator*, p. 66.
[6]For further refutation see Davidheiser, *Evolution and Christian Faith*, pp. 240–254.

cambrian period on. The evolutionist seeks to find evidence of continuity between, for example, man and beast, fish and fowl, and reptile and fish. However, in the study of fossils there is as much evidence for discontinuity as for continuity. There has been found no link between man and monkey. The Bible says that there is a flesh of man and a flesh of beast (1 Cor. 15:39). The evolutionist cannot provide the link and the Bible does not allow for such a link.

6. *Genetics.* This is the study of heredity and variations among related organisms. Why are no two fingerprints the same? Does this not suggest change occurring in the human species? And is this not an argument for evolution? Three things must be noted. First, it is readily acknowledged that mutations do take place, but they are small, and it would take numerous mutations to have any substantial effect. Further, changes tend to make the organism less well suited for its environment, thereby threatening its very survival. Finally, after generations of testing with the fruit fly, there have been no transmutations. There has not been, nor can there be, any crossing over of the "kinds" of Gen. 1. Man is a special species, he did not come from the beast.

B. Biblical Arguments for the Immediate Creation of Man

1. *The literal teaching of Scripture.* Although atheistic evolutionists disbelieve the teaching of the Bible, theistic evolutionists are in danger of impugning the character of God when they endeavor to explain the story of creation symbolically. The Scriptures taken literally give a reasonable explanation for the origin of man. Even if evolution could prove its doctrine of the survival of the fittest, it cannot account for the arrival of the first. In the Bible we are told that God "created" man (Gen. 1:27; 5:1; Deut. 4:32; Ps. 104:30; Isa. 45:12; 1 Cor. 11:9) and that he "made" and "fashioned" or "formed" him out of the dust of the ground (Gen. 1:26; 2:22; 6:6f.; Ps. 100:3; 103:14; 1 Tim. 2:13). As to his body, man was made of the dust of the ground; as to his immaterial nature, he was made of the inbreathing of God. Gen. 2:7; Job 33:4; and Eccl. 12:7 include both ideas in one statement. This conception of the origin of man taken literally from Scripture gives man a dignity of being and a position of responsibility that no other theory does, and lays the foundations for a sane system of ethics and redemption.

2. *Adam and Eve were created male and female.* If Adam and Eve were subhuman before God breathed his image into them, they would have already been male and female, but God made them male and female (Gen. 1:27; 2:7; Matt. 19:4).

3. *Eve was made directly by God.* Eve came from the side of Adam (Gen. 2:21f.; 1 Cor. 11:8). The language of Gen. 2 will not allow any other

interpretation, and if Eve was formed directly by God, it is only reasonable that Adam was formed by God as well.

4. Man comes from and goes to dust.   If the dust of Gen. 2:7 has reference to man evolving from the beast, then the returning to dust of Gen. 3:19 would mean a returning to beast. This is, of course, ludicrous.

5. Man became a living soul.   The phrase "living soul" (Gen. 2:7) is the same as that translated "living creature" (Gen. 1:21). When man was made, he became alive, not before. He was not already a living creature who became a living creature.

6. The Bible distinguishes between animal flesh and human flesh.   Paul does not allow for the mixing of beast, fish, foul, or human flesh; they are to be distinguished (1 Cor. 15:39).

II. THE ORIGINAL CHARACTER OF MAN

Scripture represents man's original condition by the phrase, "in the image and likeness of God" (Gen. 1:26f.; 5:1; 9:6; 1 Cor. 11:7; James 3:9). There does not seem to be any significant difference between the Hebrew words for "image" and "likeness," and we need not try to find any difference. But we do need to ask of what that image and likeness consisted.

A. It was not a Physical Likeness

God is spirit and does not have parts like a man. Some represent God as a great human, but they are wrong in their views. Ps. 17:15 says, "I will be satisfied with Thy likeness when I awake." But this does not suggest corporeity; rather, the context suggests likeness in righteousness (cf. 1 John 3:2f.). The "form of the Lord" was seen by Moses (Num. 12:8), but the Lord's face could not be seen (Exod. 33:20). Though man did not have a physical likeness to God since God is incorporeal, he did have a likeness insofar as he was perfect in health, had no inherited or otherwise communicated disease germs in him, and was not subject to death. God seems originally to have restricted man to a vegetarian diet (Gen. 1:29), but later he permitted the eating of meat (Gen. 9:3). It is interesting to note that in permitting the use of meat, he laid down no rules as to clean and unclean animals, though they were distinguished (Gen. 7:2). That was a later law, governing the conduct of one people and that only for a time (Lev. 11; Mark 7:19; Acts 10:15; Rom. 14:1–12; Col. 2:16).

B. It was a Mental Likeness

Hodge says:

> God is a Spirit, the human soul is a spirit. The essential attributes of a spirit are reason, conscience, and will. A spirit is a rational, moral, and therefore also a free agent. In making man after his own image, therefore, God endowed him with those attributes which belong to his own nature as a spirit. Man is thereby distinguished from all other inhabitants of this world, and raised immeasurably above them. He belongs to the same order of being as God Himself, and is therefore capable of communion with his Maker. This conformity of nature between man and God . . . is also the necessary condition of our capacity to know God, and therefore the foundation of our religious nature. If we were not like God, we could not know Him. We should be as the beasts which perish.[7]

This statement is confirmed by Scripture. In sanctification man is "being renewed to a true knowledge according to the image of the One who created him" (Col. 3:10). Of course, this renewal begins in regeneration, but it is continued in sanctification. Man's endowment with great intellectual faculties is implied in the command to cultivate the garden and keep it (Gen. 2:15), the command to exercise dominion over the earth and all the creatures of the earth (Gen. 1:26, 28), and in the statement that he gave names to all the animals on the earth (Gen. 2:19f.). This likeness to God is inalienable, and since it constitutes man's capacity for redemption, it gives value to the life even of the unregenerated (Gen. 9:6; 1 Cor. 11:7; James 3:9). How different is this conception of the original condition of man from that of the evolutionist, who thinks of the first man as only a shade above the brute— not only ignorant, but with practically no mental ability whatever.

C. It was a Moral Likeness

Some have made the mistake of holding that the image of God in which man was created consists exclusively in his rational nature; still others have been disposed to limit it to his dominion. More correctly, though, it consists in both man's rational nature and in his moral conformity to God. Quoting Hodge:

> He is the image of God, and bears and reflects the divine likeness among the inhabitants of the earth, because he is a spirit, an intelligent, voluntary agent; and as such he is rightfully invested with universal dominion. This is what the Reformed theologians were accus-

[7]Hodge, *Systematic Theology*, II, pp. 96, 97.

tomed to call the essential image of God, as distinguished from the accidental.[8]

That man had such a likeness to God is clear from the Scriptures. If in regeneration the new man "in the likeness of God has been created in righteousness and holiness of truth" (Eph. 4:24), it is undoubtedly correct to infer that originally man had both righteousness and holiness. The context in Genesis 1 and 2 bears this out. Only on this ground was it possible for man to have communion with God, who cannot look upon wickedness (Hab. 1:13). Eccl. 7:29 confirms this view. There we read that "God made men upright." This we may also infer from the statement in Gen. 1:31 that "God saw all that He had made, and behold, it was very good." The "all" includes man and would not be true if man had been morally imperfect.

What is meant by original righteousness and holiness? It is not the substance or essence of human nature, for if it were, human nature would have ceased to exist when man sinned; nor yet is it a gift from without, added to man after his creation, for man is said to have possessed the divine image by the fact of his creation, and not by a subsequent bestowal of it. Shedd elaborates:

> Holiness is more than innocence. It is not sufficient to say that man was created in a state of innocence. This would be true, if he had been destitute of a moral disposition either right or wrong. Man was made not only negatively innocent, but positively holy. Man's regenerate condition is a restoration of his primitive state; and his righteousness as regenerate is described as *kata theon*, Eph. 4:21; and as "true holiness," Eph. 4:24. This is positive character, and not mere innocency.[9]

Sometimes this is called "con-created" holiness, as opposed to holiness that some say man was endowed with by God after creation. This original holiness may be defined as a tendency of man's affections and will, though accompanied by the power of evil choice, in the direction of the spiritual knowledge of God and of divine things generally. It is distinguished from the perfected holiness of the saints, as instinctive affections and childlike innocence differ from the holiness which has developed and been confirmed by temptation.

D. IT WAS A SOCIAL LIKENESS

God's social nature is grounded in his affections. He finds the objects of his love in the trinity. As God has a social nature, so he has endowed man with a

[8]Hodge, *Systematic Theology*, II, p. 99.
[9]Shedd, *Dogmatic Theology*, II, p. 96.

social nature. Consequently, man seeks companionship. In the first place, man found this fellowship with God himself. Man "heard the sound of the Lord God walking in the garden in the cool of the day" (Gen. 3:8). This implies that man communed with his maker. God had made man for himself, and man found supreme satisfaction in communion with his Lord. But God also provided human fellowship. He created woman, for, he said, "It is not good for the man to be alone; I will make him a helper suitable for him" (Gen. 2:18). To make this a very intimate fellowship, he made the woman out of a bone taken from the man. Adam recognized that Eve was bone of his bone, and flesh of his flesh, and so he called her "woman." And because of this intimate relation between the two, "a man shall leave his father and his mother, and shall cleave to his wife; and they shall become one flesh" (Gen. 2:24). It is evident that man was made with a social nature, even as God had a social nature. Human love and social interests spring directly from this element in man's nature.

CHAPTER XVI

The Unity and Permanent Constitution of Man

I. THE UNITY OF MAN

A. THE TEACHING OF SCRIPTURE

The Scriptures clearly teach that the whole human race is descended from a single pair (Gen. 1:27f.; 2:7, 22; 3:20; 9:19). All are children of a common parent and have a common nature. Paul takes this truth for granted in his doctrine of the organic unity of mankind in the first transgression and of the provision of salvation for those in Christ (Rom. 5:12, 19; 1 Cor. 15:21f.; Heb. 2:16). This truth also constitutes the ground of man's responsibility toward his fellow man (Gen. 4:9; Acts 17:26). Attention should be called to the fact of the unity of man in another sense. In Gen. 1:26 God said, "Let Us make man," and in v. 27 we read, "Male and female He created them." Shedd says, "This implies that the idea of man is incomplete, if either the male or the female be considered by itself, in isolation from the other. The two together constitute the human species. A solitary male or female individual would not be the species man, nor include it, nor propagate it."[1] In harmony with this we have the statement in Gen. 2:21–23 that God did not make Eve out of the dust of the ground, but out of a bone taken out of Adam, and did not breathe into Eve's nostrils. Apparently her immaterial nature as well as her physical nature was taken out of Adam (1 Cor. 11:8).

B. THE TESTIMONY OF HISTORY AND SCIENCE

The teaching of Scripture is corroborated by history and science.

1. The argument from history. The history of nations and tribes in both hemispheres points to a common origin and ancestry. This is generally accepted to be somewhere in the fertile crescent region.

2. The argument from language. Secular scholars in the science of linguistics are split over the origin of language; some favor monogenesis, others

[1]Shedd, *Dogmatic Theology*, II, p. 4.

polygenesis. With increased study, the trend is toward monogenesis. There is evidence for uniformity of language with regard to phonology, grammatical structure, and vocabulary. This would mitigate against a plurality of origins, "while the case for a single beginning seems fairly strong."[2] Roucek writes, "Scholars speculate that most languages originated in one universal parent language."[3] With this the biblical accounts of the migration of the families of the three sons of Noah (Gen. 10) and of the tower of Babel (Gen. 11) agree.

3. The argument from physiology. Interracial marriages produce offspring, blood can be transfused from one race to another, organs can be transplanted, the body temperature, pulse rate, and blood pressure are within the same limits, and there is liability to the same diseases. Paul told the Athenians, "He [God] made from one, every nation of mankind to live on all the face of the earth" (Acts 17:26; cf. 1 Cor. 15:39).

4. The argument from psychology. Man shares common mental and moral characteristics. Berkhof observes:

> The soul is the most important part of the constitutional nature of man, and psychology clearly reveals the fact that the souls of all men, to whatever tribes or nations they may belong, are essentially the same. They have in common the same animal appetites, instincts, and passions, the same tendencies and capacities, and above all the same higher qualities, the mental and moral characteristics that belong exclusively to man.[4]

We have the so-called "Chaldean Genesis" with its account of creation, the traditions of the fall in Eastern countries, of longevity, of the flood, and of the tower of Babel. These are but a few of the things known by many races in different parts of the world, and they have a definite value in proving the unity of the source from which the traditions emanated. All these arguments help to confirm our conclusion as to the unity of the human race.

II. THE CONSTITUTION OF MAN

Theology is interested primarily in his psychological and moral constitution.

[2]Swadesh, *The Origin and Diversification of Language*, p. 215. Though not writing from a biblical perspective, he builds a strong case for a common origin of language in Western Asia.
[3]Roucek, *The Study of Foreign Languages*, p. 7.
[4]Berkhof, *Systematic Theology*, p. 189.

A. MAN'S PSYCHOLOGICAL CONSTITUTION

All are agreed that man has both a material and an immaterial nature. His material nature is his body; his immaterial nature is his soul and spirit. The question arises, Is man a twofold or a threefold being? Are soul and spirit one and the same, or are we to distinguish between them? Those who believe that soul and spirit are one and the same are called dichotomists; those who hold that they are not the same are called trichotomists. The Western church generally held to dichotomy, while the Eastern church generally held to trichotomy.

1. The dichotomous theory.   Strong states the theory thus:

> The immaterial part of man, viewed as an individual and conscious life, capable of possessing and animating a physical organism, is called *psuche;* viewed as a rational and moral agent, susceptible of divine influence and indwelling, this same immaterial part is called *pneuma.* The *pneuma,* then, is man's nature looking Godward, and capable of receiving and manifesting the *Pneuma hagion;* the *psuche* is man's nature looking earthward, and touching the world of sense. The *pneuma* is man's higher part, as related to spiritual realities or as capable of such relation. Man's being is therefore not trichotomous but dichotomous, and his immaterial part, while possessing duality of powers, has unity of substance.[5]

This theory is supported by a number of facts. (1) God breathed into man but one principle, the living soul (Gen. 2:7). In Job 27:3 "life" and "spirit" seem to be used interchangeably (cf. 33:18). (2) The terms "soul" and "spirit" seem to be used interchangeably in some references (Gen. 41:8 and Ps. 42:6; Matt. 20:28 and 27:50; John 12:27 and 13:21; Heb. 12:23 and Rev. 6:9). (3) "Spirit" as well as "soul" is ascribed to brute creation (Eccl. 3:21; Rev. 16:3). Though the soul or spirit in beasts is irrational and mortal, in man it is rational and immortal. (4) "Soul" is ascribed to the Lord (Isa. 42:1; Heb. 10:38). (5) The highest place in religion is ascribed to the soul (Mark 12:30; Luke 1:46; Heb. 6:19; James 1:21). (6) Body and soul (or spirit) are spoken of as constituting the whole of man (Matt. 10:28; 1 Cor. 5:3; 3 John 2), and to lose the soul is to lose all (Matt. 16:26; Mark 8:36f.). (7) Consciousness testifies that there are two elements in man's being. We can distinguish a material part and an immaterial part, but the consciousness of no one can discriminate between soul and spirit.

2. The trichotomous theory.   This theory holds that man consists of three distinct elements: body, soul, and spirit. The body is the material part of our

[5]Strong, *Systematic Theology,* p. 486.

constitution, the soul is the principle of animal life, and the spirit is the principle of our rational life. Some add to this last statement "and immortal life." This can, however, not be made an essential part of the theory. Those who take this extreme view hold that at death the body returns to the earth, the soul ceases to exist, and the spirit alone remains to be reunited with the body at the resurrection.

The trichotomous theory rests on the following considerations. (1) Gen. 2:7 does not absolutely declare that God made a twofold being. The Hebrew text is in the plural, "Then the Lord God formed man of dust from the ground, and breathed into his nostrils the breath of life [lives]; and man became a living being." We note, however, that it is not said that man became spirit and soul. And further, "living being" is the same phrase used of animals and translated "living creature" (Gen. 1:21, 24). (2) Paul seems to think of body, soul, and spirit as three distinct parts of man's nature (1 Thess. 5:23). The same thing seems to be indicated in Heb. 4:12, where the Word is said to pierce "as far as the division of soul and spirit, of both joints and marrow." (3) A threefold organization of man's nature may be implied in the classification of men as "natural," "carnal," and "spiritual," in 1 Cor. 2:14–3:4. Though Scripture seems to point to trichotomy, is it not possible that they merely intend to include the whole man? Jesus said to the young man, "You shall love the Lord your God with all your heart, and with all your soul, and with all your mind, and with all your strength" (Mark 12:30), but no one would build a fourfold division of human nature on this statement. Heb. 4:12 does not speak of the separation of the soul *from* the spirit, but of the separation itself extending to that point. The Word pierces to the dividing of the soul itself and the spirit itself. The soul and the spirit are laid open. In reference to 1 Thess. 5:27, Hiebert states, "Students of Scripture are not agreed as to whether the distinction between spirit and soul . . . is substantial or functional. Trichotomists hold to the former, dichotomists to the latter."[6]

It is probable that we are to think of man's immaterial nature as composed of a lower and a higher power. To the soul would belong man's imagination, memory, understanding; to the spirit, his powers of reason, conscience, and free will. This variation from the traditional trichotomous view makes it possible to conserve the arguments for the dichotomous view, and yet explain how some Christians are "carnal" and others "spiritual." It also coincides with the teaching that the present body is a natural or soul body and that the resurrection body will be a spiritual body (1 Cor. 15:44). In other words, man's immaterial nature is looked upon as one nature, but as composed of two parts. Sometimes the parts are sharply distinguished; at other times, by metonymy, they are used for the whole being. The unity of man's

[6]Hiebert, *The Thessalonian Epistles*, p. 253.

immaterial nature directly contradicts the view of the Gnostics, who held that the *pneuma* is part of the divine essence, and so incapable of sin; the view of the Apollinarians, who held that Christ's humanity consisted only of body and soul, while his divine nature supplied the spirit; the view of the Semi-Pelagians, who held that the human spirit had not come under the dominion of sin; and that of the Annihilationists, who hold that man by sin lost the divine element called "spirit," and regains it by regeneration; therefore, only such as are regenerated live forever, the unsaved being extinguished at death. All of these groups were or are, apparently, trichotomists.

B. MAN'S MORAL CONSTITUTION

By this we mean those powers which fit man for right or wrong action. "These powers are intellect, sensibility, and will, together with that peculiar power of discrimination and impulsion, which we call conscience."[7] Intellect enables man to discern between what is right and what is wrong; sensibility appeals to him to do the one or the other, and will decides the issue. But in connection with these powers, there is another which involves them all, and without which there can be no moral action. This is conscience. It applies the moral law to us in particular cases and urges compliance with it. It is hardly necessary in this connection to treat intellect and sensibility, but conscience and will must be considered.

1. Conscience.   Conscience is the knowledge of self in relation to a known law of right and wrong. The term "conscience" never occurs in the Old Testament, but it appears about thirty times in the New Testament. It comes from the Greek word *suneidesis*, which means "an accompanying knowledge." It is a knowing of our moral acts and states in connection with some moral standard or law which is conceived of as our true self and, therefore, as having authority over us. More specifically, conscience is discriminative and impulsive; it declares our acts and states to conform or not to conform with the standard, and it declares those acts and states which conform to be obligatory. The office of conscience is to bear witness (Rom. 2:15). The feeling of remorse and fear of punishment that follow disregard of that which conscience has pointed out as obligatory, are not properly products of conscience, but of sensibility.

Two questions are often asked concerning conscience. First, is conscience indestructible? And secondly, is it infallible? With regard to the first, Scripture teaches that conscience may be defiled (1 Cor. 8:7; Titus 1:15; cf. Heb. 9:14; 10:22) and seared (1 Tim. 4:2), but nowhere does it intimate that conscience can be destroyed. Hardened sinners are often aroused by the

---

[7]Strong, *Systematic Theology*, p. 497.

accusing, condemning testimony of conscience so that they experience great agonies of remorse. Further, the accusing conscience will probably be the chief torment of lost souls in hell.

With regard to the second question, conscience judges according to the standard given to it. If the moral standard accepted by the intellect is imperfect, the decisions of conscience, though relatively just, may be wholly unjust. Conscience is uniform and infallible, in the sense that it always decides rightly according to the law given to it. Saul, before his conversion, was a conscientious wrongdoer (Acts 24:16). His spirit and character were commendable, while his conduct was reprehensible. Paul's reason had accepted a certain interpretation of the Old Testament, and his conscience testified as to whether he conformed to it or not. The standard by which conscience judges is the intuitive knowledge of the existence of God and moral qualities with which God has endowed man. But since this knowledge has become perverted through sin, it does not form a sound basis of judgment. Conscience also judges according to the social standards which we have accepted. The only true standard for conscience is the Word of God as interpreted by the Holy Spirit (Rom. 9:1). When it judges according to other standards, its decisions are not infallible; but when it judges according to the divinely inspired Scriptures, its verdict is absolutely infallible.

2. Will. "Will is the soul's power to choose between motives and to direct its subsequent activity according to the motive thus chosen."[8] Usually human faculties are divided into three: intellect, sensibility, and will. They relate logically; the soul must know before feeling, and feel before willing. Man's will is free in the sense that man can choose to do anything in keeping with his nature. Man can will to walk, but not to fly. To walk is in keeping with his nature, but to fly is not. Man's will is not free in that he is limited to his nature. This is likewise true in the moral realm. Adam could will to sin or not to sin. After the fall, man's ability to sin became inability not to sin. Man now may desire to change (Rom. 7:18), but he is unable by merely willing to change his moral state. His evil course of action will be certain (Rom. 3:10–18) though not necessitated. Man remains "responsible for all effects of will, as well as for will itself; for voluntary affections, as well as for voluntary acts."[9] The Spirit of God works through the will of man to turn him to God, so that man wills to do God's will (John 7:17; Phil. 2:13). Man's will being brought into harmony with God's will is clearly expressed in John 1:12f.: "But as many as received Him, to them He gave the right to become children of God, even to those who believe in His name, who were born not of blood, nor of the will of the flesh, nor of the will of man, but of God."

[8]Bancroft, *Christian Theology*, p. 146.
[9]Strong, *Systematic Theology*, p. 509.

C. The Origin of the Soul

For the sake of simplicity, the term "soul" in this connection denotes man's entire immaterial nature, both soul and spirit. Three distinct theories have been held with regard to the origin of the soul: pre-existence, creationism, and traducianism.

1. The theory of pre-existence. According to this theory, souls have existed in a previous state and enter the human body at some point in the early development of the body. Some have felt that the disciples of Christ were influenced by this view when they said of the man born blind, "Who sinned, this man or his parents, that he should be born blind?" (John 9:2). This is not certain, but we know that Plato, Philo, and Origen held this view. Plato taught it to explain man's possession of ideas which he had not derived from sense; Philo, to account for the soul's imprisonment in the body; and Origen, to justify the disparity of conditions in which men enter the world. Some have held this view in order to account for inherited depravity. They suppose that it can be accounted for only on the ground of a personal act of self-determination in a previous state of being.

But the theory has no warrant in Scripture. Indeed, it contradicts Paul's teaching that all sin and death are the result of Adam's sin (Rom. 5:14–19). This theory holds that it is the result of sin in a previous existence, but we have no recollection of such a pre-existence. Surely, if we were personal entities in such an existence, we ought to be able to recall something about it; if we were not, it is inconceivable how we could commit sin and bring woe upon ourselves in the present existence.

2. The creation theory. According to this view, the soul is an immediate creation of God. It enters the body at an early stage of the development of the body, probably at conception. The body alone is propagated from past generations. This view preserves the spiritual nature of the soul. It retains the biblical distinction between body and soul by not having immortal soul spring from natural body. It also answers the question of how Christ did not inherit a sinful soul from his mother. Certain passages of Scripture that speak of God as the creator of the soul and the spirit (Num. 16:22; Eccl. 12:7; Isa. 57:16; Zech. 12:1; Heb. 12:9) are cited in support of this view. Aristotle, Ambrose, Jerome, and Pelagius, and in more recent times Anselm, Aquinas, and most of the Roman Catholic and Reformed theologians, have held this view. The Lutheran theologians have almost without exception been traducianists.[10]

To this theory we reply: (1) The references that speak of God as the creator

[10]For a good defense of creationism see Berkhof, *Systematic Theology*, pp. 199–201.

of the soul imply mediate creation. God is with equal clearness represented as also being the creator of the body (Ps. 139:13f.; Jer. 1:5); yet we do not interpret this as meaning immediate creation, but mediate. God is present in all natural generation, but mediately rather than immediately. (2) Scripture speaks of Levi being "in the loins of his father" (Heb. 7:10). This would suggest traducianism. (3) Men often resemble their ancestors in spirit as well as in body. Mullins says, "If heredity explains similar bodily traits, it more satisfactorily accounts also for the spiritual resemblances."[11] If the father begets only the body of his child, then the beast has "nobler powers of propagation than man; for the beast multiplies himself after his own image."[12] Creationism cannot account for the fact that children resemble their parents in intellectual and spiritual as well as in physical respects. Physiology properly views soul not as something added from without, but as the animating principle of the body from the beginning and as having a determining influence upon its whole development. It seems clear that the life germ carries mentality and personality, just as it carries size, color, sex, etc. Evidence points to the conclusion that normal character qualities are inherited as well as the abnormal. (4) This theory does not account for the tendency of all men to sin. God must either have created each soul in a condition of sinfulness, or the very contact of the soul with the body must have corrupted it. In the first instance, God is the direct author of sin; in the second, the indirect.

3. The traducian theory.   This theory holds that the human race was immediately created in Adam, with respect to the soul as well as the body, and that both are propagated from him by natural generation. Tertullian seems to have originated this view, though he had an overly materialistic conception of the soul. Augustine wavered in his statements regarding the origin of the soul, and some consider him a creationist while others reckon him among the traducianists. The Lutheran theologians generally have held the traducian view. The traducian theory seems best to accord with Scripture, which, as Shedd says, "teaches that man is a species, and the idea of a species implies the propagation of the *entire* individual out of it." He adds, "Individuals, generally, are not propagated in parts, but as wholes. In Gen. 1:26, 27, the man and the woman together are denominated 'man.'"[13] In Gen. 5:2 God called the two "man," that is, he treated them as a species. In Rom. 7:1 the term "person [man]" seems to be used of both husband and wife. In harmony with this, Jesus was called the "son of man," although only the woman had a part in his human origin. In Matt. 12:35 and 1 Cor. 15:21 the

---

[11]Mullins, *The Christian Religion in its Doctrinal Expression*, p. 263.
[12]Strong, *Systematic Theology*, p. 492.
[13]Shedd, *Dogmatic Theology*, II, p. 19.

term "man" likewise means both sexes. Furthermore, the likeness to himself in which Adam begat a son (Gen. 5:3) can hardly be restricted to the body. It includes the soul. "In sin my mother conceived me" (Ps. 51:5), can only mean that David inherited a depraved soul from his mother. In Gen. 46:26 we read of the persons who, according to the Hebrew term, came out of Jacob's loins. Acts 17:26 teaches that God "made from one, every nation." This most naturally means that they are descended from one pair and have one common human nature as to their whole constitution. Gen. 2:1–3 teaches that the work of creation was completed on the sixth day. This could not be the case if God daily, hourly, and momentarily created souls.

Further, this theory seems best to accord with theology. Our participation in Adam's sin is best explained by this theory. Sin came into the world by a self-determined act and is chargeable upon every individual man. This requires that the posterity of Adam and Eve should, in some way or other, partake of it. They could not partake of it as individuals, and hence they must partake of it as a race. To say that they partook of it in the person of their representative, Adam, raises more questions than it answers. We then ask, On what ground was Adam chosen as our representative? Why did not God choose an angel to represent us? We also ask, How can God condemn man for a sin which he committed in such an indirect way (Rom. 5:18)? But if God chose Adam and Eve because they were the race, then their sin was the sin of the race. Then we sinned in Adam in the same way as Levi paid tithes in Abraham (Heb. 7:9f.). In addition, the transmission of a sinful nature is best explained by the traducian theory. Numerous Scriptures intimate that we have derived our sinful nature by natural generation (Job 14:4; 15:14; Ps. 51:5; 58:3; John 3:6; Eph. 2:3).

Shedd says:

> On this scheme, the justice and propriety of each particular, and of the whole are apparent. The first sin, which it must be remembered consisted of both an internal lust and an external act, of both an inclination and a volition, is justly imputed to the common nature because it was voluntarily committed by it; is justly inherent in the common nature, because justly imputed; and is justly propagated with the common nature because justly inherent. This scheme if taken entire is ethically consistent. But if mutilated by the omission of one or more particulars, its ethical consistency is gone.[14]

4. Objections to traducianism.   Objections have been raised against the theory of traducianism. (1) It is maintained that on the traducian theory Christ must have taken into union with himself the sinful nature of Mary. To this we reply that his human nature was perfectly sanctified in and by his

[14]Shedd, *Dogmatic Theology,* II, p. 43.

conception by the Holy Spirit; or better, the human nature which he took from Mary was sanctified before he took it into union with himself (Luke 1:35; John 14:30; Rom. 8:3; 2 Cor. 5:21; Heb. 4:15; 7:26; 1 Pet. 1:19; 2:22). It was delivered from both the condemnation and corruption of sin. (2) It is held that traducianism implies a division of substance, and that all division implies extended material substance. To this we reply that this is true of divisibility by man, but not by God. He can divide and distribute a primary substance that is not visible by a method wholly different from that by which man divides a material substance. We have an example of this even in the propagation of the body. In this instance we have the derivation of physical life from specific physical life, and this is division of life. The same thing is true in the transmission of the soul of animals. (3) It is objected that if the first sin of Adam and Eve was imputed to man because of the natural headship of our first parents, then all their sinful acts ought to be imputed to their posterity as well. However, the sinful acts of the two after the fall differed from the act in the first instance. It was only the first prohibition that was of a probationary nature; their subsequent acts were of a different nature. The first sin was not a transgression of a moral law, but the subsequent sins were such transgression. The creationist says Adam ceased to represent the race after the first sin, and the traducianist says that Adam ceased to be the race-unity after that sin.

CHAPTER XVII

The Fall of Man: Background and Problems

As has been shown, Adam is the father of the whole human race. We all descended from him through natural generation. It is on the basis of this that all men have been born sinners, for Adam had already sinned when his first son was conceived. It now remains to be seen how Adam became a sinner, and what God's relation was to Adam's first sin. The background of the fall and some of the problems connected with it come to our attention.

I. THE BACKGROUND OF THE FALL

Before one can understand the fall of man, two other subjects, the law of God and the nature of sin, must be considered. We need to know about the law of God in order to understand the transgression of it, which was sin; and we need to know about the nature of sin in order to understand its origin in Adam and Eve.

A. The Law of God

Speaking generally, law is an expression of will enforced by power; it implies a lawgiver, a subject, an expression of will, and power enforcing that will. The terms "laws of nature," "laws of the mind," and so forth, are contradictions when used to denote a mode of action or an order of sequence behind which there is conceived to be no ordering will and enforcing power. "Physics derives the term 'law' from jurisprudence, instead of jurisprudence deriving it from physics."[1] Some have advocated that because the term "law" is so suggestive of a giver of law, we ought to drop it and speak of a "method" of action, or an order of sequence. But this is taking the position of agnosticism. Law is not an efficient operative cause; it presupposes a lawgiver, and is only the mode according to which the lawgiver proceeds.

1. The meaning of the law of God. The law of God, in particular, is the expression of his will enforced by his power. It has two forms: elemental law

[1] Strong, *Systematic Theology*, p. 533.

and positive enactment. Elemental law is law inwrought into elements, substances, and forces of rational and irrational creatures. It is of two types: natural or physical, and moral. Natural law relates to the material universe. It is not absolutely necessary; some other order is conceivable. Nor is natural law an end in itself; it exists for the sake of the moral order. Therefore, the physical order has only a relative constancy; God sometimes supplements it by miracles. Moral law relates to the constitution of rational and free beings. It implies a lawgiver, a free moral subject, power to enforce the command, obligation on the part of the subject to obey, and sanctions for disobedience. This law is an expression of God's moral nature and intimates that complete conformity to that holy nature is the normal condition of man (Matt. 5:48; 1 Pet. 1:16).

From this, it is clear that the law of God is not something arbitrary, since it springs from his nature; that it is not temporary, devised to meet an exigency; that it is not merely negative but also positive, demanding positive conformity to God; that it is not partial, addressed to but one part of man's being, but to body and soul alike; that it is not outwardly published, but that positive enactment is only the expression of this unwritten law of being; that it is not limited to consciousness of it, but exists whether we recognize it or not; and that it is not confined to any locality or class of people, but includes all moral creatures.[2]

Positive enactment is the expression of God's will in published ordinances. These consist of his definitely moral precepts, such as the Decalogue (Exod. 20:1-17). In the New Testament all but the fourth commandment are repeated and sanctioned. These ordinances consist also of the ceremonial legislation. Such are the offerings (Lev. 1-7), the laws of the priesthood (Lev. 8-10), and the laws of purity (Lev. 11-15). These are temporary, but only God can say how long they are binding. The period of time in which a law is in force varies. Some laws are rooted in God's essential nature, and they are eternal (Matt. 22:37-40; 1 John 5:21). Others are founded upon the permanent relations of men to each other in their present state of existence (Rom. 13:9; Gal. 5:14). Others have their foundation in certain temporal relations of men (Eph. 6:1) or conditions of society (Eph. 6:5). And others are positive laws, deriving their authority from the explicit commands of God. The ceremonial laws of sacrifice, circumcision, etc. are of this nature.

2. The purpose of the law of God. Negatively, the law was not given as a means whereby man might be saved. Paul observes, "If a law had been given which was able to impart life, then righteousness would indeed have been based on law" (Gal. 3:21). It could not make alive because it was weak "through the flesh" (Rom. 8:3). The Scriptures that promise life for keeping

[2]For a fuller discussion see Strong, *Systematic Theology*, pp. 536-542.

the law (Lev. 18:5; Neh. 9:29; Ezek. 18:5-9; Matt. 19:17; Rom. 7:10; 10:5; Gal. 3:12) speak ideally and hypothetically, as if man had no carnal nature and so were able to do God's whole will. Since, however, man is hopelessly enslaved to self, he cannot keep God's law (Rom. 8:7), and, consequently, neither life nor righteousness is possible by the law.

Positively, it was given to intensify man's knowledge of sin, to reveal the holiness of God, and to lead the sinner to Christ. Man knows that he is a sinner by the testimony of conscience, but by the published law of God he has an intensified "knowledge of sin" (Rom. 3:19f.; 7:7). Sin now takes on the form of transgression (Rom. 5:13; 7:13). Paul says, "I would not have come to know sin except through the Law" (Rom. 7:7). He does not mean that he had not known sin in any sense, but that he had not known it as exceedingly sinful. The law was also given to reveal the holiness of God (Rom. 7:12). The nature of the commandments shows this, but more particularly, the ceremonies and rituals, the tabernacle with its court, holy place, and holy of holies, and the mediation of the priesthood were intended to show the holiness of God. Approach to him was possible only on certain conditions, to certain men, and on certain occasions. The ceremonial law sets forth visibly the holiness of God. And, finally, the law was given to lead men to Christ. Christ was the end of the law for righteousness (Rom. 10:4), but he is also its aim. Paul calls the law "our tutor to lead us to Christ" (Gal. 3:24). "The Greek *paidagōgos* was not a schoolmaster, but was a slave who had charge of children from the age of seven to about eighteen. He trained the child in general deportment, took him to school each day, saw that he dressed properly, and was in almost total charge of the management of the boy."[3] The law served in like fashion to prepare those under it for the reception of Christ. This it did by revealing God's holiness and man's sinfulness, and by pointing to the cross of Christ, through its offerings, priesthood, and tabernacle, as the only way of salvation and access to God.

3. The believer's relation to the law of God.   There seems to be a distinct difference in the believer's relation to the law during the present age as compared with the past. The Scriptures teach that in the death of Christ the believer is delivered not only from the curse of the law (Gal. 3:13), that is, the penalty imposed upon him by the law, but from the law itself (Rom. 7:4; Eph. 2:14f.; Col. 2:14). It was at Calvary that Christ became the end of the law for righteousness (Rom. 10:4). That this includes the moral law as well as the ceremonial law is evident from 2 Cor. 3:7-11. It is that which was "engraved on stones," that is, the Ten Commandments, that passed away. As a result, we are told that the believer is not "under law, but under grace" (Rom. 6:14; 7:6; Gal. 4:30; 5:18), and he is exhorted, "Keep standing firm

---

[3]Kent, *The Freedom of God's Sons*, p. 105.

and do not be subject again to a yoke of slavery" (Gal. 5:1). From all of this, it is very clear that Paul does not distinguish between the ceremonial and the moral portion of the Old Testament law.

The believer has been made free from the law, but liberty does not mean license. To offset this danger of antinomianism, the Scriptures teach that we have not only been delivered from the law, but also "joined to another, to Him who was raised from the dead, that we might bear fruit for God" (Rom. 7:4). We are thus not "without the law of God but under the law of Christ" (1 Cor. 9:21; cf. Gal. 6:2). Freedom from law should not result in license, but love (Gal. 5:13; cf. 1 Pet. 2:16). The believer is, consequently, to keep his eyes on Christ as his example and teacher, and by the Holy Spirit to fulfill his law (Rom. 8:4; Gal. 5:18). This does not mean that the precepts of the Decalogue which are grounded in the character of God have no authority today. As a matter of fact, careful investigation reveals that every commandment of the Decalogue, except the fourth, is reaffirmed in the New Testament. They are repeated for our instruction as to what the will of the Lord is, but not as precepts that we are to endeavor to keep in order to become righteous. This would be useless, for, Paul says, "By the works of the Law no flesh will be justified in His sight" (Rom. 3:20). The believer of this age has received the adoption of sons, and with that adoption the mind of the Spirit (2 Cor. 1:22; 5:5; Gal. 4:5f.; Eph. 1:14). By him we have been delivered from the carnal nature (Rom. 8:2), by him we are to keep putting to death the deeds of the body (Rom. 8:13), and by him we shall produce the "fruit of the Spirit" (Gal. 5:22f.; cf. Eph. 5:9).

B. THE NATURE OF SIN

Some theologians understand sin as "lack of conformity to the moral law of God, either in act, disposition, or state,"[4] whereas others define it as "anything in the creature which does not express, or which is contrary to, the holy character of the Creator."[5] No doubt both of these are correct, for moral law is a reflection of God's character. That sin is transgression of law is clear in Scripture (Rom. 7:7–13; Gal. 3:10, 12; James 2:8–12; 1 John 3:4), and that it relates to God's character is also evident. When Isaiah saw God in his holiness, he recognized his own sinfulness (Isa. 6:1–6; cf. Job 42:5f.; Luke 5:8; Rev. 1:17). God is holy and we are to conform to his holiness; anything short of this is sin (Lev. 19:2; 1 Pet. 1:15f.). In the definition of sin several ideas are involved.

1. Sin is a specific type of evil. There are two totally different kinds of evil: physical and moral. Floods, earthquakes, droughts, wild animals, and the

[4]Berkhof, *Systematic Theology*, p. 233.
[5]Buswell, *A Systematic Theology of the Christian Religion*, I, p. 264.

like, are physical evils, not moral evils or sin. It is in this sense that it can be said that God creates evil or calamities (Isa. 45:7; cf. 54:16). Further, the evil of the mentally incompetent cannot be considered sin. Sin is a moral evil. Since man is a rational creature, he knows that when he does what he ought not to do, or omits to do what he ought to do, or is what he ought not to be, or is not what he ought to be, he is chargeable with sin. He becomes both guilty and polluted.

2. Sin is a violation of the law of God.   Sin is want of conformity to, or transgression of, the law of God. Since we are moral and rational creatures, we are of necessity subject to the law of right. The only question is, what that law may be. Hodge points out that it is not (1) our reason, for then every man is a law unto himself and then there can be no sense of guilt; (2) the moral order of the universe, for this is but an abstraction and can neither impose obligation nor inflict penalty; (3) regard for the happiness of the universe, for it is manifest that happiness is not necessarily synonymous with goodness; (4) our own happiness, for such a view makes expediency the rule of right and wrong; but (5) that it is subjection to the rule of a rational being, God, who is infinite, eternal, and immutable in his perfections.[6] The law of God is summarized in the words of Jesus, " 'You shall love the Lord your God with all your heart, and with all your soul, and with all your mind.' This is the great and foremost commandment. And a second is like it, 'You shall love your neighbor as yourself.' On these two commandments depend the whole Law and the Prophets" (Matt. 22:37–40).

Both the Old and New Testaments use various terms for sin and sinning. Some of these are: sin (Gen. 18:20; Rom. 3:23), disobedience (Rom. 5:19), iniquity (Lev. 26:40), lawlessness (Titus 2:14), transgression (Exod. 23:21; 1 Tim. 2:14), trespass (Eph. 2:1), ignorance (Heb. 9:7), godlessness (1 Pet. 4:18), wickedness (Prov. 11:31), unbelief (Rom. 11:20), unrighteousness (1 John 1:9), unjustness (Deut. 25:16), and unholiness (1 Tim. 1:9).

Several specific clarifications concerning the relation between the law and sin must be noted. (1) Failure to do what the law enjoins is as much sin as doing what it forbids. There are sins of omission as well as of commission (James 4:17; cf. Rom. 14:23). (2) To fail in one point is to be guilty of the whole (Gal. 3:10; James 2:10). One needs to break but one of God's commandments to be guilty in his sight. (3) Ignorance of a law does not excuse a man. "That slave who knew his master's will and did not get ready or act in accord with his will, shall receive many lashes, but the one who did not know it, and committed deeds worthy of flogging, will receive but few. And from everyone who has been given much shall much be required; and to whom they entrusted much, of him they will ask all the more" (Luke 12:47f.).

[6]Hodge, *Systematic Theology*, II, pp. 182f.

Ignorance of the law lessens the penalty as to degree, but not as to duration. (4) Ability to keep the law is not essential to make the non-fulfillment sin. Man's inability to fulfill the law is due to his own part in the sin of Adam, and is not an original condition. Since the law of God expresses the holiness of God as the only standard for the creature, ability to obey cannot be the measure of obligation or the test of sin. (5) The feeling of guilt is not necessary to the fact of sin. Man's moral standard may be so low and his conscience may have been so often sinned against, that he has practically no sense of sin left. This, however, does not remove the fact of sin.

3. Sin is a principle or nature as well as an act. Want of conformity to the law of God embraces want in nature as well as in conduct. Acts of sin spring from a principle or nature that is sinful. A corrupt tree can only bring forth evil fruit (Matt. 7:17f.). "For out of the heart come evil thoughts, murders, adulteries, fornications, thefts, false witness, slanders" (Matt. 15:19). Back of murder lies fierce hatred, back of adultery lies sinful lust (Matt. 5:21f., 27f.; cf. James 1:14f.). Scripture distinguishes between *sin* and *sins*, the one the nature, the other the expression of that nature. Sin is present in everyone as a nature before it expresses itself in deeds. Paul wrote, "Sin, taking opportunity through the commandment, produced in me coveting of every kind; for apart from the Law sin is dead. And I was once alive apart from the Law; but when the commandment came, sin became alive, and I died" (Rom. 7:8f.). Paul also affirmed, "Sin . . . indwells me" (v. 17), and he represented sin as reigning in the unsaved (Rom. 6:12–14). John said, "If we say that we have no sin, we are deceiving ourselves, and the truth is not in us" (1 John 1:8). The Old Testament regulation concerning sins of ignorance, or omission, and concerning general sinfulness indicates that sin is not limited to acts, but includes also the conditions from which the acts arise (Lev. 5:2–6).

The opinion of mankind in general concurs with this view. Men universally attribute both vice and virtue to dispositions and states, as well as to conscious and deliberate acts. Thus they speak of a "bad temper," and an "evil disposition." Indeed, outward acts are condemned only when they are regarded as originating in evil dispositions. Criminal law is more concerned about the motive than about the act in the crime. How this evil bent originated does not matter; the presence of it is condemned, whether inherited from our ancestors or developed in experience. Habitual disregard for a law may so deaden the voice of conscience as to make it seem altogether hushed, but that only arouses greater resentment against the man who sins with impugnity. Christian consciousness also testifies to the fact that sin is a principle as well as an act. The spiritually enlightened Christian regards his deviations from the law and character of God as due to a depravity within him and repents for it more deeply than for his acts' of sin.

4. Sin includes pollution as well as guilt.   Insofar as sin is a transgression of the law, it is guilt; insofar as it is a principle, it is pollution. The Bible clearly testifies to sin's pollution. "The whole head is sick, and the whole heart is faint" (Isa. 1:5); "the heart is more deceitful than all else and is desperately sick; who can understand it?" (Jer. 17:9); "the evil man out of the evil treasure brings forth what is evil" (Luke 6:45); "who will set me free from the body of this death?" (Rom. 7:24); "the old self, which is being corrupted in accordance with the lusts of deceit" (Eph. 4:22). These and other Scriptures form the basis for the teaching that we need to be cleansed. "Wash me thoroughly from my iniquity, and cleanse me from my sin" (Ps. 51:2); "purify me with hyssop, and I shall be clean; wash me, and I shall be whiter than snow" (Ps. 51:7); "you are already clean because of the word which I have spoken to you" (John 15:3); "that He might sanctify her, having cleansed her by the washing of water with the word" (Eph. 5:26); "and the blood of Jesus His Son cleanses us from all sin" (1 John 1:7).

This pollution shows itself in a darkened understanding (Rom. 1:31; 1 Cor. 2:14; Eph. 4:18), evil and futile imaginations (Gen. 6:5; Rom. 1:21), degrading passions (Rom. 1:26f.), unwholesome speech (Eph. 4:29), a defiled mind and conscience (Titus 1:15), and an enslaved and perverted will (Rom. 7:18f.). These are symptoms of which the corrupt nature is the source. This lack of ability to please God is also spoken of as "death." Men are said to be "dead in . . . trespasses and sin" (Eph. 2:1; cf. v. 5; Col. 2:13); that is, they are totally destitute of spiritual life.

That man is totally depraved does not mean that every man is as thoroughly corrupt as he can become, nor that he has no conscience or innate ability to distinguish between good and evil, nor that unregenerate man can have no admirable virtues of character such as kindness, nor that man is unable to see and appreciate virtue in others, nor that every man indulges in every form of sinfulness. It does mean that every person is born depraved, that depravity extends to every part of man, that unregenerate man has no spiritual good which would commend him to God, and that he is completely unable of his own strength to change his situation.

5. Sin is essentially selfishness.   It is difficult to determine what the essential principle of sin is. What makes man sin? Is it pride, unbelief, disobedience, or selfishness? Scripture teaches that the essence of godliness is love of God; is not the essence of sin the love of self? "Each of us has turned to his own way" (Isa. 53:6). There is, we grant, a proper love of self. It constitutes the basis of self-respect, self-preservation, self-improvement, and of a proper regard for others. None of these is inherently sinful. What we do mean is such an exaggerated love of self as puts self-interests ahead of God's interests.

That selfishness is the essence of sin is evident also from the fact that all the forms of sin can be traced to selfishness as their source. Thus man's natural appetites, his sensuality, selfish ambitions, and selfish affections are rooted in his selfishness. Even an idolatrous affection for others may be due to the feeling that they are in some sense a part of ourselves, and so regard for them may be only an indirect love of self. Jesus exemplified true unselfishness. He said, "I do not seek My own will, but the will of Him who sent Me" (John 5:30). Paul regarded love as "the fulfillment of the law" (Rom. 13:10). He said that Christ "died for all, that they who live should no longer live for themselves, but for Him who died and rose again on their behalf" (2 Cor. 5:15), and he represents people in the last days as being "lovers of self" (2 Tim. 3:2). These and other Scriptures represent selfishness as the essence of sin, the principle from which all else springs.

II. PROBLEMS CONNECTED WITH THE FALL

It cannot be denied that there are some difficulties connected with the account of man's fall. We shall consider the three principal ones.

A. How Could a Holy Being Fall?

Though the answer to this question is probably beyond human understanding, several things can be noted. (1) Adam and Eve were created morally free, sinless beings, with the ability to sin or not to sin. (2) The temptation to our first parents was different from that of Satan in that their temptation came from without; Satan tempted them to sin. (3) Though solicited from without, Adam made a personal decision to disobey God, and he was held responsible for his sin (1 Tim. 2:14). (4) How an unholy impulse arose in the soul of a holy, sinless being is beyond our understanding. The only satisfactory explanation is that man fell by a free act of revolt against God. Satan acted on man's God-given desire for beauty, knowledge, and food (Gen. 3:6). These desires are inherently good and not evil, when they are used properly (1 Tim. 4:4f.; cf. 1 John 2:16). Satan called for the misuse of these drives against the direct command of God not to eat of the tree. Man freely chose to disobey God and to obey the deception of the evil one. The God-given desire for beauty, knowledge, and food became an instrument Satan used in causing man to rebel. Underlying all of this was the ambition to extend his relative sovereignty to become equal with God and not submit to the absolute sovereignty of God.

B. How Could a Just God Justly Permit Man to be Tempted?

We reply that we see in this permission not so much an act of justice as one of benevolence, and this for several reasons.

1. The need for probation. God endowed man with the power of choice which enabled him to choose contrary to the known will of God, and the possession of this power seems to be the necessary condition of probation and moral development. Man was not made an automaton who would live for the glory of God without any choice in the matter. His inclination was toward God, but since he had the power of contrary choice, he could be confirmed in this inclination only by deliberate choice in the presence of the possibility of choosing the opposite. "A period of probation was essential in order to test their loyalty to God by obedience or disobedience to His command."[7] Probation was necessary even though God foreknew it would result in the fall, and it revealed his benevolence in the promise of redemption immediately after the fall.

2. The need for a tempter. Satan fell without any external temptation. He sinned deliberately, spurred on by undue ambition, and, as a result, has become what he is. Had man fallen without a tempter, he would have originated his own sin and would have himself become a Satan. This only reveals God's benevolence in leaving a possibility for man's redemption.

3. The possibility of resisting temptation. In the temptation itself there was no power to make man sin. He had as much power to choose to obey God as to choose to disobey him. The mere possibility of sinning alone has never made any man commit sin. No doubt, deliberate resistance would have caused Satan to flee then as well as now (James 4:7). It is this possibility that shows God's benevolence. By resisting temptation, man's holy nature could have been confirmed in holy character; it could have been confirmed in virtue.

C. How Could So Great a Penalty be Attached to Disobedience to So Slight a Command?

Several things can be said. It does not necessarily require some great act to prove or to disprove one's loyalty to another. A slight command involving a very small and simple act is the best test of the spirit of obedience. If a child has complied with his mother's wishes in seeming obedience in many respects, and then persists in disobeying in some other matter, whether great or small, he simply reveals his true attitude by his disobedience. Further, the external command was not insignificant. It involved God's claim to eminent authority. By means of the forbidden tree, God taught Adam that he had the right to make demands of him and expect to be obeyed. Man's obedience was to be tested in the matter of property, which was an outward and sensible

---

[7]Bancroft, *Systematic Theology*, p. 149.

sign of a right state of heart toward God. That the command was significant from God's point of view is disclosed by the severity of the penalty announced for its disobedience. How else was Adam to interpret the declaration that if he disobeyed he would surely die? And finally, Adam was not left in ignorance about the seriousness of the matter. In announcing the penalty, God made clear that it was an issue of life and death. Disobedience would be considered a deadly sin. It was a choice between life and death, between God and self.

CHAPTER XVIII

The Fall of Man: Fact and Immediate Consequences

Although human reason is forced to admit the existence of sin, it is utterly unable to account for its origin and its presence in human nature. Scripture declares that man fell into sin through Adam's transgression. We ask, how did this happen and what were the immediate consequences for our first parents?

I. THE ORIGIN OF SIN IN THE PERSONAL ACT OF ADAM

Sin is a fact; but how did it originate among men? There are various views as to this subject. The false views must be evaluated, then the true position presented.

A. Sin is Not Eternal

Cosmic dualism holds that there are two self-existent and eternal principles: good and evil. Persian speculation conceived of these two principles under the figures of light and darkness. Matter was considered inherently evil. The Gnostics and Manicheans accepted this doctrine. According to this view, sin has always existed. The good and the evil have been in conflict with each other for all eternity, and they will continue to be in conflict. They limit each other and neither is ever finally triumphant over the other. This view has grown out of the difficulty of accounting for the origin of evil and still retaining a belief in an omnipotent and holy God.

This theory, however, makes God a finite and dependent being. There cannot be two infinite things in the same category, and God cannot be both sovereign and limited by a thing which he neither created nor could prevent. This view also destroys the conception of sin as a moral evil. If sin is an inseparable part of our nature, it cannot be moral evil. And then it directly destroys human responsibility. If sin is necessary from the very constitution of man, man cannot be charged with responsibility for being sinful. Indeed, by regarding sin as a substance, the theory destroys its nature as sin. We cannot retain the doctrine of man's moral responsibility unless we can show that his sin involves guilt.

B. Sin Does Not Originate in Man's Finiteness

Leibniz and Spinoza held that sin originated in our finiteness. It is but a necessary result of the limitations of our being. God as the absolute substance is supremely good; but if other things than God are to exist, there must be in them, if they are not infinite, a minimum of evil. That is, God himself, the pantheistic God, could not create anything without limitations. This is seen in man's physical limitations; it is to be expected also in his moral nature. Some writers maintain that moral evil is the necessary background and condition of moral good. We could not know moral good if there were not also moral evil. It is an element in human education and a means to progress.

But this theory ignores the distinction between the physical and the moral. While man was created with physical weakness and limitations and could not have gone beyond these native bounds in a physical situation, it does not necessarily follow that he was created with moral weaknesses and limitations. He could have perfectly obeyed God, had he chosen to do so. Man was physically responsible only up to his ability to perform; he had no moral limitations and so was able to obey God perfectly. In other words, his sin did not originate in an imperfect moral nature. Furthermore, this view assumes the pantheistic view of the universe. In holding that God is the only substance, it makes evil a part of God as truly as the good. However, our innate convictions and the teaching of the Bible affirm that there is a personal God and that man is the author of his sin. And again, moral evil is not necessary to the existence of moral good. Strong says, "What is necessary to goodness is not the actuality of evil, but only the possibility of evil."[1]

C. Sin Does Not Originate in Sensuousness

By sensuousness we mean "of, or pertaining to, the senses." Schleiermacher held that sin had its source in our sensuous nature, which would, therefore, itself be evil. More recent writers trace moral evil to man's inheritance from an animal ancestry; the earlier theologians considered it as the result of the soul's connection with a physical organism.

But the senses are not in themselves sources of sin, though they frequently become the instruments of the carnal nature in the commission of sin. Furthermore, this doctrine leads to various absurd practices, as, for instance, asceticism, in which the power of sense is to be weakened. Instead of explaining the origin of sin, this theory really denies its existence; for if sin arises from the original constitution of human nature, we may regard it as a misfortune, but cannot consider it as guilt. And finally, the Scriptures

[1]Strong, *Systematic Theology*, p. 565.

teach that sin was not the original condition of man, but that it arose from man's deliberate, unconstrained choice.

D. Sin Originated in the Free Act of Adam

If sin is not eternal nor due to man's finiteness or sensuousness, how did it originate? The fact that it is universally present requires us to go to the fountainhead of the race for an explanation. The Scriptures teach that through one sin of one man, sin came into the world, and with it all the universal consequences of sin (Rom. 5:12–19; 1 Cor. 15:21f.). This one man was Adam and this one sin was the partaking of the fruit of the tree of the knowledge of good and evil (Gen. 3:1–7; 1 Tim. 2:13f.).

That the account of the fall in Gen. 3:1–7 is historical is evident from the fact that it is related as history, stands in a context of historical facts, and is regarded by later writers as historical. In allegorical literature characters either have no names or their names are symbolic. The names Adam and Eve are not symbolic. The narrative is straightforward and simple. Again, the garden, the rivers, the trees, and the animals are manifestly literal historical facts; how can it be imagined that surrounded by such a context the story of the fall is allegorical? Christ and the apostles treat the account as historical (John 8:44; 2 Cor. 11:3; Rev. 12:9). Furthermore, the serpent is neither a figurative designation of Satan, nor is it Satan in the form of a serpent. The real serpent was the agent in Satan's hand. This is evident from the description of this reptile in Gen. 3:1 and the curse pronounced upon it in 3:14.

The test consisted in the prohibition to eat of the tree of the knowledge of good and evil. It seems as if there may have been a life-preserving quality in the fruit of the tree of life, for when God drove Adam and Eve out of the garden, he did this "lest he stretch out his hand, and take also from the tree of life, and eat, and live forever" (Gen. 3:22). It may be that the tree of the knowledge of good and evil had in it a mysterious quality which would effect the twofold result indicated by its name.[2] It is, however, more probable that this tree merely served the purpose of a test, for the partaking of it did not give Adam the ability to tell what was good and what was evil. He still had to consult the Word of God for that. Adam knew cognitively that it was wrong to disobey and good to obey, but he did not have this knowledge experientially. A lack of knowledge of good and evil is immaturity (Isa. 7:15f.), and knowledge of it is moral maturity (2 Sam. 14:17–20). The tree of knowledge was itself good, and its fruit was good, for God made it; it was not the tree but the disobedience which had death in it. In other words, God set before man two good things: the tree of life and the tree of the knowledge of good

---

[2]For a fuller discussion from one who concurs with this position, see Custance, *The Nature of the Forbidden Fruit.*

and evil, and not one good thing and one bad thing. He forbade the partaking of one tree, not because it was bad, but because he wanted to make a simple test of man's obedience to his will.

There is nothing in this prohibition that suggests that God sought man's downfall. It is a fair and simple requirement of the creator. There is, instead, much to show that God made obedience easy. He created man without a sinful nature, placed him in an ideal environment, provided for all his temporal needs, endowed him with strong mental powers, gave him work to engage his hands and his mind, provided a life-partner for him, warned him of the consequences of disobedience, and entered into personal fellowship with him. Surely, God cannot be blamed for man's apostasy.

Satan's temptation may be summed up as appealing to man in this way: it made man desire to have what God had forbidden, to know what God had not revealed, and to be what God had not intended for him to be. Satan first sought to instill doubt of God's goodness in Eve's mind. He said, "Indeed, has God said, 'You shall not eat from any tree of the garden'?" (Gen. 3:1). When she replied that he had permitted them to eat of all the trees but the tree of the knowledge of good and evil, Satan denied the truthfulness of God's declaration that disobedience would result in death. "You surely shall not die! For God knows that in the day you eat from it your eyes will be opened, and you will be like God, knowing good and evil" (vss. 4f.). Eve apparently began to believe both these things, and then speedily took the remaining steps that led to the overt act of sin. We read that "when the woman saw that the tree was good for food, and that it was a delight to the eyes, and that the tree was desirable to make one wise, she took from its fruit and ate; and she gave also to her husband with her, and he ate" (v. 6). That is, through "the lust of the flesh and the lust of the eyes and the boastful pride of life" (1 John 2:16), she fell. To summarize, the woman fell by deception; the man by affection (Gen. 3:13, 17; 1 Tim. 2:14). It is to be noted that Adam, not Eve, is regarded as the one through whom sin was introduced into the race (Rom. 5:12, 14; 1 Cor. 15:22). Christ, the second Adam, met similar temptations, but he came forth victoriously out of them all (Matt. 4:1–11; Luke 4:1–13).

The progress leading toward the first sin seems to be something like this: Eve distrusted the goodness of God; she believed the lie of Satan; she yielded to her physical appetite; she submitted to an inordinate desire for the beautiful; and she coveted wisdom that was not intended for her. Adam, it seems, sinned because of his love for Eve and in the full light of the warning of God. But this does not trace sin to its roots. The first sin was the desire in the heart, the choosing of self-interests rather than God's interests, the preferring of self to God, the making of self the chief end rather than God. The overt act merely expressed the sin that had already been committed in the heart (cf. Matt. 5:21f., 27f.).

II. THE IMMEDIATE CONSEQUENCES OF ADAM'S SIN

Immediate, far-reaching, and fearful were the consequences of the sin of our first parents. It is difficult to suppress the desire to know what would have happened if they had not sinned, but the Scriptures are silent on the subject, and one must refrain from speculating where God has not seen fit to give definite revelation. It may be assumed, however, that the consequences of obedience would have been as great in the right direction as the consequences of disobedience have been in the wrong direction. Farther than this we cannot go. We can, however, look at what did happen to Adam and Eve and their environment as a result of their sin. The first sin had an effect on our first parents' relation to God, on their nature, on their bodies, and on their environment.

A. ITS EFFECT ON THEIR RELATION TO GOD

Before the fall, God and Adam were in fellowship with each other; after the fall, that fellowship was broken. Our first parents now had the sense of God's displeasure with them; they had disobeyed his explicit command not to eat of the tree of the knowledge of good and evil, and they were guilty. They knew that they had lost their standing before God and that his condemnation rested upon them. So instead of seeking his fellowship, they now tried to flee from him. Their guilty consciences did not permit them any rest, so they tried to shift the responsibility. Adam said that Eve, the woman whom God had given to him, had led him into sin (Gen. 3:12); Eve, in turn, accused the serpent (v. 13). Both were guilty, but both tried to shift the responsibility of their sin to others.

B. ITS EFFECT ON THEIR NATURE

When Adam and Eve came from the hand of the creator, they were not only innocent, but also holy. They had no sinful nature. Now they had a sense of shame, degradation, and pollution. There was something to hide. They were naked and could not appear before God in their fallen condition. It was this sense of unfitness that led them to make for themselves aprons of fig leaves (Gen. 3:7). They were not only ashamed to appear before God in their new condition, but also to appear before one another. They were morally ruined. God had said to Adam regarding the forbidden tree, "In the day that you eat from it you shall surely die" (Gen. 2:17). This death is first of all spiritual, a separation of the soul from God. It implies not only the inability to do anything well-pleasing to God, but also the possession of a corrupt nature. Thus, "through one man sin entered into the world" (Rom. 5:12).

That sin entered the world through Adam means that sin commenced its course in the race and man began to commit sin, that human nature became corrupt, and that man became guilty. Man was constituted a sinner (Rom. 5:19). Actual transgression proceeds from man's sinful nature.[3]

C. Its Effect on Their Bodies

When God said that for disobedience man would "surely die" (Gen. 2:17), he included the body. Immediately after the trespass, God said to Adam, "You are dust, and to dust you shall return" (Gen. 3:19). The words of Paul, "As in Adam all die" (1 Cor. 15:22), have reference primarily to physical death. Paul's subject is the physical resurrection, and he sets it over against the fact of physical death. When he wrote that "through one man sin entered into the world, and death through sin" (Rom. 5:12), he included the full concept of death: physical, spiritual, and eternal. Further, because the resurrection of the body is a part of redemption (Rom. 8:23), we can infer that the death of the body is a consequence of Adam's sin.

Yet those who reject the doctrine of original sin hold that death is a natural evil, flowing from man's original constitution, and that it is consequently no more a proof that all men are sinners than the death of brutes is a proof that they are sinners. It is sufficient to remark that men are not brutes, and that the Scriptures teach that physical death is part of the penalty of sin (Gen. 3:19; Job 5:18f.; 14:1–4; Rom. 5:12; 6:23; 1 Cor. 15:21f., 56; 2 Cor. 5:1f., 4; 2 Tim. 1:10).

What if man had not sinned? He would, no doubt, have continued in holiness and have been confirmed in holiness; holy nature would have become holy character. But what about the body? Scripture does not tell us, but it seems that the natural (soulish) body would have been changed into a spiritual body much like the changed bodies at the return of Christ (cf. Gen. 2:7 with 1 Cor. 15:44–49).

Physical illness is also due to sin. The Hebrew of Gen. 2:17 may be translated, "dying you shall die." From the moment that man ate of the forbidden tree he became a dying creature. Corruption was introduced on that very occasion. The pains which both man and woman should suffer grew out of that one apostasy. The fact that man did not die instantaneously was due to God's gracious purpose of redemption. Because of the intimate relation between mind and body, we may assume that the mental as well as the physical powers were weakened and began to decay. This is not to say that every sickness is a direct result of a personal act of sin (Job 1, 2; John 9:3; 2 Cor. 12:7), but that ultimately and finally, physical and mental sickness are a result of Adam's sin. This element of the penalty of sin alone undermines

---

[3]For a good discussion of the meaning of Rom. 5:12 see Hodge, *Commentary on the Epistle to the Romans,* pp. 144–155.

the theory of evolution. Man has not developed greater strength of body and mind, but has degenerated from a primitive perfect condition to the present enfeebled and imperfect condition.

D. ITS EFFECT ON THEIR ENVIRONMENT

We read that the serpent was cursed "more than all cattle, and more than every beast of the field" (Gen. 3:14). It is evident that animal creation has suffered as a result of Adam's sin. In the future age this curse will be removed, and the ravenous wild beasts will lie down together with the docile domestic animals (Isa. 11:6–9; 65:25; Hos. 2:18). God said, "Cursed is the ground because of you; in toil you shall eat of it all the days of your life. Both thorns and thistles it shall grow for you; and you shall eat the plants of the field; by the sweat of your face you shall eat bread, till you return to the ground" (Gen. 3:17–19). Even inanimate nature is represented as suffering the curse of man's sin. In view of this, Scripture tells us elsewhere that the time is coming when "the creation itself also will be set free from its slavery to corruption into the freedom of the glory of the children of God. For we know that the whole creation groans and suffers the pains of childbirth together until now" (Rom. 8:21f.). Isa. 35 speaks of the restoration of nature to its pristine condition and beauty. Adam and Eve were expelled from the garden and forced to make their way in this fallen world. At first they were in the most beautiful and perfect environment; now they were obliged to get along in an imperfect and almost hostile one. Their environment was decidedly changed because of sin.

CHAPTER XIX

The Fall of Man:
Imputation and Racial Consequences

Sin is both an act and a principle, both guilt and pollution. As we look about us, we see that this sin is a universal problem. History testifies to this fact in its accounts of priesthoods and sacrifices among the cultures of the world. And every man knows not only that he has come short of moral perfection, but also that every other man has done so as well. Such popular maxims as "No man is perfect," and "Every man has his price," express the conviction of all mankind that sin is universal. Christian experience uniformly testifies to the presence of sin in the heart of man, and the lack of such a consciousness in an unsaved person must be interpreted as a hardened condition.

I. THE UNIVERSALITY OF SIN

Certainly the Scriptures teach the universality of sin. "There is no man that does not sin" (1 Kings 8:46); "In Thy sight no man living is righteous" (Ps. 143:2); "Who can say, 'I have cleansed my heart, I am pure from my sin'?" (Prov. 20:9); "Indeed, there is not a righteous man on earth who continually does good and who never sins" (Eccl. 7:20); "If you then, being evil" (Luke 11:13); "There is none righteous, not even one; ... There is none who does good, there is not even one" (Rom. 3:10, 12); "That every mouth may be closed, and all the world may become accountable to God" (Rom. 3:19); "For all have sinned and fall short of the glory of God" (Rom. 3:23); "The Scripture has shut up all men under sin" (Gal. 3:22); "For we all stumble in many ways" (James 3:2); "If we say that we have no sin, we are deceiving ourselves, and the truth is not in us" (1 John 1:8). The universality of sin is shown also by the fact that condemnation rests upon all who have not accepted Christ (John 3:18, 36; 1 John 5:12, 19), and that atonement, regeneration, and repentance are universal needs (John 3:3, 5, 16; 6:50; 12:47; Acts 4:12; 17:30). When Scripture speaks of men as good, it means merely a fancied goodness (Matt. 9:12f.), or a goodness of aspiration (Rom. 2:14; Phil. 3:15).

This universal sinfulness is not limited to acts of sin; it includes also the possession of a sinful nature. The Scriptures refer the sinful acts and inclinations to their source, the corrupt nature. "There is no good tree which

185

produces bad fruit. . . . The evil man out of the evil treasure brings forth what is evil" (Luke 6:43–45); "How can you, being evil, speak what is good?" (Matt. 12:34). All men are declared to be by nature "children of wrath" (Eph. 2:3); and death, the penalty of sin, is visited even upon those who have not personally and consciously sinned (Rom. 5:12–14). It is concluded that the possession of a carnal nature is characteristic among men universally.

II. THE IMPUTATION OF SIN

If then all men are sinners, how shall we account for this situation? So universal an effect must have a universal cause. The Scriptures teach that the sin of Adam and Eve constituted all their posterity sinners (Rom. 5:19). The sin of Adam was imputed, reckoned, or charged to every member of the race. Romans 5:19 reads, "Through the one man's disobedience the many were made sinners." It is because of Adam's sin that we come into the world with a depraved nature and under God's condemnation (Rom. 5:12; Eph. 2:3). How can we be responsible for a depraved nature which we did not personally and consciously originate and how can God justly charge to our account the sin of Adam? There are various theories of the imputation of Adam's sin to his posterity.

A. The Pelagian Theory

Pelagius was a British monk who was born about A.D. 370. He propounded his doctrines at Rome in the year 409, but they were condemned by the Council of Carthage in 418. The Socinians and Unitarians advocate this general scheme of teaching. This theory holds that Adam's sin affected only himself; that every human soul is immediately created by God, and created innocent, free from depraved tendencies, and able to obey God as Adam was; that God imputes to men only those acts which they personally and consciously perform; and that the only effect of Adam's sin on his posterity is that of a bad example. Men can be saved by the law as well as by the gospel. Physical death is merely the outworking of an original law. "Death spread to all men, because all sinned" (Rom. 5:12), means that all incurred eternal death by sinning after the example of Adam. According to this view, man is well until he personally sins.

To this we reply that the theory has never been recognized as scriptural, nor formulated in a confession by any branch of the church; that the Scriptures, on the contrary, represent every human being as having inherited a sinful nature (Job 14:4, 15:14; Ps. 51:5; Rom. 5:12; Eph. 2:3); that men universally become guilty of acts of sin as soon as they come to moral consciousness (Ps. 58:3; Isa. 48:8); that no man can be saved by works (Ps. 143:2; Acts 13:39; Rom. 3:20; Gal. 2:16); and that Scripture represents man's state of apostasy as the direct result of Adam's sin (Rom. 5:15–19). Besides, Pelagianism wrongly holds that the will is simply the faculty of volitions, whereas it is also, and chiefly, the faculty of self-determination to an ultimate end; that law consists merely in positive enactment; and that each soul is immediately created by God and that it holds no relation to moral law other than that which is individual.

B. THE ARMINIAN THEORY

Arminius (1560–1609) was a professor in Holland. His interpretation is called Semi-Pelagianism. It is the view that is held by the Greek Church, the Methodist body, and other Arminian bodies. According to this theory, man is sick. As the outcome of Adam's transgression, men are by nature destitute of original righteousness and, without divine aid, utterly unable to attain it. Since this inability is physical and intellectual, not voluntary, God, as a matter of justice, bestows upon each individual at the dawn of consciousness a special influence of the Holy Spirit, sufficient to counteract the effect of their inherited depravity and to make obedience possible, if they will cooperate with the Spirit. This they are able to do. The evil tendency in man may be called sin, but it does not involve guilt or punishment. Certainly, mankind is not accounted guilty of Adam's sin. Only when men consciously and voluntarily appropriate these evil tendencies does God impute them to them as sin. "Death spread to all men, because all sinned" (Rom. 5:12), means that all suffer the consequences of Adam's sin and that all personally consent to their inborn sinfulness by acts of transgression.

To this we reply that, according to the Scriptures, man sinned in Adam and is, therefore, guilty before he commits personal sin; that man's sinful nature is due to his sin in Adam; that God is not under obligation to bestow special influences of his Spirit upon man, enabling him to cooperate in his salvation; that men do not consciously appropriate their inborn tendencies to evil at the dawn of consciousness; that ability is not the measure of obligation; and that physical death is not a matter of arbitrary decree, but the just penalty of sin. The so-called New School theory, a departure from the Old Puritan view, is much like the Arminian theory. It, too, holds that men are responsible only for their personal acts; that though all men inherit a constitution which predisposes them to sin, and all men do actually sin as soon as they come to moral consciousness, this inability is not itself sin. Since it is so much like the Arminian doctrine, the arguments against it are the same.

C. THE THEORY OF MEDIATE IMPUTATION

This theory recognizes that all men are born physically and morally depraved, and that this native depravity is the source of all actual sin, and is itself sin. The physical depravity has descended by natural propagation from

Adam, and the soul is immediately created by God, but it becomes actively corrupt as soon as it is united to the body. This native depravity is the only thing which God imputes to man, but merely as the consequence, and not the penalty, of Adam's transgression. In other words, Adam's sin is imputed mediately, and not immediately. This theory makes depravity the cause of imputation, rather than imputation the cause of depravity. Rom. 5:12 means that all sinned by having a sinful nature.

Several things must be said against this view. Scripture teaches that the reason we are depraved is that we are partakers of Adam's sin. Depravity is our fault, not mere misfortune. Depravity is a penal consequence of sin. Further, this view destroys the parallelism between Adam and Christ. Adam's sin was imputed to us, as is Christ's righteousness. It makes salvation a subjective justification rather than the imputed righteousness of Christ. This position also does away with the representative idea that one can be justly punished for the sin of another.

D. THE REALISTIC THEORY

On this view the human race was naturally and substantially in Adam when Adam sinned. In this first sin, man became corrupt and guilty, and this state was transmitted to Adam's descendants. There was an impersonal and unconscious participation by all of Adam's progeny in this first sinful act. Thus, because man was numerically one, the common, unindividualized nature committed the first sin. All men are co-sinners with Adam. In this way sin can be justly imputed and man can be justly condemned because he participated in the sin.

Though this view comes closer to the biblical doctrine of imputation than the previous views, there are still some problems which can be raised. Can man be considered guilty for a sin which was not of conscious self-determination? And can a man act before he exists? Further, if man is guilty for his participation in Adam's first sin, is he also guilty of Adam's subsequent sins? Does Christ, because of his human nature, share in this guilt? Also, does this view give us the type of parallelism required between Adam and Christ?

Of this view, Murray writes, "If we are condemned and suffer death because we are depraved and inherently sinful the only analogy or parallel to this would be that we are justified because we become inherently holy."[1] We are, however, justified by the righteousness of Jesus Christ.

E. THE FEDERAL THEORY

This view holds that Adam is both the natural and the federal head of the human race. The federal or representative headship is the specific ground of

---

[1]Murray, *The Epistle to the Romans*, I, p. 185.

the imputation of Adam's sin. When Adam sinned, he acted as a representative of the human race. God imputed the guilt of the first sin to all those whom Adam represented, the entire human race. As sin was imputed to us because of Adam's disobedience, so righteousness can be imputed to us because of Christ's obedience (Rom. 5:19). Those who hold this view argue that Adam entered into a covenant of works with God and that he spoke and acted for the entire race. There is, however, no mention of a covenant in the Genesis account. In federalism, Adam is the covenant head and his sin is imputed and assigned to his descendants; in realism, the human race actually co-sinned in Adam.

Several objections have been raised against this view. Can man be responsible for violating a covenant in which he had no part in ratifying? It is one thing to suffer the effects of someone else's sin, but can one be considered guilty of another's sin? Further, the analogy between Christ and Adam is not completely parallel, since "one person may obey in the place of others in order to save them; but one person may not disobey in the place of others in order to ruin them."[2] In other words, there can be vicarious penal sufferings, but not vicarious sinning. Guilt or sin can be imputed meritoriously but not gratuitously.

Both the realistic and the federal theory of the imputation of sin have seemingly insurmountable problems associated with them; yet they also solve certain problems. Perhaps there is a mediating position which contains both the representative concept and the natural relationship to Adam.

F. The Corporate Personality Theory

This view stresses the close association of the individual with the group to which he is attached. Any single individual can act as a representative of the group. There are Old Testament examples of this type of representation and association. A family could be destroyed because of the sin of one member (cf. Achan, Josh. 7:24-26). The family name was significant; the child could honor or dishonor the parent's name, and the name could be cast off (1 Sam. 24:21). Even the unit for religion or morality was primarily the whole, not just the individual. This theory argues on the basis of this corporate personality concept that the sin was imputed. Dodd suggests that "the moral unit was the community . . . , rather than the individual."[3]

Paul, in Rom. 5, did not seek to solve the philosophical questions which arise in either the realistic theory or the federal theory. Rather, he was using the Hebrew concept of the solidarity of the race. As Berkouwer writes, "Paul had in mind an undeniable connection and solidarity in death and guilt. At the same time, he nowhere tries to *explain* this solidarity in theoretical

[2]Shedd, *Dogmatic Theology*, II, p. 60.
[3]Dodd, *The Epistle of Paul to the Romans*, p. 79.

terms.''[4] There are some problems with this view. It faces the same problems of arbitrary imputation as does the representative or federal theory, and of involuntary or unconscious co-sinning as does the realistic theory. It does, however, contain a degree of the realistic element, and it has a representative factor as well. To quote Berkouwer again, ''Paul had a 'corporate' idea in mind when he looked at both Adam and Christ; at the same time, that very 'corporativity' can never have the character of an *explanation*.''[5]

Arguments seem to go back and forth between the realistic theory and the representative theory, or some mediating position. Some have even suggested that the parallel between the imputation of sin and the imputation of righteousness should not be considered parallel, but that the imputation of righteousness is judicial and forensic, whereas that of Adam's disobedience is personal and inherent. The fact remains that because of Adam's disobedience we were all constituted sinners, and through the obedience of Christ the believer is made righteous. Scripture does not fully explain how this is accomplished but it does declare it to be so.

[4]Berkouwer, *Sin,* p. 517.
[5]Berkouwer, *Sin,* p. 516.

CHAPTER XX

The Fall of Man:
The Nature and Final Consequences of Sin

The consequences of Adam's first sin may be considered under the following headings: depravity, guilt, and penalty.

I. DEPRAVITY

A. THE MEANING OF DEPRAVITY

Man's want of original righteousness and of holy affections toward God, and the corruption of his moral nature and his bias toward evil is called depravity. Its existence is witnessed to by both Scripture and human experience. The teaching of Scripture that all men must be born again shows the universality of its existence.

B. THE EXTENT OF DEPRAVITY

The Scriptures speak of human nature as wholly depraved. However, the doctrine of "total depravity" is easily misunderstood and misinterpreted. It is important to know both what it does not mean and what it does mean.

From the negative standpoint, it does not mean that every sinner is devoid of all qualities pleasing to men; that he commits, or is prone to, every form of sin; or that he is as bitterly opposed to God as it is possible for him to be. Jesus recognized the existence of pleasing qualities in some individuals (Mark 10:21); he said that the scribes and Pharisees did some things God demanded (Matt. 23:23); Paul asserted that some Gentiles "do instinctively the things of the Law" (Rom. 2:14); God told Abraham that the iniquity of the Amorites would grow worse (Gen. 15:16); and Paul says that "evil men and imposters will proceed from bad to worse" (2 Tim. 3:13).

From the positive standpoint, it does mean that every sinner is totally destitute of that love to God which is the fundamental requirement of the law (Deut. 6:4f.; Matt. 22:37); that he is supremely given to a preference of himself to God (2 Tim. 3:2–4); that he has an aversion to God which on occasion becomes active enmity to him (Rom. 8:7); that his every faculty is disordered and corrupted (Eph. 4:18); that he has no thought, feeling, or deed of which God can fully approve (Rom. 7:18); and that he has entered upon a line of constant progress in depravity from which he can in no wise turn away in his own strength (Rom. 7:18). Depravity has infected the whole man—mind, emotions, and will.

Depravity has produced a total spiritual inability in the sinner in the sense that he cannot by his own volition change his character and life so as to make them conformable to the law of God, nor change his fundamental preference of self and sin to supreme love for God, yet he has a certain amount of freedom left. He can, for instance, choose not to sin against the Holy Spirit, decide to commit the lesser sin rather than the greater, resist certain forms of temptation altogether, do certain outwardly good acts, though with improper and unspiritual motives, and even seek God from entirely selfish motives. Freedom of choice within these limits is not incompatible with complete bondage of the will in spiritual things. Inability consists not in the loss of any faculty of the soul, nor in the loss of free agency, for the sinner still determines his own acts, nor in mere disinclination to what is good, but in want of spiritual discernment, and therefore of proper affections. He cannot of his free will regenerate himself, repent, nor exercise saving faith (John 1:12f.). But the grace and Spirit of God are ready to enable him to repent and believe unto salvation.

II. GUILT

The fact that guilt is considered after depravity does not mean that it comes later. Both of these consequences come upon man simultaneously as a result of the fall. In a discussion of guilt, its meaning and the degrees of guilt must be considered.

A. THE MEANING OF GUILT

Guilt means the desert of punishment, or obligation to satisfy God. God's holiness, as the Scriptures show, reacts against sin, and this is "the wrath of God" (Rom. 1:18). But guilt is incurred only through self-chosen transgression, either on the part of mankind in Adam or on the part of the individual person. Guilt comes from sin in which we have had a part. Sin as pollution is unlikeness to God's character, but as guilt it is antagonism to his holy will. Both elements are ever present in the conscience of the sinner. Guilt is also an objective result of sin, for every sin, of whatever nature, is an offense against God and subject to his wrath. It must not be confounded with the subjective consciousness of it. It is primarily a relation to God, and secondarily a relation to conscience. In conscience, God's condemnation partially and prophetically manifests itself (1 John 3:20). Persistence and progress in sin will be marked by a decreased sensitivity of moral discernment and feeling.

B. THE DEGREES OF GUILT

The Scriptures recognize different degrees of guilt growing out of different kinds of sin. The principle is recognized in the Old Testament in a variety of sacrifices required for different transgressions under the Mosaic law (Lev. 4–7). It is also indicated in the variety of judgments in the New Testament (Luke 12:47f.; John 19:11; Rom. 2:6; Heb. 2:2f.; 10:28f.). The Roman Catholic Church has, however, built up an erroneous distinction between venial and mortal sins; venial sins are those which can be forgiven, and mortal sins are those which are willful and deliberate and involve death to the soul. Over against this, we may note the true differences in guilt as resulting from differences in sin. There are at least four sets of contrasting sins.

1. Sin of nature, and personal transgression. Man is a sinner by nature and by act. There is a guilt of inborn sin and there is a greater guilt when the sinful nature causes man to commit acts of personal transgression. The words of Christ, "the kingdom of heaven belongs to such as these" (Matt. 19:14), speak of the relative innocence of childhood, while his words to the scribes and Pharisees, "fill up then the measure of the guilt of your fathers" (Matt. 23:32), refer to personal transgression added to inherited depravity.

2. Sins of ignorance, and sins of knowledge. Here guilt is determined according to the amount of information the individual possesses. The greater the degree of knowledge, the greater the guilt (Matt. 10:15; Luke 12:47f.; 23:34; Rom. 1:32; 2:12; 1 Tim. 1:13–16).

3. Sins of weakness, and sins of presumption. The amount of the strength of will involved here indicates the degree of guilt. The Psalmist prayed to be kept from presumptuous sins (Ps. 19:13), and Isaiah speaks of those who "drag iniquity with the cords of falsehood, and sin as if with cart ropes" (Isa. 5:18). These are they who knowingly and determinately indulge in sin. On the other hand, Peter in his denial of Christ illustrates the sin of infirmity. He was overcome in spite of his determination to stand (Luke 22:31–34, 54–62). It is interesting to note that there was no sacrifice for willful sinning (Num. 15:30; cf. Heb. 10:26).

4. Sins of incomplete, and sins of complete hardheartedness. The degree to which the soul has hardened itself and become unreceptive to multiplied offers of the grace of God here determines the degree of guilt. A soul may turn from the love of the truth and become completely insensitive to the Spirit's promptings (1 Tim. 4:2; Heb. 6:4–6; 10:26; 2 Pet. 2:20–22; 1 John 2:19; 5:16f.).

III. PENALTY

While it is true that to a certain extent the natural consequences of sin are a part of the penalty of sin, we must remember that the full penalty is of a different nature. Depravity and guilt, as consequences of sin, rest upon mankind now, but penalty in its fullness awaits a future day.

A. THE MEANING OF PENALTY

Penalty is that pain or loss which is directly inflicted by the lawgiver in vindication of his justice, which has been outraged by the violation of law. This implies and includes the natural consequences of sin, but these by no means exhaust that penalty. In all penalty there is a personal element, that is, the holy wrath of the lawgiver, and this is only partially expressed by the natural consequences. In the light of this, it is easy to see that penalty is not essentially intended to bring about the reformation of the offender. There is a difference between discipline and punishment. Discipline proceeds from love and is intended to be corrective (Jer. 10:24; 2 Cor. 2:6–8; 1 Tim. 1:20; Heb. 12:6); but punishment proceeds from justice and so is not intended to reform the offender (Ezek. 28:22; 36:21f.; Rev. 16:5; 19:2). Neither is it primarily intended as a deterrent and preventive, though this end is sometimes secured, for it is never right to punish an individual simply for the good of society, nor will punishment do good unless the person punished deserves punishment. Punishment inflicted by law is not discipline nor remedy, but just retribution. It is not a means, but an end. A murderer is not corrected by being put to death; he is receiving a just retribution for his deed. Capital punishment is a divine mandate (Gen. 9:5f.).

B. THE CHARACTER OF PENALTY

It takes only one word to state the penalty of sin, and thus it is given in the Scriptures: death. It is a threefold death: physical, spiritual, and eternal.

1. Physical death.   Physical death is the separation of soul and body. It is represented in the Scriptures as a part of the penalty of sin. This is the most natural meaning of Gen. 2:17; 3:19; Num. 16:29; 27:3. The prayer of Moses (Ps. 90:7–11) and the prayer of Hezekiah (Isa. 38:17f.) recognize the penal character of death. The same thing is true in the New Testament (John

8:44; Rom. 4:24f.; 5:12–17; 6:9f.; 8:3, 10f.; Gal. 3:13; 1 Pet. 4:6). For the Christian, however, death is no longer a penalty, since Christ has endured death as the penalty of sin (Ps. 17:15; 2 Cor. 5:8; Phil. 1:21–23; 1 Thess. 4:13f.). For him the body sleeps, awaiting the glories of the resurrection, and the soul, absent from the body, enters consciously into the presence of the Lord Jesus.

2. *Spiritual death.*   Spiritual death is the separation of the soul from God. The penalty proclaimed in Eden which has fallen upon the race is primarily this death of the soul (Gen. 2:17; Rom. 5:21; Eph. 2:1, 5). By it man lost the presence and favor of God as well as the knowledge of and desire for God. Because of this, he needs to be made alive from death (Luke 15:32; John 5:24; 8:51; Eph. 2:5).

3. *Eternal death.*   Eternal death is simply the culmination and completion of spiritual death. It is the eternal separation of the soul from God, together with the accompanying remorse and outward punishment (Matt. 10:28; 25:41; 2 Thess. 1:9; Heb. 10:31; Rev. 14:11). This matter is examined more fully in our study of future things.

PART VI
SOTERIOLOGY

Soteriology is the doctrine of salvation. Under anthropology we have seen that every man is by nature totally depraved, guilty before God, and under the penalty of death. Soteriology deals with the provision of salvation through Christ and the application of it through the Holy Spirit. This doctrine will be treated under these two general categories. The first six chapters (XXI–XXVI) deal with the provision of salvation, covering such topics as the plan of God and the person and work of Jesus Christ. The next eight chapters (XXVII–XXXIV) concern the application of salvation. In this section the work of the Holy Spirit; the great doctrines of salvation, such as election, conversion, justification, regeneration, adoption; and other doctrines which relate to the Christian walk, such as sanctification, perseverance, and the means of grace, are considered.

CHAPTER XXI

The Purpose, Plan, and Method of God

Since salvation is the great spiritual work of God in respect to man, it is reasonable to believe that he has a definite purpose, plan, and program. It is these three which are considered in this chapter.

I. THE PURPOSE OF GOD

By his prescience God was fully aware that man would fall into sin and become utterly ruined even before he created him. Still, he created him for his glory and purpose and planned a way of redemption when he "chose us in Him [Christ] before the foundation of the world, that we should be holy and blameless before Him" (Eph. 1:4). This purpose is indicated in human nature and in the Scriptures.

A. In Human Nature

The fall of man occasioned the loss of his original innocence and holiness, but it did not rob him of all his spiritual knowledge.

1. The knowledge of God. The intuitive knowledge of the existence of some God or gods is generally acknowledged. All men have some idea or conception of God, though it may vary greatly. Concerning those who claim to be atheists, it is doubtful if any of them would consistently stand by their avowed position under every circumstance. The Scriptures declare that men have this knowledge also on the testimony of the voice of creation (Rom. 1:20; Acts 14:15–17; 17:22–31). The purpose of God to provide salvation for man is thus indicated in the remnant of the knowledge of God which he allowed man to retain.

2. The knowledge of sin. This is as universal as the knowledge of God (Rom. 1:32). In fact, it is possible to meet with men who claim to be agnostics and yet readily admit the existence of sin. The presence of evil all around them is evidence too strong to be denied. Even those who claim they are "good enough" and need no savior, do not go so far as to say they have never committed sin. The heathen may have conceptions of sin which do not harmonize with Scripture, but they believe that certain things offend the deity in which they believe. "Further, all men have moral notions, even the modern man who by theory does not believe in morality. Although the standard of moral judgments may be much lower than those set forth in the Bible, moral judgments are still constantly being made."[1]

B. IN THE SCRIPTURES

Since the New Testament is the fulfillment and explanation of the Old, we turn principally to the Old for the revelation of God's purpose. It begins with the protevangelium (Gen. 3:15) and continues until the whole program has been outlined. This revelation can be considered from the standpoint of the Law and the Prophets.

1. The Law.   By this we refer to the Mosaic legislation as found in the Pentateuch. First, the theophanies, or appearances of God to Moses, and even to the whole camp of Israel on occasion, served to confirm and develop faith in a personal God. So also did the various miracles wrought in Egypt and during the wilderness wanderings. Secondly, the specifications of divine demands with the announced penalty which would follow failure to obey, served to arouse a conviction of guilt and fear of the consequences of sin. "Through the Law comes the knowledge of sin" (Rom. 3:20). This law is called "our tutor to lead us to Christ" (Gal. 3:24). Thirdly, the establishment of a system of sacrifice and a priesthood to administer it, indicated a need of some method of removing man's guilt as well as the provision of that method by God. It takes the book of Leviticus to fully understand Hebrews.

2. The Prophets.   Through the voice of prophecy, God announced his purpose. The coming of Christ is clearly foretold. Many of the prophecies have his earthly kingdom in view, for that is also a part of God's program of salvation, but we are concerned just now about those which speak of his humiliation for the purpose of delivering us from sin. Sifting these from many others, they tell us the following: Christ was (a) to "bruise" the head of the serpent (Gen. 3:15); (b) to remove ungodliness from Jacob (Rom. 11:26f.; cf. Isa. 59:20); (c) to bear the sins of many (Isa. 53:12); and in order to do this, (d) to make his soul an offering for sin; (e) to pour out his soul until death; and (f) to be numbered with the transgressors (Isa. 53:10, 12). The experience of the cross is graphically portrayed in Ps. 22.

God's revelation is also seen in the numerous types found in the Old Testament in such persons as Adam (Rom. 5:12–21; 1 Cor. 15:45), Melchizedek (Heb. 7:1–3), and Joshua (Deut. 18:18; Acts 3:22f.); such events as

---

[1]Schaeffer, *Death in the City*, p. 112.

the brazen serpent (John 3:14–16) and the wilderness wanderings (1 Cor. 10:6, 11); such offices as prophet (Acts 3:22), priest (Heb. 3:1), and king (Zech. 9:9); such institutions as the passover (1 Cor. 5:7); and such things as incense (Rev. 8:3) and the veil (Heb. 10:20).

Paul says that God has "made known to us the mystery of His will, according to His kind intention which He purposed in Him with a view of an administration suitable to the fulness of the times, that is, the summing up of all things in Christ" (Eph. 1:9f.), and speaks of "the eternal purpose [purpose of the ages] which He carried out in Christ Jesus our Lord" (Eph. 3:11). We are left in no doubt that God has a definite purpose.

II. THE PLAN OF GOD

He who works in an orderly way in nature has not left the salvation of man to haphazard and uncertain experimentation. Scripture shows us that he has a definite plan of salvation. This plan includes the means by which salvation is to be provided, the objectives that are to be realized, the persons that are to benefit by it, the conditions on which it is to be available, and the agents and means by which it is to be applied. It may be added that he has only one plan and that all must be saved in the same way, if they are to be saved at all, whether they be moral or immoral, trained or untrained, Jew or Gentile, whether living in the Old Testament period or in the present age.

A. The Revelation of God's Plan

Scripture must be studied as a whole if we are truly to know God's plan. One may, for instance, note that Jesus said to the ruler who came to him, "If you wish to enter into life, keep the commandments" (Matt. 19:17), and undertake to save himself by good conduct. This would be to miss completely the real meaning of the passage. The Bible is to the theologian what nature is to the scientist, a source of unorganized or only partly organized facts out of which he formulates his generalizations. As it is unsafe for the scientist to draw conclusions before he has made a sufficient number of inductions, so it is unsafe for the Bible student to formulate doctrines out of isolated or insufficient proof-tests. Nowhere is this principle more important than in the study of the doctrine of salvation, for in no field are there more differences of opinion and in no study are the conclusions more far-reaching.

B. The Outline of God's Plan

Certain matters are included in God's plan. The Scriptures teach that God has provided salvation in the person and work of his Son. This Son was made to assume our flesh, die in our stead, rise again from the dead, ascend to the Father, receive the place of power at God's right hand, and appear before God in the believer's behalf. He is to come again to consummate redemption. This work of God's Son was for the purpose of saving us from the guilt, the penalty, the power, and ultimately the presence of sin. This plan embraced also the redemption of nature, which has been subjected to vanity because of man's sin. Salvation was provided for the world in some general sense, but more particularly for the elect, those who will believe in Christ and walk in his ways. Repentance is necessary for salvation, but merely as a preparation of the heart and not as a price paid for the gift of life. Faith is the only condition to salvation, and it is the gift of God. The Holy Spirit is the agent in the application of salvation to the individual soul. He uses the Word of God to bring about conviction, to point the way to Christ, and to regenerate the soul. He continues the work of sanctification in the believer's life. Salvation is not complete until the believer is resurrected and presented holy and blameless to Christ by the Holy Spirit.

III. THE METHODS OF GOD

Although God has but one plan of salvation, he has had various ways of dealing with man in regard to it, and these over a long period of time. The Scriptures intimate that this long time of preparation was needful. They state, "But when the fulness of time came, God sent forth His Son, born of a woman, born under the Law" (Gal. 4:4).

The object of this time of preparation was threefold: to disclose to man the true nature of sin and the depth of depravity to which he had fallen, to reveal to him his powerlessness to preserve or regain an adequate knowledge of God, or to deliver himself from sin by philosophy and art, and to teach him that forgiveness and restoration are possible only on the ground of a substitutionary sacrifice. History shows how imperfectly the world learned these lessons; yet a partial learning of them was necessary before God could introduce the Savior in person. The means God employed to accomplish these objectives are numerous. Though God does not change, his methods often do. He used a perfect environment, conscience, human government, inspiring promises, and the Mosaic law. At present he is using the fuller New Testament revelation, and in the future he will rule personally with a rod of iron. Under each of these tests there was a failure, and each ended in judgment. This will be the case in the present age and in the age to come. This is clearly seen on a closer examination of the Scriptures in their division of time into periods.

A. In the Old Testament Era

God placed our first parents in the garden of Eden, a most perfect environment. He had created them without a carnal nature and made every provision for their happiness and holiness. He subjected them to a simple test and warned them of the consequences of disobedience. He entered into personal fellowship with them. But when Satan came under the guise of a serpent, Eve listened to him, ate of the forbidden fruit, gave to her husband also, and he ate. As a result, they became guilty before God; their nature became corrupt; they died spiritually; and they transmitted the effects of their sin to their offspring. They did not retain the true knowledge of God, but became vain in their imaginations, and their foolish hearts were darkened. God expelled them from the garden after he had pronounced a curse upon the serpent and the ground.

Conscience now became active, and man was given the opportunity to show that the law of God written in man's nature was sufficient to bring him back to God. But Cain himself was a murderer; and though for a time there was godliness in the line of Seth, by and by all piety disappeared. All flesh corrupted its way and every imagination of the thought of the heart was only evil continually. There was no seeking after God. The voice of conscience was insufficient to cause man to seek after God and his way of salvation. God was obliged to visit the world in judgment. Only Noah and his house were saved; the rest were destroyed by the deluge that God sent as a visitation upon man for his sin.

After the flood God gave Noah information concerning human government. Murderers were to be legally executed. This is the highest function of government, and it implies every lesser function. Yet man was to rule for God, and men were to be directed by God through just and holy laws. Men, however, made a great federation and erected a tower for the purpose of idol worship. The glory and pride of man seems to have been the chief purpose in the erection of the tower of Babel. Man had ceased to rule for God and had begun to rule for himself. God, accordingly, came down in judgment upon the disobedient race and confounded their speech. Then the peoples were scattered over the face of the earth and a divided nation arose. The governments did not have God in their thinking, and man degenerated into idolatry.

God then called on Abraham to leave his country and follow him into a new land. Abraham obeyed God, and God made a covenant with him. He promised to give to him a great posterity, to give the land in which he was a stranger to his posterity, and to make him a blessing to all nations. The latter promise looked forward to the coming of Messiah, but was not limited to that event. He and his descendants were to be a spiritual blessing to the nations through all time as well. The promise was repeated to Isaac and Jacob. Jacob and his family moved to Egypt. The outcome was persecution from the Egyptians and divine deliverance from the house of bondage.

At Mount Sinai God proposed the covenant of works, and the people accepted it. They promised to do "all that the Lord has spoken" (Exod. 19:8). But it is evident that the people did not reckon with the depravity of the human heart, nor the power of Satan. Before Moses could deliver the Ten Commandments, written on two tables of stone, Israel had made an idol and had begun to worship it. The story of Israel's failure at Kadesh-barnea, under the judges, and during the monarchy are well known. Under the judges, God several times subjected them to oppressing nations, and after a short time he had the northern kingdom taken to Assyria, and about 135 years later the southern kingdom to Babylon. Some fifty or sixty thousand returned from Babylon, but their conduct was little better.

When Jesus their Messiah came, they rejected him and demanded that the Romans crucify him. Finally, God sent these same Romans to destroy their city and temple and to scatter the people over the face of the whole earth. They honored the law with their lips, but their hearts were far from God. It was proved that legal prescriptions cannot make man seek after God, nor can animal sacrifices change the heart.

B. In the Present Era

A greater change of method has taken place for the present. This is the church period. After all the previous methods, finally the Savior himself appeared. By his death he made atonement for the sins of Old Testament believers as well as for those of New Testament believers (Rom. 3:21–26). God now offers to every man salvation through Jesus Christ. Prior to this age the plan of salvation was, in many instances, but dimly apprehended; now the whole scheme is laid open to every man that will know it. All that is required of any man is to accept what God has provided in Christ. If a man by faith accepts the offer of life, he is born again of the Holy Spirit. The Holy Spirit follows up the work begun in regeneration and perfects holiness in the believer. Simple and clear as this plan is, both Scripture and observation teach us that man does not readily respond to the gospel invitation. Indeed, we are told that as the end of the age approaches, many will depart from the faith and ungodliness will abound. God will take his church home to himself and deliver the rest of earth's population over to the awful tribulation that is to come. But even in the church age unbelief is rampant and the believing are few.

C. In the Future Era

A still greater change is promised to come for the millennial period. Christ must reign in every realm into which sin has entered. He came once and offered to be Israel's king and savior, but the majority turned a deaf ear to his offers. He will come again in glory and take charge of this world by force. As the son of David, he will institute an earthly kingdom. Israel will be the center of that kingdom and Jerusalem will be the capital. All nations will come to worship at Mount Zion. The period will begin with a converted world, for Christ will judge the armies that come against him at Armageddon, judge the nations that sent them, and bind Satan. Only the saved of earth will enter into the kingdom. But many people will be born during the millennium, and they will not all become true believers. Some will yield only feigned obedience. Sin will be put down with a rod of iron, but much conformity will be only outward. The hypocrisy of many will become evident at the close of the millennium, for when Satan will be loosed for a little season, he will secure the adherence of the half-hearted believers. Judgment will fall upon the new rebellion, and Satan will be cast into the lake of fire. The kingdom, too, will not succeed in making the world righteous. Only the grace of God in the individual heart can change the life permanently in any age; and since not all will receive that grace in any age, not all will be saved.

CHAPTER XXII

The Person of Christ: Historical Views and Preincarnate State

God's method of redemption was through the seed of the woman (Gen. 3:15). The redeemer was to be born of a woman, born under the law (Gal. 4:4). He needed to be both human and divine so that he might be the mediator between man and God and reconcile man to God. Reconciliation could only be accomplished through the incarnation, God being made flesh. This chapter will deal with various historical views of the person of Christ as well as a brief study of his preincarnate state.

I. HISTORICAL VIEWS

A historical survey of views respecting the person of Christ shows that there has been a great diversity of views concerning his person; the most outstanding can be mentioned here.

A. THE EBIONITES

This group was a remnant of extreme Judaizing Christianity. They taught that Jesus, the son of Mary and Joseph, so fulfilled the Mosaic law that God chose him to be his Messiah. The consciousness that God chose him to be the Messiah came at his baptism, when he received the Holy Spirit. The deity and virgin birth of Christ were denied. The belief of Christ's deity seemed to be incompatible with monotheism. The heresy in this view is obvious.

A. THE GNOSTICS

Whereas the Ebionites demonstrated a Jewish perversion from the truth, the Gnostics represent a Gentile perversion. This system had a basic dualism running through it: the higher and the lower, the spirit and the flesh, the good and the evil. Because flesh was considered evil, surely God could not become flesh, at least not in the orthodox interpretation of the incarnation. Thus, the person of Christ was approached in one of two ways. Cerinthian Gnosticism taught that the divine Christ came upon the human Jesus at his baptism and departed shortly before Jesus' death. Docetic Gnosticism held

206

that Jesus was actually a kind of phantom, and only had the appearance of flesh. Incipient Gnosticism is touched upon in the epistles of Colossians, 1 and 2 Thessalonians, 1 John, J. ue, and Revelation. The doctrinal error as it relates to the person of Christ is strongly refuted in such passages as Col. 1:15–18; 2:9: Heb. 2:14; 1 John 2:22f.; 4:2–6, 15; 5:1–6; and 2 John 7.[1]

C. The Arians

In the early fourth century, Arius of Alexandria championed the position that though Christ may be called God, he was not true God and in no way equal with God in essence or eternity. Before time was, Christ was created. He, the *Logos* of God, was the first-born of all creation, and the agent in fashioning the world. In the incarnation, the *Logos* entered a human body, taking the place of the human spirit. Thus, Christ was neither fully God nor fully man. Such verses as Mark 13:32; John 5:19; 14:28; and 1 Cor. 15:28 were used in support. The Nicean Council, held in 325, rejected Arianism as heresy and declared that Jesus Christ was begotten, not made, and was of one substance with the Father.

D. The Apollinarians

The Nicean Council did not bring the controversy to an end, for the relationship of the two natures of Christ to one another was not clarified. There was a danger of two extremes; on the one hand, the divine nature could so absorb the human that the human would lose its identity, or on the other hand, the identities of the two natures could be so separate that Christ virtually would be two persons. Apollinaris, taking the former position, argued that Jesus had a true body and animal soul, but not a rational spirit or mind. The *Logos* filled the place of human intelligence. This view did honor to the deity of Christ, but it had the effect of destroying his full humanity. The First Council of Constantinople, held in 381, condemned this as heresy.

E. The Nestorians

Nestorius denied the real union of the two natures of Christ into one person, and implied a twofold personality. The *Logos* dwelt in the man Jesus, so that the union between the two natures was somewhat analogous to the indwelling of the Spirit. This endangered the true deity of Christ, since he was distinguished from other men in whom God dwelt only by the plenitude of his presence and the absolute control that the divine in Christ exercised over the human. The Synod of Ephesus, in 431, condemned this teaching.

[1]For a fuller discussion of the Ebionites and the Gnostics see Berkhof, *The History of Christian Doctrines*, pp. 44–50.

F. The Eutychians

The Eutychians were led to the opposite extreme from the Nestorians. They held that there were not two natures but only one nature in Christ. All of Christ was divine, even his body. The divine and the human in Christ were mingled into one, which constituted a third nature. The Eutychians were often called Monophysites because they virtually reduced the two natures of Christ to one. The Council of Chalcedon, in 451, condemned this doctrine. The Monophysite controversy then took a new turn. Some followers of this view now taught that Christ had but one will. But the Third Council of Constantinople, in 681, condemned the Monothelite doctrine, declaring that in Christ there are two distinct natures, a human and a divine, and that therefore there are of necessity two intelligences and two wills.

G. The Orthodox View

The Council of Chalcedon, in 451, established what has been the position of the Christian church. There is one Jesus Christ, but he has two natures, the human and the divine. He is truly God and truly man, composed of body and rational soul. He is consubstantial with the Father in his deity and consubstantial with man in his humanity, except for sin. In his deity he was begotten of the Father before time, and in his humanity born of the virgin Mary. The distinction between the natures is not diminished by their union, but the specific character of each nature is preserved and they are united in one person. Jesus is not split or divided into two persons; he is one person, the Son of God.

II. THE PREINCARNATE CHRIST

We approach the study of the person of Christ historically in yet another sense, and first of all note some things that show his true being in his preincarnate state. Some of these things have already been mentioned under the study of the trinity, but they bear repeating and some other things should be added here. In the eternal past, Christ "was with God," indeed, he "was God" (John 1:1). This was "before the world was" (John 17:5). He is called "the Word" (John 1:1, 14; Rev. 19:13). A word is a medium of manifestation, a means of communication, and a method of revelation. In harmony with this interpretation, we read in Heb. 1:2 that God "in these last days has spoken to us in His Son." That John conceives of the *Logos* as personal is evident from the structure of his sentence. He says *theos en ho logos*, which means that the *Logos* is God, but does not mean that he is all of God. If he had said, *ho theos en ho logos*, he would have made the terms God and *Logos* convertible terms and so have taught Sabellianism. Paul calls him "the first-born of all creation" (Col. 1:15; cf. its messianic use in Ps. 89:27). This title does not mean that Christ himself was the first one created; "what the title does mean is that Christ, existing as He did before all creation, exercises the privilege of primogeniture as Lord of all creation, the divinely appointed 'heir of all things' (Heb. 1:2). He was there when creation began, and it was for Him as well as through Him that the whole work was done."[2] We know very little of Christ's work during this period, except that the Father through him made the world (Heb. 1:2) and that he chose the believers in him before the foundation of the world (Eph. 1:4).

Scripture repeatedly declares that Christ had a part in creation. John writes that "all things came into being through Him; and apart from Him nothing came into being that has come into being" (John 1:3; cf. v. 10). Paul says that through him are all things, and we through him (1 Cor. 8:6), and that "in Him all things were created, both in the heavens and on earth, visible and invisible, whether thrones or dominions or rulers or authorities—all things have been created through Him and for Him. And He is before all things, and in Him all things hold together" (Col. 1:16f.). These Scriptures represent Christ as creator, preserver, and goal of creation. Particular attention may be called to the fact that when God was about to create man there was first a council in the Godhead. God said, "Let Us make man in Our image, according to Our likeness" (Gen. 1:26). Prov. 8:30 says, "Then I was beside Him, as a master workman."

Although the second person of the trinity often appears in the Old Testament, he is never referred to as Christ. Instead, we have the names Son, Jehovah, and the angel of Jehovah. In Ps. 2:7 Jehovah calls him his Son. More frequently he is called Jehovah. Note the usage in Gen. 19:24, "The Lord [Jehovah] rained on Sodom and Gomorrah brimstone and fire from the Lord [Jehovah] out of heaven." Undoubtedly, this is the same one who is called the Lord [Jehovah] in Gen. 18:13f., 17–20, 33. God said, "But I will have compassion on the house of Judah and deliver them by the Lord [Jehovah] their God" (Hos. 1:7). In Ps. 45:6 Jehovah calls him God. Most often he appears as the angel of the Lord [Jehovah].

His appearances in the Old Testament as the angel of the Lord are significant. As the angel of the Lord, he appeared to Hagar and told her to return and submit herself to Sarah, adding that he would multiply her posterity (Gen. 16:7–14). As such, he appeared to Abraham and stayed his hand when he was about to slay his son Isaac (Gen. 22:11–18). As the angel of God, he told Jacob that he would prosper him in the face of Laban's unfair dealings with him (Gen. 31:11–13). To Moses the angel of the Lord appeared in a flame of

[2]Simpson and Bruce, *Commentary on the Epistles to the Ephesians and the Colossians,* p. 194.

fire out of the bush and asked him not to draw near, for the ground was holy (Exod. 3:2–5). Notice that he is called God in v. 4. Then we read that the angel of God went before Israel when they left Egypt (Exod. 14:19; cf. 23:20; 32:34). Paul says that the rock that followed them was Christ (1 Cor. 10:4). When Balaam came to curse Israel, the angel of the Lord intercepted him and instructed him to say only such things as he would speak to him (Num. 22:22–35). Further, the angel of the Lord came to Gideon when he was secretly threshing wheat to hide it from the Midianites, and told him to go and deliver Israel (Judg. 6:11–24). To Manoah this angel appeared and promised him a son, whom his wife called Samson (Judg. 13:2–24). When David sinned in numbering the people, God sent the angel with a pestilence (1 Chron. 21:1–27). When Elijah fled before Jezebel, the angel of the Lord came and refreshed him under the juniper tree (1 Kings 19:5–7). No doubt it was the same person that spoke to him at Mt. Horeb (vss. 9–18). In the days when Sennacherib invaded Judah, the angel of the Lord came to the rescue of the distressed Jews and smote 185,000 Assyrians in one night (2 Kings 19:35). In Zech. 1:11 the angel of the Lord stands among the myrtle trees and receives the reports of various messengers. And in Zech. 3:1 Joshua the high priest is represented as standing before this same angel. From all these Scriptures, we learn that Christ had a distinct personal existence during the Old Testament period and that he had definite and repeated dealings with the Israelites.

CHAPTER XXIII

The Person of Christ: The Humiliation of Christ

The following Scriptures teach that the pre-existent Christ became man: "the Word became flesh" (John 1:14); "when the fulness of time came, God sent forth His Son, born of a woman" (Gal. 4:4; cf. Rom. 8:3); "who, although He existed in the form of God... emptied Himself, taking the form of a bondservant, and being made in the likeness of men" (Phil. 2:6f.); and "since then the children share in flesh and blood, He Himself likewise also partook of the same" (Heb. 2:14).

The nativity accounts (Matt. 1, 2; Luke 1, 2) give the historical record of the incarnation and trace it to the miraculous work of the Holy Spirit. That the historical Jesus was in fact the eternal Son of God whose coming was predicted in the Old Testament, was the theme of apostolic preaching (Acts 17:3; 18:5, 28). Even secular history acknowledges that Jesus Christ lived. The Roman historian Tacitus (A.D. 112) and the first-century Jewish historian Josephus both make mention of Jesus.[1] It is to the Scriptures that we must turn to determine the reasons for and the nature of the incarnation.

I. THE REASONS FOR THE INCARNATION

There are a number of reasons why God became man.

A. To Confirm God's Promises

He became man in order to confirm the promises made to the fathers and to show mercy to the Gentiles (Rom. 15:8–12). Beginning with the promise in Gen. 3:15 and continuing through the Old Testament, God at various times promised to send his Son into the world. Thus Isaiah says, "For a child will be born to us, a son will be given to us" (9:6), and "Behold, a virgin will be with child and bear a son, and she will call His name Immanuel" (7:14). Micah says, "But as for you, Bethlehem Ephrathah, too little to be among the clans of Judah, from you One will go forth for Me to be ruler in Israel. His goings forth are from long ago, from the days of eternity" (5:2). A

---

[1]Geisler, *A Popular Survey of the Old Testament*, p. 11.

careful examination of the Old Testament reveals that there are two lines of prediction concerning the coming of Christ: he was to come as a Savior from sin, and as a King in his kingdom.

The former purpose of his coming is prefigured in the sacrifices of the Old Testament (1 Cor. 5:7) and is taught in many of the Psalms (16:8–10; 22:1, 7f., 18; 41:9–11) and the Prophets (Isa. 52:14; 53:4–6; Dan. 9:26; Zech. 11:12f.; 13:1, 7). The latter purpose is foretold in many Old Testament Scriptures (Gen. 17:6, 16; 49:9f.; Deut. 17:14–20; 2 Sam. 7:12–17; Ps. 2; 8; 24; 45; 72; 89; 110; Isa. 11:1–10; Jer. 23:5; 31:31–34; Ezek. 37:15–24; Zech. 14:9). Accordingly, when he came he appeared in the double role of Savior and King; as Matthew says, he was the son of David and also the son of Abraham (Matt. 1:1). Gabriel had told Mary that the Lord God would "give Him the throne of His father David" (Luke 1:32), and he himself said, "I was sent only to the lost sheep of the house of Israel" (Matt. 15:24). However, his own received him not (John 1:11); and though the multitude acclaimed him as the son of David when he rode into Jerusalem on a donkey (Matt. 21:9), a few days later the leaders induced the multitude to ask that he be crucified. Thus he died as a substitutionary sacrifice and became the world's Savior and the cornerstone of the church (Matt. 16:18, 21; Acts 20:28; Eph. 2:20; 5:25).

B. To Reveal the Father

In the Old Testament God is revealed as creator and governor. The Old Testament reveals the unity, holiness, might, and beneficence of God. Christ completed the revelation by adding the idea of God as Father (Matt. 6:9). John wrote, "No man has seen God at any time; the only begotten God, who is in the bosom of the Father, He has explained Him" (John 1:18). Jesus taught that to see him was to see the Father (John 14:9), that the Father himself loves us (John 16:27), that the Father knows what things we have need of before we ask him (Matt. 6:8; cf. v. 32), that he will withhold no good thing from his children (Matt. 5:45; John 3:3, 5; 1 John 3:1f.). The relationship of the child of God to his heavenly Father is a precious New Testament concept.

C. To Become a Faithful High Priest

He came in order to become qualified to act as a faithful high priest. Christ came that he might enter into every human experience, apart from sin, so that he might be qualified as a high priest. The Old Testament high priests were taken from among men in order that they might faithfully represent men (Heb. 5:1f.), and Christ likewise was taken from among men for the same reasons (Heb. 5:4f.). "It was fitting for Him, for whom are all things, and through whom are all things, in bringing many sons to glory, to perfect the author of their salvation through sufferings" (Heb. 2:10). There is, then, a perfection that Christ obtained through his experiences here as a man. Note further, "He had to be made like His brethren in all things, that He might become a merciful and faithful high priest in things pertaining to God, to make propitiation for the sins of the people. For since He Himself was tempted in that which He has suffered, He is able to come to the aid of those who are tempted" (Heb. 2:17f.). "For we do not have a high priest who cannot sympathize with our weaknesses, but one who has been tempted in all things as we are, yet without sin," and it is on this ground that it is said, "Let us therefore draw near with confidence to the throne of grace, that we may receive mercy and may find grace to help in time of need" (Heb. 4:15f.). The very fact that he felt the pangs of hunger, the want of sympathy from others, that he had sleepless nights, that he was weary from the toils of life, that he felt every type of temptation that comes to man, that he was misunderstood, forsaken, persecuted, and delivered up to death, was a preparation for his present priestly ministry.

D. TO PUT AWAY SIN

He came to put away sin by the sacrifice of himself (Heb. 9:26). This truth has already been mentioned in connection with the first purpose of the incarnation, but it needs to be set out more specifically as the purpose of all purposes. Jesus said, "The Son of Man did not come to be served, but to serve, and to give His life a ransom for many" (Mark 10:45). It is clearly indicated that he needed to become a man in order to die for the sins of mankind. Hebrews reads, "But we do see Him who has been made for a little while lower than the angels, namely, Jesus, because of the suffering of death crowned with glory and honor, that by the grace of God He might taste death for every one" (2:9); and John wrote, "And you know that He appeared in order to take away sins; and in Him there is no sin" (1 John 3:5).

Several things should be noted. If Christ came to give his life a ransom for many, then we know that he came to redeem men from their sin by his death. Then we also know that his death was substitutionary and, further, that not all, but many will be saved. The idea of putting away sin seems to refer to the scapegoat of the Old Testament. On the annual Day of Atonement one goat was offered in sacrifice, and another was sent into the wilderness after the sins of the people had been confessed upon its head (Lev. 16:20-22). Thus Christ was "the Lamb of God who takes away the sin of the world" (John 1:29; cf. v. 36). As Isaiah says, "All of us like sheep have gone astray, each of us has turned to his own way; but the Lord has caused the iniquity of us all to fall on him" (53:6). And when it is said that he tasted death for every man, the thought is that he did this in place of every man.

Those who believe this truth are saved from tasting it themselves. Paul declares that he who knew no sin was made sin on our behalf, that we might become the righteousness of God in him (2 Cor. 5:21). Christ came to teach men, to aid them in material and physical respects, to give them an example, and so forth, but above all these things, he came to die for man's sins. His death is the foundational requirement of every other blessing we enjoy.

E. To Destroy the Works of the Devil

Shortly after John stated that Christ appeared to take away sin (1 John 3:5), he wrote that Christ also appeared to destroy the works of the devil (v. 8). The Bible says, "Since then the children share in flesh and blood, He Himself likewise also partook of the same, that through death He might render powerless him who had the power of death, that is, the devil" (Heb. 2:14). This was so that he "might deliver those who through fear of death were subject to slavery all their lives" (v. 15).

Christ's coming, particularly his work on the cross, brought defeat to Satan (John 12:31; 14:30). He is a vanquished foe. He has lost his hold on his subjects; some day he will be cast into the lake of fire (Rev. 20:10). Then all that he has wrought through the introduction of sin will come to an end, except for the punishment of those who have been his followers. Stott suggests, "If, then, the whole purpose of Christ's first appearing was to remove sins and to undo the works of the devil, Christians must not compromise with either sin or the devil, or they will find themselves fighting against Christ."[2]

F. To Give Us an Example of a Holy Life

Though this purpose may not be anywhere stated in so many words, it is yet implied in many references. For example, "Take My yoke upon you, and learn from Me, for I am gentle and humble in heart; and you shall find rest for your souls" (Matt. 11:29); "for you have been called for this purpose, since Christ also suffered for you, leaving you an example for you to follow in His steps" (1 Pet. 2:21); and "the one who says he abides in Him ought himself to walk in the same manner as He walked" (1 John 2:6). The writers of the Holy Scriptures were infallible teachers, but they were not infallible characters. Christ was the only one who was infallible in his teachings and in his character. It was necessary that we should have an illustration of what God wants us to be. Christ is the believer's Savior, and he is also his example. To the unsaved the Bible says, believe and live; to the saved, follow in in his steps. This order is never reversed. The most powerful incentive to

[2]Stott, *The Epistles of John*, p. 125.

holiness is not precept, but example, especially the example of one with whom we associate closely. When Moses came down from the mountain where he had spoken face to face with God, his face shone (Exod. 34:29). Similarly, the believer is being transformed into the same image of our Lord by "beholding as in a mirror the glory of the Lord" (2 Cor. 3:18).

G. To Prepare for the Second Advent

Scripture says, "Christ also, having been offered once to bear the sins of many, shall appear a second time, not to bear sin, to those who eagerly await Him, for salvation" (Heb. 9:28). There are two parts to salvation, namely, the provision of it, and the application of it; and the provision of salvation must come before there can be application of it.

Now, manifestly, much of the salvation Christ provided is presently being applied. Believers are saved from the penalty and guilt of sin the moment they accept Christ; they are being saved from the power of sin by Christ's intercession and their yielding to him of their whole being; but they are not saved from the presence of sin until they are taken to be with him. Furthermore, there is the redemption of the body. When Christ died on the cross, he died for the whole man. But bodily healing is not being granted to everyone today, and bodily immortality is wholly in the future. So is it also with the redemption of creation. On the cross, Christ purchased this whole creation, but he is holding back the actual deliverance of creation until the day when the sons of God will be revealed (Rom. 8:18–25). It is as "a Lamb standing, as if slain" (Rev. 5:6) that Christ will open the seals of the book, the title-deed to the purchased possessions. His first coming was necessary as a preparation for his second coming.

II. THE NATURE OF THE INCARNATION

There are several classical passages on this subject. In Phil. 2:6 it is to be noted that the humiliation began in Christ's attitude of mind; he thought that being equal with God was not a thing to be grasped or to be forcibly retained. His becoming man was no personal threat to him. This is an attitude of humility, for the proud are not only anxious to keep everything which they possess, but also to get everything they do not yet have. Two primary things were involved in the incarnation: Christ emptied himself, and he was made in the likeness of man.

A. He Emptied Himself

In the first place, we are told that Christ "emptied Himself" (Phil. 2:7). The Greek word is *kenoo*, and from it comes the word *kenosis*. Unfortunately, many have wrongly interpreted the act which it describes. They say that Christ emptied himself of his relative attributes—his omniscience, omnipotence, and omnipresence—while retaining his immanent attributes—his holiness, love, and truth. It is taught that he had deep knowledge, but not complete; was powerful, but not all-powerful.

This, however, is not the case. Christ repeatedly asserted his divine knowledge. We read that "He knew all men," that "He Himself knew what was in man" (John 2:24f.), and that he knew "all the things that were coming upon Him" (John 18:4). As for his power, we not only read that he rebuked the wind, miraculously fed the hungry, healed the sick, cast out demons, and raised the dead, but that he frequently called on the people to believe him for his works' sake, if they would not believe his words (John 6:36; 10:25, 37f.; 14:11; 15:24). John presented several selected miracles from the ministry of Christ so that his readers might "believe that Jesus is the Christ, the Son of God; and that believing" they might "have life in His name" (John 20:31). Surely, the works of Elijah and Elisha did not indicate that they were God incarnate, since they performed them through the power of the Spirit; but we are called on to believe that Christ is God because of the works which he did. This can only be the case if he wrought them, at least many of them, by the power of his own deity. Christ worked miracles through his own inherent power (Matt. 9:28), the apostles performed them in the name of Christ, and Christ at times performed miracles in the power of the Holy Spirit, and not his own (Matt. 12:28).

Several things did happen in the humiliation of Christ. In some manner his divine glory was veiled, but not surrendered (John 1:14; 2:11; 17:5). He willingly left the riches of heaven to take on human poverty (2 Cor. 8:9). He took on unglorified human flesh which was subject to weakness, pain, temptation, and limitation. He voluntarily chose not to use his prerogatives of deity, such as his omnipotence, omnipresence, and omniscience, to make his way easier. He wearied, travelled from one point to another, and grew in wisdom and knowledge. Thus, though he did not surrender his divine attributes, he willingly submitted to not exercising certain attributes of deity so that he could identify with man. As Walvoord writes, "The act of kenosis ... may ... be properly understood to mean that Christ surrendered no attribute of Deity, but that He did voluntarily restrict their independent use in keeping with His purpose of living among men and their limitations."[3]

It is evident that the Scriptures teach, when taken as a whole, that Christ merely surrendered the independent exercise of some of his relative or transitive attributes. He did not surrender the absolute or immanent attributes in any sense; He was always perfectly holy, just, merciful, truthful, and faith-

---

[3]Walvoord, *Jesus Christ Our Lord*, p. 144.

ful; and he always loved with all the intensity of his being. But he emptied himself by giving up the independent exercise of his relative attributes. Thus he was omniscient, omnipotent, and omnipresent as the Father granted him the exercise of these attributes. This is involved in his giving up the glory which he had with the Father before the world was (John 17:5) and his taking on the form of a servant (Phil. 2:6). That this is the true view is evident from the fact that Jesus speaks of the things that the Father had shown him (John 5:20; 8:38), taught him (John 8:28), and given him to do (John 5:36) as well as from the fact that the Father had given him certain authority (John 10:18), that the Father had "anointed Him with the Holy Spirit and with power" (Acts 10:38), that he, at least at times, cast out demons by the Holy Spirit (Matt. 12:28), that he by the Holy Spirit gave commandments to the apostles (Acts 1:2), and that he offered himself to God through the eternal Spirit (Heb. 9:14). As Müller observes:

> By taking the form of a servant He emptied Himself. Nothing is mentioned of any abandonment of divine attributes, the divine nature or the form of God, but only a divine paradox is stated here: He emptied Himself by taking something to Himself, namely the manner of being, the nature or form of a servant or slave. At His incarnation He remained 'in the form of God' and as such He is Lord and Ruler over all, but He also accepted the nature of a servant as part of His humanity.[4]

B. He was Made in the Likeness of Men

Though he existed in the form of God, he came to be in the likeness of men (Phil. 2:7). The one who was and is by nature God, became man. John declared that "the Word became flesh" (John 1:14; cf. 1 John 4:2f.; 2 John 7). Christ was given a human body (Heb. 10:5) so that God could dwell among us (John 1:14). In Christ "all the fullness of Deity dwells in bodily form" (Col. 2:9). That Christ took on flesh does not mean that he took on sinful flesh. Paul asserts that God sent "His own Son in the likeness of sinful flesh" (Rom. 8:3).

Concerning the expression "sinful flesh," Murray clarifies it, saying Paul "is using the word 'likeness' not for the purpose of suggesting any unreality in respect of our Lord's human nature. That would contradict Paul's express language elsewhere in this epistle and in his other epistles. He is under the necessity of using this word here because he uses the term 'sinful flesh' and could not have said that Christ was sent in 'sinful flesh'. That would have contradicted the sinlessness of Jesus for which the New Testament is jealous throughout."[5]

[4]Muller, *The Epistles of Paul to the Philippians and to Philemon*, p. 82.
[5]Murray, *The Epistle to the Romans*, I, p. 280.

Other Scriptures which speak of the incarnation are Rom. 1:3; Gal. 4:4; 1 Tim. 3:16; and Heb. 2:14. Not only did Christ become man, but while being in the form of God, he took on the form of a servant (Phil. 2:7). Hendriksen explains, "The text cannot mean that 'he *exchanged* the form of God for the form of a servant,' as is so often asserted. He took the form of a servant while he retained the form of God! It is exactly that which makes our salvation possible and achieves it."[6]

[6]Hendriksen, *Exposition of Philippians*, p. 109.

CHAPTER XXIV

The Person of Christ: The Two Natures and the Character of Christ

The study of the purpose and nature of the incarnation leads easily into an analysis of the two natures possessed by Christ: the human nature and the divine nature. What kind of person was Jesus Christ of Nazareth?

I. THE HUMANITY OF CHRIST

The humanity of Christ has seldom been questioned. There were heresies, like Gnosticism, that denied the reality of his body, and Eutychianism, which made even the body of Christ divine, but for the most part the early church held to the humanity as well as the deity of Christ. The departures from the biblical doctrine were in the direction of a denial of the deity of Christ rather than of his humanity. Since Christ must become a true man if he is to atone for the sins of men, the question of his humanity is not merely an academic one, but a most practical one. What are the proofs of his humanity?

A. He Had a Human Birth

Jesus was born of a woman (Gal. 4:4). This fact is confirmed by the narratives of the virgin birth (Matt. 1:18–2:11; Luke 1:30–38, 2:1–20). Because of this, he is called "the son of David, the son of Abraham" (Matt. 1:1) and is said to be "born of the seed of David according to the flesh" (Rom. 1:3). For the same reason, Luke traces his descent back to Adam (Luke 3:23–38). This was in direct fulfillment of the promise made to Eve (Gen. 3:15) and to Ahaz (Isa. 7:14). On several occasions he is referred to as Joseph's son, but as will be noticed, in each case this is done by those who were not his friends or who were as yet imperfectly acquainted with him (Luke 4:22; John 1:45; 6:42; cf. Matt. 13:55). When there is danger that the reader may regard such designations as the true intent of the writer, some explanatory statement is added to show that that is not the case. Thus we read in Luke 3:23 that he was "supposedly" the son of Joseph, and in Rom. 9:5 that Christ is of Israel "according to the flesh."

One important question has been raised in this connection: if Christ was born of a virgin, did he then also inherit a sinful nature from his mother? Scripture is clear concerning his separateness from sin. It declares that he "knew no sin" (2 Cor. 5:21); that he is "holy, innocent, undefiled, separated from sinners" (Heb. 7:26); and that "in Him there is no sin" (1 John 3:5). At the annunciation Gabriel spoke of Jesus as "the holy offspring" (Luke 1:35). Satan had nothing in Christ (John 14:30); he has no claim on the sinless son of God. "It is sin which gives Satan his hold on men, but there is no sin in Jesus as in others."[1] Through the miraculous overshadowing of the Holy Spirit, Jesus was born sinless.

B. He Had a Human Development

Jesus had the ordinary development of human beings. Thus we are told that he "continued to grow and become strong, increasing in wisdom; and the grace of God was upon Him" (Luke 2:40), and that he "kept increasing in wisdom and stature, and in favor with God and men" (Luke 2:52). Christ's physical and mental development are not to be explained as primarily due to his deity, but as the result of the ordinary laws of human growth. However, the fact that he had no carnal nature and that he abstained from acts of sin undoubtedly materially assisted in it. His mental development cannot be ascribed totally to his learning in the schools of the day (John 7:15), but must be attributed largely to his training in a godly home, his regular attendance at the synagogue (Luke 4:16), his visits to the temple (Luke 2:41, 46), his study of the Scriptures (Luke 4:17), and also to his use of the Scriptures in his temptation, and his communion with the Father (Mark 1:35; John 4:32–34).

C. He Had the Essential Elements of Human Nature

That he had a human body is clear from such statements as "She poured this perfume upon My body" (Matt. 26:12); "but He was speaking of the temple of His body" (John 2:21); he "partook" of "flesh and blood" (Heb. 2:14); "a body Thou hast prepared for Me" (Heb. 10:5); and "through the offering of the body of Jesus Christ" (Heb. 10:10). Even after his resurrection he said, "Touch Me and see, for a spirit does not have flesh and bones as you see that I have" (Luke 24:39).

Not only did Christ have a physical, human body, he also had other necessary properties of human nature, such as rationality and voluntariness. He could reason and will. Scripture speaks of him as having a soul and/or spirit: "My soul is deeply grieved" (Matt. 26:38; cf. Mark 8:12; John 12:27; 13:21); "Jesus, perceiving in His spirit" (Mark 2:8); and "Father, into Thy

---

[1]Morris, *The Gospel According to John*, p. 660.

hands I commit My spirit" (Luke 23:46). In saying that he took on our nature, we must always distinguish between a human nature and a sinful nature; Jesus had the former, but not the latter.

D. He Had Human Names

Human names were given him. The name "Jesus," which means "Savior" (Matt. 1:21), is but the Greek of the Old Testament "Joshua" (cf. Acts 7:45; Heb. 4:8). He is called "son of Abraham" (Matt. 1:1) and "son of David," the latter occurring frequently in Matthew (1:1; 9:27; 12:23; 15:22; 20:30f.; 21:9, 15). The name "Son of Man" occurs over 80 times in the New Testament. This name is repeatedly applied to Ezekiel (2:1; 3:1; 4:1, etc.), and once to Daniel (8:17). It is used prophetically of Christ in Dan. 7:13 (cf. Matt. 16:28). That this name was regarded by the Jews as referring to the Messiah is evident from the fact that the high priest rent his garment when Christ applied this prophecy in Daniel to himself (Matt. 26:64f.). The Jews understood this phrase to mean the Messiah (John 12:34), and to call Christ the Son of Man was equivalent to calling him the Son of God (Luke 22:69f.). The expression implies not only that he is truly human, but also that he is the representative of all humanity (cf. Heb. 2:6–9).

E. He Had the Sinless Infirmities of Human Nature

Thus, he was weary (John 4:6), hungry (Matt. 4:2; 21:18), thirsty (John 19:28); he slept (Matt. 8:24; cf. Ps. 121:4); he was tempted (Heb. 2:18; 4:15; cf. James 1:13); he was dependent upon his Father for strength (Mark 1:35; John 6:15; Heb. 5:7); and he wrought miracles (Matt. 12:28), taught (Acts 1:2), and offered himself to God by the Holy Spirit (Acts 10:38; Heb. 9:14). "Christians have in heaven a high priest with an unequalled capacity for sympathizing with them in all the dangers and sorrows and trials which come their way in life, because He Himself, by virtue of His likeness to them, was exposed to all these experiences."[2] Again, it must be born in mind that to speak of the infirmities of Christ's nature does not imply sinful infirmities.

F. He Is Repeatedly Called a Man

Jesus applied this human designation to himself (John 8:40). John the Baptist (John 1:30), Peter (Acts 2:22), and Paul (1 Cor. 15:21, 47; Phil. 2:8; cf. Acts 13:38) called him a man. So thoroughly was he recognized as a man (John 7:27; 9:29; 10:33), that he was known as a Jew (John 4:9); that he was

[2]Bruce, *The Epistle to the Hebrews*, p. 85.

thought to be older than he really was (John 8:57); and that he was accused of blasphemy for calling himself anything but a man (John 10:33). Even after his resurrection, he had the appearance of a man (John 20:15; 21:4f.). Furthermore, he today exists as a man in heaven (1 Tim. 2:5), will come again (Matt. 16:27f.; 25:31; 26:64f.), and will judge the world in righteousness as a man (Acts 17:31).

II. THE DEITY OF CHRIST

The Scriptures and arguments used earlier in the discussion of the trinity to prove Christ's equality with the Father also prove the reality of his divine nature in the incarnate state.

He possesses the attributes of deity; divine offices and prerogatives belong to him; things which are in the Old Testament said of Jehovah are in the New said of Christ; names of deity are given to him; he sustains certain relations to God that prove his deity; divine worship was rendered to and accepted by him during the time of his earthly life; and Christ was conscious of being God incarnate and represented himself as being such. The above is a summary statement of what was considered earlier under the discussion of the trinity.

III. THE TWO NATURES IN CHRIST

This is an area of deep mystery. How can there be two natures and yet but one person? Though this is a difficult concept to understand, the Scriptures, nevertheless, encourage a consideration of the mystery of God, even Christ (Col. 2:2f.), and Jesus indicates that a true knowledge of him is possible through divine revelation (Matt. 11:27). The study of the person of Christ is very difficult because in this respect his is unique; there is no other being like him, and so we cannot reason from the known to the unknown.

A. THE PROOF OF THEIR UNION

First, certain misconceptions must be clarified. The union between the two natures is not comparable to the marriage relationship, for the two parties to that union remain, after all, two distinct persons. Nor are the natures united by the kind of tie that unites believers to Christ. Nor did the divine nature dwell in Christ in the same way that Christ dwells in the believer, for then he would have been but a man filled with God and not God himself. The suggestion of a dual personality in Christ is unscriptural. Neither did the *Logos* occupy the place of the human mind or spirit in Christ, for in that case Christ would have united himself with an imperfect humanity. Neither did the two natures combine to form a third, for then Christ would not have been true man. Nor yet did Christ gradually take on the divine nature, for in that case the reality of his deity would have been dependent upon the conscious appropriation of it by the humanity of Christ and not a fact *per se*. The church at large has definitely condemned these various views as unscriptural and therefore unacceptable.

If the above misconceptions are in error, how can we show that the two natures are inseparably bound together so as to constitute but one person with two consciousnesses and two wills? Though there are two natures, there is but one person. And though the attributes of one nature are not to be attributed to the other nature, the two natures are attributed to the one person. Christ can not be properly described as deity possessing humanity, nor humanity indwelt by deity. In the former case, humanity would not have its proper place, nor would deity in the latter. The second person of the trinity assumed humanity with all its attributes. It follows that Christ's personality resides in his divine nature, because the Son did not unite with a human person but with human nature. Christ's human nature was impersonal apart from the incarnation; this, however, is not true of the divine nature. So complete was this union into one person that, as Walvoord observes, "Christ at the same moment has seemingly contradictory qualities. He can be weak and omnipotent, increasing in knowledge and omniscient, finite and infinite,"[3] and we might add, localized and omnipresent.

Jesus speaks of himself as a single person; he does not evidence a split personality. Further, the individuals with whom he came in contact thought of him as one person with a single and undivided personality. What about his self-consciousness? Jesus evidently was aware at all times of his deity in his divine self-consciousness. It was fully operative at all times, even in infancy. "There is evidence, however, that the human nature developed and with it a human self-consciousness came into play."[4] Sometimes he would act from his human self-consciousness, at other times from his divine, but the two were never in conflict.

The same thing is true of his will. No doubt the human will desired to avoid the cross (Matt. 26:39), and the divine desired to avoid being made sin (2 Cor. 5:21). In the life of Jesus his will was to do the Father's will (Heb. 10:7, 9). This he fully accomplished.

B. The Nature of Their Union

If, then, the two natures of Christ are indissolubly united in the one person, what, in the second place, is the nature of this union? The answer has

[3]Walvoord, *Jesus Christ Our Lord*, p. 116.
[4]Walvoord, *Jesus Christ Our Lord*, p. 118.

already, in large measure, been anticipated in the preceding paragraphs. No exact psychological analysis of the unique personality of Christ is possible, though the Scriptures do give some indication.

1. It is not theanthropic.   The person of Christ is theanthropic, but not his nature. That is, one may speak of the God-man when he wishes to refer to the person; however, one cannot speak of the divine-human nature, but must say the divine and human nature in Christ. This is evident from the fact that Christ had an infinite intelligence and will and a finite intelligence and will; he had a divine consciousness and human consciousness. His divine intelligence was infinite; his human intelligence increased. His divine will was omnipotent; his human will had only the power of unfallen humanity. In his divine consciousness he said, "I and the Father are one" (John 10:30); in his human consciousness he said, "I am thirsty" (John 19:28). It must be emphasized that he is still the God-man.

2. It is personal.   The union of the two natures in Christ is called the hypostatic union. That is, the two natures or substances constitute one personal subsistence. Because Christ did not unite with a human person but with a human nature, the seat of the personality of Christ is in the divine nature.

3. It included the human and divine qualities and acts.   Both human and divine qualities and acts may be ascribed to the God-man under either of his names. Thus we have human qualities and characteristics ascribed to Christ under divine titles: "He will be great, and will be called the Son of the Most High" (Luke 1:32); "they would not have crucified the Lord of Glory" (1 Cor. 2:8); "the church of God which He purchased with His own blood" (Acts 20:28). From these we see that God was born and that God died. There are also divine qualities and characteristics ascribed to Christ under his human names: "He who descended from heaven, even the Son of Man" (John 3:13); "what then if you should behold the Son of Man ascending where He was before?" (John 6:62); "the Christ according to the flesh, who is over all, God blessed forever" (Rom. 9:5); the Christ who died is the Christ who "fills all in all" (Eph. 1:23; cf. Matt. 28:20); the one by whom God will judge the world is the man (Acts 17:31; cf. Matt. 25:31f.).

4. It insures the constant presence of both humanity and deity.   The humanity of Christ is present with his deity in every place. This fact adds preciousness to the thought that Christ is in his people. He is there in his deity, and by the union of his humanity with his deity, also in his humanity.

IV. THE CHARACTER OF CHRIST

As has been noted, one of the purposes of the incarnation was that Christ might set for us an example (Matt. 11:29; 1 Pet. 2:21; 1 John 2:6). It is, therefore, important to study his character in order to know the standard, the ideal, of the Christian's walk. To cast our eyes upon this wonderful person is to say with Isaiah, "Woe is me, for I am ruined! Because I am a man of unclean lips, and I live among a people of unclean lips; for my eyes have seen the King, the Lord of hosts" (Isa. 6:5). John says, "These things Isaiah said, because he saw His glory, and he spoke of Him" (John 12:41). Peter responded in similar fashion as Isaiah when he said, "Depart from me, for I am a sinful man, O Lord!" (Luke 5:8). What was so unique about Christ that would make men like Isaiah and Peter respond in the manner they did?

A. He was Absolutely Holy

He was that "holy offspring" (Luke 1:35), "the Holy and Righteous One" (Acts 3:14), God's "holy servant Jesus" (Acts 4:27). He was holy in nature, for the prince of this world had nothing in him (John 14:30), and he was "without sin" (Heb. 4:15). He was holy also in conduct, for he was separate from sinners (Heb. 7:26). He always did the things well-pleasing to his Father (John 8:29). He "committed no sin, nor was any deceit found in His mouth; and while being reviled, He did not revile in return; while suffering, He uttered no threats, but kept entrusting Himself to Him who judges righteously" (1 Pet. 2:22f.). No one accepted the challenge when he bade his enemies, "Which one of you convicts Me of sin?" (John 8:46). Yet he was "tempted in all things as we are" (Heb. 4:15).

We are to be holy because he is holy (1 Pet. 1:16). However far we may fall from being like Christ, we have no excuse for choosing a lower ideal than the Scriptures hold out for us. If we with unveiled face behold "as in a mirror the glory of the Lord, [we] are being transformed into the same image from glory to glory, just as from the Lord, the Spirit" (2 Cor. 3:18; cf. Ps. 34:5). Christ is our example of sinless perfection, and it is nothing short of absolute perfection. He has shown us how to be holy.

B. He Had Genuine Love

Paul says that "the love of Christ . . . surpasses knowledge" (Eph. 3:19). Christ's love goes out, in the first place, toward his Father (John 14:31). Christ's love is directed also to the Scriptures, in this case the Old Testament. He received these as relating truthfully the events and doctrines of which they treat (Matt. 5:17f.). He used Scripture in time of temptation (Matt. 4:4, 7, 10); he expounded certain prophecies in it as referring to himself (Luke 4:16–21; 24:44f.); and he declared that the Scriptures cannot be broken (John 10:35).

Christ's love also goes out to men, to men in general. When Jesus looked upon the rich young ruler, he loved him (Mark 10:21). He was accused of being "a friend of tax-gatherers and sinners" (Matt. 11:19). He so loved the lost that he laid down his life for them (John 10:11; 15:13; Rom. 5:8). More particularly, he loves his own. John speaks of "Him who loves us, and released us from our sins by His blood" (Rev. 1:5). He loved his disciples to the end (John 13:1); he loved them as much as the Father loved him (John 15:9); he loves his own so much that he gave his life for them (Eph. 5:2, 25); and he loves them so much that no one can separate them from his love (Rom. 8:37–39).

C. He was Truly Humble

This is seen primarily in his humiliation. Though equal with God, he emptied himself, took on the form of a servant, was made in the likeness of men, and then further humbled himself and went to the ignominious death of the cross (Phil. 2:5–8). His humility is also seen in his conduct while on earth. He who was rich, for our sakes became poor (2 Cor. 8:9). He was born in a stable, for there was no room for him in the inn (Luke 2:7); he had no place to lay his head when he went about teaching and healing (Luke 9:58), so that certain women whom he had healed of evil spirits and infirmities ministered unto him of their substance (Luke 8:2f.); he had Peter catch a fish to supply the money needed for him and Peter for the temple tax (Matt. 17:27); and he was buried in a borrowed tomb (Matt. 27:59f.). Further, he associated with the lowly. He was called "a friend of tax-gatherers and sinners" (Matt. 11:19; cf. Luke 15:2). He welcomed the anointing by a woman who was a sinner (Luke 7:37f.) and forgave her sins (vss. 47f.). In fact, the disciples were of lowly origin, and yet he revealed to them the great mysteries of the kingdom (Matt. 13:11, 16f.). Additionally, he engaged in the most menial service. He "did not come to be served, but to serve, and to give His life a ransom for many" (Matt. 20:28). In fact, he washed the feet of his disciples (John 13:14). Though he was the master of his disciples (Matt. 23:10; John 13:14), he really wanted to be recognized as their friend (John 15:13–15).

D. He was Thoroughly Meek

He himself said, "For I am gentle and humble in heart" (Matt. 11:29), and Paul exhorts the Corinthians "by the meekness and gentleness of Christ"

(2 Cor. 10:1). His meekness is seen in his not breaking the bruised reed, nor putting out the smoldering wick (Matt. 12:20; cf. Isa. 42:3). Examples of this may be seen in his gentle dealings with the repentant sinner (Luke 7:37-39; 48-50), in his accommodating himself to doubting Thomas (John 20:29), and in his tenderness toward Peter subsequent to Peter's denial of him (Luke 22:61; John 21:15-23). Perhaps more clearly still is his meekness seen in his gentle dealings with Judas the betrayer (Matt. 26:50; John 13:21) and with those who crucified him (Luke 23:34). He did not quarrel, nor cry out, nor did anyone hear his voice in the streets (Matt. 12:19; cf. Isa. 42:2). In like manner, the servant of the Lord "must not be quarrelsome, but be kind to all, able to teach, patient when wronged, with gentleness correcting those who are in opposition" (2 Tim. 2:24f.).

E. HE WAS PERFECTLY BALANCED

He was grave without being melancholy, joyful without being frivolous. He took life seriously. Isaiah speaks of his life: "He was despised and forsaken of men, a man of sorrows, and acquainted with grief; and like one from whom men hide their face, He was despised, and we did not esteem Him. Surely our griefs He Himself bore, and our sorrows He carried; yet we ourselves esteemed Him stricken, smitten of God, and afflicted" (Isa. 53:3f.; cf. Ps. 69:9; Rom. 15:3; Heb. 2:10). In addition to being sorrowful, Jesus was joyful. He said, "These things I have spoken to you, that My joy may be in you, and that your joy may be made full" (John 15:11), and "These things I speak in the world, that they may have My joy made full in themselves" (John 17:13). We never read that Jesus laughed, though in his teaching he sometimes introduced the humorous and the ridiculous (Matt. 19:24; 23:24; Luke 7:31-35). That he wept is clear (Luke 19:41; John 11:35). He sorrowed over those who willingly rejected his free salvation (Matt. 23:37; John 5:40). He bore our griefs and sorrows and seemed to have appeared older than he was (John 8:57). His joy was largely the joy of anticipation (Heb. 12:2; cf. Isa. 53:11), the joy of seeing the multitude of souls saved and with him forever in glory.

F. HE LIVED A LIFE OF PRAYER

Jesus prayed often. Luke mentions eleven occasions when Jesus prayed. He often prayed before his disciples, but he is never said to have prayed with them. He spent long seasons in prayer, sometimes whole nights (Matt. 14:23; Luke 6:12). At other times he arose early and sought seclusion for prayer (Mark 1:35). He prayed before engaging in great tasks: before entering upon a missionary tour in Galilee (Mark 1:35-38), before choosing the twelve apostles (Luke 6:12f.), and before he went to Calvary (Matt. 26:38-

46). He also prayed after great successes (John 6:15). While he prayed for himself, he never forgot to pray also for his own (Luke 22:32; John 17). He prayed earnestly (Luke 22:44; Heb. 5:7), perseveringly (Matt. 26:44), believingly (John 11:41f.), and submissively (Matt. 26:39). The writer to the Hebrews says, "In the days of His flesh, when He offered up both prayers and supplications with loud crying and tears to Him who was able to save Him from death, and who was heard because of His piety" (Heb. 5:7). If the Son of God needed to pray, how much more do we need to wait upon God.

G. He was an Incessant Worker

Jesus said, "My Father is working until now, and I Myself am working" (John 5:17), and "We must work the works of Him who sent Me, as long as it is day; night is coming, when no man can work" (John 9:4). Beginning early in the morning (Mark 1:35; John 8:2), he continued until late at night (Matt. 8:16; Luke 6:12; John 3:2). It is interesting to follow him through a typical busy day (Matt. 12:22–13:53; Mark 3:20–4:41). He forgot about food (John 4:31–34), rest (Mark 6:31), and his own death pains (Luke 23:41–43) when he had the opportunity of helping a needy soul. His work consisted of teaching (Matt. 5–7), preaching (Mark 1:38f.), casting out demons (Mark 5:12f.), healing the sick (Matt. 8, 9), saving the lost (Luke 7:48; 19:9), raising the dead (Matt. 9:25; Luke 7:14; John 11:43), and calling and training his workers (Matt. 10; Luke 10). As a worker, he was characterized by courage (John 2:14–17; 3:3; 19:10f.), thoroughness (Matt. 14:36; John 7:23), impartiality (Matt. 11:19), and tact (Mark 12:34; John 4:7–30).

CHAPTER XXV

The Work of Christ: His Death

The work of Christ has specific reference to the death, resurrection, ascension, and exaltation of Christ. These four events will be considered in the chronological order in which they occurred. First, we consider our Lord's death. The death of Christ is considered a "work" that he performed because it did not come upon him unavoidably or unawares, but rather it resulted from a definite choice on his part, when he could have avoided it. It is also a "work" because of what it accomplished for the beneficiaries of that death. This usage of the term "work" is clearly justified by the biblical conception of the purpose and meaning of Christ's death.

I. THE IMPORTANCE OF THE DEATH OF CHRIST

Contrary to the facts in the case of ordinary men, the death of Christ rather than the earthly life of Christ is of supreme importance. This is evident from many considerations.

A. IT IS FORETOLD IN THE OLD TESTAMENT

The death of Christ is the subject of many types and prophecies in the Old Testament. We can trace a scarlet cord through the whole Bible: the sacrifice of Abel (Gen. 4:4), the ram on Mount Moriah (Gen. 22:13), the sacrifices of the patriarchs in general (Gen. 8:20; 12:8; 26:25; 33:20; 35:7), the Passover lamb in Egypt (Exod. 12:1–28), the Levitical sacrifices (Lev. 1–7), Manoah's offering (Judg. 13:16–19), Elkanah's yearly sacrifice (1 Sam. 1:21), Samuel's offerings (1 Sam. 7:9f.; 16:2–5), David's offerings (2 Sam. 6:18), Elijah's offering (1 Kings 18:38), Hezekiah's offerings (2 Chron. 29:21–24), the offerings in the days of Joshua and Zerubbabel (Ezra 3:3–6) and Nehemiah (Neh. 10:32f.). These all point to the one great offering to be made by Christ.

Further, there are prophecies that point forward to the death of Christ. The Psalms prophesy the betrayal of Christ (Ps. 41:9; cf. John 13:18; Acts 1:16), the crucifixion and the attendant events (Ps. 22:1, 7f., 18; cf. Matt. 27:39f., 46; Mark 15:34; John 19:23f.), and the resurrection (Ps. 16:8–11;

cf. Acts 2:25–28). Isaiah writes, "He was pierced through for our transgressions, He was crushed for our iniquities" (53:5). Daniel indicates that after sixty-nine weeks Messiah will be cut off and have nothing (9:26). Zechariah foretells the selling of Christ for thirty pieces of silver and the investment of that sum in a potter's field (11:12f.; cf. Matt. 26:15; 27:9f.). Zechariah also predicts the striking of the shepherd (13:7) and the opening of a fountain for sin and impurity (13:1). Thus it is clear that the death of Christ is an important part of the teaching of the Old Testament.

B. It is Prominent in the New Testament

The last week of our Lord's earthly life occupies about one-fifth of the narratives in the four Gospels. Similarly, the Epistles are filled with references to this historic event. Manifestly, the death and resurrection of our Lord were esteemed of supreme importance by the Holy Spirit, the author of Scripture.

C. It is the Chief Purpose of the Incarnation

As has been stated earlier, Christ did not come primarily to set us an example or to teach us doctrine, but to die for us (Mark 10:45; Heb. 2:9, 14; 9:26; 1 John 3:5). His death was not an afterthought nor an accident, but the accomplishment of a definite purpose in connection with the incarnation. The incarnation is not an end in itself; it is but a means to an end, and that end is the redemption of the lost through the Lord's death on the cross.

D. It is the Fundamental Theme of the Gospel

The term "gospel" means "good news." Accordingly, the term is used in various ways. The four accounts of the earthly life of Jesus are called Gospels; all the revelation of God to his creatures is called the gospel; and more narrowly it is used of the "good news" of salvation. Paul says that the gospel consists of the death of Christ for our sins, his burial, and resurrection (1 Cor. 15:1–5). The death of Christ for man's sin is good news; it implies that man does not need to die for his sin. The Mosaic law, the Sermon on the Mount, the teaching and example of Christ, all show to us our sin and reveal to us the need of a Savior, but they do not provide the remedy for sin. This remedy is found only in the death of Christ.

E. It is Essential to Christianity

Other religions base their claim to recognition on the teaching of their founders; Christianity is distinguished from all of them by the importance it assigns to the death of its founder. Take away the death of Christ as interpreted by the Scriptures, and you reduce Christianity to the level of the ethnic religions. Though we would still have a higher system of ethics, were we to take away the cross of Christ, we would have no more salvation than these other religions. Take away the cross, and the heart of Christianity is gone. The subject of apostolic preaching was Christ and him crucified (1 Cor. 1:18, 23; 2:2; Gal. 6:14).

F. IT IS ESSENTIAL TO OUR SALVATION

The Son of Man must be lifted up if man is to be saved (John 3:14f.); the grain of wheat must fall into the ground and die if it is to bring forth fruit (John 12:24). God cannot pardon sin merely on the ground of the sinner's repentance. That would be impossible for a righteous God to do. God can pardon only when the penalty is first paid. In order that God might be able to pardon a sinner and to remain righteous at the same time, Christ paid the sinner's penalty (Rom. 3:25f.). Christ repeatedly said that he must suffer many things, be killed, and be raised the third day (Matt. 16:21; Mark 8:31; Luke 9:22; 17:25; John 12:32-34). The two men who were in the tomb after Christ had arisen reminded the women who came to anoint the body that Christ said that he must be crucified and arise again (Luke 24:7). Paul sought to prove to the Thessalonians the necessity of Christ's death (Acts 17:3). From God's standpoint, the death of Christ is an absolute necessity if man is to be saved.

G. IT IS OF SUPREME INTEREST IN HEAVEN

When Moses and Elijah appeared on the Mount of Transfiguration, they conversed with Christ "of His departure which He was about to accomplish at Jerusalem" (Luke 9:31). The four living creatures and the twenty-four elders sang a song of the redemption accomplished through the death of Christ (Rev. 5:8-10). Even the angels around the throne, though not in need of redemption themselves, joined in the song of the Lamb who was slain (Rev. 5:11f.). Since those who have the veil of human limitations completely removed from their eyes and have entered into the fuller truths of redemption through the blood of Christ extol Christ's death above all else, we who are yet in the flesh ought to probe into the full and true meaning of the death.

II. MISINTERPRETATIONS OF THE DEATH OF CHRIST

In order to obtain a clearer apprehension of the scriptural doctrine of the death of Christ, it is well to look first at the erroneous views of this truth that have been put forward. Many times this subject has been approached with bias and philosophical predilection, and the results have been an unscriptural doctrine of the atonement.

A. The Accident Theory

This view sees no significance in the death of Christ. He was a man and, as such, subject to death. His principles and methods did not appeal to the people of his day and so they killed him. It may have been unfortunate that so good a man was killed, but nevertheless his death had no meaning for anyone else. This is a common humanistic approach.

However, his death was no mere accident. It was clearly foretold in the Old Testament (Ps. 22; Isa. 53: Zech. 11). Christ foretold repeatedly that he would die by force (Matt. 16:21; 17:22f.; 20:18f.; Mark 9:31; Luke 9:44; 22:21f.; John 12:32f.; 15:20). Christ came with a definite purpose of dying, and so his death was no accident.

B. The Martyr Theory

This theory, also called the Example Theory, holds that Christ's death was that of a martyr. He was killed because he was faithful to his principles and to what he considered his duty by men who did not agree with him in these respects. He is an example of fidelity to truth and duty. This view assumes that the only thing needed to save man is to reform him. Christ's example is to teach man to repent of his sins and to reform.

This theory, however, (1) ignores the fundamental idea of the atonement wherein the atonement has to be made to God (Exod. 12:13, 23; Rom. 3:24f.; Heb. 2:17; 9:11–14; 1 John 2:2; 4:10); (2) makes Christ's example sufficient to save, whereas his example is intended for believers only (Matt. 11:29; 1 Pet. 2:21, 24; 1 John 2:6); (3) logically leads to a perversion of every fundamental doctrine of Scripture, such as inspiration, sin, the deity of Christ, justification, regeneration, and eternal retribution; and (4) furnishes no satisfactory explanation of Christ's unmartyrlike agony in Gethsemane and on the cross, and the Father's withdrawal from him (Matt. 26:37–39; 27:46; John 12:27; cf. Paul's behavior in suffering, Phil. 1:20–23, and Stephen's, Acts 7:55–60). Even if the death of Christ as thus interpreted did move men to moral improvement, it cannot atone for the sins already past, nor yet save the sinner (John 6:53; Acts 20:28; 1 Cor. 11:25; 1 Pet. 1:19; Rev. 7:14).

C. The Moral Influence Theory

This theory, also called the Love of God Theory, holds that Christ's death is the mere natural consequence of his taking human nature upon himself, and that he merely suffered in and with the sins of his creatures. The love of God manifested in the incarnation, the sufferings and death of Christ, are to soften human hearts and lead them to repentance. The atonement is not for the purpose of satisfying divine justice, but rather of expressing divine love.

This view of the atonement is woefully deficient, for it presents Christ as suffering with the sinner rather than in the sinner's stead. To this theory we reply that (1) though Christ's death is an expression of God's love (John 3:16; Rom. 5:6–8), man knew that God loved him long before Christ came (Deut. 7:7f.; Jer. 31:3; cf. Mal. 3:6); (2) a mere stirring of the emotions does not lead to repentance; (3) this theory contradicts the representations of Scripture that God must be propitiated before he can forgive (Rom. 3:25f.; Heb. 2:17; 9:14; 1 John 2:2; 4:10); (4) it grounds the death of Christ in the love of God rather than in his holiness; and (5) on this theory it is difficult to explain how the Old Testament believers were saved, since they did not have this object lesson of the love of God. The atonement must not be reduced to a play in which the actor appears to be moved by sincere motives, when in reality he is merely working upon the emotions of the audience. "While men are influenced deeply by the demonstration of love at Calvary, they must also come to terms with the wrath of God against sin which is revealed at the Cross."[1]

D. The Governmental Theory

This theory agrees with the preceding three in holding that there is no principle in the divine nature that needs propitiating. Rather, God, in order to maintain respect for his law, made an example of his hatred of sin in the death of Christ. In that death he showed that sin is offensive to him and that it will be punished if it is not repented of. Christ did not suffer the precise penalty of the law, but God graciously accepted what he did suffer as a substitute for our penalty. It was, in effect, a token payment but not a full payment. This bearing of substituted suffering on the part of Christ takes such a hold on the hearts of men that they repent, and since repentance is the only condition to forgiveness, God secures the salvation of the sinner by the death of Christ. This theory is the usual Arminian view of the atonement. Theologians who hold this position are not comfortable with the legal concept of substitution. Taylor writes that Paul "did not look upon the death of Christ as that of a substitute. The alleged substitutionary element in his thought is rather to be discerned in his teaching about the representative aspect of Christ's work."[2] The same writer later states, "His work is a ministry accomplished on our behalf, but not in our stead."[3] Although

---

[1]Purkiser, *God, Man, and Salvation,* pp. 407–408.
[2]Taylor, *The Atonement in New Testament Teaching,* p. 59.
[3]Taylor, *The Atonement in New Testament Teaching,* p. 184.

hesitant to use the legal concept of substitution, Purkiser writes:

> If there is a penal substitutionary dimension to the sacrifice of Christ, it rests in the fact that He experienced judgment as only God can experience it. This was possible because He knew holy love and fully comprehended the nature of sin and the just punishment due sinners. On the Cross He suffered because He knew the facts of our alienation from the Father. His sufferings therefore were substituted for our deserved punishment. To that degree we can speak of penalty in this substitutionary deed.[4]

About this theory several things must be said. (1) Proper regard for law can only be maintained so long as the penalty is equivalent. Christ did not suffer the identical penalty, but he did suffer the equivalent penalty due the sinner. The infinite one could exhaust the infinite curse put upon the sinner, something a finite person could not do. (2) This theory does not explain why the example had to be a sinless person, nor does it account for the intensity of the suffering (Matt. 27:46; Mark 15:23; Luke 22:44). (3) It does not do justice to the many passages which speak of Christ's death as truly substitutionary (1 Pet. 1:18f.). And finally, (4) this theory is based on the good of society rather than on the justice of God. God must punish sin, not merely make a token display of justice. Christ bore our sins in our stead.

E. THE COMMERCIAL THEORY

This theory, held by many conservatives, holds that sin violates the divine honor, and since it is committed against an infinite being, it deserves infinite punishment. It further holds that God's honor requires him to punish sin, while the love of God pleads for the sinner, and that this conflict between the divine attributes is reconciled by the voluntary sacrifice of Christ. In this manner, the divine claims are satisfied and God is free to pardon the sinner. This theory teaches that Christ suffered the exact equivalent for the deserved sufferings of the elect. Anselm, who developed this view, through the dissemination of it was able to put an end to the theory that Christ paid the ransom to Satan, a theory which had been held by such men as Justin Martyr and Origen. This view rightly gets back to God and to his honor, rather than centering the atonement in either how it relates to man's sense of justice or how it relates to Satan's false claims. Smeaton has written of Anselm and this view, "He knows no court but that of God Himself, and the harmony of His attributes. In this great transaction there is no human nor angelic public before which God makes a governmental display: His public is Himself, or His own perfections, which are inviolable."[5]

[4]Purkiser, *God, Man, and Salvation*, p. 403.
[5]Smeaton, *The Apostles' Doctrine of the Atonement*, p. 514.

While this view has many things to commend it, there are several items of weakness. (1) It suggests a conflict between the attributes of God. (2) It places the honor of God above the holiness of God. (3) It does not place sufficient emphasis on the active obedience of Christ and his holy life. (4) It limits the atonement to the elect. And finally, (5) it speaks of the substitution in quantitative terms rather than qualitative. The infinitely holy Son of God gave his life and died in man's stead so that all who respond in faith will not die but will have abundant life (John 10:10).

In most of the theories presented there is a measure of truth, and they are true as far as they go, but they do not go far enough. It is true that Christ died as a result of his loyalty to what he believed, that the death of Christ was an expression of the love of God, and that the death of Christ removed the stain from God's honor. But these are, after all, only partial explanations of Christ's death and secondary in significance in comparison with the main idea of his death. What is the true meaning and extent of his death?

III. THE TRUE MEANING OF CHRIST'S DEATH

The prophet Isaiah gives the heart of the truth when he declares, "But the Lord was pleased to crush Him, putting Him to grief; if He would render Himself as a guilt offering" (53:10). In giving a definition of the atonement, several items must be noted.

A. IT IS VICARIOUS

It is evident that Christ did not die for his own sin (John 8:46; Heb. 4:15; 1 Pet. 2:22). Everywhere it is said that he died for the sins of others. "The sufferings of Christ were not just the sympathetic sufferings of a friend, but the substitutionary sufferings of the Lamb of God for the sin of the world."[6] Isaiah writes, "But He was pierced through for our transgressions, He was crushed for our iniquities; the chastening of our well-being fell upon Him, and by His scourging we are healed. . . . But the Lord has caused the iniquity of us all to fall on Him" (53:5f.). Note some of the other Scriptures: "But God demonstrates His own love toward us, in that while we were yet sinners, Christ died for us" (Rom. 5:8); "Christ died for our sins according to the Scriptures" (1 Cor. 15:3); "He made Him who knew no sin to be sin on our behalf, that we might become the righteousness of God in Him" (2 Cor. 5:21); "He Himself bore our sins in His body on the cross, that we might die to sin and live to righteousness; for by His wounds you were healed" (1 Pet. 2:24); and "Christ also died for sins once for all, the just for the unjust, in order that He might bring us to God" (1 Pet. 3:18). Jesus himself said, "For

[6]Berkhof, *Systematic Theology*, p. 376.

even the Son of Man did not come to be served, but to serve, and to give His life a ransom for many" (Mark 10:45) and "I am the good shepherd; the good shepherd lays down His life for the sheep" (John 10:11). He died in our stead as the true Passover lamb (Exod. 12; 1 Cor. 5:7) and was the true sin-offering (Isa. 53:10), of which the ones in the Old Testament economy were but types (Lev. 6:24–30; Heb. 10:1–4; cf. also the scapegoat, Lev. 16:20–22).

There are objections brought against this interpretation of his death, the first lexical and the second and third moral. It is said that the Greek preposition *anti* may mean "instead," but that the preposition *huper*, which is nearly always used when the sufferings and death of Christ are spoken of, means "in behalf of," "with the view to the benefit of," and never "instead of." That *anti* means "instead of," is evident from its use in Matt. 5:38; 20:28; Mark 10:45; Luke 11:11; Rom. 12:17; 1 Thess. 5:15; Heb. 12:16; 1 Pet. 3:9. The term *huper* is used often in phrases which relate to the atonement. Some of these are: "This cup which is poured out for you is the new covenant in My blood" (Luke 22:20); "greater love has no one than this, that one lay down his life for his friends" (John 15:13); "in that while we were yet sinners, Christ died for us" (Rom. 5:8); "He who did not spare His own Son, but delivered Him up for us all" (Rom. 8:32); "He made Him who knew no sin to be sin on our behalf" (2 Cor. 5:21); Christ tasted "death for every one" (Heb. 2:9); and "for Christ also died for sins once for all, the just for the unjust" (1 Pet. 3:18; cf. John 6:51; 2 Cor. 5:14; Gal. 3:13; Eph. 5:2, 25).

What is the significance of the preposition *huper*? Though this preposition often means "in behalf of" or "for the benefit of," it can also mean "in the stead of." This is the case in 1 Cor. 15:3; 2 Cor. 5:14; and Gal. 1:4, where the idea of substitution cannot be denied. It is evident that Christ died both for the benefit of the sinner as well as in his stead. Both ideas are contained in the preposition *huper*, whereas *anti* has special reference to substitution.

It is further objected that it is immoral for God to punish an innocent one, and that for that reason alone Christ's death is not substitutionary. But the error in this view lies in the assumption that God and Christ are two beings as different from each other as two individual men. If this were the case, then there might be some point to this objection. Since, however, Christ is God incarnate, the substitute is God himself. It is not unjust for the judge to pay the penalty himself, if he chooses to do so. Furthermore, Jesus volunteered to be the substitute. He declared, "I lay down My life for the sheep. . . . The Father loves Me, because I lay down My life that I may take it again. No one has taken it away from Me, but I lay it down on My own initiative. I have authority to lay it down, and I have authority to take it up again" (John 10:15, 17f.).

Closely related to this objection is the third. It is said that satisfaction and forgiveness are mutually exclusive. It is held that if a substitute pays the debt we owe, God cannot collect the debt also from us but is morally bound to let us go free; that is, on this theory God does not exercise mercy in forgiving us, but merely does his duty. But this objection is likewise removed by the fact that the one who pays the debt is not a third party, but the judge himself. Forgiveness is, therefore, still optional with him and may be offered upon terms agreeable to himself. The terms which God has laid down are repentance and faith. The obedience of Christ, therefore, does not make ours unnecessary, but still requires us to meet the terms before we can become the beneficiaries of his atoning death.

B. It is Satisfaction

Since holiness is God's fundamental attribute it is only reasonable that he should be given some satisfaction to remove the outrage of sin. The death of Christ supplies this satisfaction.

1. It satisfies the justice of God. Man has sinned against God and has incurred his displeasure and condemnation. God rightly exacts the penalty of a broken law. He cannot free the sinner until the demands of justice are satisfied. God must visit sin with punishment. God will not, apart from substitution, clear the guilty (Exod. 34:7; Num. 14:18). Only through Christ's death could God be just while justifying the sinner (Rom. 3:25f.). In whatever God does, his justice must be maintained; Christ's death fully satisfied the just demands of God. As in the case of state criminals, if the offender suffers the penalty prescribed by the law, he is no longer liable to condemnation. "No further punishment can justly be demanded for that offence. This is what is called the perfection of Christ's satisfaction. It perfectly, from its own intrinsic worth, satisfies the demands of justice."[7]

2. It satisfies the law of God. But Christ's death is not merely a satisfaction of the justice of God, it is also a satisfaction of the law of God. The law of God is grounded in the very nature of God, and transgression of that law brings with it a penalty. "It is inviolable exactly because it is grounded in the very nature of God and is not . . . a product of His free will."[8] The sinner could not meet the demands of divine law, but Christ, as our representative and substitute, did. Thus God made provision for a vicarious satisfaction through the active and passive obedience of Christ (Rom. 8:3f.). By his obedience and sufferings and his life of perfect righteousness, Jesus fulfilled all the demands of the law. Paul speaks of Israel, saying, "Not knowing about

---

[7]Hodge, *Systematic Theology*, II, p. 482.
[8]Berkhof, *Systematic Theology*, p. 370.

God's righteousness, and seeking to establish their own, they did not subject themselves to the righteousness of God. For Christ is the end of the law for righteousness to everyone who believes" (Rom. 10:3f.).

3. *It is involved in atonement.* Involved in the thought of "satisfaction" are a number of other terms found frequently in the Scriptures. Thus the death of Christ is an atonement and a propitiation. Lev. 6:2-7 speaks of individual atonement for individual sin: "When a person sins and acts unfaithfully against the Lord, . . . he shall bring to the priest his guilt offering to the Lord, . . . and the priest shall make atonement for him before the Lord; and he shall be forgiven for any one of the things which he may have done to incur guilt." Lev. 4:13-20 makes reference to national atonement for national transgression: "If the whole congregation of Israel commits error, . . . and they become guilty; . . . Then the elders of the congregation shall lay their hands on the head of the bull before the Lord, and the bull shall be slain before the Lord. . . . So the priest shall make atonement for them, and they shall be forgiven." From these passages it is evident that the bull or ram must die, and that forgiveness is possible only on the ground of the death of a substitute. The Hebrew word for atonement in these and similar passages is *kaphar*, often translated "to make atonement." It means literally "to cover over" so as not to be seen. Hoeksema writes of the expiatory nature of the Old Testament sacrifices: "They were called sin offerings or trespass offerings, and are said to bear the sins of the offender, to make expiation for sin, to be a propitiation, and to cover the sins of the people in the sight of God. And their fruit is the forgiveness of sins."[9] The thought of covering sins from the eye of God is suggested in verses such as "Hide Thy face from my sins, and blot out all my iniquities" (Ps. 51:9); "For Thou hast cast all my sins behind Thy back" (Isa. 38:17); and "Thou wilt cast all their sins into the depths of the sea" (Mic. 7:19).

4. *It is involved in propitiation.* In the Septuagint this Hebrew word *kaphar* is translated by a Greek word which has a slightly different emphasis. The word is rendered in Greek *exilaskomai*, which means "to propitiate, to appease." Evidently the thought is, if the sin has been covered or removed, then God's wrath against that sin has been appeased or satisfied. Because of this truth, the translators of the Septuagint are justified in making this translation.

The term *exilaskomai* itself does not occur in the New Testament, but the verb *hilaskomai* occurs twice (Luke 18:13; Heb. 2:17), the noun *hilasmos* twice (1 John 2:2; 4:10), and the adjective *hilasterion* twice (Rom. 3:25; Heb. 9:5). The New Testament has much to say about the wrath of God (John

[9]Hoeksema, *Reformed Dogmatics*, p. 389.

3:36; Rom. 1:18; 5:9; Eph. 5:6; 1 Thess. 1:10; Heb. 3:11; Rev. 19:15). Corresponding to this thought, the New Testament represents Christ's death as appeasing God's wrath. Paul says, God set him forth "publicly as a pro-pitiation" (Rom. 3:25), and Hebrews uses this term for the mercy seat at the tabernacle (Heb. 9:5). John declared that Christ "is the propitiation for our sins; and not for ours only, but also for those of the whole world" (1 John 2:2; cf. 4:10); and Hebrews states that Christ became a merciful and faithful high priest "to make propitiation for the sins of the people" (2:17). The tax-gatherer's prayer was literally, "God be propitious to me, the sinner" (Luke 18:13). By his death, Christ appeased God's holy wrath against sin.

5. It is involved in reconciliation.   Closely connected with the idea of propitiation is the thought of reconciliation. The two ideas seem to be related to each other as cause and effect; Christ's death "propitiated" God, and as a result God is "reconciled" (Rom. 5:10; 2 Cor. 5:18f.; Eph. 2:16). The verb *katallasso* occurs six times in the New Testament (Rom. 5:10; 1 Cor. 7:11; 2 Cor. 5:18–20), and the noun *katallage* four times (Rom. 5:11; 11:15; 2 Cor. 5:18f.). *Diallassomai* appears once (Matt. 5:24). In all these occurrences the thought is that of reconciliation. Berkouwer states that Paul uses this term to refer "to the relationship of peace which is brought about by the death of Christ, to the communion in contrast with the previous enmity, to the reconciliation as the removal of all obstacles, to the access to the Father."[10] In the Scriptures the term reconciliation is applied to both God and man (Rom. 5:10; 2 Cor. 5:18–20).

The thought is something like this. At first God and man stood face to face with each other in perfect harmony. In sinning, Adam turned his back upon God. Then God turned his back upon Adam. Christ's death has satisfied the demands of God and now God has again turned his face toward man. It remains for man to turn around and face God. Since God has been reconciled by the death of his Son, man is now entreated to be reconciled to God. In the largest sense of that word, God has reconciled to himself, not only man, but also all things in heaven and on earth (Col. 1:20). Due to this reconciliation, God sends temporal blessings upon the unsaved (Matt. 5:45; Rom. 2:4), extends an opportunity to man to repent (2 Pet. 3:9), and will deliver heaven and earth from the results of the fall (Rom. 8:19–21).

C. It is a Ransom

The death of Christ is represented as the payment of a ransom. The idea of ransom is that of the payment of a price in order to set another held in bond-age free. Thus Jesus said that he had come to give his life a ransom for many

[10]Berkouwer, *The Work of Christ*, p. 255.

(Matt. 20:28; Mark 10:45), and the work of Christ is spoken of as a redemption (Luke 1:68; 2:38; Heb. 9:12). In these references we have the word *lutrosis*. The verb *lutroomai* occurs in Luke 24:21; Titus 2:14; 1 Pet. 1:18. The compound *apolutrosis* occurs ten times (Luke 21:28; Rom. 3:24; 8:23; 1 Cor. 1:30; Eph. 1:7, 14; 4:30; Col. 1:14; Heb. 9:15; 11:35). Deissmann says,

> When anybody heard the Greek word *lutron*, "ransom," in the first century, it was natural for him to think of the purchase-money for manumitting slaves. Three documents from Oxyrhynchus relating to manumissions in the years 86, 100 and 91 or 107 A.D. make use of the word.[11]

This ransom is not paid to Satan, but to God. The debt that requires cancelling is due to God's attribute of justice; Satan has no legal claims against the sinner, and so does not need to be paid before the sinner can be set free. As Shedd has well stated, "God's mercy ransoms man from God's justice."[12]

Scripture teaches that we are redeemed through the death of Christ. This redemption is (1) from the penalty of the law, or as Paul says in Gal. 3:13, "from the curse of the Law," by Christ's having become a curse for us; (2) from the law itself, by our being made dead to the law by the body of Christ (Rom. 7:4), so that we are no longer under it but under grace (Rom. 6:14); (3) from sin as a power, by Christ's death to sin and our death to it in him (Rom. 6:2, 6; Titus 2:14; 1 Pet. 1:18f.), so that we need no longer submit to the domination of sin (Rom. 6:12–14); (4) from Satan, who held man in captivity (2 Tim. 2:26), likewise through Christ's death on the cross (Heb. 2:14f.); and (5) from all evil, both physical and moral, including our present mortal body (Rom. 8:23; Eph. 1:14), to be fully granted at the return of Christ (Luke 21:28). The term "redemption" alludes sometimes to the payment of a debt and sometimes to the liberation of a captive. Christ's sacrifice provided for both.

IV. THE EXTENT OF CHRIST'S DEATH

This also is a subject about which there is much difference of opinion. Did Christ die for the whole world, or only for the elect? If for the whole world, then why are not all saved? And if for the whole world, in what sense? If for the elect only, then what about the justice of God? The answer to these

[11]Deissmann, *Light from the Ancient East*, pp. 327–328.
[12]Shedd, *Dogmatic Theology*, II, p. 398.

questions is bound up with one's conception of the order of the decrees. Those who take the supralapsarian view naturally hold that Christ died only for the elect; those who hold the sublapsarian view hold that Christ died, at least in some sense, also for the whole world.

A. Christ Died for the Elect

The Scriptures teach that Christ died primarily for the elect. Paul writes that God "is the Savior of all men, especially of believers" (1 Tim. 4:10); and Jesus said, "The Son of Man did not come to be served, but to serve, and to give His life a ransom for many" (Matt. 20:28) and "I ask on their behalf; I do not ask on behalf of the world, but of those whom Thou hast given Me, for They are Thine" (John 17:9). Scripture further declares, "Christ also loved the church and gave Himself up for her" (Eph. 5:25) and "Who has saved us, and called us with a holy calling, not according to our works, but according to His own purpose and grace which was granted us in Christ Jesus from all eternity" (2 Tim. 1:9; cf. Rev. 13:8). He died for the elect, not only in the sense of making salvation possible for them, but also in the sense of providing it for them when they believe.

B. Christ Died for the Whole World

This is clear from several passages: "Behold, the Lamb of God who takes away the sin of the world!" (John 1:29); "Who gave Himself as a ransom for all" (1 Tim. 2:6); "For the grace of God has appeared, bringing salvation to all men" (Titus 2:11); "He might taste death for every one" (Heb. 2:9); "The Lord is ... not wishing for any to perish but for all to come to repentance" (2 Pet. 3:9); and "He Himself is the propitiation for our sins; and not for ours only, but also for those of the whole world" (1 John 2:2). There is a necessary order in a man's salvation; he must first believe that Christ died for him before he can appropriate the benefits of his death to himself. Although Christ died for all in the sense of reconciling God to the world, not all are saved, because their actual salvation is conditioned on their being reconciled to God (2 Cor. 5:18-20).

The sense in which Christ is the Savior of the world may be thus summarized: His death secured for all men a delay in the execution of the sentence against sin, space for repentance, and the common blessings of life which have been forfeited by transgression; it removed from the mind of God every obstacle to the pardon of the penitent and restoration of the sinner, except his willful opposition to God and rejection of him; it procured for the unbeliever the powerful incentives to repentance presented in the cross, by means of the preaching of God's servants, and through the work of the Holy Spirit; it provided salvation for those who do not willfully and personally sin (i.e., those who die in infancy or those who have never been mentally responsible) and assured its application to them; and it makes possible the final restoration of creation itself. We conclude that the atonement is unlimited in the sense that it is available for all; it is limited in that it is effective only for those who believe. It is available for all, but efficient only for the elect.

CHAPTER XXVI

The Work of Christ: His Resurrection, Ascension, and Exaltation

The objective aspect of our salvation includes more than the death of Christ; it includes also his resurrection, ascension, and exaltation. Each of these contributes significantly to the plan of redemption.

I. THE RESURRECTION OF CHRIST

We look now at the importance, nature, credibility, and results of Christ's resurrection.

A. THE IMPORTANCE OF CHRIST'S RESURRECTION

The resurrection of Christ is of paramount importance for several reasons.

1. It is the fundamental doctrine of Christianity. Many admit the necessity of the death of Christ who deny the importance of the bodily resurrection of Christ. But that Christ's physical resurrection is vitally important is evident from the fundamental connection of this doctrine with Christianity. In 1 Cor. 15:12–19 Paul shows that everything stands or falls with Christ's bodily resurrection. If Christ has not risen, preaching is vain (v. 14), the Corinthians' faith was vain (v. 14), the apostles were false witnesses (v. 15), the Corinthians were yet in their sins (v. 17), those fallen asleep in Jesus have perished (v. 18), and Christians are of all men most to be pitied (v. 19). All through the book of Acts the emphasis of the apostolic preaching was upon the resurrection of Christ (2:24, 32; 3:15, 26; 4:10; 10:40; 13:30–37; 17:31). This can be noted in Paul's Epistles as well (Rom. 4:24f.; 6:4, 9; 7:4; 8:11; 10:9; 1 Cor. 6:14; 15:4; 2 Cor. 4:14; Gal. 1:1; Eph. 1:20; Col. 2:12; 1 Thess. 1:10; 2 Tim. 2:8), and other New Testament Epistles (1 Pet. 1:21; 3:21; Rev. 1:5; 2:8). The resurrection is clearly an essential part of the gospel.

2. It has an important part in the application of salvation. God raised him up and exalted him to his own right hand that he might be the head over all things to the church (Eph. 1:20–22). It was necessary for him to rise before he could baptize the believer in the Holy Spirit (John 1:33; Acts 1:5;

2:32f.; 11:15–17; 1 Cor. 12:13; cf. John 14:16–19; 15:26; 16:7). His death, resurrection, and ascension are preparatory to his bestowing gifts on men (Eph. 4:7–13). And he must rise to be a Prince and Savior, to give repentance and remission of sins to Israel (Acts 5:31). Paul sums it all up when he says that while Christ's death reconciled us to God, his present life perfects our salvation (Rom. 5:8–10). The resurrection is essential to the application of the salvation provided for in the death of Christ.

3. It is important as an exhibition of divine power.   The standard of divine power often expressed in the Old Testament was the power with which the Lord brought Israel out of the land of Egypt. The annual Passover was a reminder of God's mighty hand (Exod. 12). In the New Testament the standard power is the power God exhibited in the resurrection of Christ. It was impossible for Christ to be held in death's power (Acts 2:24). This same power which raised Christ from the dead is available to Christians. Paul prayed that the believers might know "what is the surpassing greatness of His power toward us who believe. . . . in accordance with the working of the strength of His might which He brought about in Christ, when He raised Him from the dead, and seated Him at His right hand in the heavenly places" (Eph. 1:19f.).

B. The Nature of Christ's Resurrection

That it was a bodily resurrection has been repeatedly assumed in this study, but we need to present the proof of this assumption.

1. It was an actual resurrection.   The theory that Jesus did not actually die, but that he merely fell into a swoon from which the cool air of the tomb and the spices revived him, is a gross perversion of the plain meaning of biblical terms. That Christ actually died, is evident from the fact that the centurion and the soldiers declared him to be dead (Mark 15:45; John 19:33); that the women came with the expectation of anointing a dead body (Mark 16:1); that blood and water flowed from his opened side (John 19:34); that the disciples assumed he was dead and his resurrection greatly surprised them (Matt. 28:17; Luke 24:37f.; John 20:3–9); that he did not appear to his disciples on the third day in a weakened condition, but as a mighty conqueror of death; and that Christ himself declared that he was dead but now is alive forevermore (Rev. 1:18).

2. It was a bodily resurrection.   Some who claim to believe in the resurrection of Christ refuse to believe that his was a bodily resurrection. They explain his death and resurrection as being merely the two sides of the one experience; in his death he passed out of his physical life, and in his resurrection he passed into his spiritual life. Thus his death and resurrection are declared to be simultaneous events. The appearances of Christ are explained as those of his spirit or as mere subjective hallucinations.

Several things prove that Christ arose bodily. Jesus himself declared after his resurrection that he had flesh and bones (Luke 24:39). Matthew declared that the women who met Christ on the resurrection morning held him by the feet (Matt. 28:9). David prophesied by the Spirit that Christ's flesh would not see corruption (Ps. 16:10; Acts 2:31). The tomb was empty and the grave-clothes were in order when the disciples examined the tomb (Mark 16:6; John 20:5–7). Christ partook of food in the presence of his disciples after he had arisen (Luke 24:41–43). Jesus was recognized by his own after the resurrection, even to the imprint of the nails (Luke 24:34–39; John 20:25–28). Jesus predicted that he would rise bodily (Matt. 12:40; John 2:19–21). The angels in the tomb declared that he had arisen as he had said (Luke 24:6–8). And finally, many Scriptures would be unintelligible on the theory that his was a spiritual resurrection (John 5:28f.; 1 Cor. 15:20; Eph. 1:19f.).

3. *It was a unique resurrection.* The son of the widow of Zarephath (1 Kings 17:17–24), the Shunammite's son (2 Kings 4:18–37), Jairus' daughter (Mark 5:22–43), the young man of Nain (Luke 7:11–17), Lazarus (John 11:1–44), Tabitha (Acts 9:36–43), and Eutychus (Acts 20:7–12) undoubtedly all died again. Surely, they did not receive the resurrection body as Christ did. Concerning Christ's resurrection body, several things must be mentioned. (1) It was a real body. It could be and was touched (Matt. 28:9); it had flesh and bones (Luke 24:39). (2) It was recognized as the same body, not another. Christ himself mentioned his opened side (John 20:27). It appears that these marks of his passion will be visible even at his second coming (Zech. 12:10; Rev. 1:7). At different times we are told that his own recognized him after the resurrection (Luke 24:41–43; John 20:16, 20; 21:7). (3) Yet his body was in some respects different after the resurrection. He passed through closed doors (John 20:19), and undoubtedly he did not need to eat and sleep after that time. (4) He is now alive forevermore (Rom. 6:9f.; 2 Tim. 1:10; Rev. 1:18).

C. The Credibility of Christ's Resurrection

The resurrection of Christ was a miracle, and the kind of evidence needed to prove this fact is the same as that which is needed to prove any other miracle. Inasmuch as all miracles involve a departure from the usual operations of natural law, miracles are not to be proved by reference to such laws. They have valid proof of their occurrence, but it is not proof such as the naturalist insists upon as necessary. What are some of the proofs of Christ's resurrection?

1. The argument from testimony.   In what has just been said it is implied that the unusual manifestations of God's power are not to be deduced from the usual ones. They must be established on other grounds, the argument from testimony being one of these. Three things are necessary to make a testimony trustworthy: the witnesses must be competent first-hand witnesses, they must be sufficient in number, and they must have a good reputation.

The apostles qualify in all these respects. They repeatedly refer to the fact that they were eyewitnesses (Luke 24:33-36; John 20:19, 26; 21:24; Acts 1:3, 21f.). That is, they did not base their teaching on the reports of others. Again, the Scriptures affirm that there were more than five hundred who saw the risen Lord (1 Cor. 15:3-8). The Old Testament requires only two or three witnesses to establish a case (Deut. 17:6; Matt. 18:16), and this is true in the church as well (2 Cor. 13:1; 1 Tim. 5:19). As to the character of the witnesses, it is sufficient to say that neither the Scriptures nor any honorable opponent has ever assailed them on ethical grounds. The apostles could not have had any ulterior motive for proclaiming so stupendous a fact. They proclaimed Christ's resurrection at the risk of their lives. The disbelieving disciples believed when they saw the risen Christ and became indefatigable heralds of the resurrection. The events on the resurrection morning and during the forty days immediately thereafter seem to have taken place in the following order: early that morning three women came to the tomb and saw the angels (Matt. 28:1-8; Mark 16:1-7; Luke 24:1-8); they separated at the tomb, Mary Magdalene going to tell John and Peter (John 20:1f.), and the other two going to tell the other disciples, who probably were at Bethany (Luke 24:9-11). Then Peter and John ran to the grave ahead of Mary and returned without seeing the Lord (John 20:3-10).

Following this, we have twelve appearances of Christ, apparently in this order: to Mary, who came to the tomb after Peter and John had already left it (Mark 16:9; John 20:11-18), to the other women on the way (Matt. 28:9f.), to the two on the way to Emmaus (Mark 16:12f.; Luke 24:13-33), to Simon Peter (Luke 24:34; 1 Cor. 15:5), to the ten apostles (John 20:19-24), to the eleven disciples (John 20:26-29), to the apostles at the Sea of Tiberias (John 21:1-14), to the apostles on the mount in Galilee (Matt. 28:16-20), to more than five hundred brethren at the same time (1 Cor. 15:6), to James (1 Cor. 15:7), to the disciples on the mount of the ascension (Mark 16:19; Luke 24:50f.; Acts 1:9), and to Paul (1 Cor. 15:8).

2. The argument from cause and effect.   Every effect has a cause. There are a number of effects in Christian history that must be traced to the bodily resurrection of Christ for their cause. (1) There is the empty tomb. The Scriptures tell us that the tomb was empty. Surely if this were not true, someone would have shown that the disciples were deceivers, that the tomb was not empty. The lie invented by the chief priests and the elders of that day, that the disciples came and stole the body while the soldiers slept, has been accepted by some moderns as the truth. But the evidence for the resurrection of Christ is established by the fact that the Lord's grave-clothes were found undisturbed; only the napkin that had been around his head had been removed and laid to one side (John 20:5-7). Surely, this could not have been the case had the disciples come and stolen the body.

(2) The Lord's Day is another effect of the resurrection. It is a remarkable thing that the apostles who were Jews should turn from the observance of their time-honored Sabbath Day, which had been given in Eden and been made a sign of their covenant relation with God (Exod. 31:13; Ezek. 20:12, 20), to Sunday worship. The origin of the Lord's Day can be accounted for only on the ground that the apostles changed it in honor of Christ's physical resurrection and with his approval. (3) The Christian church is an effect which is traceable to the same event. Great was the impression made upon the disciples by the life of Christ among them, but all their hopes were blasted when he was crucified. Nothing could have inspired these discouraged disciples to assemble themselves together for meditation and the worship of a master whom they regarded as dead. Certainly nothing could have induced them to proclaim his name to their fellow Jews in the face of persecution but the absolute assurance that Christ had risen from the dead. Their assemblies were the beginnings of the Christian church. Thus the Christian church can be accounted for only on the assumption of the physical resurrection of our Lord.

(4) And finally, the New Testament itself is an effect of the resurrection. How could this book ever have been written if there had been no resurrection? Evans says, "If Jesus had remained buried in the grave, the story of His life and death would have remained buried with Him."[1] The New Testament is obviously an effect of Christ's resurrection.

D. THE RESULTS OF CHRIST'S RESURRECTION

What are the results of Christ's resurrection?

1. It attests to Christ's deity. Paul teaches that Christ "was declared with power to be the Son of God by the resurrection from the dead" (Rom. 1:4). Christ had pointed forward to his resurrection as a sign that would be given the people of Israel (Matt. 12:38-40; John 2:18-22), and Paul declares that it was a sign of his deity.

[1]Evans, *The Great Doctrines of the Bible*, p. 91.

2. It assures the acceptance of Christ's work. Paul writes that Christ "was delivered up because of our transgressions, and was raised because of our justification" (Rom. 4:25). We can have the confidence that God has accepted Christ's sacrifice because he has risen from the dead.

3. It has made Christ our high priest. Through his resurrection from the dead, he became the intercessor, executive, and protector of his people (Rom. 5:9f.; 8:34; Eph. 1:20–22; 1 Tim. 2:5f.). He not only delivers from bondage, but he also intercedes for his people in times of need.

4. It provided for many additional blessings. By Christ's resurrection provision has been made for the personal realization of the salvation which he has provided in his bestowal of repentance, forgiveness, regeneration, and the Holy Spirit (John 16:7; Acts 2:33; 3:26; 5:31; 1 Pet. 1:3). Again, his resurrection is made the basis of assurance to the believer that all necessary power for life and service is available to him (Eph. 1:18–20). If God could raise Christ from the dead, he is able to supply all the needs of the believer (Phil. 3:10). The resurrection of Christ is a guarantee that our bodies too will be raised from the dead (John 5:28f.; 6:40; Acts 4:2; Rom. 8:11; 1 Cor. 15:20–23; 2 Cor. 4:14; 1 Thess. 4:14). And again, the resurrection of Christ is God's concrete proof that there will be a judgment of the godly and ungodly (Acts 10:42; 17:31; cf. John 5:22). The day of judgment has been appointed, and so has the judge. On these facts, God has given assurance unto all men, in that he has raised Christ from the dead. Finally, the resurrection of Christ prepared the way for him to sit on the throne of David in the coming kingdom (Acts 2:32–36; 3:19–25).

II. THE ASCENSION OF CHRIST

The ascension and exaltation of Christ must be distinguished from each other. The ascension of Christ refers to his going back to heaven in his resurrection body, the exaltation of Christ is the act of the Father by which he gave to the risen and ascended Christ the position of honor and power at his own right hand.

A. The New Testament Teachings

The New Testament abundantly teaches that Christ ascended to heaven after his resurrection. Matthew and John do not narrate the fact of the ascension, and Mark speaks of it only in one verse, and that in the disputed ending of Mark (16:19). Luke, in his Gospel (24:50f.) and in the Acts (1:9), gives some details of the event. Though the historical narrative is sketchy, this does not leave us without teaching on the ascension. Though John does not narrate the fact of Christ's bodily return to heaven, he represents Christ as having clearly predicted it (6:62; 20:17; cf. 13:1; 15:26; 16:10, 16f., 28). Paul spoke of it (Eph. 4:8-10; Phil. 2:9; 1 Tim. 3:16), as did Peter (1 Pet. 3:22) and the writer to the Hebrews (4:14). It is evident, therefore, that the early church regarded the ascension as a historical fact.

B. Objections to the Ascension of Christ

Modern criticism objects to the reality of the ascension mainly on two grounds. First, it contends that our knowledge of the universe excludes the belief that heaven is a definite place above and beyond the stars. But Scripture does not indicate where heaven is, even though it represents it as a place as well as a state. Heaven is where God dwells, where the angels and the spirits of just men are, and where Christ went in a true body. Such a body must occupy space. The angels, not being infinite, cannot be ubiquitous; they must be in some definite place. Likewise Christ said, "I go to prepare a place for you" (John 14:2). Secondly, modern criticism argues that a tangible or palpable body is not adapted to a superterrestrial abode. But this is ignoring the fact that the stars and the planets are superterrestrial, and yet they are material. Paul says, "There are also heavenly bodies and earthly bodies" (1 Cor. 15:40). Admit the bodily resurrection of Christ, and the question of Jesus' bodily departure from this earth is not difficult. In fact, the bodily ascension of Christ is a necessary historical presupposition to belief in his bodily return, since he is to come back to earth as he went away, and to belief in our own bodily resurrection, since we shall be like him.

III. THE EXALTATION OF CHRIST

The Scriptures likewise speak of Christ's exaltation. Luke mentions it several times (Acts 2:33; 5:31); Paul teaches it (Rom. 8:34; Eph. 1:20; Phil. 2:9; Col. 3:1); the writer to the Hebrews mentions it (10:12); and Jesus himself intimates it (Matt. 22:41-45; Rev. 3:21; cf. Ps. 110:1).

A. Things Embraced in the Exaltation of Christ

A number of things are embraced in the exaltation of Christ. Christ was "crowned with glory and honor" (Heb. 2:9). This glory appears in his present "body of His glory" (Phil. 3:21). John saw him in this body on the Isle of Patmos (Rev. 1:12-18). Both the glory and the honor are seen in his receiving a name that is above every name (Phil. 2:9). The Lord refers to his new name (Rev. 3:12; 19:12f., 16). With this new name went also his enthronement at the right hand of the Father (Matt. 28:18; Heb. 10:12). Stephen saw him standing there (Acts 7:55f.). Some day Christ will sit upon his own throne (Matt. 25:31). In this act was included also, no doubt, his appointment as head of his body, the church (Eph. 1:22). Now he directs the affairs of his church. He serves as high priest (Heb. 4:14; 5:5–10; 6:20; 7:21; 8:1–6; 9:24), offering his own blood (1 John 2:1f.), and praying for the keeping and unifying of his own (Luke 22:32; John 17). Today, angels, authorities, and powers are all subject to him (1 Pet. 3:22). Indeed, all things have been put under his feet (Eph. 1:22). In this sense, he is today King in a kingdom (Col. 1:13; Rev. 1:9).

B. Results of the Ascension and Exaltation of Christ

The results of his ascension and exaltation may be treated together. (1) He is now not merely in heaven, but is spiritually present everywhere. He fills all (Eph. 4:10). Thus he is an ideal object of worship for all mankind (1 Cor. 1:2). (2) He has "led captive a host of captives" (Eph. 4:8). This may mean that the Old Testament believers are no longer in Hades, but have been transferred to heaven. Clearly, the New Testament believer goes directly into the immediate presence of Christ when he dies (2 Cor. 5:6–8; Phil. 1:23). (3) He has entered upon his priestly ministry in heaven (Heb. 4:14; 5:5–10; 6:20; 7:21; 8:1–6; 9:24). (4) He has bestowed spiritual gifts upon his own (Eph. 4:8–11). These are both personal gifts to individuals (1 Cor. 12:4–11) and gifts to his church (Eph. 4:8–13). (5) He has poured out his Spirit upon his people (John 14:16; 16:7; Acts 2:33), is giving repentance and faith to men (Acts 5:31; 11:18; Rom. 12:3; 2 Tim. 2:25; 2 Pet. 1:1), and is baptizing believers into the church (John 1:33; 1 Cor. 12:13). These are the results of his ascension and exaltation. It is evident that we cannot stop with the death of Christ, important as that is, if we are to have a complete redemption; the physical resurrection, ascension, and exaltation of Christ must also be historical facts.

CHAPTER XXVII

The Work of the Holy Spirit

Just as the work of Christ is important in the accomplishment of salvation, so also is the work of the Holy Spirit. The deity and personality of the Holy Spirit were considered in the chapter on the trinity. It was there noted that the Holy Spirit is deity. This was proven by the fact that attributes of deity are ascribed to him and that works of deity are performed by him, and by his relationship to the other members of the trinity. It was further noted that the Holy Spirit is a person. Personal pronouns refer to him, he is given names of personality, and attributes of personality are ascribed to him. He does personal acts, is associated in a personal way with the other persons of the trinity, and is susceptible of personal treatment. Having considered his deity and personality, we move to his work. Though our primary purpose at this point is to clarify his work as it relates to salvation and the Christian experience, we must also look at his work in relation to the world, to the Scriptures, and to Christ.

I. HIS RELATIONSHIP TO THE WORLD

A. In Creation and Preservation

It is interesting that creation is ascribed to all three persons of the trinity: the Father (Rev. 4:11), the Son (John 1:3), and the Holy Spirit. Gen. 1:2 demonstrates the active involvement of the Spirit at creation. Elihu tells Job, "The Spirit of God has made me, and the breath of the Almighty gives me life" (Job 33:4), and Job responds to Bildad, "By His breath [Spirit] the heavens are cleared" (Job 26:13). The Psalmist suggests the work of the Spirit in creation, "By the word of the Lord the heavens were made, and by the breath [Spirit] of His mouth all their host" (Ps. 33:6). The Spirit is not only involved in creation but also in preservation. Both are mentioned in Ps. 104:30, "Thou dost send forth Thy Spirit, they are created; and Thou dost renew the face of the ground." Isa. 40:7 suggests the active involvement of the Spirit, "The grass withers, the flower fades, when the breath [Spirit] of the Lord blows upon it." In discussing the whole matter of the greatness of God's creative and providential activities, Isaiah asks, "Who has directed the

Spirit of the Lord, or as His counselor has informed Him?" (40:13). It seems evident that expressions such as his Spirit (breath), Spirit (breath) of his mouth, Spirit (breath) of the Lord, Spirit of his Son, and Spirit of Jesus, all have reference to the Holy Spirit, the third person of the trinity (Job 26:13; Ps. 33:6; Isa. 40:7; Gal. 4:6; Acts 16:7, respectively).

B. IN THE AFFAIRS OF NON-BELIEVERS

In addition to his providential governance in creation, the Spirit is active in the non-believing world in three general areas: he actively works through individuals to accomplish his purposes, he convicts the world of sin and the need of salvation, and he restrains and controls the direction of evil. God anointed Cyrus, the pagan king of Persia, with the Holy Spirit to accomplish his service, though Cyrus did not know God (Isa. 44:28–45:6). Concerning King Saul, Kuyper writes:

> There is no reason to consider Saul one of God's elect. After his anoint-
> ing the Holy Spirit comes upon him, abides with him, and works upon
> him as long as he remains the Lord's chosen king over His people. But
> as soon as by wilful disobedience he forfeits that favor, the Holy Spirit
> departs from him and an evil spirit from the Lord troubles him.[1]

It is no wonder that David, having sinned and knowing well what had happened to Saul, requested of the Lord, "Do not take Thy Holy Spirit from me" (Ps. 51:11). This work of the Spirit upon Cyrus and Saul is something completely distinct from regeneration. We must also recognize that the Spirit came upon Old Testament believers in such fashion as this for special ministry (cf. Bezalel, Exod. 31:2f.; Othniel, Judg. 3:9f.; Jephthah, Judg. 11:29).

In addition to this sovereign ministry upon the unbeliever as well as believer, Scripture speaks of the Spirit's work in the unbeliever's heart to cause him to turn to the Lord. Various terms are used to express this minis-try. He is spoken of as a witness. Peter and the apostles said, "And we are witnesses of these things; and so is the Holy Spirit" (Acts 5:32). Jesus said of his witnessing ministry, "The Spirit of truth . . . will bear witness of Me" (John 15:26). It would appear that the enlightening of John 1:9 and the drawing of John 6:44 and 12:32 have reference to the work which the Father and the Son do through the Spirit. Finally, he convicts. Jesus said of the Spirit, "He . . . will convict the world concerning sin, and righteousness, and judgment" (John 16:8). For the unbeliever to attribute these works of the Spirit to the activities of Satan is to blaspheme against the Spirit, a sin for

---

[1]Kuyper, *The Work of the Holy Spirit*, p. 39.

which there is no forgiveness (Mark 3:29). Willful sin against the knowledge of the truth is to insult the Spirit of grace (Heb. 10:29). After the Spirit had striven with evil men during the antediluvian period, God said, "My Spirit shall not strive with man forever" (Gen. 6:3). One hundred twenty years later God destroyed the earth with the deluge. To resist the Spirit is a dreadful sin (Acts 7:51; cf. also Acts 6:10).

The Spirit also restrains evil. It is common knowledge that conscience, daylight, and government among other things serve as restraints for evil. The presence of godly people also confines and represses evil. The restrainer of 2 Thess. 2:6–8 seems to have reference to the Holy Spirit. During the great tribulation, the Spirit's ministry of restraining evil and hindering the revelation of the man of lawlessness will be withdrawn. Evil will be allowed to run rampant.

II. HIS RELATIONSHIP TO SCRIPTURE AND TO CHRIST

A. To Scripture

The Holy Spirit is both the author and the interpreter of Scripture. As Peter indicates, "Men moved by the Holy Spirit spoke from God" (2 Pet. 1:21). At the close of each of the seven letters to the churches in the Revelation, Jesus said, "He who has an ear, let him hear what the Spirit says to the churches" (2:7, 11, etc.). "It was the Spirit who was to guide the apostles into all the truth, and show them things to come (John 16:13)."[2] Such statements as "The Holy Spirit rightly spoke through Isaiah the prophet to your fathers" (Acts 28:25) and "The Spirit foretold by the mouth of David concerning Judas" (Acts 1:16), clearly reveal the apostles' commitment to the Spirit's authorship of Scripture (cf. also Heb. 3:7; 10:15). It was he who revealed to the New Testament apostles and prophets matters undiscoverable through human philosophy and the natural reasoning processes of the human mind (Eph. 3:5).

Not only is the Spirit the author of Scripture, he is also the interpreter. Paul prayed that God might give to the Ephesian believers "a spirit of wisdom and of revelation in the knowledge of Him" (Eph. 1:17). That this is the Holy Spirit is suggested from Isa. 11:2. Paul also writes that God has given to us "the Spirit who is from God, that we might know the things freely given to us by God" (1 Cor. 2:12). The Spirit takes Christ's words and discloses them to believers (John 16:14). He teaches us, "combining spiritual thoughts with spiritual words" (1 Cor. 2:13). John reminds his readers that they all had "an anointing from the Holy One" (1 John 2:20), and he further

2Evans, *The Great Doctrines of the Bible,* p. 119.

writes, "The anointing which you received from Him abides in you, and you have no need for any one to teach you; but . . . His anointing teaches you about all things" (v. 27). Thus the same Spirit who wrote Scripture, interprets it.

B. To Christ

The Spirit was active in the life of Christ. Several things can be noted which relate to the earthly ministry of Christ. Our Lord was conceived of the Spirit (Luke 1:35). He was anointed by the Spirit at his baptism (Matt. 3:16; cf. Isa. 61:1; Luke 4:18). The Spirit, given without measure (John 3:34), equipped him for his messianic ministry, and it was at this point that Jesus "began His ministry" (Luke 3:23). Immediately after the baptism, "Jesus, full of the Holy Spirit, returned from the Jordan and was led about by the Spirit in the wilderness for forty days, while tempted by the devil" (Luke 4:1f.; cf. Matt. 4:1; Mark 1:12). Peter informed Cornelius "how God anointed Him with the Holy Spirit and with power" (Acts 10:38). It was through the Spirit that Jesus performed his miracles (Matt. 12:28). Further, the Spirit was active in his crucifixion and his resurrection (Heb. 9:14; Rom. 1:4; 8:11).

When Jesus ascended, he requested of the Father that he would send the Spirit (John 14:16, 26; 15:26). The Spirit was to be Jesus' replacement so that the disciples would not be left as orphans (John 14:18; 16:7-15). Before Jesus left, he prepared the disciples to receive the Spirit (Luke 24:49; John 20:22; Acts 1:8). Kuyper summarizes:

> The same Holy Spirit who performed His work in the conception of our Lord, who attended the unfolding of His human nature, who brought into activity every gift and power in Him, who consecrated Him to His office as the Messiah, who qualified Him for every conflict and temptation, who enabled Him to cast out devils, and who supported Him in His humiliation, passion, and bitter death, was the same Spirit who performed His work in His resurrection, so that Jesus was justified in the Spirit (I Tim. iii. 16), and who dwells now in the glorified human nature of the Redeemer in the heavenly Jerusalem.[3]

III. HIS RELATIONSHIP TO THE BELIEVER

The ministry of the Holy Spirit to the believer can be briefly stated under several terms. Some of these doctrines will be considered more fully in later chapters. We consider first those which relate to salvation, then those which relate to the Christian life.

[3]Kuyper, *The Work of the Holy Spirit*, p. 110.

A. The Work of the Spirit at Salvation

1. He regenerates.   It is through the ministry of the Spirit that a person is born again (John 3:3–8), for it is the Spirit who gives life (John 6:63). Paul speaks of the "renewing by the Holy Spirit" (Titus 3:5).

2. He indwells.   Closely related to the regenerating ministry of the Spirit is his indwelling. Concerning the coming of the Comforter, Christ said, "You know Him because He abides with you, and will be in you" (John 14:17). So important is the indwelling of the Spirit that if a person does not have him, he does not belong to Christ (Rom. 8:9). To the scandal-torn Corinthian church Paul said, "The Spirit of God dwells in you" (1 Cor. 3:16; cf. 6:19). The indwelling of the Spirit guarantees the resurrection (Rom. 8:11).

3. He baptizes.   Christ baptizes believers in the Spirit into the body of Christ (Matt. 3:11; Mark 1:8; Luke 3:16; John 1:33; Acts 1:5; 11:16). Paul writes, "For by one Spirit we were all baptized into one body, whether Jews or Greeks, whether slaves or free, and we were all made to drink of one Spirit" (1 Cor. 12:13). This baptism takes place at the moment of salvation. The rite of water baptism symbolizes Spirit baptism (Rom. 6:3f.; cf. also Eph. 4:5; Col. 2:12).

4. He seals.   God seals the believer with the Holy Spirit (Eph. 1:13f.; 4:30). Paul writes that God "sealed us and gave us the Spirit in our hearts as a pledge" (2 Cor. 1:22). Sealing speaks of several things: security, ownership, and a guarantee. The Spirit is the spirit of adoption and he "bears witness with out spirit that we are children of God" (Rom. 8:16; cf. Gal. 4:6). These four works of the Spirit occur simultaneously and at the moment of believing faith.

B. The Continuing Work of the Spirit in the Believer

After conversion, the Spirit continues to have an active ministry in the life of believers. Several items can be noted.

1. He fills.   Believers are commanded to "be filled with the Spirit" (Eph. 5:18). At conversion the believer is indwelt by the Spirit; during his life he needs to be controlled by the same Spirit. Men, like the seven administrators of the early Jerusalem church (Acts 6:3) and Barnabas (Acts 11:24), were full of the Spirit. On the day of Pentecost it seems that the indwelling and the filling were concurrent events (Acts 2:4; cf. the experience of Paul, Acts 9:17), the former being a once-for-all experience, and the latter a way of life under the control of the Spirit. The filling ministry of the Spirit can be divided into the general filling ministry, which relates to control and spiritual growth and maturation, and into the special fillings, which relate to special movings of the Spirit. Peter was filled with the Spirit when he spoke (Acts 4:8; cf. 4:31; 13:9), but surely he was already full of the Spirit before he spoke. We can assume that he was living a Spirit-filled life when in critical times he was filled in a unique and special way with the Spirit.

2. He guides. The believer is commanded to walk in the Spirit and be led by the Spirit (Gal. 5:16, 25). This will enable him, on the one hand, not to fulfill the lusts of the flesh, and on the other hand, keep him from enslavement to legalism (Gal. 5:16–18; cf. Rom. 8:14). The early church enjoyed the leadership of the Spirit; the Spirit disciplined (Acts 5:9), directed (Acts 8:29), appointed (Acts 13:2), made decisions (Acts 15:28), and prohibited (Acts 16:6f.).

3. He empowers. The believer is engaged in a battle: the flesh against the Spirit, and the Spirit against the flesh. It takes the indwelling Spirit of God to provide the victory (Rom. 8:13; Gal. 5:17). The Spirit is the secret to victory. This was true in Old Testament times as well, for Zech. 4:6 reads, " 'Not by might nor by power, but by My Spirit,' says the Lord of hosts." It is the Spirit who produces in us the fruit of the Spirit (Gal. 5:22f.; cf. Eph. 5:9; Phil. 1:11).

4. He teaches. Jesus promised the coming of the Spirit to guide them into truth (John 14:26; 16:13). Each believer has the Spirit and, therefore, he does not need some additional special revelation or mystical insight (1 John 2:20, 27). The one who inspired Scripture is the one able to illumine the minds of spiritual people to the understanding of Scripture (1 Cor. 2:13).

In addition to the above items, the Spirit sovereignly gives spiritual gifts to believers (1 Cor. 12:4, 7–11; cf. Rom. 12:6–8; Eph. 4:11; 1 Pet. 4:10f.). He also intercedes for believers before the Father (Rom. 8:26). The Spirit of God does a blessed work in the life of each believer, and believers are cautioned not to grieve the Spirit through careless sinning (Eph. 4:30), not to tempt the Spirit by lying (Acts 5:9), not to quench the Spirit by restraining his ministries (1 Thess. 5:19), not to insult the Spirit by minimizing the atoning work of the blood of Jesus Christ (Heb. 10:29), and not to resist the Spirit by refusing to obey his directives (Acts 7:51).

CHAPTER XXVIII

Election and Vocation

In treating election and calling as the application of Christ's redemption, we imply that they are, in God's decree, logically subsequent to the decree of redemption. As has been noted previously, supralapsarianism suggests the following order of decrees: (1) the decree to save certain people and reprobate others; (2) the decree to create both; (3) the decree to permit the fall of both; (4) the decree to provide in Christ redemption for the elect; and (5) the decree to send the Spirit to apply this redemption to the elect. Some theologians unite (4) and (5) into one decree. We reject supralapsarianism, for surely God did not decree to save or to reprobate before he decreed to create. Again, as was noted earlier, it is better to understand the decrees in the following order: (1) the decree to create man; (2) the decree to permit the fall; (3) the decree to elect some of the fallen to salvation; (4) the decree to provide redemption for the elect; and (5) the decree to send the Spirit to apply this redemption to the elect. But even this view, called sublapsarianism, has a basic drawback in that it does not allow for unlimited atonement. It is best to enlarge (4) to read: the decree to provide redemption sufficient for all, and then to exchange the order of (3) and (4) so that the decree to provide redemption would come before the decree to elect. For our purposes, then, we will assume the following order: God decreed (1) to create man; (2) to permit the fall; (3) to provide in Christ redemption sufficient for all; (4) to elect some to salvation; and (5) to send the Spirit to secure the acceptance of redemption on the part of the elect.

I. THE DOCTRINE OF ELECTION

Assuming the above order of the decrees, we still have different perspectives concerning the definition of election. Is election the sovereign act of God whereby he chose some to salvation solely on the basis of sovereign grace apart from the merits or acts of the individual, or is it the sovereign act of God whereby he chose those whom he foreknew would respond to his gracious invitation? What is a working definition of election?

A. The Definition of Election

The election under consideration relates to election in its redemptive aspect. The Scriptures speak of an election that relates to a nation (Rom. 9:4; 11:28); one that relates to a particular office (Moses and Aaron, Ps. 105:26; David, 1 Sam. 16:12; 20:30; Solomon, 1 Chron. 28:5; the apostles, Luke 6:13–16; John 6:70; Acts 1:2, 24; 9:15; 22:14); and one that relates to the unfallen angels (1 Tim. 5:21). In its redemptive aspect, election means that sovereign act of God whereby he graciously chose in Jesus Christ for salvation all those whom he foreknew.

Election is a sovereign act of God; he is under no obligation to elect anyone, since all have lost their standing before God. Even after Christ died, God was not obligated to apply that salvation, except as he owed it to Christ to keep the agreement with him as to man's salvation. Thus, election is a sovereign act because it is not due to any constraint laid upon God. It is an act of grace, in that he chose those who were utterly unworthy of salvation. Man deserved the exact opposite, but in his grace God chose to save some. He chose them "in Christ" (Eph. 1:4). He could not choose them in themselves because they deserved judgment, so he chose them in the merits of another. Furthermore, he chose those whom he foreknew. But how do foreknowledge and predestination relate to election?

At this point we move into one of the great mysteries of our Christian faith. The Christian church is divided on the understanding of this doctrine especially as it relates to divine sovereignty and human responsibility coupled with the righteousness and holiness of God and the sinfulness of man. Scripture indicates that election is based on foreknowledge (1 Pet. 1:1f.; cf. Rom. 8:29), but the actual meaning of foreknowledge is debated. Is it merely prescience or foresight, or does it relate more closely to actual choice? Does God, in his foreknowledge, perceive what each man will do in response to his call and then elect him to salvation in harmony with this knowledge? Or does foreknowledge mean that God, from eternity past, looked with favor upon some and then elected them to salvation? Both of these positions must be set forth with arguments for and against.

B. Election Based on Prescience

In this position,[1] God in his foreknowledge foresaw those who would respond to his offer of salvation and actively elected them to salvation. That is, election is that sovereign act of God in grace whereby he chose in Christ for salvation all those whom he foreknew would accept him. Though we are nowhere told what it is in the foreknowledge of God that determines his

[1]This is the position held by Thiessen.

choice, the repeated teachings of Scripture that man is responsible for accepting or rejecting salvation suggest that it is man's response to the revelation which God made of himself that is the basis of his election. The elect are those whom God foresees will respond personally to the gospel.

Closely related to election is predestination or foreordination. The Greek verb occurs several times in the New Testament (Acts 4:28; Rom. 8:29f.; 1 Cor. 2:7; Eph. 1:5, 11). It carries the idea of marking off or appointing beforehand. Though election and predestination are similar in meaning, they may perhaps be distinguished in this manner: in election God has determined to save those who accept his Son and the proffered salvation; and in foreordination or predestination he has resolved to effectively accomplish that purpose. Thus Paul writes, "Whom He foreknew, He also predestined to become conformed to the image of His Son" (Rom. 8:29), and "He predestined us to adoption as sons through Jesus Christ to Himself" (Eph. 1:5; cf. v. 11).

1. Arguments for this view of election. This position can be argued along several lines.

a. Scripture teaches that God's salvation bringing grace has appeared to all men, not merely the elect (Tit. 2:11). Though mankind is hopelessly dead in trespasses and sins and can do nothing to obtain salvation, God, by prevenient grace, has restored to all men sufficient ability to make a choice in the matter of submission to God. This grace operates on the will before one turns to God. God, in common grace, gives mankind many blessings of life, health, friends, fruitful seasons, prosperity, the delay of judgment, the presence and influence of the Bible, the Holy Spirit, and the church. In addition to these he has restored to the sinner the ability to make a favorable response to God. Thus God, in his grace, has made it possible for all men to be saved. There is no merit in this transaction; it is all of God.

b. The Bible clearly and unequivocally teaches that Christ died for all (1 Tim. 2:6; 4:10; Heb. 2:9; 2 Pet. 2:1; 1 John 2:2; 4:14). God does not desire "for any to perish but for all to come to repentance" (2 Pet. 3:9; cf. Ezek. 18:32). The invitation to salvation is to all, to "whoever" (John 3:15f.; 4:13f.; 11:26; 12:46; Acts 2:21; 10:43). It is difficult to conceive of a universal invitation to which only the few have the ability to respond.

c. There are numerous exhortations to turn to God (Isa. 31:6; Joel 2:13f.; Matt. 18:3; Acts 3:19), to repent (Matt. 3:2; Luke 13:3, 5; Acts 2:38; 17:30), and to believe (John 6:29; Acts 16:31; 1 John 3:23). Paul writes, "For the grace of God has appeared, bringing salvation to all men" (Tit. 2:11). This results in the freeing of the will in the matter of salvation. In this way man can make an initial response to God, as a result of which God can give him repentance and faith. If man will turn to God on the basis of prevenient grace, then God will turn to him (Jer. 31:18ff.) and grant him repentance (Acts 5:31; 11:18; 2 Tim. 2:25) and faith (Rom. 12:3; 2 Pet. 1:1).

d. Scripture bases election on foreknowledge (Rom. 8:28–30; 1 Pet. 1:1f.), and to say that God foreknew all things because he had arbitrarily determined all things is to ignore the distinction between God's efficient and his permissive decrees. God foresaw that sin would enter the universe but he did not efficiently decree it. Surely he can also foresee how men will act without efficiently decreeing how they will act. God knows how man will respond to the gospel invitation, but he does not arbitrarily necessitate that response.

e. In this discussion the justice of God must also be considered. It is admitted that God is under no obligation to provide salvation for anyone, since all are responsible for their present lost condition. Further, God is not obliged to save anyone even though Christ has provided salvation sufficient for all. But is it not difficult to see how God can choose some from the mass of guilty and condemned men, provide salvation for them and efficiently secure their salvation, and yet do nothing about all the others? God would not be partial if he permitted all men to go to their deserved doom; but how can he be other than partial if he selects some from this multitude of men and does things for them and in them which he does not do for others, if there is not something about the two classes that makes the difference? Common grace has been extended to all, and everyone has the ability restored to him to be "willing to do His will" (John 7:17). The salvation bearing the grace of God has appeared to all men; but some receive the grace of God in vain. Only if God makes the same provisions for all and makes the same offers to all, is he truly just.

f. Acceptance of this view of election tends logically to great missionary endeavor. Christ sent his disciples into all the world, and he instructed them to preach the gospel to every creature. If election means that all those whom God has arbitrarily chosen will certainly be saved and that all those whom he has not chosen will not be saved, why should the Christian be overly concerned about preaching the gospel to every creature? But the knowledge that salvation is available to all stimulates and motivates missionary activity.

2. Objections to this view of election. Certain objections have been raised against this understanding of election. These must be addressed.

a. There are statements that the Father gave certain ones to Christ (John 6:37; 17:2, 6, 9), and it is assumed that this was an arbitrary act of God by which the rest were left to perish. But it is more probable that he did this because of what he foresaw they would do, than merely to exercise sovereign authority.

b. Christ said, "No one can come to Me, unless the Father who sent Me draws him" (John 6:44). This verse, however, must be read in light of another statement by Christ, "And I, if I be lifted up from the earth, will draw all men to Myself" (John 12:32). There issues a power from the cross of Christ that goes out to all men, though many continue to resist that power.

c. Paul writes that God works in us both to will and to work for his good pleasure (Phil. 2:13). It is assumed that there is nothing a sinner can do until God does these things in him. But this text is not addressed to unbelievers, but to believers. Jesus plainly said to some of the Jews, "You are unwilling to come to Me, that you may have life" (John 5:40), clearly implying that they could if they would.

d. In Rom. 9:10-16 God is said to have chosen Jacob rather than Esau, even before they were born and before they had done either good or bad. But two things should be noted. Though it is said that they had not yet done either good or bad, it is not said that God did not know who would do the good and who would do the bad. Esau consistently chose the profane things of life, and Jacob, though far from constant in the things of God, chose the more spiritual things. Further, the choice of Jacob rather than Esau was a choice to outward and national privilege, not a choice to salvation directly. Scripture declares that not all the descendants of Israel (Jacob) are Israel, and not all the children of Abraham are children of promise. A descendant of Esau can be saved as readily as a descendant of Jacob.

e. Acts 13:48 reads, "As many as had been appointed to eternal life believed." That this cannot refer to an absolute decree is evidenced by the fact that in v. 46 Paul had already declared that the Jews by their own personal choice rejected the message. Thus God had ordained to salvation those whom he foresaw would believe. It is also possible that the verb "appointed" should be understood as in the middle voice, meaning "as many as set themselves to eternal life believed."

f. Again, Eph. 1:5-8; 2:8-10 represent salvation as originating in the choice of God and as being all of grace. But this does not contradict the view being presented. God must take the initiative, and he does in prevenient grace. If it were not for the operation of his grace upon the heart of the sinner, no man could be saved. But this prevenient grace does not save the man, it merely enables him to choose whom he will serve.

g. Scripture teaches that repentance and faith are gifts of God (Acts 5:31; 11:18; Rom. 12:3; Eph. 2:8-10; 2 Tim. 2:25). But it would seem very strange if God should call upon all men everywhere to repent (Acts 17:30; 2 Pet. 3:9) and believe (Mark 1:14f.) when only some may receive the gift of repentance and faith.

h. Finally, some claim that if predestination is not unconditional and absolute, then God's whole plan is uncertain and liable to miscarriage. But this could only be true if God had not foreknown the outcome and had not adopted it as his plan. God has foreseen all that will happen and has accepted these eventualities into his program. His plan is certain though not all the events in it are necessitated.

C. ELECTION BASED ON CHOICE

The second approach to election is to understand foreknowledge as actively looking with favor upon some and then electing them to salvation. Election is that sovereign act of God whereby he chose out from the sinful human race certain to be the recipients of his special saving grace. It is solely his sovereign pleasure and on account of no foreseen merit in those chosen. In this approach foreknowledge is not mere prescience, but more closely related to actual choice. For God to foreknow is for God to choose. His foreknowledge is his choice. Further, the term "know," with its various cognates, often carries the idea of "to know intimately," "to know with appreciation," "to know lovingly." Examples of this can be found in both the Old and New Testaments. God declares, "You only have I chosen [known] of all the families of the earth" (Amos 3:2). Keil suggests that the term "acknowledge" be used in this verse. He writes, "Acknowledgment on the part of God is not merely taking notice, but is energetic, embracing man in his inmost being, embracing and penetrating with divine love." He continues by saying that it "not only includes the idea of love and care, as in Hos. xiii. 5, but expresses generally the gracious fellowship of the Lord with Israel, as in Gen. xviii. 19, and is practically equivalent to electing, including both the motive and the result of election."[2] The sons of Eli "did not know the Lord and the custom of the priests with the people" (1 Sam. 2:12f.). Surely this does not mean that they were unaware of God or his Levitical regulations; rather they did not acknowledge or have proper respect and appreciation for God and his regulations. The verb "know" is used in similar fashion in the New Testament. Paul writes of our obligation to know (appreciate) our spiritual leaders (1 Thess. 5:12). John writes, "By this we know that we have come to know Him, if we keep His commandments" (1 John 2:3). Surely this is more than to be cognizant of God; it is rather to have a loving relationship with God, to acknowledge him. With this in mind, can we not interpret God's foreknowledge as God, in eternity past, looking with favor upon some and then electing them to salvation? Foreknowledge is antecedent to election, and both are determinative acts of God; the former is not passive knowledge, but active.

1. Arguments for this view of election. Ultimate reasons for election are beyond the scope of the human mind. We finally leave the understanding of it with a wise, sovereign, and loving God. We rest ourselves in the words of

[2]Keil, *The Twelve Minor Prophets*, I, p. 259.

Deut. 29:29, "The secret things belong to the Lord our God, but the things revealed belong to us and to our sons forever, that we may observe all the words of this law." But there are several arguments or proofs which can be given in support of this doctrine.

a. There are clear biblical statements in support of election. Acts 13:48 reads, "As many as had been appointed to eternal life believed" (cf. Rom. 8:27–30; Gal. 4:9; Eph. 1:5, 11; 1 Thess. 1:4; 1 Pet. 1:1f.; 2:9).

b. The whole process of salvation is a gift of God (Rom. 12:3; Eph. 2:8–10). Granted, man must respond to the gospel, but even his ability to respond is a gift of God. To the Philippians Paul wrote, "God . . . is at work in you, both to will and to work for His good pleasure" (2:13).

c. There are verses which speak of men having been given to Christ (John 6:37; 17:2) and of the Father drawing men to Christ (John 6:44).

d. There are examples in Scripture of the sovereign calling of God upon individuals, such as Paul (Gal. 1:15) and Jeremiah (Jer. 1:5; cf. Ps. 139:13–16).

e. It is on the basis of election that the appeal to a godly life is made (Col. 3:12; 2 Thess. 2:13; 1 Pet. 2:9).

f. Election is portrayed as being from all eternity. God "has saved us, and called us with a holy calling, not according to our works, but according to His own purpose and grace which was granted us in Christ Jesus from all eternity" (2 Tim. 1:9).

Two items, both of which come from human experience, must be added. Christians universally thank God for their salvation, not themselves. And further, why pray to God for the salvation of others, if we do not expect God to work sovereignly in their loves to respond to the gospel? Thus by intercession for the salvation of others and by giving thanks for salvation, Christians everywhere acknowledge and confess God's sovereignty in salvation. In all of this, we recognize a mystery in God's sovereign working in the free will of man.

2. *Objections to this view of election.*   Several objections may be raised to this view of the doctrine of election.

a. It makes foreknowledge and election virtually the same. It is argued that to foresee is merely to know beforehand. God foresaw that sin would enter the world, but he did not necessitate it, he merely permitted it. In the same fashion, it is argued, God foresaw how man would respond when presented with the claims of Christ, and then elected those whom he foresaw would respond favorably. It has been demonstrated, however, that for God to know someone is often more than just to have a knowledge of the person. Rather, it speaks of having a personal relationship with. Thus, foreknowledge is active, not passive. Further, the doctrine of election retains the sovereignty of God. He can determine to save whomsoever he will. Luke reports of the response to the gospel at Antioch of Pisidia, "As many as had been appointed to eternal life believed" (Acts 13:38).

b. It is argued that if election is limited by God, surely the atonement must be limited as well. This, however, is contrary to the many Scriptures which teach unlimited atonement (John 1:29; 3:16; 1 Tim. 2:6; Heb. 2:9; 1 John 2:2). Man remains responsible for rejecting the atonement. It is available to all, but man willfully turns aside from it. That some men reject it, limits the effectiveness of it, but not its availability. An illustration could be used of those who crucified our Lord. It was ordained by God that Christ be crucified, but the men who actually did it will be held responsible (Acts 2:23; 4:27f.). Jesus said, "It is inevitable that stumbling blocks come; but woe to that man through whom the stumbling block comes!" (Matt. 18:7). Ryrie counsels:

> Balance is the great need in considering this doctrine. While one must not lose sight of the reality of responsibility, that responsibility must not obscure the full meaning of grace. Grace concerns origins, responsibility concerns reactions. God originated His plan of salvation and based it entirely on grace (for sinful man could not merit His favor); yet man is entirely responsible for acceptance or rejection of God's grace.[3]

Salvation is available for all; it is unlimited. But it is effectively limited by man's rejection of it.

c. It makes God responsible for reprobation. Why God did not elect some to salvation is a deep mystery. But let us remember that election deals not with innocent creatures, but with sinful, guilty, vile, and condemned creatures. That any should be saved is a matter of pure grace (Eph. 2:8). Those not included in election suffer only their due reward. We should rather praise God for saving any, than charge him with being unfair or unjust in saving just the few. God does not delight in the death of the wicked (Ezek. 33:11), and he is not willing that any should perish (2 Pet. 3:9), but man's iniquities have brought him separation from God (Isa. 59:2). The decree of reprobation, if it indeed can be spoken of in that fashion, is a decree to do nothing, a decree to leave the sinner to himself, to his own self-hardening and self-destruction. It is not correct to say that God elects some to hell. When Peter writes, "They stumble because they are disobedient to the word, and to this doom they were also appointed" (1 Pet. 2:8), his teaching is that they were appointed, not to disobedience, but *to stumble* because they are disobedient. In like manner Paul's conclusion, "So then He has mercy on whom He desires, and He hardens whom He desires" (Rom. 9:18), must be understood. God leaves man to his own destructive and self-hardening ways, and in that sense he hardens man's heart.

[3]Ryrie, *The Grace of God*, p. 85.

d. Further, election discourages evangelism. It is asked, if only the elect will be saved, why evangelize? Those who are elect to salvation will be saved; those who are not elect will not be saved; therefore, why evangelize? Several things should be noted. (1) The last command of Christ was to communicate the gospel to the world (Acts 1:8). This command is our mandate. God has chosen evangelism as the method through which his election finds its fulfillment (Acts 13:48; 18:10). (2) This doctrine gives the Christian encouragement as he shares his faith. Paul writes, "For this reason I endure all things for the sake of those who are chosen, that they also may obtain the salvation which is in Christ Jesus and with it eternal glory" (2 Tim. 2:10). (3) The child of God who begins to comprehend the great love of God toward him in choosing him for salvation has renewed motivation to share this great truth of salvation with others. Paul declares, "The love of Christ controls us" (2 Cor. 5:14), and he continues a few verses on, "We are ambassadors for Christ, as though God were entreating through us; we beg you on behalf of Christ, be reconciled to God" (v. 20).[4]

e. It portrays God as partial and arbitrary. Perhaps on the surface this objection seems valid, but two things must be noted. First, it has nothing to do with partiality, because there is nothing in man which commends him to God. Second, to speak of election as arbitrary, indirectly accuses God of not being wise, free, and loving. Election is done by a wise and loving God.

f. Finally, this view of election instills pride within the elect. But surely this is not so. Human works and effort bring about pride (Luke 18:11f.; Rom. 4:2; Eph. 2:9); the sovereign grace of God causes worship.

Whichever of these two approaches to the doctrine of election might seem more appropriate and biblical to us, our response should be that of the apostle, "Oh, the depth of the riches both of the wisdom and knowledge of God! How unsearchable are His judgments and unfathomable His ways!" (Rom. 11:33). We conclude with Paul, "To Him be glory forever. Amen" (v. 36; cf. Isa. 55:8f.).

II. THE DOCTRINE OF VOCATION

This is the doctrine of God's call. The grace of God is magnified not only in the provision of salvation, but also in the offer of salvation to the undeserving. We may define God's call as that act of grace by which he invites men to accept by faith the salvation provided by Christ.

A. THE PERSONS CALLED

The Scriptures indicate that salvation is offered to all. It is offered to the "predestined" (Rom. 8:30), to "all who are weary and heavy-laden" (Matt.

---

[4]For a full discussion of this, see Packer, *Evangelism and the Sovereignty of God.*

11:28), to "whoever believes in Him" (John 3:16; cf. 3:15; 4:14; 11:26; Rev. 22:17), to "all the ends of the earth" (Isa. 45:22; cf. Ezek. 33:11; Matt. 28:19; Mark 16:15; John 12:32; 1 Tim. 2:4; 2 Pet. 3:9), and to "as many as you find" (Matt. 22:9).

At this point two questions arise: (1) If some are elect and others not, is the call of God sincere for all? If the call of God is sincere for all, is it compatible with the doctrine that the sinner by nature is unable to obey? It must be remembered that the inability is a moral inability, not a physical inability. Man's inability is because of his own evil will, for which man himself is responsible. The question is further asked, how is this call compatible with election? But the difficulty is the same whether we speak of God's permitting men to reject the call or whether we speak of God's foreknowing that some would reject it. (2) A second question relates to the efficacy of the call. Is the call irresistible? This term might leave a wrong impression of God bringing outside pressure on the human mind. But surely we acknowledge that God works in man to do his will (Phil. 2:13). God is able to work sovereignly in the hearts of men to cause them to respond personally and by their own volition to the call of God to salvation. The coming together of sovereignty and free will as they relate to the call of God are shown in an amazing way by John, "He came to His own, and those who were His own did not receive Him. But as many as received Him, to them He gave the right to become children of God, even to those who believe in His name, who were born not of blood, nor of the will of the flesh, nor of the will of man, but of God" (John 1:11–13).

B. The Object of the Call

Briefly stated, God does not call men to reformation of life, to good works, to baptism, to church involvement, etc. These are all proper things in themselves, but they are merely the sure fruit of that to which he does call men. The things to which he calls men are repentance (Matt. 3:2; 4:17; Mark 1:14f.; Acts 2:38; 17:30; 2 Pet. 3:9) and faith (Mark 1:15; John 6:29; 20:30f.; Acts 16:31; 19:4; Rom. 10:9; 1 John 3:23).

C. The Means of the Call

God has a variety of means by which to call men. (1) He calls men through the Word of God (Rom. 10:16f.; 1 Thess. 2:13; 2 Thess. 2:14). (2) He also calls men by his Spirit (John 16:8; Heb. 3:7f.; cf. Gen. 6:3). The Holy Spirit urges the sinner to come and accept Christ. (3) God uses his servants to call men (2 Chron. 36:15; Jer. 25:4; Matt. 22:2–9; Rom. 10:14f.). Jonah is a good example of God's use of human messengers to bring a city to repentance. The Word of God must be brought to the unsaved by regenerated persons, persons who can testify to the power of the Word and the Spirit in their own lives (1 Thess. 1:5). And (4) God calls by his providential dealings with men. His goodness is intended to bring men to repentance (Jer. 31:3; Rom. 2:4), but if that does not succeed, then his judgments are to do it (Ps. 107:6, 13; Isa. 26:9).

CHAPTER XXIX

Conversion

What is the logical order in the experience of salvation? There is, of course, no chronological sequence; conversion, justification, regeneration, union with Christ, and adoption, all take place at the same instant. Sanctification alone is both an act and a process. But there is a logical sequence, and we shall follow the order just indicated. This is done because the Scriptures appeal to man to turn to God (Prov. 1:23; Isa. 31:6; 59:20; Ezek. 14:6; 18:32; 33:9–11; Joel 2:12f.; Matt. 18:3; Acts 3:19; Heb. 6:1). Conversion is that turning to God, and it represents the human response to the call of God. It consists of two elements: repentance and faith. The Scriptures never ask man to justify himself, to regenerate himself, or to adopt himself. God alone can do these things, but man by God's enablement can turn to God. The church at Jerusalem acknowledged, "Well then, God has granted to the Gentiles also the repentance that leads to life" (Acts 11:18; cf. 2 Tim. 2:25). It seems clear that repentance and faith lead to justification, and justification leads to life, and not the reverse (Rom. 5:17f.). We look, then, at the two elements in conversion.

I. THE ELEMENT OF REPENTANCE

Although repentance and faith are closely linked together we need to consider each by itself.

A. The Importance of Repentance

The importance of repentance is not always recognized as it should be. Some call upon the unsaved to accept Christ and to believe, without ever showing the sinner that he is lost and needs a Savior. But the Scriptures lay much stress on the preaching of repentance. Repentance was the message of the Old Testament prophets (Deut. 30:10; 2 Kings 17:13; Jer. 8:6; Ezek. 14:6; 18:30). It was the keynote of the preaching of John the Baptist (Matt. 3:2; Mark 1:15), of Christ (Matt. 4:17; Luke 13:3–5), of the twelve as such (Mark 6:12), and in particular of Peter on the day of Pentecost (Acts 2:38; cf. 3:19). It was also fundamental to the preaching of Paul (Acts 20:21; 26:20).

The dispensational change has not made repentance unnecessary in this age; it is definitely a command to all men (Acts 17:30). This is what Paul said at Athens, the farthest removed from a Jewish environment. Repentance is something in which all heaven is supremely interested (Luke 15:7, 10; 24:46f.). It is the fundamental of fundamentals (Matt. 21:32; Heb. 6:1), because it is an absolute condition of salvation (Luke 13:2–5).

B. THE MEANING OF REPENTANCE

Repentance is essentially a change of mind, taking the word in a broad sense. It has, however, three aspects: an intellectual, an emotional, and a volitional aspect. Let us look at each of these more carefully.

1. The intellectual element.   This implies a change of view. It is a change of view with regard to sin, God, and self. Sin comes to be recognized as personal guilt, God as the one who justly demands righteousness, and self as defiled and helpless. The Scriptures speak of this aspect of repentance as the knowledge of sin (Rom. 3:20; cf. Job 42:5f.; Ps. 51:3; Luke 15:17f.; Rom. 1:32). Repentance also involves a change of mind concerning Christ. Peter called upon the Jews to see Christ not as a mere man, an imposter, or a blasphemer, but as the promised Messiah and Savior (Acts 2:14–40).

2. The emotional element.   This implies a change of feeling. Sorrow for sin and a desire for pardon are aspects of repentance. There is intense emotion in David's prayer, "Be gracious to me, O God, according to Thy lovingkindness; according to the greatness of Thy compassion blot out my transgressions" (Ps. 51:1). Paul writes, "I now rejoice, not that you were made sorrowful, but that you were made sorrowful to the point of repentance; for you were made sorrowful according to the will of God, in order that you might not suffer loss in anything through us. For the sorrow that is according to the will of God produces a repentance without regret" (2 Cor. 7:9f.). Other verses which show emotion to be a part of repentance are Matt. 21:32; 27:3 (cf. Ps. 38:18).

3. The volitional element.   This element implies a change of will, disposition, and purpose. This is the inward turning from sin. There is a change of disposition to seek pardon and cleansing. Peter said, "Repent, and let each of you be baptized in the name of Jesus Christ for the forgiveness of your sins" (Acts 2:38), and Paul writes, "Or do you think lightly of the riches of His kindness and forbearance and patience, not knowing that the kindness of God leads you to repentance?" (Rom. 2:4). The volitional element of repentance is contained in both these verses.

Confession of sin (Ps. 32:5; 51:3f.; Luke 15:21; 18:13; 1 John 1:9) and reparations for wrongs done to men (Luke 19:8) are fruits of repentance, but they do not constitute repentance. We are not saved *for* repenting but *if* we repent. Repentance is not a satisfaction rendered to God, but a condition of the heart necessary before we can believe unto salvation. Furthermore, true repentance never exists apart from faith. That is, one cannot turn from sin without at the same time turning to God. Conversely, we may say that true faith never exists without repentance. The two are inseparably bound together.

C. The Means to Repentance

A word should also be said about the means to repentance. On the divine side, repentance is the gift of God. Paul writes, "If perhaps God may grant them repentance leading to the knowledge of the truth" (2 Tim. 2:25; cf. Acts 5:31; 11:18). On the human side, it is brought about by various things. Jesus teaches that miracles (Matt. 11:20f.), even the coming of one from the dead (Luke 16:30f.), are insufficient to produce repentance. But the Word of God (Luke 16:30f.), the preaching of the gospel (Matt. 12:41; Luke 24:47; Acts 2:37f.: 2 Tim. 2:25), the goodness of God toward his creatures (Rom. 2:4; 2 Pet. 3:9), the chastisement of the Lord (Heb. 12:10f.; Rev. 3:19), belief of the truth (Jonah 3:5–10), and a new vision of God (Job 42:5f.) are definite means that God uses to produce repentance.

II. THE ELEMENT OF FAITH

As in the case of repentance, so in the case of faith, the doctrine does not receive the attention that it deserves. A man's life is governed by what he believes and in what he has faith, and his religion by the person in whom he believes. Evans says, "The Syrophoenician woman (Matt. 15) had perseverance; the centurion (Matt. 8), humility; the blind man (Mark 10), earnestness. But what Christ saw and rewarded in each of these cases was faith."[1] This is true, and it ought to cause us to consider the place of faith in life. Let us consider it as an element of conversion.

A. The Importance of Faith

The Scriptures declare that we are saved by faith (Acts 16:31; Rom. 5:1; 9:30–32; Eph. 2:8), enriched with the Spirit by faith (Gal. 3:5, 14), sanctified by faith (Acts 15:9; 26:18), kept by faith (Rom. 11:20; 2 Cor. 1:24; 1 Pet. 1:5; 1 John 5:4), established by faith (Isa. 7:9), and healed by

[1]Evans, *The Great Doctrines of the Bible,* p. 144.

faith (Acts 14:9; James 5:15). We walk by faith (2 Cor. 5:7) and surmount difficulties by faith (Mark 9:23; Rom. 4:18–21; Heb. 11:32–40). God declares faith necessary in order to please him (Heb. 11:6) and regards unbelief as a great sin (John 16:9; Rom. 14:23) and as putting a limit upon the manifestations of his power (Mark 6:5f.). Faith makes us a constant blessing to others (John 7:38); it leads us to put forth an effort in behalf of others (Mark 2:3–5); it induces perseverance in service (Matt. 15:28); and it obtains help for others (Acts 27:24f.). Surely, these benefits reveal the importance of faith.

B. The Meaning of Faith

Let us first distinguish between some terms that are sometimes confounded. Such are the terms "belief," "hope," "the faith," and "faith." The word "belief" is often used in the same sense as the word "faith"; but many times it serves to denote only one element of faith, namely the intellectual. We must guard against a loose use of this term. Hope has to do exclusively with the future, while faith has to do with the past, the present, and the future. Hope has been defined as desire plus expectation, but scriptural hope has in it also the elements of knowledge and assurance. It rests upon a truth revealed in the Scriptures. By "the faith" we mean the sum total of Christian doctrine as contained in the Scriptures (Luke 18:8; Acts 6:7; 1 Tim. 4:1; 6:10; Jude 3). Trust is a characteristic Old Testament word for the New Testament "believe" or "faith."

What then is faith? It is not easy to formulate a simple and adequate definition. In conversion, faith is the turning of the soul to God, as repentance is the turning of the soul from sin. But we need to make a closer study of this turning to God. We may say that the Scriptures represent faith as an act of the heart. It therefore involves an intellectual, an emotional, and a volitional change. Men believe with the heart to be saved (Rom. 10:9f.). The Scriptures emphasize the intellectual aspect of faith in such references as Ps. 9:10; John 2:23f.; and Rom. 10:14. Nicodemus had faith in this sense of the term when he came to Jesus (John 3:2), and the demons, we are told, believe, for they know the facts concerning God (James 2:19). It is, no doubt, in this sense also that Simon Magus believed (Acts 8:13), for there are no indications that he repented and appropriated Christ. We conclude, therefore, that faith must be more than intellectual assent. Let us look at the three aspects necessary to faith.

1. The intellectual element. This element includes belief in the revelation of God in nature, in the historical facts of Scripture, and in the doctrines taught therein as to man's sinfulness, the redemption provided in Christ, the conditions to salvation and to all the blessings promised to God's children.

While this element of faith is greatly disparaged in our day, it is nevertheless fundamental to the other constituents of faith. Paul says, "So faith comes from hearing, and hearing by the word of Christ" (Rom. 10:17). We know that there is a God; therefore, we believe in his existence (Rom. 1:19f.); we need to know the gospel in order to believe in Christ (Rom. 10:14). Scriptural faith, therefore, is not the acceptance of a working hypothesis in religion, it is belief based on the best of evidence. The Psalmist wrote, "Those who know Thy name will put their trust in Thee; for Thou, O Lord, hast not forsaken those who seek Thee" (Ps. 9:10).

2. The emotional element.   This is emphasized in such Scriptures as Ps. 106:12f., "Then they believed His words; they sang His praise. They quickly forgot His works; they did not wait for His counsel"; Matt. 13:20f., "And the one on whom seed was sown on the rocky places, this is the man who hears the word, and immediately receives it with joy; yet he has no firm root in himself, but is only temporary, and when affliction or persecution arises because of the word, immediately he falls away"; and John 8:30f., where the writer distinguishes between the many who believed on him and those who merely believed him. Compare also the scribe's assent to Jesus' statement as to what is the greatest commandment without accepting him as Savior (Mark 12:32–34); and John 5:35, "He was the lamp that was burning and was shining, and you were willing to rejoice for a while in his light." All these references intimate a partial and temporary acceptance of the truth of God, as distinguished from a complete appropriation of its message and its Christ.

We may define the emotional element of faith as the awakening of the soul to its personal needs and to the personal applicability of the redemption provided in Christ, together with an immediate assent to these truths. But it must not stop here, for while the emotional element is certainly to be recognized as a constituent of faith, it must not be treated as if it were the sole characteristic of faith.

3. The voluntary element.   This element of faith is the logical outgrowth of the intellectual and the emotional. If a man accepts the revelation of God and his salvation as true and comes to assent to it as applicable to himself personally, he should logically go on to appropriate it to himself. Each preceding term logically leads on to the succeeding; a man is not saved unless his faith has all three of these elements in it. The voluntary element, however, is so comprehensive that it presupposes the other two. Certainly, no one can be saved who does not voluntarily appropriate Christ, and no one can get an answer to prayer who does not wholeheartedly embrace the promises of God.

The voluntary element includes the surrender of the heart to God and the appropriation of Christ as Savior. The former is brought out in such Scriptures as "Give me your heart, my son, and let your eyes delight in my ways" (Prov. 23:26); "Come to Me, all who are weary and heavy-laden, and I will given you rest. Take My yoke upon you, and learn from Me" (Matt. 11:28f.); and "If anyone comes to Me, and does not hate his own father and mother and wife and children and brothers and sisters, yes, and even his own life, he cannot be My disciple" (Luke 14:26). That the Greek term *pisteuo* (to believe or trust) is used in the sense of surrender and commitment is seen in such statements as "But Jesus, on His part, was not entrusting Himself to them, for He knew all men" (John 2:24); "They were entrusted with the oracles of God" (Rom. 3:2); and "I had been entrusted with the gospel" (Gal. 2:7). The Scriptures frequently emphasize that man should count the cost before deciding to follow Christ (Matt. 8:19–22; Luke 14:26–33). The thought of surrender is also implied in the exhortation to accept Jesus as Lord. The command is "Believe in the Lord Jesus" (Acts 16:31), and we must confess "Jesus as Lord" (Rom. 10:9) to be saved. To believe in him as Lord is to recognize him as Lord, and we cannot recognize him as Lord until we ourselves abdicate. This note in faith is often overlooked or even referred to a later time of consecration, but the Scriptures connect it with the initial experience of salvation.

The appropriation of Christ as Savior is abundantly taught in Scripture: "But as many as received Him, to them He gave the right to become children of God, even to those who believe in His name" (John 1:12); "But whoever drinks of the water that I shall given him shall never thirst; but the water that I shall give him shall become in him a well of water springing up to eternal life" (John 4:14); "Unless you eat the flesh of the Son of Man and drink His blood, you have no life in yourselves. He who eats My flesh and drinks My blood has eternal life; and I will raise him up the last day" (John 6:53f.); and "Behold, I stand at the door and knock; if any one hears My voice and opens the door, I will come in to him, and will dine with him, and he with Me" (Rev. 3:20).

C. THE SOURCE OF FAITH

As with repentance, there is a divine and a human side of faith.

1. The divine side. The writer to the Hebrews speaks of Jesus as being "the author and perfecter of faith" (Heb. 12:2). Clearly, faith is a gift of God (Rom. 12:3; 2 Pet. 1:1), sovereignly given by the Spirit of God (1 Cor. 12:9; cf. Gal. 5:22). Paul speaks of the whole aspect of salvation as being a gift of God (Eph. 2:8), and surely that includes faith.

2. The human side. Both the spoken and the written word of God produce faith. The Bible says, "So faith comes from hearing, and hearing by the word of Christ" (Rom. 10:17), and "Many of those who had heard the message believed" (Acts 4:4). Not only is the word of God a means of faith, so is prayer (Mark 9:24; Luke 22:32). The disciples requested of the Lord, "Increase our faith" (Luke 17:5). Further, the exercise of the faith we have will be a means whereby our faith will grow (Matt. 25:29; cf. Judg. 6:14).

D. THE RESULTS OF FAITH

The results of faith are several.

1. *Salvation.*   Our whole salvation is dependent upon faith. From start to finish we are saved by faith, be it justification (Rom. 5:1), adoption (Gal. 3:5, 14; 4:5f.), or sanctification (Acts 26:18). Peter tells us that we are "protected by the power of God through faith" (1 Pet. 1:5).

2. *Assurance.*   It is true that assurance comes by the witness of the Holy Spirit (Rom. 8:16; 1 John 3:24; 4:13), but, nevertheless, God refers the soul to the promises in the Word of God, and assurance comes when we believe them. Closely connected with assurance is peace (Isa. 26:3; Rom. 5:1) and rest (Heb. 4:3), with the resulting joy (1 Pet. 1:8).

3. *Good works.*   Faith necessarily leads to good works. We have been saved apart from works (Rom. 3:20; Eph. 2:9), but yet "for good works" (Eph. 2:10). Jesus said, "Let your light shine before men in such a way that they may see your good works, and glorify your Father who is in heaven" (Matt. 5:16). James emphasizes the manifestation of faith in "works" (James 2:17–26). Paul stresses the insufficiency of the works of the law (Gal. 2:16; 3:10); yet he also emphasizes that "works" are the outgrowth of faith (Titus 1:16; 2:14; 3:8). These good works are the fruit of the Spirit (Gal. 5:22f.; Eph. 5:9).

CHAPTER XXX

Justification and Regeneration

The next doctrines to be considered are justification and regeneration.

I. THE DOCTRINE OF JUSTIFICATION

Conversion is followed by justification. While the Scriptures lay great stress on the doctrine of justification, in the course of history it became greatly perverted and practically discarded. It is the glory of the Protestant Reformation that it restored this doctrine to its rightful place. We are more or less disappointed when we search for the doctrines of regeneration and sanctification in the Reformers; these doctrines did not receive sufficient emphasis until the days of the Wesleyan Revival. But we may rejoice that the Reformation did give back to the church the fundamental doctrine of justification. Several aspects of this doctrine need to be considered.

A. THE DEFINITION OF JUSTIFICATION

By nature, man is not only a child of the evil one, but also a transgressor and a criminal (Rom. 3:23; 5:6-10; Eph. 2:1-3; Col. 1:21; Titus 3:3). In regeneration man receives a new life and a new nature; in justification, a new standing. Justification may be defined as that act of God whereby he declares righteous him who believes in Christ. Ladd suggests, "The root idea in justification is the declaration of God, the righteous judge, that the man who believes in Christ, sinful though he may be, is righteous—is viewed as being righteous, because in Christ he has come into a righteous relationship with God."[1]

Justification is a declarative act. It is not something wrought in man, but something declared of man. It does not make upright or righteous, but declares righteous. Several things are involved.

1. The remission of the penalty. The penalty for sin is death: spiritual, physical, and eternal (Gen. 2:17; Rom. 5:12-14; 6:23). If man is to be saved,

---

[1]Ladd, *A Theology of the New Testament*, p. 437.

275

this penalty must first be removed. It was removed by and in the death of Christ, who bore the punishment of our sins in his own body on the tree (Isa. 53:5f.; 1 Pet. 2:24). Since Christ has borne man's penalty for sin, God now remits it in the case of him who believes in Christ (Acts 13:38f.; Rom. 8:1, 33f.; 2 Cor. 5:21). This is the forgiveness of sins (Rom. 4:7; Eph. 1:7; 4:32; Col. 2:13).

The death of Christ made forgiveness possible, but not necessary, since Christ died voluntarily and not of necessity. God is still entitled to say on what conditions man may receive forgiveness. This he has done in declaring that he forgives those who repent and believe on his son. David said, "How blessed is he whose transgression is forgiven, whose sin is covered! How blessed is the man to whom the Lord does not impute iniquity" (Ps. 32:1f.). "The doctrine of justification means that God has pronounced the eschatological verdict of acquittal over the man of faith in the present, in advance of the final judgment."[2]

2. *The restoration to favor.*   The sinner has not merely incurred a penalty, but he has also lost God's favor (John 3:36; Rom. 1:18; 5:9; Gal. 2:16f.). Justification is more than acquittal; the remission of the penalty is one thing, restoration to favor is another. The justified man becomes a friend of God (2 Chron. 20:7; James 2:23). He is made an heir of God and a fellow-heir of Christ (Rom. 8:16f.; Gal. 3:26; Heb. 2:11).

3. *The imputation of righteousness.*   Since justification is setting one right before law, the sinner must not only be pardoned for his past sins, but also supplied with a positive righteousness before he can have fellowship with God. This need is supplied in the imputation of the righteousness of Christ to the believer. To impute is to reckon to one. Paul asked Philemon to reckon Onesimus' debt to him (Philem. 18). David declares that man blessed "to whom the Lord does not impute iniquity" (Ps. 32:2). Paul says of this statement that David "speaks of the blessing upon the man to whom God reckons righteousness apart from works" (Rom. 4:6). How can God do that? By imputing to the believer the righteousness of Christ. "He made Him who knew no sin to be sin on our behalf, that we might become the righteousness of God in Him" (2 Cor. 5:21). Christ "became to us wisdom from God, and righteousness and sanctification, and redemption" (1 Cor. 1:30). This righteousness of God is revealed in the gospel, and it is from faith to faith (Rom. 1:17). We should observe that this is not God's attribute of righteousness, for our faith has nothing to do with that, but with the righteousness which God has provided for the one who believes in Christ. Thus, God restores us to favor by imputing to us Christ's righteousness. This is the wedding gar-

---

[2]Ladd, *A Theology of the New Testament*, p. 446.

ment that is ready for everyone who accepts the invitation to the feast (Matt. 22:11f.; cf. Luke 15:22–24).

The justified person, therefore, has had his sins pardoned and the penalty of his sins remitted; he has also been restored to God's favor by the imputation of the righteousness of Christ. He is not yet righteous in himself, though the adjective *dikaios* sometimes is used of righteous conduct, but he is righteous in the forensic sense, from the legal standpoint. The Roman Catholic Church defines justification as the remission of sin and infusion of new habits of grace. Thus, justification is treated as a subjective experience and not as an objective relationship. It was against this view that the Reformers contended. They insisted that justification is something different from sanctification, that the former is a declarative act, setting forth the sinner's relation to the law and justice of God, and the latter an efficient act, changing the inward character of the sinner. That this is the correct view is evident from many Scriptures.

B. The Method of Justification

As early as the days of Job, we find man asking the question, "How then can a man be just with God? Or how can he be clean who is born of woman?" (Job 25:4). The Psalmist pleads with the Lord and says, "Do not enter into judgment with Thy servant, for in Thy sight no man living is righteous" (Ps. 143:2). Fortunately, Old Testament seekers after God did not wait until Paul was born to find an answer to their question. Paul reminds us that Abraham was justified by faith fourteen years before he was circumcised (Rom. 4:1–5, 9–12; cf. Gen. 15:6; 16:15f.; 17:23–26) and that David rejoiced in the fact of an imputed righteousness (Rom. 4:6–8). The New Testament doctrine of justification is not an innovation; it is a truth already known in Old Testament times, and righteousness was obtained in the same manner in those days as in the New Testament dispensation. What is the method of justification?

1. It is not by works of the law. Negatively, justification is not by the works of the law. It is true that Jesus referred the rich young ruler to the law when he asked how he might inherit eternal life (Mark 10:17–22), but it is evident that he did this simply to demonstrate to the young man that salvation is impossible on that basis. He that would be justified by works must continue in all things that are written in the law (Gal. 3:10; James 2:10). This no one has done nor can do. Paul declares that by the works of the law no flesh is justified in his sight (Rom. 3:20; Gal. 2:16). The law merely serves to reveal sin (Rom. 3:20; 7:7) and to impel the convicted soul to flee to Christ (Gal. 3:24). Jesus, on another occasion, taught that "the work of God" is to "believe in Him whom He has sent" (John 6:29). Men are not

saved by doing the best they can, unless that doing is believing on the Lord
Jesus.

2. *It is by the grace of God.*   Two Scriptures may be quoted: "Being justified as a gift by His grace through the redemption which is in Christ Jesus"
(Rom. 3:24) and "Being justified by His grace we might be made heirs according to the hope of eternal life" (Titus 3:7). These denote the source of our justification. It is not for works of righteousness which we have done, but according to his mercy that he saved us (Titus 3:5; cf. Eph. 2:4f., 8). Justification thus
originates in the heart of God. Realizing not only our lack of righteousness,
but also our inability to attain it, he in his kindness determined to provide a
righteousness for us. It was his grace that led him to provide it; he was under
no obligation whatsoever to do it. In his grace he had regard to our guilt,
and in his mercy, to our misery.

3. *It is by the blood of Christ.*   Not only is the believer justified by his
grace, but also by the blood of Christ. Paul wrote, "Having now been justified by His blood, we shall be saved from the wrath of God through Him"
(Rom. 5:9). The Bible further says, "According to the Law, one may almost
say, all things are cleansed with blood, and without shedding of blood there
is no forgiveness" (Heb. 9:22). This sets forth the ground of our justification. Because Christ has borne the punishment of our sins in his own body,
God is able to remit the penalty and to restore us to his favor. In justification,
sins are not excused but punished in the person of Christ, the substitute. The
resurrection of Christ is one proof that his death on the cross has satisfied
God's claims against us (Rom. 4:25; 1 John 2:2). The gift of the Holy Spirit
is another. "The Spirit Himself bears witness with our spirit that we are
children of God" (Rom. 8:16; cf. Gal. 4:5f.).

4. *It is by faith.*   The Bible says, "Therefore having been justified by faith,
we have peace with God through our Lord Jesus Christ" (Rom. 5:1), and
"With the heart man believes, resulting in righteousness, and with the
mouth he confesses, resulting in salvation" (Rom. 10:10). It further declares
that "a man is not justified by the works of the Law but through faith in
Christ Jesus" (Gal. 2:16; cf. Acts 13:38f.; Rom. 3:28; Gal. 3:8, 24). This is
the condition of our justification, not the meritorious ground of it. "If this
were the case, faith would have to be regarded as a meritorious work of
man."[3] The apostle is consistently opposed to a justification by works (Rom.
3:27f.; Gal. 2:16). It is not *for* faith that we are justified, but *by* faith. Faith
is not the price of justification, but the means of appropriating it. It is evident
that the Old Testament saints were justified as well as the New Testament
believers (Acts 13:38f.; Rom. 4:5–12; Gal. 3:8).

[3]Berkhof, *Systematic Theology*, p. 521.

C. The Results of Justification

These can be summed up briefly. (1) There is the remission of penalty (Rom. 4:7f.; 2 Cor. 5:19). The condemnation is gone (Rom. 8:1, 33f.), and there is peace with God (Rom. 5:1; Eph. 2:14-17). (2) There is the restoration to God's favor (Rom. 4:6; 1 Cor. 1:30; 2 Cor. 5:21). (3) There is the imputation of Christ's righteousness (Rom. 4:5). The believer is now clothed in a righteousness not his own, but provided for him by Christ, and is therefore accepted into fellowship with God. (4) There is heirship. Paul says, "That being justified by His grace we might be made heirs according to the hope of eternal life" (Titus 3:7). (5) There is also a direct result in practical living. Justification leads to righteous living. Scripture speaks of "having been filled with the fruit of righteousness which comes through Jesus Christ, to the glory and praise of God" (Phil. 1:11). John writes, "Little children, let no one deceive you; the one who practices righteousness is righteous, just as He is righteous" (1 John 3:7). It is this that James emphasizes; he is concerned that a man have such a faith as will result in works, that is, a living faith (James 2:14-26). (6) The justified man is assured that he will be saved from the coming wrath of God (Rom. 5:9; 1 Thess. 1:10). And (7) he is also assured of glorification (Matt. 13:43; Rom. 8:30; Gal. 5:5). These results are directly connected with justification.

II. THE DOCTRINE OF REGENERATION

The doctrine of regeneration follows logically the doctrine of justification.

A. The Meaning of Regeneration

Justification is with a view to reigning in life, and is spoken of as "justification of life" (Rom. 5:18). From the divine side, the change of heart is called regeneration, the new birth; from the human side, it is called conversion. In regeneration, the soul is passive; in conversion, it is active. Regeneration may be defined as the communication of divine life to the soul (John 3:5; 10:10, 28; 1 John 5:11f.), as the impartation of a new nature (2 Pet. 1:4) or heart (Jer. 24:7; Ezek. 11:19; 36:26), and the production of a new creation 2 Cor. 5:17; Eph. 2:10; 4:24). This new spiritual life affects the believer's intellect (1 Cor. 2:14; Eph. 1:18; Col. 3:10), will (Phil. 2:13; 2 Thess. 3:5; Heb. 13:21), and emotions (Matt. 5:4; 1 Pet. 1:8).

B. The Necessity of Regeneration

Scripture repeatedly declares that a man must be regenerated before he can see God. These claims of the Word of God are supported by reason and conscience.

Holiness is the indispensable condition to acceptance into fellowship with God. Scripture commands, "Pursue peace with all men, and the sanctification without which no one will see the Lord" (Heb. 12:14). But all humanity is by nature depraved, and when it arrives at moral consciousness, becomes guilty of actual transgression. In its condition by nature, therefore, mankind cannot have fellowship with God. Now this moral change in man can be brought about only by an act of the Spirit of God. He regenerates the heart and communicates to it the life and nature of God. The Scriptures represent this experience as a new birth, whereby a man becomes a child of God. Jesus said, "Truly, truly, I say to you, unless one is born again, he cannot see the kingdom of God" (John 3:3; cf. 1:12; 1 John 3:1). By nature all men are "sons of disobedience" (Eph. 2:2), "children of wrath" (Eph. 2:3), "sons of this age" (Luke 16:8), and "children of the devil" (1 John 3:10; cf. Matt. 13:38; 23:15; Acts 13:10). This latter term is especially used of the Christ rejectors in John 8:44. Only the new birth can produce that holy nature within sinners that makes fellowship with God possible.

C. The Means of Regeneration

Scripture represents regeneration as the work of God. But there are a number of means and agencies involved in the experience.

1. The will of God. We are born of the will of God (John 1:13). James writes, "In the exercise of His will He brought us forth by the word of truth" (James 1:18).

2. The death and resurrection of Christ. The new birth is conditioned on faith in the crucified Christ (John 3:14–16), and the resurrection of Christ is equally involved in our regeneration (1 Pet. 1:3).

3. The Word of God. James teaches that we were brought forth "by the word of truth" (1:18; cf. 1 Pet. 1:23). Paul speaks of "the washing of water with the word" (Eph. 5:26; cf. Titus 3:5). Some see baptism as a necessary prerequisite to regeneration, but this makes salvation dependent upon works. Clearly, Cornelius was born again before he received baptism (Acts 10:47). Acts 2:38 must be understood in the sense of being baptized because of the forgiveness of sins, rather than in order that they would be forgiven; just as John baptized because of repentance, rather than in order that those who were being baptized would repent (Matt. 3:11).

4. The ministers of the Word. God uses people in the redemptive process. Their contribution, however, consists simply in the proclamation of the truth and the appeal to decision for Christ (Rom. 10:14f.; 1 Cor. 4:15; Philem. 10; cf. Gal. 4:19).

5. *The Holy Spirit.*   The real efficient agent in regeneration is the Holy Spirit (John 3:5f.; Titus 3:5; cf. Acts 16:14; Rom. 9:16; Phil. 2:13). Truth does not in itself constrain the will; besides, the unregenerate heart hates the truth until it is worked upon by the Holy Spirit.

D. The Results of Regeneration

The Scriptures declare that there are a number of definite results that follow regeneration. They are of such a nature that they serve as tests to whether a soul has been regenerated. (1) He who is born of God overcomes temptation (1 John 3:9; 5:4, 18). The present tense of all of these verbs indicates a life of habitual victory. Consequently, the regenerated person practices righteousness. This, however, is not to suggest sinless perfection. (2) The attitude of the regenerated is different. He habitually loves the brethren (1 John 5:1), God (1 John 4:19; 5:2), God's Word (Ps. 119:97; 1 Pet. 2:2), his enemies (Matt. 5:44), and lost souls (2 Cor. 5:14). (3) The regenerated person also enjoys certain privileges of a child, as the supply of his needs (Matt. 7:11; cf. Luke 11:13), a revelation of the Father's will (1 Cor. 2:10–12; Eph. 1:9), and being kept (1 John 5:18). (4) The man born of God is also an heir of God and a fellow-heir with Jesus Christ (Rom. 8:17). While the actual possession of the inheritance is for the most part still future, the child of God has even now a token of that inheritance in the gift of the Holy Spirit (Eph. 1:13f.). It is, of course, clear that these results are not directly visible to the world, but they are, nevertheless, very real to the one who has been born into the divine family.

CHAPTER XXXI

Union with Christ and Adoption

This is the last point in the consideration of the application of salvation in its beginning. The believer's union with Christ and his position by adoption must be analyzed.

I. THE BELIEVER'S UNION WITH CHRIST

The regenerated soul is brought into a vital union with Christ. This is not to deny that there is, first of all, a federal or representative union with Christ. By this legal union Christ, as the second Adam (1 Cor. 15:22), assumes those broken obligations which the first Adam failed to discharge, and fulfills them all in behalf of mankind. The results of this union with Christ are the imputation of our sins to him and of his righteousness to us, and all the forensic benefits involved in them. We are now, however, concerned with the believer's vital union with Christ.

A. THE NATURE OF THIS UNION

The Scriptures represent the union of the believer with Christ in various ways. There are first the analogies drawn from earthly relationships. Such is the union of a building and its foundation (Eph. 2:20-22; Col. 2:7; 1 Pet. 2:4f.), the union between husband and wife (Rom. 7:4; Eph. 5:31f.; Rev. 19:7-9), the union between the vine and the branches (John 15:1-6), the union between the head and the body (1 Cor. 6:15, 19; 12:12; Eph. 1:22f.; 4:15f.), and the union between Adam and his descendants (Rom. 5:12, 21; 1 Cor. 15:22, 49; cf. also the union between the shepherd and the sheep, John 10:1-18; Heb. 13:20; 1 Pet. 2:25).

1. The scriptural representations. There are also the many direct statements of this fact. Frequently, it is said that the believer is "in Christ." Jesus spoke of the believers as in him (John 14:20), and in his Epistles Paul again and again speaks of believers as being in Christ (Rom. 6:11; 8:1; 2 Cor. 5:17; Eph. 2:13; Col. 2:11f.). This is likewise true of the Johannine Epistles (1 John 2:6; 4:13; cf. 2 John 9). Often it is also said that Christ is in th believer (John 14:20; Rom. 8:10; Gal. 2:20; Col. 1:27). Indeed, Jesus declares that both he and the Father dwell in the believer (John 14:23). The believer is, furthermore, represented as partaking of Christ (John 6:53, 56f.; 1 Cor. 10:16f.) and of the divine nature (2 Pet. 1:4), and as being one spirit with the Lord (1 Cor. 6:17). God's seed remains in him (1 John 3:9).

2. The negative side. To understand what this union is not, certain concepts must be discarded. First, this union is not the mystical union of the pantheist. Scripture knows of no union between God or Christ and the unregenerated. Nor is it a mere moral union, a union of love and sympathy, as between friends. Jonathan's soul was knit with the soul of David (1 Sam. 18:1), but the believer's union with Christ transcends all such union of interests and purpose. Nor yet is it a union of essence by which the human personality is destroyed or absorbed into Christ or God. This view was held by some of the mystics, but the Scriptures represent the relationship between Christ and the believer as an "I" and "you" relationship, even in the case of those farthest advanced in the Christian life (Phil. 3:7–14). Nor finally, is it a physical and material union, which some claim to procure by participating in the ordinances of the church. The ordinances, according to Scripture, do not secure this union, for they are represented as presupposing the union is already in existence.

3. The positive side. What is this union? (1) We may say positively that it is a spiritual union. "The one who joins himself to the Lord is one spirit with Him" (1 Cor. 6:17; cf. 12:13; Rom. 8:9f.; Eph. 3:16f.). The Holy Spirit is the author of this union. (2) It is a vital union. Paul writes, "It is no longer I who live, but Christ lives in me; and the life which I now live in the flesh I live by faith in the Son of God, who loved me, and delivered Himself up for me" (Gal. 2:20), and "You have died and your life is hidden with Christ in God. When Christ, who is our life, is revealed, then you also will be revealed with Him in glory" (Col. 3:3f.). The life of Christ is the life of the believer. (3) It is a complete union. Again Paul writes, "Now you are Christ's body, and individually members of it" (1 Cor. 12:27), and "Because we are members of His body" (Eph. 5:30; cf. 1 Cor. 6:15). Each part of the body is both a means and an end. The hands exist for the eyes, and the eyes for the hand. Each part exists for the head, and the head for each part. (4) It is an inscrutable union. Scripture says, "This mystery is great; but I am speaking with reference to Christ and the church" (Eph. 5:32), and "The riches of the glory of this mystery among the Gentiles, which is Christ in you, the hope of glory" (Col. 1:27). That Gentiles should be accepted and incorporated into the body is a mystery. (5) And finally, it is indissoluble. Jesus said, "I give eternal life to them, and they shall never perish; and no one is able to snatch them out of My hand" (John 10:28). Paul asks, "Who shall separate us from the love of Christ? Shall tribulation, or distress, or persecution, or famine, or nakedness, or peril, or sword?"; then he answers, "In all these things we overwhelmingly conquer through Him who loved us" (Rom. 8:35, 37; cf. vss. 38f.). Christ gives to us eternal life, which means that we shall never perish; in addition to this, he holds us in his hand, and this assures us that no one shall snatch us out of his hand.

B. The Method of This Union

How is this union between Christ and the Christian established? Scripture has little to say directly on this subject. But some things may be noted. This union originated in the purpose and plan of God. Scripture says, "Just as He chose us in Him before the foundation of the world" (Eph. 1:4), and "Even as Thou gavest Him authority over all mankind, that to all whom Thou hast given Him, He may give eternal life" (John 17:2). It begins in Christians when we are made alive together with Christ (Eph. 2:5). Paul speaks of our having become "united with Him in the likeness of His death" (Rom. 6:5). And in 1 Cor. 12:13 we are told that we have been baptized into one body by the Holy Spirit. 1 Cor. 6:17 refers to the fact of our being joined to the Lord, but it does not say how we were thus joined. Surely, only God can take a person and engraft him into Christ. It is as those who have been made alive that we are made to partake in this life-union with Christ.

C. The Consequences of This Union

There are four of them. (1) Union with Christ means eternal security (John 10:28-30). Nothing is able to separate the believer from the love of God, which is in Christ Jesus our Lord (Rom. 8:38f.). When Jesus speaks of taking away the branch that abideth not in him, he must mean the person who is only nominally in Christ (John 15:6), for "if we have become united with Him in the likeness of His death, certainly we shall be also in the likeness of His resurrection" (Rom. 6:5). (2) Union with Christ also means fruitfulness (John 15:5). This is the fruit of the Spirit (Gal. 5:22f.; cf. Rom. 6:22; 7:4; Eph. 5:9). Pruning is one of the Lord's methods of increasing the production of fruit in the branch that abides in him (John 15:1f.). (3) Union with Christ means endowment for service. Believers are members of Christ and, as such, have various offices and endowments (1 Cor. 12:4-30). It is the head that directs that service. This union with Christ brings with it, logically, cooperation among the members. It leads to unity in the body in the midst of diversity. (4) Last of all, union with Christ means fellowship with Christ. We are taken into his confidence and made acquainted with his purposes and plans (Eph. 1:8f.).

II. THE BELIEVER'S ADOPTION

The doctrine of adoption is purely Pauline, and we give to it the last place. The other New Testament writers associate the blessings which Paul connects with adoption with the doctrines of regeneration and justification. The Greek word rendered "adoption" occurs but five times in the Scriptures, and it is only in Paul's writings (Rom. 8:15, 23; 9:4; Gal. 4:5; Eph. 1:5). Once Paul applies the term to Israel as a nation (Rom. 9:4); once he refers the full realization of adoption to the future coming of Christ (Rom. 8:23); and three times he declares it to be a present fact in the life of the Christian.

A. THE DEFINITION OF ADOPTION

As the Greek word indicates, adoption is literally "placing as a son." Evans has well summarized, "Regeneration has to do with our change in nature; justification, with our change in standing; sanctification, with our change in character; adoption, with our change in position."[1] This word is used of believers when the question of rights, position, and privilege is involved. John's emphasis is on the relationship of believers as children of God; we are born of God and grow into maturity (John 1:12f.; 1 John 3:1). Paul's emphasis is more on position; we are sons of God, and we have been adopted into the family of God.

It would appear that Paul regarded the Old Testament believers as "children," but nevertheless as "minors"; but the New Testament believers he regarded as both "children" and "adult sons." The chief advantages of sonship, according to Paul, are deliverance from the law (Gal. 4:3–5) and the possession of the Holy Spirit, the Spirit of adoption and sonship (Gal. 4:6; cf. Rom. 8:15f.). We may summarize: In regeneration we receive new life; in justification, a new standing; and in adoption, a new position.

B. THE TIME OF ADOPTION

Adoption has a threefold time-relationship. (1) In the councils of God it was an act in eternity past (Eph. 1:5). Before he ever began with the Hebrew race, yes, before creation, he predestined us to this position. (2) In personal experience it becomes true of the believer at the time of his accepting Jesus Christ. Scripture declares, "You are all sons of God through faith in Christ Jesus" (Gal. 3:26), and "Because you are sons, God has sent forth the Spirit of His Son into our hearts" (Gal. 4:6). Before salvation, the Gentile was a slave and the Jew a minor; through adoption, both have legal standing as

[1]Evans, *The Great Doctrines of the Bible*, p. 161.

sons of God (Gal. 4:1–7). (3) But the full realization of sonship awaits the coming of Christ. It is at that time that the adoption will be fully consummated (Rom. 8:23). Then our bodies will be delivered from corruption and mortality and be made like unto his own glorious body (Phil. 3:20f.).

C. THE RESULTS OF ADOPTION

Perhaps first among them is deliverance from the law (Rom. 8:15; Gal. 4:4f.). The believer is no longer under guardians and managers, but is free from such bondage. Next may be mentioned the pledge of the inheritance. This is the Holy Spirit himself (Gal. 4:6f.; cf. Eph. 1:11–14). The Father starts his sons out with the investiture of the Spirit. It is the initial payment of the full inheritance which he will receive when Christ comes. Then there is the witness of the Spirit, or assurance (Rom. 8:15f.; Gal. 4:6). If the believer appreciates these high endowments, he will spontaneously enter into fellowship with the Father. That is, he will manifest a filial spirit in relation to the Father (Rom. 8:15; Gal. 4:6). This will naturally be followed by a walk in the Spirit, for the believer will be led by the Spirit (Rom. 8:14; cf. Gal. 5:18). The result will be greater and greater conformity to the image of God's Son (Rom. 8:29). And for the future, the believer has the prospect of one day being made manifest as a son (Rom. 8:19). These are the glorious results of salvation.

CHAPTER XXXII

Sanctification

The importance of this doctrine appears from such a statement as, "Pursue peace with all men, and the sanctification without which no one will see the Lord" (Heb. 12:14). This Scripture does not so much stress the realization of absolute holiness in life, as the pursuit of it. Peter writes, "Like the Holy One who called you, be holy yourselves also in all your behavior" (1 Pet. 1:15). The differences in teaching current today make it especially necessary that we look carefully at the teaching of Scripture regarding this doctrine. Let us consider the definition, the time, and the means of sanctification.

I. THE DEFINITION OF SANCTIFICATION

The noun "sanctification" is found several times in the New Testament (Rom. 6:19, 22; 1 Cor. 1:30; 1 Thess. 4:3f., 7; 2 Thess. 2:13; 1 Tim. 2:15; Heb. 12:14; 1 Pet. 1:2). There are several other words closely related to it: holiness (Rom. 1:4; 2 Cor. 7:1; 1 Thess. 3:13), holy (Acts 7:33; 1 Cor. 3:17; 2 Cor. 13:12), saint (1 Cor. 16:1; Eph. 1:1; Phil. 4:21), sanctuary (Heb. 8:2), and sanctify or hallow (Matt. 6:9; John 17:17; Heb. 13:12). The verb "to sanctify" has at least three meanings: to render or acknowledge to be venerable, to hallow (Luke 11:2; 1 Pet. 3:15); to separate from things profane and dedicate to God, to consecrate (Matt. 23:17; John 10:36; 17:19; 2 Tim. 2:21); and to purify (Eph. 5:26; 1 Thess. 5:23; Heb. 9:13). The adjective "holy" is used of things (mountain, 2 Pet. 1:18; kiss, 1 Cor. 16:20), the Spirit (Rom. 5:5), the Father (John 17:11; 1 Pet. 1:15), the law (Rom. 7:12; 2 Pet. 2:21), angels (Mark 8:38), believers (Eph. 1:1; Heb. 3:1), Old Testament prophets (2 Pet. 3:2), and so forth. Often the adjective is used as a substantive and is translated "saints." In this way it is used of angels (Jude 14), believers (Jude 3; Rev. 8:3), or both (1 Thess. 3:13). What does it mean to be a saint and to have been sanctified?

Broadly speaking, we may define sanctification as a separation to God, an imputation of Christ as our holiness, purification from moral evil, and conformation to the image of Christ.

A. SEPARATION TO GOD

Separation to God presupposes separation from defilement. This pertains to
inanimate things in particular. Thus Hezekiah charged the Levites to sanctify
the house of Jehovah by carrying forth the filthiness out of the holy place
(2 Chron. 29:5, 15–19). Usually, we have the positive idea of separation or
dedication to God. In this sense, the tabernacle and the temple were sanctified
with all their furniture and vessels (Exod. 40:10f.; Num. 7:1; 2 Chron.
7:16). A man might sanctify his house or a part of his field (Lev. 27:14–16).
The Lord sanctified Israel's firstborn to himself (Exod. 13:2; Num. 3:13).
The Father sanctified the Son (John 10:36), and the Son sanctified himself
(John 17:19). Christians are sanctified at the time of their conversion (1 Cor.
1:2; 1 Pet. 1:2; Heb. 10:14). Jeremiah was sanctified before he was born
(Jer. 1:5), and Paul speaks of having been separated from his mother's womb
(Gal. 1:15).

B. IMPUTATION OF CHRIST AS OUR HOLINESS

Imputation of Christ as our holiness accompanies the imputation of Christ
as our righteousness. He is made unto us both righteousness and sanctification (1 Cor. 1:30). Paul says believers "have been sanctified in Christ Jesus"
(1 Cor. 1:2). This holiness is obtained by faith in Christ (Acts 26:18). The
"washing of water with the word" preceded this sanctification (Eph. 5:26).
The believer is thus reckoned holy as well as righteous, because he is clothed
with the holiness of Christ. In this sense, all believers are called "saints,"
irrespective of their spiritual attainments (Rom. 1:7; 1 Cor. 1:2; Eph. 1:1;
Phil. 1:1; Col. 1:2). In the case of the Corinthians, their unsaintly character
is especially evident (1 Cor. 3:1–4; 5:1f.; 6:1; 11:17–22). The Hebrew
believers were saints, yet immature (Heb. 2:11; 3:1; 5:11–14).

C. PURIFICATION FROM MORAL EVIL

Purification from moral evil is, in reality, but another form of separation.
The priests were asked to sanctify themselves before drawing near to God
(Exod. 19:22), and the believer today is asked to separate himself from the
ungodly in general (2 Cor. 6:17f.), from false teachers and doctrines (2 Tim.
2:21; 2 John 9f.), and from his own evil nature (Rom. 6:11f.; Eph. 4:25–32;
Col. 3:5–9; 1 Thess. 4:3, 7). Paul writes, "Beloved, let us cleanse ourselves
from all defilement of flesh and spirit, perfecting holiness in the fear of God"
(2 Cor. 7:1). It will be noticed that in some passages sanctification is treated
as a single act and in others as a continuous process; in some the purification
is more of an outward nature, while in others it is essentially inward. In all of

these, it is considered as an act of man and not as an act of God. God has already set apart to himself everyone who believes in Christ; now the believer sets himself apart to God for God's use.

D. Conformation to the Image of Christ

Conformation to the image of Christ is the positive aspect of sanctification, as purification is the negative, and separation and imputation of Christ's holiness are the positional. There are several Scriptures that deal with this phase of sanctification. Paul writes, "For whom he foreknew, He also predestined to become conformed to the image of His Son, that He might be the first-born among many brethren" (Rom. 8:29); "that I may know Him, and the power of His resurrection and the fellowship of His sufferings, being conformed to His death" (Phil. 3:10); and "But we all, with unveiled face beholding as in a mirror the glory of the Lord, are being transformed into the same image from glory to glory, just as from the Lord, the Spirit" (2 Cor. 3:18; cf. Gal. 5:22f.; Phil. 1:6). And John says, "Beloved, now we are children of God, and it has not appeared as yet what we shall be. We know that, when He appears, we shall be like Him, because we shall see Him just as He is" (1 John 3:2). Clearly, this is a process extending throughout life and coming to full fruition only when we shall see the Lord.

II. THE TIME OF SANCTIFICATION

Sanctification is both an act and a process. In this, it is different from justification, which is an act that takes place once, and is not a process. Let us consider the three time elements in sanctification.

A. The Initial Act of Sanctification

This is positional sanctification. The Scriptures teach that the moment a man believes in Christ he is sanctified. This is clear from the fact that believers are called saints in the New Testament irrespective of their spiritual attainments (1 Cor. 1:2; Eph. 1:1; Col. 1:2; Heb. 10:10; Jude 3). Of the Corinthians, Paul explicitly says that they "were sanctified" (1 Cor. 6:11), though he also declared that they were "still fleshly" (1 Cor. 3:3). In 2 Cor. he urged them to be "perfecting holiness in the fear of God" (7:1). In Ephesians he speaks of the "equipping of the saints" (4:12) and exhorts his readers to walk "as is proper among saints" (5:3). In Thessalonians he affirms that his readers are already sanctified (2 Thess. 2:13), though he also prays for their sanctification (1 Thess. 5:23f.).

According to Heb. 10:10, sanctification and the offering of Christ stand or fall together. The suffering of Christ was done without the gate "that He might sanctify the people through His own blood" (Heb. 13:12). Thus, Christ's death was necessary for the sanctification of his people. When a person accepts Christ, he has his being in Christ; he is hid with Christ in God (Col. 3:3). Christ has been made unto the Christian, sanctification (1 Cor. 1:30). It is not Christ *plus* sanctification; Christ *is* the believer's sanctification. The believer is now complete in him (Col. 2:10). He is an heir to the righteousness and holiness of Christ, these being imputed to him because of his relationship to Christ, not because of any work he may have done or any merit he may have achieved. He stands before God, Christlike (Rom. 8:29; 1 Cor. 1:30). In positional sanctification there is no second work of grace, no progress, no growth. Because of this positional relationship with Christ, the believer is enjoined to walk "as is proper among saints" (Eph. 5:3).

B. The Process of Sanctification

As a process, sanctification continues throughout life. On the basis of what the believer has done at conversion, he is admonished to do the same actually in his own experience. Because he has "put off" and "put on," he is now to "put off" and "put on" (Col. 3:8–13). Where the initial surrender has not been adhered to, there is need first of a definite presentation of the life to God before practical holiness is possible (Rom. 6:13; 12:1f.); but when the believer is wholly dedicated to God, progress in sanctification is assured. Then the Holy Spirit will put to death the deeds of the body (Rom. 8:13), work in him obedience to the Word (1 Pet. 1:22), produce the fruit of the Spirit (Gal. 5:22f.), and use him in God's service. Then he will "grow in the grace and knowledge of our Lord and Savior Jesus Christ" (2 Pet. 3:18), "increase and abound in love" (1 Thess. 3:12), cleanse himself "from all defilement of flesh and spirit, perfecting holiness in the fear of God" (2 Cor. 7:1), and be transformed into the image of Christ (2 Cor. 3:18; Eph. 4:11–16). Paul declared, "I press on in order that I may lay hold of that for which I was laid hold of by Christ Jesus" (Phil. 3:12).

This does not mean some type of sinless perfection. "Perfect" or "blameless" is used of several people in Scripture; yet it does not mean sinless. It is used of Noah (Gen. 6:9); yet, that Noah was not sinlessly perfect is evident from his shameful drunkenness (Gen. 9:20–27). Likewise, Job was called "perfect" or "blameless" (Job 1:1), but he was in many ways imperfect. When he came to understand God more fully, he abhorred himself and repented in dust and ashes (Job 42:6). God told Abram to walk before him and be perfect (Gen. 17:1). Jesus commanded, "You are to be perfect, as your heavenly Father is perfect" (Matt. 5:48). If this refers to absolute sinlessness and likeness to God, then no Christian has ever yet attained to this precept. It is clear from the context that Jesus is exhorting his followers to be like the Father in displaying love to both good and bad. Paul disclaims being already perfect in one breath and in the next claims to be perfect (Phil. 3:12, 15). It is evident that one is positional perfection and the other experiential perfection. Positionally, he was perfect since the day that he believed in Christ; experientially, he was perfect only to a limited degree. The same Greek word is used in both verses, except that the first is a verb and the second an adjective. Col. 1:28; 4:12; and Heb. 12:23 hold out perfection as a goal to be attained in the end, but not in this life. It is clear from these and other Scriptures that absolute perfection is not to be expected in this life.

We come to the same conclusion by another line of argument. Some use 1 John 3:8f. in support of sinless perfection. John writes there, "The one who practices sin is of the devil; for the devil has sinned from the beginning. . . . No one who is born of God practices sin, because His seed abides in him; and he cannot sin, because he is born of God." Attention to the Greek tenses removes the possibility that this is sinless perfection, for they are all the present tense. Accordingly, the meaning is, he that habitually sins is of the devil; he that is of God does not repeatedly sin. If this is not the meaning, then John contradicts himself in this very Epistle, for he tells the believer what to do in case he sins. "My little children, I am writing these things to you that you may not sin. And if anyone sins, we have an Advocate with the Father, Jesus Christ the righteous; and He Himself is the propitiation for our sins" (1 John 2:1f.). The believer is enjoined not to sin, but if he sins he has a remedy. John further says that if we walk in the light, "the blood of Jesus His Son cleanses us from all sin" (1 John 1:7). And again, "If we say that we have no sin, we are deceiving ourselves, and the truth is not in us" (1:8). Surely, we must conclude that John does not teach sinless perfection.

The same may be said concerning the teaching that we have died to sin (Rom. 6:1–10). It is clear that this is an objective experience in which the believer is identified with Christ. If this were an absolute experiential death, why then does Paul insist that we need yet to "consider" ourselves dead to sin and alive to God (v. 11)? One who is absolutely dead does not need to consider himself dead; he simply is dead apart from any such reckoning.

We must beware of concluding that the defeated, imperfect life is the normal life. If sinless perfection is an unscriptural doctrine, so also is sinful imperfection. The Scriptures, so far from condoning sin in the life of the believer, definitely prohibit it and demand that we live an overcoming life. The answer to Paul's question, "Are we to continue in sin?" (Rom. 6:1), is most emphatically, "May it never be! How shall we who died to sin still live in it?" (v. 2). The apostle warns the Corinthians that those who live in sin shall not "inherit the kingdom of God" (1 Cor. 6:10).

C. COMPLETE AND FINAL SANCTIFICATION

Complete and final sanctification awaits the sight of Christ. No matter how much progress we may have made in the life of holiness, entire conformity to Christ will only be realized when "the perfect comes" and "the partial will be done away" (1 Cor. 13:10). We have been saved from the guilt and the penalty of sin, are being saved from the power of sin, and will ultimately be saved from the very presence of sin. Our salvation from the presence of sin will take place when we shall see the Lord, either at death (Heb. 12:23) or at his coming (1 Thess. 3:13; Heb. 9:28; 1 John 3:2; Jude 21). There will be no further possibility of sinning after that (Rev. 22:11). The body of the believer will then be glorified (Rom. 8:23; Phil. 3:20f.) and become a perfect instrument of obedience to God. The prospect of this complete conformation to the image of Christ should impel us to put away now all unholy things from our lives (1 John 3:2f.).

III. THE MEANS OF SANCTIFICATION

This question will be more fully treated later, but it must receive a preliminary consideration here. There are two parties that have to do with man's sanctification: God and man. However, it is not God the Father only, but the triune God that has a part in the work. God the Father sanctifies the believer in that he reckons the holiness of Christ to him (1 Cor. 1:30), works in him that which is well-pleasing in his sight (Heb. 13:21), and disciplines him (Heb. 12:9f.; 1 Pet. 4:17f.; 5:10). Christ sanctifies the believer by laying down his life for him (Heb. 10:10; 13:12), and by producing holiness in him by the Spirit (Rom. 8:13; Heb. 2:11). The Holy Spirit sanctifies the believer in that he frees him from the carnal nature (Rom. 8:2), strives against the manifestation of it (Gal. 5:17), puts to death the old nature as the believer yields it to him for crucifixion (Rom. 8:13), and produces the fruit of the Spirit (Gal. 5:22f.). Thus, there is a definite function of each member of the trinity in our sanctification.

In himself man can do nothing to achieve sanctification. Even in the believer, God must take the initiative. Paul says, "It is God who is at work in you, both to will and to work for His good pleasure" (Phil. 2:13). But there are definite means that man may employ in his sanctification. Here, as elsewhere, faith in Christ is the first step to take (Acts 26:18). He who believes in Christ is sanctified positionally, for Christ is at that moment made unto him sanctification (1 Cor. 1:30). Next must come the pursuit of holiness. He who does not follow after sanctification shall not see God (2 Cor. 7:1; Heb. 12:14). This should lead him to study the Scriptures, for they disclose the state of the heart and point out the remedy for failure (John

17:17, 19; Eph. 5:26; 1 Tim. 4:5; James 1:25). The divinely instituted ministry also has its part in pointing out the need for holiness and urging the pursuit of it (Eph. 4:11–13; 1 Thess. 3:10). The definite surrender of the life to God constitutes the supreme condition of practical sanctification (Rom. 6:13, 19–21; 12:1f.; 2 Tim. 2:21). Since God must make man holy, if he is ever to be holy, man must yield himself to God that he may accomplish this work in him.

CHAPTER XXXIII

Perseverance

If properly understood, this is a very comforting doctrine, but it must not be abused or misinterpreted. The Scriptures teach that all who are by faith united to Christ, who have been justified by God's grace and regenerated by his Spirit, will never totally nor finally fall away from the state of grace, but certainly persevere therein to the end. This does not mean that everyone who professes to be saved is eternally saved. Nor even does it mean that everyone who manifests certain gifts in Christian service is necessarily eternally saved. The doctrine of eternal security is applicable only to those who have had a vital experience of salvation. Concerning such, it affirms that they shall never totally nor finally fall away from the state of grace. This is not equivalent to saying that they shall never backslide, never fall into sin, and never fail to show forth the praises of him who called them out of darkness into his marvelous light. It merely means that they will never totally fall away from the state of grace into which they have been brought, nor fail to return from their backsliding in the end.

I. PROOF OF THE DOCTRINE

This truth is not a matter of speculation, but of revelation. Human opinion has very little value in this connection, except as it is steeped in the declarations and principles of the Word of God. Some of the chief proofs of this doctrine as found in the Scriptures can be enumerated.

A. The Purpose of God

Isaiah says, "The Lord of hosts has sworn saying, 'Surely, just as I have intended so it has happened, and just as I have planned so it will stand'" (14:24; cf. Job 23:13). The Scripture teaches that God has purposed to save those whom he has justified. Paul declares in answer to the question, "Who shall separate us from the love of Christ?", "I am convinced that neither death, nor life, nor angels, nor principalities, nor things present, nor things to come, nor powers, nor height, nor depth, nor any other created thing, shall be able to separate us from the love of God, which is in Christ Jesus our Lord" (Rom. 8:35, 38f.). Earlier in the chapter he had expressed God's purpose for the saved, which is as follows, "For whom He foreknew, He also predestined to become confirmed to the image of His son, that He might be the first-born among many brethren; and whom He predestined, these He also called; and whom He called, these He also justified; and whom He justified, these He also glorified" (vss. 29f.). That is, in the councils of God there is an unfailing sequence with regard to everyone whom he foreknows. The revelation of this fact led the apostle to express himself with certainty, as we have indicated. Paul further states, "For the gifts and the calling of God are irrevocable" (Rom. 11:29). Jesus gave utterance of the same, saying, "My sheep hear My voice, and I know them, and they follow Me; and I give eternal life to them, and they shall never perish; and no one shall snatch them out of My hand. My Father, who has given them to Me, is greater than all; and no one is able to snatch them out of the Father's hand. I and the Father are one" (John 10:27–30). Morris comments, "It is one of the precious things about the Christian faith that our continuance in eternal life depends not on our feeble hold on Christ, but on His firm grip on us."[1]

B. The Mediatorship of Christ

This is a continued and effective mediatorship. It is conceivable that God might purpose to keep a man eternally, but that the conditions of security might fail. We are saved by the blood of Christ, and our Lord's resurrection testifies that that sacrifice was accepted by the Father (Rom. 1:4; 4:25). But does his work avail perpetually? Paul says, "God demonstrates His own love toward us, in that while we were yet sinners, Christ died for us. Much more then, having now been justified by His blood, we shall be saved from the wrath of God through Him. For if while we were enemies, we were reconciled to God through the death of His Son, much more, having been reconciled, we shall be saved by His life" (Rom. 5:8–10). His present ministry avails to keep us saved, as his past work availed to save us in the first place. The author of the Hebrews wrote, "Hence, also, He is able to save forever those who draw near to God through Him, since He always lives to make intercession for them" (Heb. 7:25). In John 17 Jesus prayed, among other things, that the Father would keep those who believe and that they might enjoy the blessings of eternal fellowship with him. Surely the prayer of Christ will not go unanswered. Christ presently is at the right hand of God interceding for us (Rom. 8:34).

C. God's Ability to Keep

It is one thing to be willing to keep secure, but another to be able to do so. God is represented as qualifying in both respects. Paul asserts, "I am confi-

---

[1]Morris, *The Gospel According to John*, p. 521.

dent of this very thing, that He who began a good work in you will perfect it until the day of Christ Jesus" (Phil. 1:6), and "I know whom I have believed and I am convinced that He is able to guard what I have entrusted to Him until that day" (2 Tim. 1:12). Scripture further speaks of believers as those "who are protected by the power of God through faith for a salvation ready to be revealed in the last time" (1 Pet. 1:5; cf. Rom. 16:25; Jude 24). Thus, in Scripture the Lord's desire and ability to settle and keep us saved are definitely affirmed.

D. The Nature of the Change in the Believer

Scripture tells us that the believer has been regenerated, and that in regeneration he becomes a new creature and receives a new life. Paul says, "If any man is in Christ, he is a new creature; the old things passed away; behold, new things have come" (2 Cor. 5:17). Having believed on the Lord Jesus, we are looked upon by God as if we had been crucified together with him (Rom. 6:6), and also as if we had risen from the dead with him in newness of life. The believer has received not only a new life, but eternal life. Jesus said, "I give eternal life to them" (John 10:28). He also said, "As Moses lifted up the serpent in the wilderness, even so must the Son of Man be lifted up; that whoever believes may in Him have eternal life" (John 3:14f.; cf. v. 16), and further, "He who believes in the Son has eternal life; but he who does not obey the Son shall not see life, but the wrath of God abides on him" (John 3:36). Boettner says:

> The nature of the change which occurs in regeneration is a sufficient guarantee that the life imparted shall be permanent. Regeneration is a radical and supernatural change in the inner nature, through which the soul is made spiritually alive, and the new life which is implanted is immortal. And since it is a change in the inner nature, it is in a sphere in which man does not have control. No creature is at liberty to change the fundamental principles of its nature, for that is the prerogative of God as Creator. Hence nothing short of another supernatural act of God could reverse this change and cause the new life to be lost. The born-again Christian can no more lose his sonship to the heavenly Father than an earthly son can lose his sonship to an earthly father.[2]

II. OBJECTIONS TO THE DOCTRINE

There are several objections to this position which can be noted.

---

[2]Boettner, *The Reformed Doctrine of Predestination*, p. 184.

A. That It Induces Laxness and Indolence

It is charged that the doctrine of eternal security induces laxness in conduct and indolence in service.

1. Laxness in conduct. It is argued, if every believer is eternally secure, why then be holy in conduct; why not have a so-called good time in this world? But those who raise this objection show that they do not grasp the true nature of regeneration and the exact nature of the doctrine of perseverance. Regeneration is a change in the inner nature, and the new life is eternal life. This is the true view of regeneration. Furthermore, the doctrine of eternal security does not imply that a man can do wrong and go unpunished. It does state, however, that the man who is born again will seek to live a new life. John writes, "No one who is born of God practices sin, because His seed abides in him; and he cannot sin, because he is born of God" (1 John 3:9). This means that he does not habitually sin; and it is certainly true that the experience of the new birth is here represented as resulting in an overcoming life. If a man habitually lives in sin, we conclude that he has never been saved (cf. Rom. 6:1f.; 2 Tim. 2:19; 2 Pet. 1:10f.; 1 John 2:3f., 29; 3:14; 5:4).

2. Indolence in service. Assurance of a right relation with God brings with it a joy and praise that seeks expression in devoted service. Whereas the soul that is never sure of its security is timid and halfhearted, the believer who has the confidence that he is eternally secure in God's keeping is impelled to do something for others. In service as in morality, "My sheep hear My voice, and I know them, and they follow Me" (John 10:27). This is not an exhortation, but a statement of fact. All these verbs are in the present tense; his sheep habitually hear his voice, he continually knows them, and they habitually follow him. Not by a man's professions, but by his fruits do we know him (Matt. 7:16).

B. That It Robs Man of His Freedom

It is said that the teaching of eternal security makes man an automaton, that he no longer is conceived of as having the power to choose. But such a view reveals an erroneous conception of freedom. Freedom is not necessarily the ability to choose between right and wrong, but the ability to choose the right. God is perfectly free, and he is unable to choose or to do wrong. The new life in the believer impels him to choose the right and reject the wrong. Paul asks the Philippians to work out their salvation with fear and trembling, but bases that exhortation on the fact that "it is God who is at work in you, both to will and to work for His good pleasure" (Phil. 2:13). The doctrine of perseverance does not rob a man of his freedom; it rather recognizes that a saved man has a freedom to do what he ought to do that an unsaved man does not possess.

C. That Scripture Teaches the Contrary

It is said that the Scriptures show that certain men were saved and yet perished in the end. Saul in the Old Testament and Judas Iscariot in the New Testament are favorite examples. But this merely emphasizes that one must be careful judging the outward appearance. The rocky soil in the parable of the sower brought forth shoots quickly, but the plant endured only for a season. When persecution and tribulation arose, it withered quickly (Mark 4:16f.). The same thing is true of those sown among the thorns; there seemed to be real life there, but the cares of the age, the deceitfulness of riches, and the lusts of other things entering in, choked the word (vss. 18f.). Jesus declared that not everyone who said, "Lord, Lord," would enter into the kingdom, not even if he could boast of having prophesied in his name, of having cast out demons in his name, or of having done many mighty works in his name. Such are the people who only seem to have the gift of God (Luke 8:18). Only he who had had a personal acquaintance with him would enter the kingdom (Matt. 7:21–23). John uses the argument of continuance with the people of God as a proof of regeneration, and failure to continue as a proof that the ones separating themselves are not of them. "They went out from us, but they were not really of us; for if they had been of us, they would have remained with us; but they went out, in order that it might be shown that they all are not of us" (1 John 2:19; cf. John 6:66f.; 2 Pet. 2:20–22). Surely, Judas Iscariot was never saved. Jesus said in connection with the washing of the disciples' feet, " 'He who has bathed needs only to wash his feet, but is completely clean; and you are clean, but not all of you.' For He knew the one who was betraying Him; for this reason He said, 'Not all of you are clean' " (John 13:10f.). The bath made the disciples clean; they were all clean, except Judas; therefore, it is clear that Judas had not had the bath. He was unregenerated. We may not be able to say just why Christ chose and tolerated in his company one who was unsaved, but we have the statement of Christ himself to the effect that this was the case. In the case of Saul, Scripture does not give enough information to establish his relation to God, but to say he lost his salvation is to go beyond what Scripture reveals to us.

D. That There are Many Warnings

It is urged that the Scriptures contain many warnings and exhortations to the saved. Can it really be that those who are eternally secure need yet to be warned? What is the force of these warnings? Outstanding among these

Scriptures are Heb. 6:4–6 and 10:26–31. It seems that the people mentioned in these verses were being enticed to turn back to Judaism. They were losing their faith and confidence in the promises of the gospel and were looking back to what they had forsaken. It is a dangerous thing for a person to become actively involved in Christian things and with Christian people without actually turning from darkness to light and from the kingdom of Satan to the kingdom of Christ. If such an unregenerate person should turn away, his chances of returning are very remote (cf. 2 Pet. 2:20–22). Another Scripture which is brought up in this connection is Matt. 24:13, which says, "But the one who endures to the end, it is he who shall be saved." To this we simply reply that that has nothing to do with the main argument. If a man is saved, he will continue; if he is not saved, he will not continue. If he continues to the end, he will ultimately be saved. In other words, this Scripture indicates the reward of enduring; it does not raise the question as to whether a truly saved man will continue to the end.

Another Scripture that is thought to indicate the possibility of falling away is Ezek. 18:24, "But when a righteous man turns away from his righteousness, commits iniquity, and does according to all the abominations that a wicked man does, will he live?" It is clear from the whole context in this chapter that the prophet is speaking of legal righteousness and outward fidelity to duty (cf. 33:12–20). If this statement were to be taken in a literal sense, then salvation would be by works and not by grace. This makes it clear that the life in view here is not eternal life, but life on earth, prolonged and cut short as a result of obedience or disobedience. The last one to be mentioned is John 15:1–6, especially v. 6, which speaks of casting forth the branches that do not bear fruit, and of their being cast into the fire. Can this be done to a true believer? The answer is that in these verses the Lord is trying to teach one main lesson, and one should not press the other analogies of the vine and the branches. He is merely teaching that every true branch is bearing some fruit; if a branch is not bearing some fruit, it is evident that there is no life union between it and the vine. That is, the person thus represented is unsaved. Of course, such a branch is cast forth. It was brought into union with Christ, but the union did not become vital; therefore, it will experience separation and the judgment in the end.

CHAPTER XXXIV

The Means of Grace

God uses many different means to bring people to himself for fellowship and salvation, and all of these may be considered, in the wider sense, means of grace. But we concur with Berkhof, who has written:

> Fallen man receives all the blessings of salvation out of the eternal fountain of the grace of God, in virtue of the merits of Jesus Christ and through the operation of the Holy Spirit. While the Spirit can and does in some respects operate immediately on the soul of the sinner, He has seen fit to bind Himself largely to the use of certain means in the communication of divine grace. The term "means of grace" is not found in the Bible, but it is nevertheless a proper designation of the means that are indicated in the Bible.[1]

Reformed theology has largely limited the phrase "means of grace" to two, the Word of God and the sacraments.[2] The sacraments are, in Reformed theology, baptism and the Lord's Supper. Though in a certain sense what is involved in the remembrance of Christ at the communion service is a source of spiritual blessing and benefit, the Lord's Supper should be considered more as an ordinance than as a sacrament. The same is true of baptism. In our considerations we will limit the phrase "means of grace" to the Word of God and prayer.

I. THE WORD OF GOD

By the Word of God we here mean the Bible, consisting of the canonical books of the Old and New Testaments. These divinely inspired books are "profitable for teaching, for reproof, for correction, for training in righteousness" (2 Tim. 3:16). This Word of God represents itself to us as a means of grace in various ways, and it does this under several symbols. The Bible is a "hammer which shatters a rock" (Jer. 23:29), a judge of "the thoughts and intentions of the heart" (Heb. 4:12), a mirror to reveal the true condition of

---

[1]Berkhof, *Systematic Theology*, p. 604.
[2]Hoeksema, *Reformed Dogmatics*, pp. 631–726.

man (James 1:25), a laver for the washing of the defiled (John 15:3; Eph.
5:26), seed (Luke 8:11; 1 Pet. 1:23), food for the hungry (Job 23:12), a lamp
for the traveler (Ps. 119:105), and a sword for the soldier (Eph. 6:17; Heb.
4:12).

A. IT IS A MEANS OF SALVATION

How is the Bible a means to salvation? Paul says that the gospel is "the power
of God for salvation" (Rom. 1:16) and that God was pleased by "the foolish-
ness of the message preached to save those who believe" (1 Cor. 1:21). He
makes it clear that the thing to be preached is "Christ crucified" (v. 23). To
Timothy he says, "From childhood you have known the sacred writings
which are able to give you the wisdom that leads to salvation through faith
which is in Christ Jesus" (2 Tim. 3:15). Peter speaks of the believer having
been "born again not of seed which is perishable but imperishable, that is,
through the living and abiding word of God" (1 Pet. 1:23). The Psalmist
says, "The law of the Lord is perfect, restoring the soul" (Ps. 19:7).

The gospel is the death, burial, and resurrection of Christ, according to the
Scriptures (1 Cor. 15:3f.), and the preaching of the apostles was permeated
with Scripture (Acts 2:16–21, 25–28, 34f.; 3:12–16; 13:16–41; 17:2f.).
Surely, experience corroborates that the Bible is a means of drawing people to
Christ. God honors his Word, and through it people come to a saving knowl-
edge of Christ.

B. IT IS A MEANS OF SANCTIFICATION

The Word of God is also a means of sanctification. This concept is set forth in
Scripture under such symbols as a mirror, a laver, a lamp, and a sword. The
Bible reveals the state of the heart and its need of cleansing (2 Cor. 3:18;
James 1:23–25); it is the water of purification (Ps. 119:9, 11; John 15:3;
Eph. 5:26); it is the lamp to guide the wandering feet in the paths of righ-
teousness (Ps. 119:105; Prov. 6:23; 2 Pet. 1:19); and it is the sword to
overcome the enemy (Eph. 6:17; Heb. 1:12). Jesus prayed to the Father,
"Sanctify them in the truth; Thy word is truth" (John 17:17). There is a
very direct relation between the reading and study of the Word and growth
in grace. A close study of Christian biography reveals that the great men of
God were constant readers of the Scriptures. The Lord's word to Joshua has
perpetual significance, "This book of the law shall not depart from your
mouth, but you shall meditate on it day and night, so that you may be
careful to do according to all that is written in it; for then you will make your
way prosperous, and then you will have success" (Josh. 1:8; cf. Deut.
17:18–20).

A word may here be added in explanation of the power of the Word.

Though the Word of God is said to be "living and active" (Heb. 4:12), to be the wisdom and power of God, and to convince, convert, and sanctify the soul, it produces spiritual results only as attended by the Spirit of God. Peter declared that the prophets "preached the gospel . . . by the Holy Spirit sent from heaven" (1 Pet. 1:12). Paul prays that "the God of our Lord Jesus Christ, the Father of glory, may give to you a spirit of wisdom and of revelation in the knowledge of Him" (Eph. 1:17). It seems clear that though the Word has the necessary efficacy to do its work, the soul does not have the necessary susceptibility until empowered by the Holy Spirit (1 Cor. 2:14–16).

II. PRAYER

No one can read the Bible without being impressed with the large place given to prayer in its pages. Beginning with the conversation between God and Adam, all through the Old Testament and the New there are examples of men who prayed. Prayer, however, is in Scripture not simply held out as a privilege, but is laid out as a command (Gen. 18:22f.; 1 Sam. 12:23; 2 Kings 19:15; Ps. 5:2; 32:6; Jer. 29:7; Matt. 5:44; 26:41; Luke 18:1; 21:36; Eph. 6:18; 1 Thess. 5:17, 25; 1 Tim. 2:8; James 5:13–16). Ezra regarded prayer as more important than a band of soldiers and horsemen (Ezra 8:21–23); Christ regarded it as more necessary than food and sleep (Mark 1:35; Luke 6:12); and the apostles put it ahead of preaching (Acts 6:4). We now inquire into the nature, problems, and methods of prayer.

A. The Nature of Prayer

Prayer may be defined as the communication of the individual with God. The communication may take on many forms. True prayer is characterized by confession. There are many Old Testament examples of this (1 Kings 8:47; Ezra 9:5–10:1; Neh. 1:2–11; 9:5–38; Dan. 9:3–19). Prayer is also adoration (Ps. 45:1–8; Isa. 6:1–4; Matt. 14:33; 28:9; Rev. 4:11). This is the first point in the so-called Lord's Prayer (Matt. 6:9). Similar to adoration is communion. Abraham's prayer for Sodom and Gomorrah is an example (Gen. 18:33). God agreed to converse with the Levitical high priest from above the mercy-seat (Exod. 25:22), and Moses is represented as communing with God on Mt. Sinai (Exod. 31:18). Another form of prayer is thanksgiving. The songs of Moses (Exod. 15:1–18), of Deborah (Judg. 5), and of David (2 Sam. 23:1–7) are essentially songs of thanksgiving. The Scriptures abound in exhortations to give thanks (Ps. 95:2; 100:4; Eph. 5:20; Phil. 4:6; Col. 4:2).

Only after glorifying God in prayer are we ready to think of ourselves. First there is petition, or the making known of our requests. Both by example and precept are we encouraged to ask for things of God (Dan. 2:17f.; 9:16–19; Matt. 7:7–11; John 14:13f.; 15:16; 16:23f.; Acts 4:29f.; Phil. 4:6). Supplication is the urging of our request. Daniel made petition and supplication to God (Dan. 6:11); Israel will have the spirit of supplication poured out upon her (Zech. 12:10); the Canaanite woman urged her request and was heard (Matt. 15:22–28); and the elect who cry to God day and night will be heard speedily (Luke 18:1–8). Paul exhorts not only to prayer, but to perseverance in prayer (Eph. 6:18; 1 Tim. 2:1). Finally, prayer is intercession. The Lord is looking for intercessors (Isa. 59:16); Samuel considered it a sin to cease praying for disobedient Israel (1 Sam. 12:23); Job was requested to pray for his "comforters" (Job 42:8); Paul exhorts that intercessions be made for all men (1 Tim. 2:1); and the early church gathered together for definite intercession (Acts 12:5). Certain classes are specifically mentioned in Scripture as objects of intercession: rulers (1 Tim. 2:2), Israel (Ps. 122:6), the unsaved (Luke 23:34; Acts 7:60), new converts (2 Thess. 1:11), all saints (Eph. 6:18; 1 Tim. 2:1; James 5:16), backsliders (1 John 5:16), Christian workers (Eph. 6:19f.; 1 Thess. 5:25), and our enemies (Matt. 5:44).

B. The Relation of Prayer to Providence

We assert that prayer changes things, but how does that statement harmonize with the sovereign plan and purpose of God? Does prayer effect a change in God's mind, and if so, does not then God make his plan contingent on man? How can God answer prayer consistently with the fixity of natural law? Considering this from a negative standpoint, several things should be noted. (1) The reflex influence upon the man who prays is not the sole effect of prayer. Some hold that prayer has only a subjective value: a man has a burden upon his heart, and when he puts this into words, addressing it to God, he feels relieved. But prayer has this value only when the man who prays believes that God listens to his prayer and will answer it. (2) Nor must we suppose that prayer involves the suspension of the laws of nature. God no more suspends the laws of nature when he answers prayer than an airplane does that when it ascends into the sky. And further, (3) we must not think that prayer acts directly upon nature, as if it were a physical force. Prayer influences God to act upon nature; otherwise there would be no discrimination in answers to prayer. None of these negative views reveals the correct conception of the relation of prayer to its answer.

The positive answer to this question involves a right view of God's foreknowledge and foreordination. Let us be reminded again that God has set certain general bounds within which his universe is to operate. Within these bounds, he has given man freedom to act. For instance, the believer has the power of the Spirit in his life and may cooperate largely or only in a small degree with the Spirit in the accomplishment of God's work. God foreknew what each man would do in respect to prayer and embraced that in his foreordination. Thus, when a man prays, he only carries out what God knew he would do and what God set him down to do. Where man fails to cooperate with God within the bounds of his predetermined will, there God works by reason of his sovereignty apart from prayer. In doing so, however, he does not set aside any law of nature, but rather counteracts it by higher and stronger law. His will is the law of nature, and when his will changes in any particular instance, the law of nature involved is overcome by his law.

C. The Method and Manner of Prayer

It is clear that not all that men call prayer is true prayer. Even the disciples realized their deficiency in this respect and so asked Jesus to teach them to pray (Luke 11:1). Our Lord's compliance with that request confirms the conviction of the disciples. Paul expressed the same feeling when he declared that "we do not know how to pray as we should," and then added, "but the Spirit Himself intercedes for us with groanings too deep for words" (Rom. 8:26). What is the scriptural method and manner of prayer?

1. The addressee in prayer.   Scripture teaches that we are to pray to the Father (Neh. 4:9; John 16:23; Acts 12:5; 1 Thess. 5:23), and to the Son (Acts 7:59; 1 Cor. 1:2; 2 Cor. 12:8f.; 2 Tim. 2:22), but there is no clear indication in Scripture of prayer to the Holy Spirit. Although there is no command to pray to the Spirit, neither is there any prohibition. Since the Spirit is deity, surely he can be worshipped as deity, and prayer is a form of worship. The Bible speaks of the "fellowship of the Holy Spirit" (2 Cor. 13:14); this may imply prayer. Primarily, however, the Spirit's part in our prayer is that of praying in us (Rom. 8:26; Jude 20), rather than receiving our prayers. The normal manner seems to be to pray to the Father, on the merits of the Son, in or through the Holy Spirit.

2. Posture in prayer.   The Scriptures prescribe no particular posture, but illustrate and teach many postures. There is standing (Mark 11:25; Luke 18:13; John 17:1), kneeling (1 Kings 8:54; Luke 22:41; Acts 20:36; Eph. 3:14), lying prostrate on the ground (Matt. 26:39), lying down in bed (Ps. 63:6), walking on the water (Matt. 14:30), sitting down (1 Kings 18:42), and hanging on the cross (Luke 23:43). All this indicates that it is not the posture of the body that is significant, but the attitude of the heart. There are, however, more indications that men either stood or knelt when they prayed than that they approached God in some other posture.

3. The time of prayer.   The Scriptures teach that we should pray always (Luke 18:1; Eph. 6:18), but also that we should have stated times for prayer

(Ps. 55:17; Dan. 6:10; Acts 3:1). Though these are all examples of the practice of others and are not precepts, they at least indicate the desirability of regularity of prayer. Besides, they teach us to pray before meals (Matt. 14:19; Acts 27:35; 1 Tim. 4:4f.), and they teach that special occasion should drive us to special prayer (Luke 6:12f.; 22:39–46; John 6:15). Scripture exhorts, "Let us therefore draw near with confidence to the throne of grace, that we may receive mercy and may find grace to help in time of need" (Heb. 4:16). Thus, the Lord is available any time day or night to receive the prayers of his children.

4. *The place of prayer.*   Closely related to the time of prayer is the place of prayer. The Scriptures encourage secret prayer, in the closet, away from all the disturbing elements around us (Dan. 6:10; Matt. 6:6). Jesus, by his example, teaches us to select a solitary place, a desert place (Mark 1:35), or a mountaintop (Matt. 14:23). The Scriptures also encourage united prayer, prayer-fellowship with those who agree with us (Matt. 18:19f.; Acts 1:14; 12:5; 20:36). There are also examples of prayer before the unsaved. Paul and Barnabas prayed before the rest of the prisoners (Acts 16:25), and Paul prayed before the passengers on the fateful trip to Rome (Acts 27:35). There is, in fact, no place where prayer may not be made, since Paul admonishes us to pray in every place (1 Tim. 2:8).

5. *Decorum in prayer.*   The subject of decorum in prayer is often overlooked, but Jesus makes mention of it. He taught that men should not be of a sad or gloomy countenance even when they fast, but anoint their heads and wash their faces (Matt. 6:16–18). That is, he objected to all pretense with no reality. Likewise, he requested that we "do not use meaningless repetition, as the Gentiles do, for they suppose that they will be heard for their many words. Therefore do not be like them" (Matt. 6:7f.). Decorum requires also order in the public assembly. Paul exhorts, "Let all things be done properly and in an orderly manner" (1 Cor. 14:40). This applied to tongues (1 Cor. 14:27), and no doubt to prayer as well. Orderliness in the prayer sessions recorded in Acts is implied (Acts 1:24–26; 4:24–31; 12:5, 12; 13:1–3).

6. *The condition of the heart.*   The most important question as to the manner of prayer is the condition of the heart of the one praying. "If you abide in Me, and My words abide in you" (John 15:7), is the all-inclusive condition to answered prayer. What does this mean? To abide in him implies freedom from known sin (Ps. 66:18; Prov. 28:9; Isa. 59:1f.), unselfishness in our requests (James 4:2f.), asking according to his will (1 John 5:14), forgiveness of those who have wronged us (Matt. 6:12; Mark 11:25), asking in Christ's name (John 14:13f.; 15:16; 16:23f.), praying in the Spirit (Eph. 6:18; Jude 20), asking in faith (Matt. 21:22; James 1:6f.), and earnestness and perseverance in our supplications (Luke 18:1–8; Col. 4:12; James 5:16).

PART VII

ECCLESIOLOGY

There are no evidences of an organized religious life in the earliest accounts of the Scriptures. The nearest approach to it was the family. The father acted as priest and leader in the worship of God. This seems to be the case with Adam (Gen. 4:24f.), Noah (Gen. 6:18), Job (Job 1:5), Abraham (Gen. 12:1–3), Isaac (Gen. 26:2–5), and Jacob (Gen. 28:13–15).

With the organization of the nation under Moses, the religious life of Israel underwent a change. The twelve tribes were organized into a nation, a people of God (Exod. 19:6). This theocracy involved the total life of the people, their political, social, and religious life. God was the chief ruler; the priests, kings, and prophets were merely the executors of God's will. The bond of this union was circumcision, the law, and the tabernacle and temple worship.

With the coming of Christ and his rejection by the nation of Israel, God set Israel aside for this age and founded the church of Jesus Christ. The following chapters concern themselves with such matters as the founding, organization, ordinances, and mission of the church.

CHAPTER XXXV

Definition and Founding of the Church

There are many things in the New Testament that indicate the importance of the doctrine of the church. For example, Christ loved the church and gave himself for her (Eph. 5:25); the primary purpose of God for this age is the building of the church (Matt. 16:18; Acts 15:14); Paul considered it his greatest sin that he had persecuted the church (1 Cor. 15:9; Gal. 1:13, 23; 1 Tim. 1:13); and this apostle suffered many things for the church (Col. 1:24). It is fitting that after the doctrine of salvation, a study of the kind of organized life God has planned for his saved people during this age should be undertaken.

I. THE DEFINITION OF THE CHURCH

There is need of a clear understanding of the New Testament conception of the church. First, we must consider what the church is not, then what it is.

A. THE CHURCH IS NOT A CONTINUATION OF THE OLD ECONOMY

While there is a connection between the saved of all ages (John 10:16; Rom. 11:16, 24; 1 Pet. 2:9), and there is a people of God throughout the various ages, Christianity is not new wine poured into old wineskins. Rather, it is new wine in new wineskins (Matt. 9:17). That the church is not a continuation of the old system is seen from several arguments. First, Israel and the church are not synonymous terms. Paul distinguished between Jews, Gentiles, and the church (1 Cor. 10:32). Further, Paul speaks of the church as one new man (Eph. 2:15; cf. Col. 3:11), composed of believing Jews and believing Gentiles. And finally, God has yet a future for Israel. Paul, in Rom. 11, outlines the chronology of God's future dealings with Israel. She is the olive branch which has now been broken off while the wild olive has been grafted into the trunk. It is during the time of the wild olive branch that the church is God's instrument on earth. That the kingdom did not come in the days of Christ is attested to by the question of the disciples, "Lord, is it at this time You are restoring the kingdom to Israel?" (Acts 1:6). The counsel of James at the Jerusalem Council (Acts 15:13-21) suggests that the early church saw itself as something quite different than a continuation of Israel.

B. The Church is Not a Continuation of the Synagogue

Admittedly, there are marked similarities between the church and the synagogue, but there are also marked dissimilarities. Jesus said, "I will build My church" (Matt. 16:18). This could not refer to the synagogue because the synagogue was already in existence. When the apostles preached in the synagogues, their message was evangelistic, calling for repentance and faith. According to New Testament evidence, the nucleus from the synagogue who believed formed a local body of believers quite apart from the synagogue. Further, when the church did begin, the believers met initially in the temple area, not in a synagogue.

C. The Church is Not Coterminal with the Interregnum

The interregnum began and will end at points different from the origin and rapture of the church. The interregnum began when the Lord was rejected by his own, and when he began to declare the purpose and plan of God for the coming age. This approximates the time when Jesus began telling the parables of the mysteries of the kingdom (Matt. 13). This period will end with the coming of the Lord in glory to establish his earthly kingdom (Rev. 19), when the tares are gathered out and burned, and the true children of the kingdom remain to enjoy the millennial blessings (Matt. 13:24–30, 36–43). The church, however, began at Pentecost, some time after the beginning of the interregnum, and the rapture of the church will take place at a time prior to the great tribulation period and the millennial reign of Christ. We conclude that, though the church is a part of the kingdom of God, it is not to be equated as one and the same. It is not even to be equated exactly with the mystery form of the kingdom, for there also it is just a part of the larger kingdom.

D. The Church is Not a Denomination

We often speak of various denominations as churches, but this use of the term "church" does not occur in the Scriptures. Some of the denominations claim to be the only true church, but it must be remembered that the Word warns against such divisions (1 Cor. 1:11–17). There may be many denominations, but there is only the one true universal church. All of the redeemed of this age are members of this one spiritual body.

E. The Church is Considered in Two Senses

We note, then, positively what the church is. The term "church" is used in two senses: the universal sense and the local sense.

1. In the universal sense. In the universal sense the church consists of all those who, in this age, have been born of the Spirit of God and have by that same Spirit been baptized into the body of Christ (1 Cor. 12:13; 1 Pet. 1:3, 22-25). That the term is used in this universal sense is evident because Christ spoke of building his church, not churches (Matt. 16:18); Paul grieved because he had persecuted the church (1 Cor. 15:9; Gal. 1:13; Phil. 3:6); Christ is said to have loved the church and to have given himself for her (Eph. 5:25); our Lord is purifying and sanctifying the church (Eph. 5:26f.); he is the head of the church (Eph. 1:22; 5:23; Col. 1:18); he has set gifted men in the church (1 Cor. 12:28); the church is making known to the rulers and authorities in the heavenly places the manifold wisdom of God (Eph. 3:10); and the whole company of believers of this age is called the church of the firstborn who are enrolled in heaven (Heb. 12:23). In all these Scriptures the Greek word *ekklesia* is used. In itself this term means simply a body of called-out people, as an assembly of citizens in a self-governing state; but the New Testament has filled it with a spiritual content, so that it means a people called out from the world and from sinful things. Although the word occurs over 100 times in the New Testament, it is used in the secular sense only in Acts 19:32, 39, 41, and of the assembly of the Israelites only in Acts 7:38 and Heb. 2:12. It is interesting to note that the English word "church" comes from the Greek word *kuriakos*, which means "belonging to the Lord." This adjective occurs only twice in the New Testament; it is used of the Lord's Supper (1 Cor. 11:20), and of the Lord's Day (Rev. 1:10). We might, therefore, give as a secondary definition of the term "church" the following: a group of people called out from the world and belonging to the Lord. Yet, the former definition recognizes more clearly the fact of the new birth as an essential requirement of membership in the true church. Membership is not, however, hereditary or by compulsion but by a personal decision of faith in Christ.

This universal conception of the church is seen in the figures under which it is represented. The church is called a building of God (1 Cor. 3:9, 16f.; 2 Cor. 6:16; Eph. 2:20-22; 1 Tim. 3:15). Christ is the cornerstone of this building (Matt. 16:18; 1 Cor. 3:11; 1 Pet. 2:6f.) and dwells in it by his Spirit (1 Cor. 3:16; 6:19). The believer performs priestly service in this temple (Heb. 13:15f.; 1 Pet. 2:9; Rev. 1:6). It is also called the body of Christ (Rom. 12:4; 1 Cor. 12:12-27; Eph. 1:22f.; 3:6; 4:4, 12, 16; 5:23, 30; Col. 1:18, 24; 2:19; 3:15). Under this figure, the church is represented as an organism, as having a vital connection with Christ, as under the superintendence of Christ, as being a unit, although made up of Jews and Gentiles, as having a diversity of gifts among the members, and as ideally cooperating in the performance of one common task. And it is called the bride of Christ (2 Cor. 11:2f.; Eph. 5:24f., 32). As the bride of Christ, the church is in the position of espousal to him; as such, she is to be faithful to Christ (James

4:4), to prepare for the wedding ceremonies (Rev. 19:7f.), to be married some day to Christ (John 3:29), and to reign with him (Rev. 19:6–20:6). Other figures used are vine (John 15:1ff.) and flock (John 10:1ff.; Heb. 13:20; 1 Pet. 2:25).

2. In the local sense.   In the local sense the word "church" is used of the group of professed believers in any one locality. Thus, we read of the church in Jerusalem (Acts 8:1; 11:22), in Ephesus (Acts 20:17), in Cenchrea (Rom. 16:1), and in Corinth (1 Cor. 1:2; 2 Cor. 1:1). We read of the church of the Laodiceans (Col. 4:16) and of the Thessalonians (1 Thess. 1:1; 2 Thess. 1:1). Sometimes the term is in the plural, as in the churches of Galatia (Gal. 1:2), of Judea (1 Thess. 2:14), and of Asia (Rev. 1:4). The local churches together are to be a faithful replica of the true church, the universal church.

It is interesting that the figures used of the church are used equally of the individual believer, the local church, and the universal church. The figures of bride, body, building, and flock are used of the church universal (Eph. 5:25; 1:23; 2 Cor. 6:16; Heb. 13:20, respectively), of the local church (2 Cor. 11:2; 1 Cor. 12:12–27; 1 Cor. 3:16; Acts 20:28, respectively), and of the individual believer (Rom. 7:4; Rom. 6:12; 1 Cor. 6:19; Luke 15:4–10, respectively).

II. THE FOUNDING OF THE CHURCH

Since the founding of the universal church and of local churches are coincident, they will be treated together in this section. The peculiarities of the one or the other will be noted in the proper connections. Connected with the biblical conception of the nature of the church are the ideas of the time and manner of its founding. One must have a clear apprehension of both elements of truth in order to have a true biblical view of the church. Let us note several things that are pertinent here.

A. THE TIME OF ITS FOUNDING

There is some confusion at this point. Those who hold that the church is but the spiritual Israel of the New Testament, in other words, a continuation of Old Testament Israel, necessarily believe that the church was begun in Old Testament times. Others hold that it began with the preaching of Christ. But these positions are shown to be unscriptural on the basis of Christ's own statement. Christ declared at Caesarea Philippi that the church was still future, for he said, "Upon this rock I will build My church" (Matt. 16:18). Those who hold that Peter is the rock will have to admit that the church did not come into existence in the Old Testament, and so also those who hold that the rock is Peter's confession of Jesus as the Christ, the Son of the living

God. It seems difficult to believe that Jesus merely meant that he would make a new beginning in the development of the church, for he was dealing with the founding, not the rebuilding, of it. Others hold that there was a church for the period of the Acts that is not the church of today. Some of these suggest that the present Christian church began when the book of Acts closed, others teach that it began when Paul said at Antioch of Pisidia, "Behold, we are turning to the Gentiles" (Acts 13:46). But what does Scripture teach?

That the church, both universal and local, was founded on the day of Pentecost (Acts 2), is clear from a number of things. We must go back to the statement concerning the manner in which the church was to be founded. Paul expressed it succinctly when he wrote, "For by one Spirit we were all baptized into one body, whether Jews or Greeks, whether slaves or free, and we were all made to drink of one Spirit" (1 Cor. 12:13). By the body, Paul means the church (v. 28; Eph. 1:22f.). This baptism of the Spirit places the believer in the church, the body of Christ. This baptism is mentioned in all four Gospels and the Acts. The four references in the Gospels (Matt. 3:11; Mark 1:8; Luke 3:16; John 1:33) are practically the same, namely, the promise of the coming baptism. In Acts 1:5, Jesus repeats the promise and says that it will be fulfilled in a few days; and in Acts 11:15-17, Peter refers back to Pentecost as the fulfillment. 1 Cor. 12:13 refers to the baptism as a past experience. Thus, it is evident that the baptism of the Spirit occurred on the day of Pentecost and that the church was founded on that day. This same conclusion is made necessary by the fact that the church would not have been possible before the ascension and exaltation of Christ (Eph. 1:19-23).

The local church was founded at the same time. We read that there were 120 waiting for the promise of the Spirit when the day of Pentecost came. These 120 were the first ones to be baptized with the Spirit, and they became the charter members of the Jerusalem church. In response to the preaching of Peter and the other apostles, 3,000 received the word, were baptized, and were added to the church (Acts 2:14, 41). A little later this local church had grown to 5,000 (Acts 4:4). It is clear that the believers acted as a corporate unit. They had a definite doctrinal standard, the apostles' teaching; they had fellowship with one another as believers; they observed the ordinances of baptism and the Lord's Supper; they met for public worship; and they contributed to the support of the needy (Acts 2:42-47). Surely, these are the marks of an organized local church, even if the organization was only loose as yet.

B. The Founding of Other Local Churches

It is evident that other such churches arose in Judea (Gal. 1:22; 1 Thess. 2:14), though there is no specific reference to them in the Acts. A local church also sprang up in the city of Samaria (Acts 8:1–24), and possibly in many villages of Samaria (Acts 8:25). Soon there was a church started in Antioch in Syria (Acts 11:20–30; 13:1). This church became the home-base for Paul's missionary journeys (Acts 13:1–3; 14:26–28; 15:36–41; 18:22f.). There were a number of prophets and teachers in this church, but they recognized the need of counsel with the Jerusalem church in regard to the conditions on which the Gentiles might be received into fellowship (Acts 15:1–35). Finally, as a result of the missionary labors of Paul and the other apostles, and the early Christians in general, local churches were established in Asia Minor, Macedonia, Greece, Italy, Spain, and many other areas of the Mediterranean world. It seems that in some sense the early church evangelized its own generation.

CHAPTER XXXVI

The Foundation of the Church, the Manner of the Founding, and the Organization of Churches

Several items come under consideration at this point: the foundation of the church, the manner of its founding, and the New Testament organization of churches.

I. THE FOUNDATION OF THE CHURCH

At this point we consider the founding of the universal and the local church.

A. THE UNIVERSAL CHURCH

Jesus said to Peter, "And I also say to you that you are Peter, and upon this rock I will build My church" (Matt. 16:18). It is clear from this passage that the church is the Lord's, for he calls it "my church." It is "the church of God which He purchased with His own blood" (Acts 20:28). It is called the church of Jesus Christ, and he is the head over it (Eph. 5:23; Col. 1:18). In the Revelation, Christ is portrayed as the Lord of the churches, walking among the lampstands (Rev. 1:12–20), with the power to remove the local church (2:5) or judge those in it (2:16). Clearly, "the church as the new creation of God rests upon the person and work of Jesus Christ."[1] Christ said that he would build his church upon "this" rock. Opinions vary as to what or who this rock is. The following possibilities have been suggested: (1) The term "rock" refers to Peter. Christ is the principal foundation and founder, but Peter is the one whom Christ delegated to found the church. (2) Others suggest that the term "rock" refers to the apostles and that Peter is simply the spokesman for the group. (3) Still others feel that in light of such verses as Rom. 9:33; 1 Cor. 10:4; and 1 Pet. 2:8 this could only refer to Christ himself as the rock (cf. Matt. 7:24–27). (4) Then there are those who refer it to Peter's confession of the deity of Christ. Thus, the New Testament church is built upon the confession that Jesus is the Christ.

The view that the rock refers to Peter seems to have the best support. Several arguments can be set forth. (1) The name "Peter" does mean "rock."

[1]Saucy, *The Church in God's Program*, p. 60.

315

The Lord surnamed him "Cephas," meaning "rock," the Greek term being "Peter." To argue that Christ is called a rock elsewhere in Scripture, and therefore it must refer to him, is to ignore that "rock" could be used of different persons, even as "light" is used of both believers (Matt. 5:14) and Christ (John 9:5). (2) Historically, Peter was used in the founding of the church. He opened the door of the gospel to the Jews (Acts 2:14–41), to the Samaritans (Acts 8:14–17), and to the Gentiles (Acts 10:24–48). (3) Christ used the masculine form of "rock" in naming Peter, and the feminine form in speaking of the foundation of the church. This has caused some to argue that the rock and Peter are not the same. However, it was necessary linguistically to express it this way, because rock in the feminine form speaks of bedrock or boulder; whereas in naming a person, Christ must of necessity use the masculine form for a male. And finally, (4) the apostles are spoken of as the foundation of the church (Eph. 2:20), Jesus himself being the chief cornerstone. We conclude that "the 'rock' upon which Christ predicted that he would build his church has reference to the apostle Peter as leader and representative of the apostles."[2] To take the position that Peter is the rock is not to ignore that Christ is the ultimate and final foundation, the foundation par excellence. But Christ used men in the founding of the church. Further, it is not to ignore the importance of the confession. A person without this confession cannot be a part of the body of Christ. Anyone who desires to be a living stone (1 Pet. 2:5) within this living temple must confess to the deity of Christ, even as Peter did.

Whatever position one might take on this debated subject, three things are clear: Christ is building his church, he is using human instruments, and these human instruments must confess to the deity of Jesus Christ. The authority of binding and loosing was not given to Peter only, but also to the rest of the apostles (Matt. 16:19; 18:18; John 20:23). This seems to be a declarative power much like that of Jeremiah (Jer. 1:10).

B. The Local Church

It is self-evident that on Pentecost the church universal and the local church at Jerusalem were both founded, and at that time they were one and the same. As the disciples moved into other areas, other local churches were founded. As individuals turned to the Lord in various areas, they banded together and formed local bodies of believers. They were started by believers who preached the gospel, and were founded upon Christ. Paul writes of the Corinthian church, "According to the grace of God which was given to me, as a wise master builder I laid a foundation, and another is building upon it. But let each man be careful how he builds upon it. For no man can lay a

[2]Saucy, *The Church in God's Program*, p. 63.

foundation other than the one which is laid, which is Jesus Christ" (1 Cor. 3:10f.). Thus, Paul claims, the foundation he laid was Jesus Christ. Jesus Christ must be the foundation, the Word of God must be the rule of faith and practice, and the Spirit of God must be the administrator. Only those who freely confess that Jesus is the Christ should be allowed to become members of the local body. Only those who are, for all appearances, members of the universal body should be admitted into the local church.

II. THE MANNER OF THE FOUNDING

The universal or true church is not the product of man's effort. It was not organized, but born. In Heb. 12:23 this church is called "the church of the first-born" (first-born is a plural adjective, meaning "first-born ones"). That is, the new birth is the first condition in the founding of this church. The second is the baptism of the Spirit. Scripture declares, "For by one Spirit we were all baptized into one body, whether Jews or Greeks, whether slaves or free, and we were all made to drink of one Spirit" (1 Cor. 12:13). This baptism occurred initially on the day of Pentecost (Acts 1:4f.; 2:1f.; 11:15-17). The Lord alone can baptize with the Holy Spirit (Mark 1:8), and he alone can add to this church (Acts 2:47; cf. 5:14; 11:24). Christ said that he would build his church (Matt. 16:18). All those in this age who believe are baptized into the church, the body of Christ.

The local church sprang up in a most simple way. At first there was no organization, but merely a simple bond of love, fellowship, doctrine, and cooperation. Gradually, however, the earlier loose arrangement under the apostles was superseded by a close organization. Because members were already members of the true church, they felt impelled to organize local churches in which the invisible realities in Christ might be worked out for the common good and the salvation of the unsaved.

In the beginning there was but one local church, the church at Jerusalem. It seems that the meetings were held in various homes, but there was but one church. The membership grew to 3,000 and then 5,000, while the Lord added to them daily (Acts 2:41, 47; 4:4; 5:14). The apostles were the leaders of the church.

Later, other local churches were founded in new places as the gospel was preached and believed, as in Judea and Samaria (Acts 8), no doubt being patterned after the one in Jerusalem. The exact manner of the founding is not recorded. Paul directs Titus to "appoint elders in every city" (Titus 1:5), which seems to indicate that where a group of believers had been formed in a community, elders were appointed as leaders (cf. Acts 14:23). In the early church, when a person responded to the gospel of Jesus Christ, he was added to the church. There was no question whether he ought to join the local assembly; this was taken for granted.

III. THE ORGANIZATION OF CHURCHES

Very little is said of the organization between churches, but we have considerable information on the organization of the local church.

A. THE FACT OF ORGANIZATION

There are indications that very early in Jerusalem the church had at least a loose kind of organization, and there is conclusive evidence that soon thereafter local churches were definitely organized. That there must have been a simple organization even in the church in Jerusalem is evident from a number of things. The believers adhered to a definite doctrinal standard (Acts 2:42), met for spiritual fellowship, united in prayer, practiced baptism, observed the Lord's Supper, kept account of the membership, met for public worship, and provided material help for the needy of their number (Acts 2:41–46). The apostles were the leaders in this church, but soon they added seven men to take care of the ministration to the poor (Acts 6:1–7). On the day of Pentecost they were assembled in the upper room (Acts 1:13; 2:1), wherever that may have been. More often, however, they seem to have met in some home of a Christian (Acts 2:46; 12:12), though for some services apparently they still visited the temple (Acts 2:46; 3:1). All these factors indicate the beginnings of organization in the Jerusalem church.

1. They had church officers.   There are, besides the example of the first church, many other indications that the Scriptures teach the propriety and necessity of organizing local groups of believers into churches. Paul and Barnabas, when retracing their steps from Derbe, "appointed elders for them in every church" (Acts 14:23). The original suggests that this was done by a show of hands under apostolic direction. Titus was asked to appoint elders (Titus 1:5). Further, the Jerusalem church appointed stewards to look after the needs of the poor (Acts 6:1–7). There must have been a way of ascertaining the sentiment of the people, and a regulation that stated who was entitled to vote on the question. In the church at Ephesus there were elders (Acts 20:17), in the church at Antioch, prophets and teachers (Acts 13:1), and in the church at Philippi, overseers and deacons (Phil. 1:1). Later, the church at Ephesus had both overseers and deacons (1 Tim. 3:1, 8).

2. They had stated times of meeting.   The disciples met on the first day of the week immediately following Christ's resurrection (John 20:19, 26). In his first letter to the Corinthians, Paul instructs the readers to lay by them in store as the Lord has prospered them on the first day of the week (1 Cor. 16:2), that is, on that day the collection was to be taken. On Paul's last journey to Jerusalem, he stopped at Troas and met with the disciples there on the first day of the week (Acts 20:7). And in the Revelation, John indicates that he was in the Spirit on the Lord's Day (1:10). There must have been an action taken with regard to the day to be observed, and business transactions presuppose an organization.

3. They regulated church decorum. They regulated church decorum (1 Cor. 14:26–40) and exercised church discipline. Jesus had given instructions that in the case of a believer who refused to bow to private admonition, the dispute was to be referred to the church for discipline (Matt. 18:17). Paul requests the Corinthians most definitely to exercise church discipline (1 Cor. 5:13). He gives similar instructions to the church at Rome (Rom. 16:17; cf. 2 Thess. 3:6–15). In 3 John 9f. we are told that Diotrephes acted high-handedly in church discipline. Here, again, organization is presupposed, for it is necessary to draw the line in such matters between those who may vote and those who may not. It would appear that the majority ruled in matters of discipline (2 Cor. 2:6).

4. They raised money for the Lord's work. Writing to the Corinthian church from Ephesus, Paul stated that he had already given orders to the churches of Galatia, and then he gave them instructions to contribute to the collection for the saints (1 Cor. 16:1f.). They were to give systematically, proportionately, and purposefully. They were to give on the first day of the week, as each may prosper, for the saints. In 2 Cor. Paul urges them to give liberally (2 Cor. 8:7–9; 9:6) and cheerfully (2 Cor. 9:7). He commends the Macedonian churches for their great liberality in this connection (2 Cor. 8:1–5), and urges the Corinthian church to follow their example (2 Cor. 8:6–9:5). In Romans Paul tells of the offering which he is taking to Jerusalem (15:25–28). Before Felix, Paul refers to this offering which he had brought to his nation (Acts 24:17). Thus, the churches in Galatia, Macedonia, and Achaia entered into an organized effort to raise funds for the poor in Judea.

5. They sent letters of commendation to the other churches. This was done when Apollos left Ephesus for Corinth (Acts 18:24–28). It is also implied in Paul's sarcastic question, whether he will have to bring letters of commendation when he returns to Corinth (2 Cor. 3:1). Rom. 16:1f. is probably a sample of such a letter concerning Phoebe. Insofar as this practice grew, it must have become necessary to ascertain the mind of the church as to who was worthy of such a letter. Organization is to be presupposed in such a procedure. The Council at Jerusalem rendered a decision with reference to the conditions on which Gentiles might be admitted into fellowship and sent a letter (Acts 15:22–29). This, too, presupposes an organization of some sort or other.

B. The Officers of the Church

An organization implies officers. Everything was very simple at the beginning, but there were two or perhaps three distinct offices in the early churches. This evidence comes to us partly by way of reference to the officials of churches and partly by way of the teaching concerning the appointment and duties of the officers.

1. Pastor, elder, overseer.   These three terms denote one and the same office in the New Testament. In Acts 20:17, 28 the elders of the church at Ephesus are said to have been made overseers (or bishops) over the flock, with the purpose that they should feed (shepherd or pastor) the church of God. Here we have the terms elders, overseers, and pastors all used of the same men. In 1 Pet. 5:1f. the duties of a pastor are assigned to "the elders among you." That is, the two were one and the same. Both John (2 John 1; 3 John 1) and Peter (1 Pet. 5:1) were apostles, and yet they call themselves elders. Surely, this did not imply an office inferior to that of pastor or overseer. In Titus 1:5-9 the terms "elder" and "overseer" are used interchangeably. The Greek term "shepherd" occurs several times in the New Testament, but only in Eph. 4:11 is it translated "pastor." Its real meaning is that of shepherd (cf. Matt. 9:36; 26:31; Luke 2:8; John 10:2; Heb. 13:20; 1 Pet. 2:25). As has been pointed out, the elders and overseers in the church at Ephesus had been entrusted with the work of shepherding the flock, that is, they had been made pastors in the church. Paul addresses the church at Philippi, "To all the saints in Christ Jesus who are in Philippi, including the overseers and deacons" (Phil. 1:1). If there had been elders and pastors in that church, distinct from the overseers, Paul would have addressed only a part of the officials of the church, an unlikely supposition.

2. Deacons.   The word comes from the Greek *diakonos* (Phil. 1:1; 1 Tim. 3:8). It is used in the general sense of servant (Mark 10:43; John 2:5; 12:26). The verb form is translated "to minister" or "to serve" (Matt. 4:11; 20:28; Rom. 15:25). The term is also used in a non-technical way of any minister of the gospel (1 Cor. 3:5; 2 Cor. 6:4; Eph. 6:21; Col. 1:7; 1 Tim. 4:6). The term, however, is also used in a technical way and, as such, is usually translated "deacon." This special meaning is found in Phil. 1:1; 1 Tim. 3:8-13; and perhaps Rom. 16:1. It may be that the seven men chosen to minister to the poor widows of the early church in Acts 6:1-6 are to be regarded as the first deacons, but this is not certain. It is significant that deacons must have the same high spiritual qualifications as overseers (1 Tim. 3:8-13). Therefore, it seems that deacons may have helped in the spiritual work of the church as well as in the material.

The function of the office of deacon is not clear in Scripture, but it appears that it had to do with the administering of relief funds. The elders were responsible for the spiritual needs of the community of the faithful and the deacons cared primarily for the physical needs. The qualifications for those holding this office are similar to those of the elder, except that the requirements concerning the ability to teach and hospitality, though mentioned for the elder, are not required for a deacon. This would suggest that these are not the responsibilities of the deacon. The qualification, not "found of sordid gain," suggests that the deacon was involved in the financial activities of the church. It is safe to say that the requirements for deacon seem particularly appropriate for those handling the material and financial needs of the organization.

3. *Deaconesses.* That certain women functioned in some type of official capacity in the early church seems clear. Phoebe is called a servant, that is, deaconess (Rom. 16:1), and in Paul's discussion of church officers (1 Tim. 3:1–13) he lists women (v. 11). It seems proper that there should be certain women devoted to caring for the sick, making arrangements for the common meals, lending aid in the distribution of alms, and, in general, help where a woman's role could best be utilized.

The interpretation of "women" in 1 Tim. 3:11 has been variously understood. Some see it as the deacons' wives. If this is the case, it seems strange that the elders' wives are not mentioned. Because they are mentioned in the midst of Paul's discussion of the deacons, it is probable that the women refer to a subgroup within the larger diaconate. Further, it is of interest that "likewise" is used, as it is with deacons (v. 8; cf. v. 2), indicating that these women held a special office within the church. Also, the requirements for office are closely parallel to those of deacon.

We conclude that the deacons had the primary responsibility of the material and financial needs of the church, and that certain women, called "deaconesses," worked with the deacons in areas where they function more adequately than the men. Because the diaconate was not a governing body, women could serve on it.

C. The Government of the Church

There are three basic types of church government: the episcopal, the presbyterial, and the congregational. The episcopal type is the government of the church by bishops or overseers, in reality, by three different orders of ministers: bishops or overseers, priests, and deacons. The presbyterial is the government of the church by presbyters or elders. It usually provides for the following courts: the session, the presbytery, the synod, and the general assembly. There is but one order in the ministry, namely, pastors, ruling elders or elders, and deacons. Both pastors and ruling elders take part in the meetings of the presbytery, synod, and general assembly. The congregational type of church government vests all legislative authority in the local church. District and general organizations are merely advisory in power and instituted simply for the purpose of cooperating in missionary work, educational work, and so forth.

Each of these forms seeks to find its support in Scripture. The episcopal form finds support in passages that speak of the authority of apostles or their delegates (Acts 14:23; 20:17, 28; Titus 1:5). But there are no longer apostles or delegated apostolic authority. What is available today are their instructions concerning church government as contained in Scripture. The presbyterial form finds support in such matters as the conduct of the Jerusalem Council (Acts 15:6) and the ordination of Timothy (1 Tim. 4:14). But even in these cases, there is indication that the congregation was involved. Early church government is a combination of the congregational and the presbyterial forms. The congregation chose their leaders, and the leaders acted in accordance with directives and suffrage of the people. Acts 6 gives information on the selection of officers (vss. 1–6). The term translated "appointed" in Acts 14:23 means "raise the hand." Evidently, Paul and Barnabas conducted some form of congregational vote in the selection of elders. Even at the Jerusalem Council the apostles, elders, and the congregation were involved in the decision-making process. Several items can be mentioned which point to congregational government in the early church. (1) Each church elected its own officers and delegates (Acts 6:1–6; 15:2f.). (2) Each church had the power to carry out its own church discipline (Matt. 18:17f.; 1 Cor. 5:13; 2 Cor. 2:6; 2 Thess. 3:6, 14f.). (3) The church, together with its officers, rendered decisions (Acts 15:22), received delegates (Acts 15:4; 18:27), and sent out solicitors (2 Cor. 8:19) and missionaries (Acts 13:3f.; 14:26). The local congregation was actively involved in all the affairs of the church. Whatever delegated authority there was, did not ignore the needs of the body.

CHAPTER XXXVII

The Ordinances of the Church

There are two rites of the church: baptism and the Lord's Supper. These rites are called ordinances or sacraments. In addition to the two accepted by most Protestant churches, the Roman Catholic Church adds five: ordination, confirmation, matrimony, extreme unction, and penance. In Roman Catholic theology "each of the sacraments confers or increases sanctifying grace. This sanctifying grace is known as sacramental grace inasmuch as it carries with it a right to the supernatural helps necessary and useful for the accomplishment of the purpose of each sacrament."[1] Though the Reformed churches accept only the two rites, baptism and the Lord's Supper, they also see them as means of grace. Berkhof writes, "As signs and seals they are means of grace, that is, means of strengthening the inward grace that is wrought in the heart by the Holy Spirit."[2] In order to avoid the mysticism and sacramentarianism characterized by the term "sacrament," it is perhaps better to use the term "ordinance" for the two rites of the church. An ordinance can be defined as an outward rite instituted by Christ to be administered in the church as a visible sign of the saving truth of the Christian faith. There is no special grace effected by either baptism or the Lord's Supper, though as we are obedient to Christ's commands and remember Christ and his sacrifice on our behalf, we do grow in the grace of the Lord Jesus. This, however, does not come through the ordinance itself. We now consider the two ordinances.

I. BAPTISM

From the preaching of John the Baptist and throughout the historical and doctrinal sections of the New Testament, the reader is continually confronted with baptism. It can be considered from several perspectives.

A. ITS INSTITUTION

Jesus commanded his followers shortly before his ascension, "Go therefore and make disciples of all the nations, baptizing them in the name of the

---

[1]Clarkson, *et al., The Church Teaches,* p. 257.
[2]Berkhof, *Systematic Theology,* p. 618.

Father and the Son and the Holy Spirit, teaching them to observe all that I commanded you" (Matt. 28:19f.; cf. Mark 16:15f.). And this is precisely what the disciples did after the coming of the Holy Spirit (Acts 2:41; 8:12, 38; 9:18; 10:48; 16:15, 33; 18:8). The challenge of Peter was, "Repent, and let each of you be baptized in the name of Jesus Christ" (Acts 2:38). It would seem that as the apostles preached the gospel and people responded, they were immediately baptized. Thus, repentance, faith, and baptism were very closely related. Clearly, though, baptism did not contribute to salvation; rather, it followed immediately. Cornelius was baptized after having received the Spirit (Acts 10:44–48). Bruce makes an aside, "The idea of an unbaptized Christian is simply not entertained in the NT."[3]

New Testament baptism is distinguished from John's baptism (Acts 10:37; 13:24; 18:25; 19:3). John the Baptist's baptism was a baptism of repentance in preparation for entrance into the promised kingdom which had been predicted by the prophets (Mal. 3:1; 4:5f.; Matt. 3:1–12; Mark 1:2–8; Luke 3:2–17; John 1:19–36). New Testament baptism relates more to the believer's identification with Christ.

B. Its Significance

The ordinance of baptism is a symbol of the believer's identification with Christ in his death, burial, and resurrection (Rom. 6:3f.; Col. 2:12; 1 Pet. 3:21). In baptism the believer testifies that he was in Christ when Christ was judged for sin, that he was buried with him, and that he has arisen to new life in him. It symbolizes that the believer is identified which Christ, for he is baptized in (or "into") the name of the Lord Jesus (Acts 2:38; 8:16). This was done while the penitent called upon the name of the Lord (Acts 22:16). This was an open and public confession of the lordship of Christ (Rom. 10:9f.). But before water baptism must come instruction (Matt. 28:19), repentance (Acts 2:38), and faith (Acts 2:41; 8:12; 18:8; Gal. 3:26f.), for water baptism does not effect identification, but presupposes and symbolizes it.

Several passages, on the surface, seem to teach that baptism saves. Four key ones are: "He who has believed and has been baptized shall be saved; but he who has disbelieved shall be condemned" (Mark 16:16); "Repent, and let each of you be baptized in the name of Jesus Christ for the forgiveness of your sins; and you shall receive the gift of the Holy Spirit" (Acts 2:38); "Arise, and be baptized, and wash away your sins, calling on His name" (Acts 22:16); and "Corresponding to that, baptism now saves you" (1 Pet. 3:21). But in all these cases, faith must come first. The biblical order is repentance, belief, baptism. John's statement, "I baptize you in water for

[3]Bruce, *Commentary on the Book of the Acts*, p. 77.

repentance" (Matt. 3:11) is the same Greek construction as Peter's "Be baptized . . . for the forgiveness of your sins" (Acts 2:38). Surely John assumed repentance came first; likewise, forgiveness comes before baptism. Scripture is abundantly clear that purification from sin is not the result of baptism (Acts 15:9; 1 John 1:9), but the act of baptism is so very closely related to the act of faith that they are expressed often as one act. Saucy states,

> The blessings of the gospel are received through faith. Nevertheless, when that saving faith goes on to be expressed in an objective manner through baptism, God uses this act to confirm the realities of salvation. The faith of the individual is strengthened as it is openly expressed, and the saving acts of salvation are sealed and ratified with additional force to the heart of the believer.[4]

Not only does baptism symbolize the identification of the convert with Christ, it also is the visible means of identifying the penitent with the local body of believers. As he becomes a member of the body of Christ, he should also identify himself with the local assembly. When an individual responds to the call of salvation, he should, as the New Testament believers did, be baptized and be initiated into the Christian community (Acts 2:41).

C. Its Mode

There are currently three common modes of baptism: sprinkling, pouring or effusion, and immersion. Within these forms are certain variations such as triune baptism and baptizing forward or backward. There is general agreement that the term "baptize" means "to dip," and immersion suits the meaning of the term best. Further, history argues for immersion. Pouring and sprinkling came about because of water shortages and as a convenience for the aged and infirm. The significance of baptism as a symbol of our identification in the death, burial, and resurrection of Christ is best portrayed by immersion. Also, that the convert went into the water and came out of it seems to imply immersion (Acts 8:38f.; cf. Mark 1:10; John 3:23). We must be careful not to make the mode more important than the truth it symbolizes; and whereas immersion symbolizes our identification with Christ best, certain external considerations might make other modes necessary.

D. Its Subjects

Baptism is reserved for those who personally and willingly repond to the call of salvation. In the New Testament, it involved those who were to be taught

---

[4]Saucy, *The Church in God's Program*, p. 198.

(Matt. 28:20), who had received the Word (Acts 2:41), and who had received the Spirit (Acts 10:47). Some households were baptized (Acts 10:48; 16:15, 33; 18:8; 1 Cor. 1:16), and this has been construed to mean that even infants were baptized. It has been suggested that infant baptism of this nature answers to circumcision in the Old Testament. In answer to this, we say that "household" does not necessarily demand that there were infants; and further, in these cases mentioned above, those who were baptized were those who heard the Word (Acts 10:44) and believed (Acts 16:31, 34). Nowhere does Scripture teach that infants were baptized. Dedication of the child to the Lord by his parents is to be preferred above infant baptism.

II. THE LORD'S SUPPER

This second ordinance is called by several names. (1) In 1 Cor. it is called the Lord's Supper (11:20). (2) It is also called "the breaking of bread" (Acts 2:42), a common phrase for partaking of a common meal. (3) It is rendered "communion," from the Authorized Version translation of *koinonia* in 1 Cor. 10:16, "Is not the cup of blessing which we bless a sharing (communion) in the blood of Christ? Is not the bread which we break a sharing (communion) in the body of Christ?" And (4) finally, it is called the "Eucharist," from the Greek word for thanksgiving, taken from the giving of thanks before the partaking of the elements. The common meal eaten before the partaking of the elements was called the *agape* or love-feast (Jude 12).

A. ITS INSTITUTION

Paul writes, "For I received from the Lord that which I also delivered to you, that the Lord Jesus in the night in which He was betrayed took bread" (1 Cor. 11:23), and then he goes on into considerable detail concerning the Lord's Supper. The historical account of the institution of the Last Supper can be found in the three Synoptics (Matt. 26:26–28; Mark 14:22–24; Luke 22:17–20). Though we do not read about the practice of this ordinance as much as we do of baptism, it is not absent in the life of the early church. This was a vital part of the life of the infant church in Jerusalem. It is clearly linked with three other activities: doctrinal teaching, fellowship, and prayer (Acts 2:42). In this verse each of the four has the definite article which suggests that each was a specific and integral part of the corporate meetings of the church. Paul writes that he received of the Lord what he had delivered to the Corinthians (1 Cor. 11:23). This suggests that in the establishment of the Corinthian church he had introduced the Lord's Supper to them. He was in 1 Cor. simply reminding them of teachings concerning the communion service which he had given to them when he established the church. It can be inferred from this that Paul instituted the Lord's Supper in all the churches which he founded, and no doubt the other apostles did likewise.

B. Its Significance

1. It is memorial to Christ.   Jesus said, "Do this in remembrance of Me" (1 Cor. 11:24). It is not to be just a memorial to his death, as to a martyr, but to him as a living person. It is of significance that the believers met together on the first day of the week, resurrection day, to break bread (Acts 20:7). Jesus is to be commemorated as the one who ever lives and is ever present with his own (Matt. 28:20).

2. It is a pledge of the new covenant.   The sign of the new covenant is the cup. It symbolizes the blood which was shed by our Lord in the ratification of the new covenant. Jesus said, "This cup which is poured out for you is the new covenant in My blood" (Luke 22:20; cf. 1 Cor. 11:25). Matthew's Gospel reads, "This is My blood of the covenant, which is to be shed on behalf of many for forgiveness of sins" (Matt. 26:28). This new covenant thus provides for the believer the forgiveness of sins (Heb. 10:16–18). It is a better covenant than the old Mosaic one (2 Cor. 3:6–18; Heb. 7:22; 12:24). Thus, the partaking of the communion elements reminds us anew of the perfect forgiveness which we have in Christ.

3. It is a proclamation of Christ's death.   Paul writes, "For as often as you eat this bread and drink the cup, you proclaim the Lord's death until He comes" (1 Cor. 11:26). As believers meet together in remembrance of Christ, they are actively proclaiming to the world the death of Christ. Both the fact of his death and the significance of it are proclaimed by the members of his body as they partake of the meal together.

4. It is a prophecy of Christ's coming.   This ordinance is to be practiced until Christ comes (1 Cor. 11:26). Not only does this rite look back upon his death, it looks forward to his return for his own. At the Last Supper, Jesus told his disciples, "But I say to you, I will not drink of this fruit of the vine from now on until that day when I drink it new with you in My Father's kingdom" (Matt. 26:29). Hendriksen writes of this statement, "We see, therefore, that communion not only points back to what Jesus Christ has done for us but also forward to what he is still going to mean for us."[5] Partaking together reminds the believer of the joyful reunion and unending jubilation which await us when we meet the Lord.

---

[5]Hendriksen, *Exposition of the Gospel According to Matthew*, p. 911.

5. *It is a fellowship with Christ and his own.* This is a private time when the redeemed gather for fellowship around Jesus Christ. The table reminds the worshipper of the provisions which Christ has made for his own. We sit at the table of the Lord rather than at the table of demons (1 Cor. 10:21). Christ is the unseen host at the meal. Further, the believer is reminded of Christ's humility and our responsibility to serve one another. It was at the Lord's Supper that Jesus washed the disciples' feet, an act of humility, devotion, and love. Jesus said, "If I then, the Lord and the Teacher, washed your feet, you also ought to wash one another's feet. For I gave you an example that you also should do as I did to you" (John 13:14f.).

If Christ is present in the fellowship of believers at the communion service, what is the nature of his presence? Several views have been advanced. The Roman Catholic Church teaches that the literal body and blood of Christ are present in the bread and the wine. At consecration, the elements literally become the body and blood of Christ. This interpretation, called "transubstantiation," is to be rejected on several grounds. (1) Christ was present when he said that the elements were his body and his blood. Clearly, he was using figurative language. (2) The use of "is" in "this is My body" (1 Cor. 11:24) is figurative, meaning "this represents my body." (3) Jesus himself said that to eat of his body and drink of his blood was to come to him and believe (John 6:35; cf. vss. 53–58). (4) This idea of literally eating human flesh and drinking human blood would be abhorrent to the Jewish mind. Surely, the Jews in Jesus' day would have reacted strongly against such a thought. Drinking of blood was strictly forbidden (Gen. 9:4; Lev. 3:17; Acts 15:29). And (5) the Passover itself, the feast from which the elements were taken, was a symbolic feast of the deliverance of Israel from Egyptian bondage (Exod. 12). Thus, the symbolism of the elements in the communion service would be in keeping with the symbolism used in the Passover feast.

Another view of the presence of Christ is called "consubstantiation." According to this view, the position of the Lutheran church, the communicant partakes of the true body and blood of Christ in, with, and under the bread and the wine. The elements themselves remain unchanged, but the mere partaking of them after the prayer of consecration communicates Christ to the participant along with the elements. It is considered a literal partaking of Christ. This view, however, has the same problems associated with it as does transubstantiation. Jesus laid down the true principle, "It is the Spirit who gives life; the flesh profits nothing; the words that I have spoken to you are spirit and are life" (John 6:63).

Seeking to avoid the sacramental and mystical meaning of Christ's presence in the elements, others have held that the communion service is nothing more than a memorial commemorating Christ's death. Though Christ is present spiritually, the actual eating and drinking of the elements signifies the participants' faith in him and in his redemptive work. This view rejects the bodily presence of Christ in the elements.

The Reformed position is somewhere between that of consubstantiation and that of a memorial. In some manner, there is a dynamic presence of Christ in the elements made effective in the believer as he partakes. According to Paul, the cup is a "sharing in the blood of Christ" and the bread is a "sharing in the body of Christ" (1 Cor. 10:16). The elements are the symbols of his presence. Saucy writes, "Partaking of His presence is therefore not a physical eating and drinking, but an inner communion with His person which uses the outward action as an expression of inward spiritual faith."[6] His presence in the supper is similar to his presence in the Word. It is perhaps best to see the communion service as primarily a memorial, while at the same time acknowledging the presence of Christ in our midst as we partake of the elements which symbolize his body and blood. Surely, the receiving of the elements can symbolize a spiritual reception of and communion with Christ.

C. Its Participants

The conditions of participating in the Lord's Supper are regeneration and a life of obedience to Christ. That regeneration is a condition is evident from the fact that the Lord gave the ordinance to his disciples (Matt. 26:27), the disciples observed it among themselves (Acts 2:42, 46; 20:7; 1 Cor. 11:18–22), and each participant is asked to examine himself as to whether or not he is qualified to partake of the communion elements (1 Cor. 11:27–29). That a life of obedience is a condition, is evident from the fact that persons who fall into sin are to be excluded from the church (1 Cor. 5:11–13; 2 Thess. 3:6, 11–15), as also those who teach false doctrine (Titus 3:10; 2 John 10f.) and promote divisions and dissensions (Rom. 16:17). Baptism preceded the partaking of the Lord's Supper in the life of the early church as far as we know, but there is no command to that effect, nor is there any proof that believers were excluded from the Lord's Supper until they were baptized. Nor is there any proof that local church membership was a condition. This is "the table of the Lord," not the church's table. This is evident from the fact that the individual is asked to examine himself as to his fitness to come to the table; the church is not authorized to sit in judgment upon believers, except in the case of disorderly conduct, false teaching, or participation in unscriptural practices.

[6]Saucy, *The Church in God's Program*, p. 224.

CHAPTER XXXVIII

The Mission and Destiny of the Church

Having now considered the church in its foundation, organization, and ordinances, it is fitting that we should also give some thought to its mission and its destiny.

I. THE MISSION OF THE CHURCH

As we function in the church and plan the programs of the local church, a primary question which needs to be asked is, What is the mission of the church? In other words, what is the church to be doing? What are the scriptural mandates for the church? Several can be suggested.

A. To Glorify God

Man's chief purpose is to glorify God. This is no more true of the individual than it is of the church as a whole. The Scriptures repeatedly point this out as the primary purpose of the church (Rom. 15:6, 9; Eph. 1:5f., 12, 14, 18; 3:21; 2 Thess. 1:12; 1 Pet. 4:11). So fundamental is this duty that if faithfully performed, there will also be the carrying out of the other purposes of the church. How is God glorified? (1) We glorify God by worshipping him (John 4:23f.; cf. Phil. 3:3; Rev. 22:9). (2) We glorify God by prayer and praise. The Psalmist writes, "He who offers a sacrifice of thanksgiving honors Me" (Ps. 50:23). (3) Further, we also glorify him by living a godly life. Jesus said, "By this is My Father glorified, that you bear much fruit, and so prove to be My disciples" (John 15:8). Peter declares that we are to "proclaim the excellencies of Him who has called you out of darkness into His marvelous light" (1 Pet. 2:9; cf. Titus 2:10).

B. To Edify Itself

Paul tells us that God gave the church apostles, prophets, evangelists, pastors, and teachers "for the equipping of the saints for the work of service, to the building up of the body of Christ; until we all attain to the unity of the faith, and of the knowledge of the Son of God, to a mature man, to the measure of the stature which belongs to the fulness of Christ. As a result, we are no longer to be children, tossed here and there by waves, and carried about by every wind of doctrine, by the trickery of men, by craftiness in deceitful scheming; but speaking the truth in love, we are to grow up in all aspects into Him, who is the head, even Christ, from whom the whole body, being fitted and held together by that which every joint supplies, according to the proper working of each individual part, causes the growth of the body for the building up of itself in love" (Eph. 4:12–16). Clearly, this means the indoctrination of the members of the church, in order that they might mature to the fullest and be able to stand against the heresies around them. This is the building up of the body in Christ (Col. 2:7). The public church service is intended to do this (1 Cor. 14:26), but the individuals are also to build themselves up in the most holy faith (Jude 20) and "grow in the grace and knowledge of our Lord and Savior Jesus Christ" (2 Pet. 3:18). Paul challenges us to use proper materials in erecting God's spiritual temple (1 Cor. 3:10–15) and warns us against using improper materials. Thus, the church is to indoctrinate its members, develop the graces of the Christian life in them, and teach them to cooperate with one another in the service of Christ.

C. To Purify Itself

Christ gave himself for the church "that He might sanctify her, having cleansed her by the washing of water with the word, that He might present to Himself the church in all her glory, having no spot or wrinkle or any such thing; but that she should be holy and blameless" (Eph. 5:26f.). There is a purging that the Father performs (John 15:2), chiefly through divine chastening (1 Cor. 11:32: Heb. 12:10). There is a purging that the believer should perform (1 Cor. 11:28–31; 2 Cor. 7:1; 1 John 3:2), but there is also a purging that the local church is asked to perform (Matt. 18:17). The early church provides an example for the carrying out of church discipline, and the present church is not excused from this duty (Acts 5:11; Rom. 16:17; 1 Cor. 5:6–8, 13; 2 Cor. 2:6; 2 Thess. 3:6, 14: Titus 3:10f.; 2 John 10). Divisions, heresies, immoralities, and the like, are mentioned as causes for discipline. Discipline is part of the bride's making herself ready (Rev. 19:7).

D. To Educate its Constituency

As seen above, God's gift to the church of apostles, prophets, evangelists, pastors, and teachers, is for "the equipping of the saints for the work of service" (Eph. 4:12). Jesus gave the great commission, not only that men should be made disciples and be baptized, but also that thereafter they should be taught "to observe all" that he had commanded them (Matt. 28:20). There can, therefore, be no doubt as to whether the church should carry on a program of teaching and training for its own members, both young and old. The church must teach its membership in God's truth. It must devote itself to the apostles' doctrine. Paul directs the believers at Philippi to be interested in all types of worthy knowledge. He says, "Finally, brethren, whatever is true, whatever is honorable, whatever is right, whatever is pure, whatever is lovely, whatever is of good repute, if there is any excellence and if anything worthy of praise, let your mind dwell on these things" (Phil. 4:8; cf. 2 Tim. 2:2).

E. To Evangelize the World

The great commission directs the church to go into all the world and make disciples of all nations (Matt. 28:19; Luke 24:46–48; Acts 1:8). The Scriptures do not direct us to convert the world, but to evangelize it. By this is meant that the church is debtor to the whole world, that is, that the church is under obligation to give the whole world an opportunity to hear the gospel and to accept Christ. We know that not all the world will respond to the gospel call, but the church is by duty bound to give the whole world an opportunity to know about him and to accept his salvation. God is today calling out from among the Gentiles a people for his name (Acts 15:14), and he does it through the church and by his Spirit. This is to go on until "the fulness of the Gentiles has come in" (Rom. 11:25). No one knows when that will be, but that is the definite objective of Christ in which the church is to participate. Evangelization begins in a study of needs (John 4:28–38; cf. Matt. 9:36–38), and so every church should study missions. It finds expression in missionary intercession (Matt. 9:38), missionary contributions (Phil. 4:15–18), the sending of missionaries (Acts 13:1–3; 14:26; Rom. 10:15), and in going forth into the mission fields (Rom. 1:13–15; 15:20).

F. To Act as a Restraining and Enlightening Force in the World

Jesus said that believers are the salt of the earth and the light of the world (Matt. 5:13f.). By their influence and testimony, they hold back the development of lawlessness (cf. 2 Thess. 2:6f.). God holds back judgment because of the presence of the godly among the wicked (Gen. 18:22–33). Believers are to make known God's righteous requirements of man and the need for repentance and regeneration. To this end, God has made his people the custodians of his truth (2 Cor. 5:19; Gal. 2:7; 1 Tim. 1:11; 3:15). In the Scriptures, men are always to find the truth concerning God and spiritual things, should they desire to know these things. But more than that, the church is to hold forth the Word of life to the world (Phil. 2:16) and to contend for the truth (Jude 3). Few worldly communities realize the true worth of the people of God in their midst. But surely, not many of the ungodly would want to live in a world where there were no Christian influence.

G. To Promote All That is Good

While the believer is to separate from all worldly alliances (2 Cor. 6:14–18), he is yet to support all causes that seek to promote the social, economic, political, and educational welfare of the community. Paul said, "So then, while we have opportunity, let us do good to all men, and especially to those who are of the household of the faith" (Gal. 6:10). Here we note that we have a primary duty toward fellow-believers, but that we also have a duty toward the rest of the world. It is necessary to be clear as to the place of this ministry toward the world. Jesus' practice is the best example to follow. He always subordinated physical and other material help to the spiritual. He went about doing good and healing all that were oppressed of the devil, though he never lost sight of his principal mission (Acts 10:38–43). The work of reformation, including philanthropy, must be definitely subordinated to the work of evangelization. The Christian should make all his charity and kindnesses bear testimony to Christ. Jesus may have fed five thousand as a humanitarian act, but he certainly did it primarily as a testimony to his own power and deity. When Jesus turned the water to wine he showed kindness to the wedding party, but he also "manifested His glory" (John 2:11). It appears that he healed the man born blind in order to win his soul (John 9:35–38). In other words, the Christian should make all his good works testify to Christ.

II. THE DESTINY OF THE CHURCH

The details of that destiny will be discussed under the study of eschatology, but mention must here be made of the prospects for the church in a general way.

A. The Church Will Not Convert the World

According to the Scriptures, the church is not to win the whole world to Christ, nor to rise to a position of world influence in social, economic, and political life. Scripture predicts that lawlessness will increase and that "most people's love will grow cold" (Matt. 24:12). Paul writes, "But the Spirit explicitly says that in later times some will fall away from the faith, paying attention to deceitful spirits and doctrines of demons" (1 Tim. 4:1; cf. 2 Tim. 3:1–9). There will be no mass turning to the Lord, but life will continue much as usual. This is indicated by Christ's statement, "And just as it happened in the days of Noah, so it shall be also in the days of the Son of

Man: they were eating, they were drinking, they were marrying, they were being given in marriage, until the day that Noah entered the ark, and the flood came and destroyed them all" (Luke 17:26f.). That the world will not be converted is taught by the parable of the tares (Matt. 13:24–30, 36–43) and the parable of the dragnet (Matt. 13:47–50). Good and evil will continue to the end of the age.

B. THE CHURCH WILL OCCUPY A PLACE OF BLESSING AND HONOR

The Scriptures give us some definite teaching in support of this.

1. The church will be united to Christ.   The church is called the bride of Christ (2 Cor. 11:2; Eph. 5:27), and in the Revelation her union with Christ at the marriage of the Lamb is foretold (19:7). This can only mean that she will be brought into the most intimate relation with him. The ideas of fellowship and of co-ownership are involved in the conception (Rom. 8:16f.).

2. The church will reign with Christ.   As his bride, she will be at his side and share in his authority in his worldwide kingdom on earth (1 Cor. 6:2; Rev. 1:6; 2:26f.; 3:21; 20:4, 6; 22:5). She will even have a part in the judging of angels (1 Cor. 6:3). Having suffered with Christ in the day of his rejection, the church will reign with him in the day of his glorification (2 Tim. 2:11–13). Those who suffer with him will be glorified with him (Rom. 8:17). The duration of the reign is first specified as one thousand years (Rev. 20:4–6), but later on it is said that his servants shall reign forever and ever (Rev. 22:5). That is, they shall reign with him the thousand years, or the millennium, and this is but the beginning of a reign that shall last through eternity.

3. The church will be an eternal testimony.   She will witness throughout eternity to God's wisdom and goodness (Eph. 3:10, 21). Her very presence with Christ will speak of his grace and power in saving and keeping her in the midst of an evil generation. Thus, Christ will be eternally glorified in the church.

PART VIII
ESCHATOLOGY

Every system of theology has its eschatology. If there is a beginning, there is also an end, not in the absolute sense in which the universe was non-existent before creation, but in the sense of an exchange of that which is temporal for that which is external. Under this head, we shall consider the biblical doctrines of the last things. These are the doctrines of the second coming of Christ, of the resurrections, of the judgments, of the millennium, and of the final state.

CHAPTER XXXIX

Personal Eschatology and the Importance of the Second Coming of Christ

Eschatology can be divided into two broad areas: personal and general eschatology. General eschatology covers the sweep of future events from the return of Jesus Christ on to the creation of the new heavens and new earth. Personal eschatology relates to the individual from the time of physical death until he receives his resurrection body. In this study we will consider personal eschatology only briefly, and give more extensive treatment to general eschatology. The focus of this chapter will be personal eschatology and the importance of the second coming of Christ.

I. PERSONAL ESCHATOLOGY

This can be considered under two headings: physical death and the intermediate state.

A. Physical Death

Physical death is not to be confused with spiritual or eternal death. Spiritual death is that spiritual state in which one finds oneself before salvation. It is spoken of as being "dead" in trespasses and sins (Eph. 2:1, 5). Jesus said, "Truly, truly, I say to you, an hour is coming and now is, when the dead shall hear the voice of the Son of God; and those who hear shall live" (John 5:25). Thus, a person is considered spiritually dead before he comes alive in Christ at salvation. Eternal death is that eternal judgment which comes at death upon those who have never been made spiritually alive. It is the eternal judgment of God which comes upon those who have never, in their lifetime, "passed out of death into life" (John 5:24; cf. Rev. 20:10). This is called "the second death, the lake of fire" (Rev. 20:14).

Spiritual death and eternal death relate to the soul; physical death has to do with tbe body. Physical death is the separation of the soul from the body; it is the termination of physical life. It is described in several ways in Scripture: the separation of body and soul (Eccl. 12:7; Acts 7:59; James 2:26), the loss of the soul or life (Matt. 2:20; Mark 3:4; John 13:37), and departure (Luke 9:31; 2 Pet. 1:15). It should not, however, be thought of as annihilation, cessation of being, or non-existence; rather, it is a change in relationships. There is a severance of the natural relationship between soul and body. The body decays in the grave and returns to dust (Gen. 3:19), and the soul continues on.

Physical death bears a relationship to sin because Adam was not subject to physical death until after the fall. Physical death is a result of man's spiritual death (Rom. 5:21; 6:23; 1 Cor. 15:56). Physical death is not something natural in the existence of man. It is a judgment (Rom. 1:32; 5:16) and a curse. Christ has delivered the believer from the power of death. Scripture records that Christ partook of flesh and blood "that through death He might render powerless him who has the power of death, that is, the devil; and might deliver those who through fear of death were subject to slavery all their lives" (Heb. 2:14f.).

Though death is a common enemy, through Christ the believer needs no longer to fear it. Death for the believer is entrance into the presence of Christ. He is absent from the body and present with the Lord (2 Cor. 5:8). Death to the believer is "to depart and be with Christ" (Phil. 1:23). The sting of death has been removed (1 Cor. 15:55–57) and the Christian falls asleep in Jesus (1 Thess. 4:14). In stark contrast to the believer, the unbeliever has no such comforting hope. He faces condemnation and eternal judgment away from the presence of the Lord (John 3:36; 2 Thess. 1:9; Rev. 20:10).

B. The Intermediate State

Physical death relates to the physical body; the soul is immortal and as such does not die. While Scripture declares that God alone has immortality (1 Tim. 6:16; cf. 1:17), man is immortal in the sense that his soul never dies. That the soul is immortal, even after physical death, is confirmed by Scripture. In answer to the Sadducees' question concerning the resurrection, Jesus responded by quoting what God had said to Moses in Exod. 3:6, "I am the God of Abraham, and the God of Isaac, and the God of Jacob" (Matt. 22:32). He further commented, "God is not the God of the dead but of the living" (v. 32), the point being that if God was the God of Abraham in Moses' day, then Moses was yet alive. The story of Lazarus and the rich man also indicates the immortality of the soul (Luke 16:19–31), as does the mention of souls under the altar (Rev. 6:9f.).

But what happens to the soul after death, but before the resurrection? We look first at the scriptural evidence, then at four unscriptural positions.

1. The scriptural evidence.   Though the Bible does not give a great deal of information, it does give sufficient material to draw certain conclusions. In the first place, the believer is with Christ. Paul said that he would "prefer rather to be absent from the body and to be at home with the Lord" (2 Cor.

5:8; cf. v. 6). Further, Paul had the "desire to depart and be with Christ" (Phil. 1:23). This was the encouragement which Jesus gave to the penitent man on the cross next to him, "Truly I say to you, today you shall be with Me in Paradise" (Luke 23:43). That paradise was heaven is clear from 2 Cor. 12:3f. Not only is the believer with the Lord and in heaven, but he is in fellowship with other believers. Hebrews speaks of the "general assembly and church of the first-born who are enrolled in heaven" (12:23). Believers are alive, conscious, and happy (Luke 16:19–31; Rev. 14:13). This state between death and the resurrection is a condition to be preferred above the present state. Paul calls it "very much better" (Phil. 1:23). He asserted that he would "prefer rather to be absent from the body and to be at home with the Lord" (2 Cor. 5:8). A careful study of 2 Cor. 5:1–9 suggests that the believer prefers to be raptured and translated rather than to die and enter into the intermediate state. He would rather be clothed with the resurrection body than to be unclothed. But the unclothed state is to be preferred over the present physical state, for even if unclothed, the believer is present with the Lord.

In the story of Lazarus and the rich man, Lazarus was in Abraham's bosom, comforted; the rich man was in agony (Luke 16:19–31). From this we gather that the unsaved individual is also in a temporary state undergoing conscious torment, while awaiting the great white throne judgment (Rev. 20:11–15).

2. Purgatory. In Roman Catholic theology, souls which are completely pure at death are allowed to enter heaven, to enter into the presence of God, the beatific vision. Those souls which are not perfectly pure and are in need of cleansing go to a place for purging. This place, called "purgatory," is for the purging away of the guilt of venial sins. It is not a place of probation, but a place of purging or cleansing. Believers there suffer in that they are for a time losing out on the joys of heaven and their souls are being afflicted. Several Scriptures are used in support of this doctrine (Zech. 9:11; Matt. 12:32; 1 Cor. 3:13–15). Against this position are the facts that there is no solid scriptural support for it and that Christ fully paid our penalty. We cannot add anything to the merits of Christ (Heb. 1:3). Granted, there are temporal punishments for sin in this life, but Scripture nowhere teaches explicitly or implicitly that these sufferings continue after death. The primary support for purgatory is found in the noncanonical book of 2 Maccabees (12:42–45).

3. Soul-sleep. Those who hold this view maintain that after death the soul lapses into a state of sleep or unconscious repose. This is argued in several ways. Scripture often represents death as sleep (Matt. 9:24; John 11:11; 1 Thess. 4:13). Further, some references seem to teach that the dead are unconscious (Ps. 146:4; Eccl. 9:5f., 10; Isa. 38:18). And finally, no one who has returned from the dead has reported concerning this temporary state. But in answer to these objections, first, sleep is used of a believer. It is a euphemistic expression taken from the similarity in appearance between a dead body and a sleeping person (cf. James 2:26). Further, the scriptural evidence is that believers who die enjoy a conscious communion with Christ. The verses which suggest the unconscious condition of the soul are viewed from the perspective of the living. From the vantage point of the living, the dead have gone to sleep.

4. Annihilationism. This teaching relates primarily to the unsaved. According to this doctrine, there is no conscious existence at all for the wicked after death. Most who hold this position teach that at death the unsaved individual simply ceases to exist. Biblical terms such as death, destruction, and perish are interpreted to mean "deprived of existence" or "reduced to non-existence" (John 3:16; 8:51; Rom. 9:22). But, in answer to this view, we say that God does not annihilate what he has created. Life is the opposite of death; if death is merely cessation of being, then life is just prolonged existence. But eternal life is a quality of life, not merely quantity. Further, death and destruction is punishment; it is hard to see how annihilation could be termed punishment. Scripture is clear that the unsaved will continue to exist forever (Eccl. 12:7; Matt. 25:46; Rom. 2:5–10; Rev. 14:11). Again, there are degrees of punishment, and annihilationism does not allow for this (Luke 12:47f.; Rom. 2:12; Rev. 20:12).

5. Conditional immortality. According to this doctrine, the soul is not created or born with immortality, but receives it upon confession of faith in Christ. It comes as a gift of God. The one who dies without Christ simply ceases to exist because he has not received the gift of immortality. Those who hold this position argue that God alone has immortality (1 Tim. 6:16), and he gives it to those who respond to his call. They further teach that Scripture nowhere speaks of the immortality of the soul. But we answer that this doctrine confuses immortality with eternal life. The eternal life received at salvation is more than eternal existence; it is rather a quality of life, a richness of life in the presence of Christ. It is true that God alone has inherent immortality; nevertheless, man did receive derived immortality at creation. He is born as an immortal being.

We conclude that at death the believer enters into the presence of Christ. He remains with the Lord in a state of conscious blessedness until the time of the resurrection, at which time he will receive his body of glory. The unbeliever enters into a state of conscious torment until the resurrection, at which time he will be cast into the lake of fire. The doctrines of purgatory, soul-sleep, annihilationism, and conditional immortality cannot be considered biblical doctrines.

II. THE IMPORTANCE OF THE SECOND COMING OF CHRIST

The early church was keenly interested in the doctrine of the return of Christ. The apostles had held out the possibility of his returning in their day, and the next generations kept alive the blessed hope as something that was imminent. Not until the third century was there any great exception to this rule, but from the time of Constantine onward, this truth began to be rejected until it was almost entirely set aside. It is only during the last 100 years or so that this doctrine has been revived in the church. Though there is still indifference and opposition to it, there is a growing and healthy interest in this biblical truth. While devout Christians say, "Amen. Come, Lord Jesus" (Rev. 22:20), unbelievers and scoffers continue to say, "Where is the promise of His coming? For ever since the fathers fell asleep, all continues just as it was from the beginning of creation" (2 Pet. 3:4). The unbelief of the scoffer does not reduce the importance of this doctrine; rather, many things indicate its importance.

A. Its Prominence in the Scriptures

Throughout the Scriptures there is a prominent place given to the second coming of Christ. Though the first and second advents are often so closely merged in the Old Testament prophecies as to make it difficult to bring forward a specific promise that deals with the second coming alone, there are some references that clearly do so (Job 19:25f.; Dan. 7:13f.; Zech. 14:4; Mal. 3:1f.). The New Testament mentions this doctrine more than three hundred times. Whole chapters are devoted to the subject (Matt. 24, 25; Mark 13; Luke 21; cf. 1 Cor. 15). Some books are practically given over to this subject (1 Thess.; 2 Thess.; Rev.). It ranks with other major doctrines in emphasis.

B. It is a Key to the Scriptures

We speak of prayer and a teachable spirit as keys to the understanding of the Word of God, but in addition to these, the recognition of the fundamental character of the doctrine of the Lord's return is a key to the Scriptures. Many biblical doctrines, ordinances, promises, and types cannot be fully understood except in the light of the doctrine of the Lord's return. Take the case of biblical doctrine. Christ is prophet, priest, and king, but no one can properly understand his kingly office apart from the recognition of the truth of his second coming. Salvation is represented as past, present, and future, but no adequate view of the future aspect can be held apart from a belief in the Lord's return. John's teaching concerning two resurrections (Rev. 20:4–15) presents a conundrum apart from this doctrine. The Davidic covenant (2 Sam. 7:12–16; Ps. 89:3f.) remains inexplicable to one who rejects the truth of Christ's return. The prophecy concerning the restoration of nature and the animal world (Isa. 11:6–9; 65:25; Rom. 8:20–22) becomes absurd if interpreted apart from a reference to the second advent. The prediction of the bruising of Satan's head (Gen. 3:15) loses its real point if it is not associated with the return of Christ.

Many types of Scripture lose their most attractive features if they are not viewed in the light of Christ's return. Enoch's ministry and translation is one of these (Gen. 5:22–24; Heb. 11:5; Jude 14). The story of Noah drops down to the level of mere historical fact if it has no typical meaning, as does the high priest's blessing of the people on the day of atonement (Heb. 9:28).

The same thing is true of many of the promises of Scripture. The Lord's coming is a key to many of the Psalms (Ps. 2; 22; 45; 72; 89; 110). Peter declares that all the holy prophets speak of the times of restoration and the coming of Christ (Acts 3:19–24). Besides this, there are many definite promises of his return in the New Testament (Matt. 16:27; John 14:3; 1 Thess. 4:13–18; Heb. 10:37; James 5:8; Rev. 1:7; 22:12, 20). In these, the Christian is challenged to be ready for his return, comforted by the fact of his return, admonished to console the bereaved by the truth of his return, asked to bear oppression in the light of his return, exhorted to retain confidence because shortly he will return, and assured that his return will bring blessings and rewards to all who look for him. Surely, some of the most precious incentives to godliness are lost by rejecting the truth of the Lord's return.

The same thing is true of the ordinances; they lose their full meaning for the one who rejects the truth of the Lord's return. Baptism implies resurrection with Christ to newness of life, and this new life in Christ Jesus will be made manifest when he who is our life shall appear in glory (Col. 3:1–4). So also the Lord's Supper has a bearing upon the second advent. Paul says, "For as often as you eat this bread and drink this cup, you proclaim the Lord's death until He comes" (1 Cor. 11:26). And Jesus said, "But I say to you, I will not drink of this fruit of the vine from now on until that day when I drink it new with you in My Father's kingdom" (Matt. 26:29).

C. It is the Hope of the Church

The Lord's coming is set before us as the great hope of the church. Neither death nor the conversion of the world is the hope of the believer, but according to the Scriptures, the Lord's return is. Paul said, "I am on trial for the hope and resurrection of the dead!" (Acts 23:6; cf. 26:6–8; Rom. 8:23–25; 1 Cor. 15:19; Gal. 5:5) and "Looking for the blessed hope and the appearing of the glory of our great God and Savior, Christ Jesus" (Titus 2:13). Peter wrote, "Blessed be the God and Father of our Lord Jesus Christ, who according to His great mercy has caused us to be born again to a living hope through the resurrection of Jesus Christ from the dead" (1 Pet. 1:3; cf. 2 Pet. 3:9–13). And John said, "Beloved, now we are the children of God, and it has not appeared as yet what we shall be. We know that, when He appears, we shall be like Him, because we shall see Him just as He is. And every one who has this hope fixed on Him purifies himself, just as He is pure" (1 John 3:2f.).

D. It is the Incentive to Biblical Christianity

The coming of Christ is the great incentive to biblical Christianity. A sincere belief in this doctrine has had much to do with orthodoxy, for those who have entertained this hope most heartily and intelligently have never denied the deity of Christ, nor questioned the authority of the Bible, nor declined from the faith that was once delivered to the saints. But this is not all. The acceptance of this truth also induces self-purification (Matt. 25:6f.; 2 Pet. 3:11; 1 John 3:3); it inspires watchfulness and perseverance (Matt. 24:44; Mark 13:35f.; 1 Thess. 5:6; 1 John 2:28); it challenges the backslider to return (Rom. 13:11f.); it constitutes a warning to the ungodly (2 Thess. 1:7–10); and it is a stay in adversity and bereavement (1 Thess. 4:13–18; 5:11; 2 Tim. 2:12; Heb. 10:35–39; James 5:7). It is clear that the blessed hope was the incentive to apostolic Christianity. The men who had heard Jesus say that he would come again, could not be again seduced by the allurements of this world. They longed for his coming, lived for it, sought to lead others to him and to the hope of his return.

E. It Has a Marked Effect on Christian Service

The Scriptures furnish in the promises and prospects of his return the greatest stimulus to service (Matt. 24:45–51; Luke 19:13; 1 Cor. 3:11–15; 2 Cor. 5:10f.). In them is disclosed to us the divine purpose and program of service (Acts 1:8; 15:13–18; Rom. 11:22–32). And then, this truth itself constitutes the basis of the most effective appeals for the acceptance of Christ and for the consecration of life to God. Paul certainly so used it (Rom. 13:11f.; 2 Thess. 1:7–10). Thus, we conclude that the second coming of Christ is a most important doctrine.

CHAPTER XL

The Second Coming of Christ:
The Nature of His Coming
and the Purpose of His Coming in the Air

There are several questions which come to mind in connection with the doctrine of the return of Christ. First, what is the nature of his coming? Then we ask, are there phases to his coming? And, if so, what are they? Having determined that there will be several phases of the return of Christ, other questions arise which relate to his coming in the air, the judgment of the nations, the coming of Christ to rule, the resurrections, and many other such questions. In this chapter we will look first at the nature of his coming, then continue with a study of the purpose of his coming in the air.

I. THE NATURE OF CHRIST'S COMING

All who believe that the Bible is the Word of God believe also in the second coming of Christ, but there is a vast difference of opinion as to what is meant by the Lord's return. It is necessary, therefore, to examine this question in the light of the Scriptures.

A. THE SCRIPTURAL TEACHING

There is much teaching concerning the return of Christ in the Bible. Jesus declared that he would return personally (John 14:3; 21:22f.), unexpectedly (Matt. 24:32–51; 25:1–13; Mark 13:33–37), suddenly (Matt. 24:26–28), in the glory of his Father with his angels (Matt. 16:27; 19:28; 25:31), and triumphantly (Luke 19:11–27). The men in white clothing testified at Christ's ascension that he would come personally, bodily, visibly, and suddenly (Acts 1:10f.). The testimony of the apostles is very extensive. Peter testifies that he will come personally (Acts 3:19–21; 2 Pet. 3:3f.) and unexpectedly (2 Pet. 3:8–13). Paul testifies that he will come personally (Phil. 3:20f.; 1 Thess. 4:16f.), suddenly (1 Cor. 15:51f.), in glory and accompanied by the angels (2 Thess. 1:7–10; Titus 2:13). Hebrews testifies that he will come personally (9:28) and speedily (10:37). James states that he will come personally (5:7f.). John writes that he will come personally (1 John 2:28; 3:2f.) and suddenly (Rev. 22:12). And Jude cites Enoch to show that he will come publicly (vss. 14f.). The biblical evidence is clear and sufficient.

B. Some Erroneous Interpretations

Despite the unambiguous and ample evidence, there are many erroneous interpretations of it. It is necessary, therefore, to refute such teachings before proceeding further with the study of this doctrine. Five of these will be dealt with briefly.

1. The coming of the Holy Spirit.   It is taught by some that the return of Christ is the coming of the Holy Spirit on the day of Pentecost. Some have referred Matt. 16:28, "Truly I say to you, there are some of those who are standing here who shall not taste death until they see the Son of Man coming in His kingdom," to Pentecost. Likewise, some interpret John 16:16, "A little while, and you will no longer behold Me; and again a little while, and you will see Me," to have been fulfilled when the Spirit came. The promise in Matthew more naturally means Christ's reappearance after his resurrection. Jesus promised that he would send the Comforter, but he does not send himself (John 14:16; 15:26). Indeed, he declared that the Spirit's descent was conditioned on his withdrawal (John 16:7). In Acts 2:33 Jesus is represented as pouring out the Spirit from the right hand of God. This was on the day of Pentecost. In Acts 3:19–21, after the day of Pentecost, Peter called on Israel to repent in order that God might send Christ, "whom heaven must receive until the period of restoration of all things." Many other promises of Christ's return were uttered after the day of Pentecost; therefore, these two things are not interchangeable.

2. The conversion of the soul.   This is held by some, but it is also unscriptural. Jesus spoke of both the Father and the Son coming to dwell in the believer (John 14:23), and immediately afterward he promised that the Comforter would come and teach them all things (John 14:26). The Holy Spirit is the Spirit of Jesus (Acts 16:7) and the Spirit of Christ (Rom. 8:9; 1 Pet. 1:11), but Christ and the Holy Spirit are never confused. Paul makes a statement which is easily misunderstood, "The Lord is the Spirit" (2 Cor. 3:17). We acknowledge there is an identity of essence and power, just as Christ said of his relationship with the Father, "I and the Father are one" (John 10:30). This, however, does not mean one and the same person, but one and the same being. Additionally, Christ and the Spirit are virtually the same in that Christ communicates himself at conversion and at other times by means of the Spirit. The Holy Spirit is his Spirit. The animating dynamic of the Lord's indwelling and influence in the believer is the Spirit of God (Rom. 8:9f.; Gal. 2:20; 4:6; Phil. 1:19; cf. Acts 20:28 with Eph. 4:7, 11). It is interesting that Paul uses the phrases "the Spirit," "the Spirit of God," "the Spirit of Christ," "Christ," "the Spirit of Him who raised Jesus from the dead," and "His Spirit" interchangeably in Rom. 8:9–11.

Certainly all the authors of the Epistles were converted when they wrote; yet they spoke of the Lord's coming as still future. Therefore, the coming of Christ into the life of a repentant sinner is not his coming in the eschatological sense of that term.

3. The destruction of Jerusalem. There are some who believe that the coming of Christ is the destruction of Jerusalem in A.D. 70. Matt. 16:28 is interpreted in that manner. We may admit that the prophecy concerning the destruction of this city is intimately connected with the predictions concerning our Lord's return in Matt. 24, Mark 13, and Luke 21, and that this event may be called a coming of the Lord in judgment, but at the same time we are forced to recognize the predictions of a future personal return of the Savior. The book of Revelation and 1 John were both written a number of years after the destruction of Jerusalem; yet each of them has a number of definite predictions of the Lord's second coming (1 John 2:28; 3:2f.; Rev. 1:7; 3:11; 22:12, 20). We may add that at the destruction of Jerusalem Israel was scattered, but at the return of Christ Israel will be gathered to Palestine.

4. The coming of death. Some have taken Matt. 24:42, "Therefore be on the alert, for you do not know which day your Lord is coming," to refer both to death and to the return of Christ. Granted that when the believer dies, the Lord takes his soul to himself, this is not to be confused with the return of Christ. We must not apply Scriptures that speak of Christ's return to death. In reality the two are very different. Death is in the Bible treated as an enemy (1 Cor. 15:25f.: Heb. 2:14f.), but the Lord's return is represented as a blessed hope (Titus 2:13). At death the grave is occupied; at the Lord's return the grave is abandoned (John 5:28f.; 1 Thess. 4:16). The disciples understood the Lord's reference to his coming to imply exemption from death for John (John 21:21–23). If death and the second coming are the same, then we may substitute the word "death" for the second "coming." Anyone who will make this experiment with such Scriptures as Matt. 16:27f., 1 Thess. 4:16f., and Rev. 1:7, will recognize the absurdity of this interpretation.

5. The conversion of the world. Some think the reference is to world conversion when they pray, "Thy kingdom come" (Matt. 6:10). They hold that as the world accepts the principles of Christ, Christ comes. But the Scriptures teach that there will be a great falling away from the faith in the last days (Luke 18:8; 2 Thess. 2:3–12; 1 Tim. 4:1); that difficult times will exist (2 Tim. 3:1); that sound doctrine will not be tolerated and damnable heresies will be introduced (2 Tim. 4:1–4; 2 Pet. 2:1f.); and that the conditions of the days of Noah and of Lot will again prevail (Luke 17:26–30). This does not look like a converted world at the time of Christ's return. Besides, the Scriptures represent Christ's coming as something sudden, as the lightning (Matt. 24:27), and unexpected, as a thief (Matt. 24:43; 1 Thess. 5:2), and the resurrection as "in the twinkling of an eye" (1 Cor. 15:52). This too does not fit in with the idea of a gradual conversion of the world. And further, the Bible associates the conversion of the world with Christ's return, but it represents it as taking place after the event (Isa. 2:2–4; Zech. 8:21–23; Acts 15:16–18; Rom. 11:12, 25). This point will be considered further in another connection, but it is clear that the coming of Christ is not the conversion of the world.

C. THE PHASES OF CHRIST'S COMING

Anyone who comes to the truth of the Lord's second coming for the first time is perplexed by the seemingly contradictory descriptions of it. He reads that Christ will come for his own and that he will come visibly to the whole world, that he will judge men in general and that he will come to judge the works of believers. He reads about an out-resurrection of saved ones, a marriage supper, a conflict with the Antichrist and his forces, a binding of Satan, a setting up of an earthly kingdom, and judgment before the great white throne. How shall he reconcile all these statements; what is the order of the events in this composite picture? Many despair of finding any definite program through this prophetic labyrinth, and many even denounce all who think that they can come to anything that is at all final. We believe that the key to this question is that there are two phases to his coming. Thus, we find that he will come into the air and that some things will take place in the air, and we find that he will come to the earth and that some things will take place on the earth. These two comings must be distinguished.

1. His coming in the air.   Paul writes, "For the Lord Himself will descend from heaven with a shout, with the voice of the archangel, and with the trumpet of God; and the dead in Christ shall rise first. Then we who are alive and remain shall be caught up together with them in the clouds to meet the Lord in the air" (1 Thess. 4:16f.). 2 Thess. 2:1 speaks of our gathering together with him. This same idea is expressed in John 14:3, "And if I go and prepare a place for you, I will come again, and receive you to Myself; that where I am, there you may be also." In this coming Christ does not come all the way to the earth, but he gathers his own in the air. The dead in Christ are raised, and those living are changed (1 Cor. 15:51–54). This coming is to be distinguished from his coming to earth.

2. His coming to earth.   In Zech. 14:4 we are told that "His feet will stand on the Mount of Olives, which is in front of Jerusalem on the east." In Acts 1:11 the men in white clothing assert that Jesus will return in "just the same way" as they had "watched Him go into heaven." He left Mt. Olivet visibly, and he will return visibly to Mt. Olivet. Matt. 19:28 speaks of his sitting upon his glorious throne and his twelve disciples sitting upon twelve thrones judging the twelve tribes of Israel. Matt. 24:29–31 and 25:31–46 imply his coming down to earth. Zech. 12:10–14 represents the house of David, the inhabitants of Jerusalem, and all the families of Israel that remain, as mourning when they see him whom they had pierced. And Rev. 1:7 says, "Behold, He is coming with the clouds, and every eye will see Him, even those who pierced Him; and all the tribes of the earth will mourn over Him." When he comes back to earth he will come with his own (Joel 3:11; 1 Thess. 3:13; Jude 14). This in itself presupposes two aspects to his coming: one in which his own are caught up to him and another in which his own return with him.

II. THE PURPOSE OF HIS COMING INTO THE AIR

We now come to a study of the first phase of his coming. We ask, what is the purpose of his coming in the air? Several answers can be given.

A. To Receive His Own

Jesus will come to receive his own to himself. Jesus said, "I will come again, and receive you to Myself; that where I am, there you may be also" (John 14:3). Jesus longs for the closest fellowship, but "while we are at home in the body we are absent from the Lord" (2 Cor. 5:6). When the believer falls asleep in Jesus, he is "absent from the body," but at "home with the Lord" (2 Cor. 5:8). But this too is not the ideal condition, for it is apart from the body. When Jesus returns, he will receive the believer to himself in bodily form. From this time forth the believer "shall always be with the Lord" (1 Thess. 4:17). But since "flesh and blood cannot inherit the kingdom of God" (1 Cor. 15:50), it is evident that certain changes must take place before he can receive us unto himself. These must be considered next.

1. The prerequisites. "His own" are now either in his presence in spirit (2 Cor. 5:8; Phil. 1:23; Heb. 12:23; Rev. 6:9) and conscious (Luke 16:19–31; Rev. 6:9), and their bodies are in the grave, or they are yet "at home in the body," while "absent from the Lord" (2 Cor. 5:6). But to be with Christ in spirit is not the ultimate goal of redemption; Christ has redeemed the body as well as the soul (Rom. 8:23; Eph. 1:14; 4:30), and he will some day change the body "of our humble state into conformity with the body of His glory" (Phil. 3:21). Two things are necessary before he can receive us to himself. First, the dead in Christ must be raised; then, second, the living believers must be changed. Let us look at these two in more detail.

(1) The dead must be raised. When the Lord shall descend from heaven, the dead in Christ shall be raised (1 Thess. 4:16). Because Jesus is "the resurrection and the life" (John 11:25), he who believes on him "shall live even if he dies" (v. 25). Whoever believes on him shall never die. Paul writes, "This perishable must put on the imperishable, and this mortal must put on immortality" (1 Cor. 15:53). These Scriptures indicate what will take place in the believers at his coming; the dead will be made alive and the living will have their lives made immortal.

There is no general resurrection at which all the dead will arise at the same time. Though John 5:28f. may at first glance seem to imply one general resurrection, it does not say that some will come forth to life and others to judgment, but that some will come forth to a resurrection of life and others to a resurrection of judgment. That both are said to occur in an hour presents no difficulty. John's last hour (1 John 2:18) has already lasted for about nineteen hundred years. It is easy to think of two resurrections taking place in one hour. Dan. 12:2 also seems to refer to two bodily resurrections. "There is to be a resurrection unto life and a resurrection unto death."[1]

According to Rev. 20:4-7, there is a space of one thousand years between the first and the second resurrection. Some have suggested that the first resurrection of Rev. 20 is spiritual salvation (cf. John 5:24-26), which is followed by the general resurrection. If one has attained to the first resurrection (or spiritual resurrection), he need not fear the second death. However, language will not allow for that interpretation. Note the words of Alford, the noted Greek scholar:

> If, in a passage where *two resurrections* are mentioned, where certain *psuchai exesan* at the first, and the rest of the *nekros exesan* only at the end of a specified period after that,—if in such a passage the first resurrection may be understood to mean *spiritual* rising with Christ, while the second means *literal* rising from the grave;—then there is an end of all significance in language, and Scripture is wiped out as a definite testimony to any thing. If the first resurrection is spiritual, then so is the second, which I suppose none will be hardy enough to maintain: but if the second is literal, then so is the first, which in common with the whole primitive Church and many of the best modern expositors, I do maintain, and receive as an article of faith and hope.[2]

We may add that it is this resurrection (*ten exanastasin ten ek nekron*) to which Paul sought to attain (Phil. 3:11); there was no need of striving to

---

[1]Young, *The Prophecy of Daniel*, p. 256.
[2]Alford, *The Greek Testament*, IV, pp. 732-733.

attain to the general resurrection, since Scripture abundantly shows that all men will ultimately be raised, whether they desire to be or not.

But even in the first resurrection there are phases. Our Lord's resurrection (1 Cor. 15:23), the rapture of the church when Christ comes for his own (John 14:3; 1 Cor. 15:51-54; 1 Thess. 4:14-17; 2 Thess. 2:1), the resurrection of the two witnesses in the tribulation (Rev. 11:11f.), and the resurrection of Old Testament saints and tribulation believers (Dan. 12:2; Rev. 20:4f.) are all different phases of the first resurrection. Even the resurrection of certain saints at the resurrection of Christ might be considered part of this larger group (Matt. 27:52f.).

(2) The ones living and believing in Christ must be changed. After stating that the dead in Christ will rise first when the Lord descends in the air, Paul adds, "Then we who are alive and remain shall be caught up together with them in clouds to meet the Lord in the air" (1 Thess. 4:17). But inasmuch as "flesh and blood cannot inherit the kingdom of God" (1 Cor. 15:50), the bodies of the living will be changed. Paul explains, "Behold, I tell you a mystery; we shall not all sleep, but we shall all be changed, in a moment, in the twinkling of an eye, at the last trumpet; for the trumpet will sound, and the dead will be raised imperishable, and we shall be changed" (1 Cor. 15:51f.). Perhaps Paul has the living in mind in Phil. 3:20f., when he writes, "For our citizenship is in heaven, from which also we eagerly wait for a Savior, the Lord Jesus Christ; who will transform the body of our humble state into conformity with the body of His glory." The exact nature of the change spoken of is nowhere revealed, but the possibility of being caught up without dying is illustrated in the translation of Enoch (Gen. 5:24; Heb. 11:5) and of Elijah (2 Kings 2:11-18).

The question immediately arises, will all the saved be taken at the rapture? To this we may reply that the nature of the church would seem to require that everyone who belongs to it should be taken. The church is a temple (1 Cor. 3:16f.; 2 Cor. 6:16; Eph. 2:20f.; 1 Pet. 2:5). Will any part of the building in which the Spirit dwells be left behind? Further, the church is Christ's bride (2 Cor. 11:2; Eph. 5:24, 32; Rev. 19:6-9). Will any part of his bride be left behind? It is also Christ's body (1 Cor. 12:12-27; Eph. 1:22f.; 4:12; 5:29f.; Col. 1:18, 24; 2:19). Surely, he will not leave a part of his body behind. That all the living believers will be taken at the rapture is no more improbable than that all those who have fallen asleep in Christ will be raised at that time. Some would maintain on the basis of Phil. 3:11, "In order that I may attain to the resurrection from the dead," that Paul taught a partial resurrection; however, this is not an expression of doubt, but of humility and hope. In enumerating the order of the resurrection, Paul says, "Christ the first fruits, after that those who are Christ's at His coming, then comes the end, when He delivers up the kingdom to the God and Father"

(1 Cor. 15:23f.). Note that "those who are Christ's" are all grouped together as being raised at the same time; there is no division among them.

2. *The manner.*   A careful reading of the Scriptures discloses that the transference of the believers into Christ's presence is not the whole of the receiving of his own to himself. It is that, but it is ultimately the receiving of the church into the marriage relationship. The church is the bride. She is now in the position of betrothal or espousal (2 Cor. 11:2); ultimately, Christ will "present to Himself the church in all her glory, having no spot or wrinkle or any such thing" (Eph. 5:27). John writes, "And I heard, as it were, the voice of a great multitude and as the sound of many waters and as the sound of mighty peals of thunder, saying, 'Hallelujah! For the Lord our God, the Almighty, reigns. Let us rejoice and be glad and give the glory to Him, for the marriage of the Lamb has come and His bride has made herself ready.' And it was given to her to clothe herself in fine linen, bright and clean; for the fine linen is the righteous acts of the saints" (Rev. 19:6–8). Jesus Christ will come as the bridegroom to take the church to be his bride. John the Baptist was the friend of the bridegroom (John 3:29) and as such prepared the way for the coming of Christ.

B. To Judge and Reward

Both of these are associated with the return of Christ.

1. *The believer's judgment.*   Christ will come to judge the works of believers and to bestow the rewards. The believer will not be judged with regard to his sins (John 5:24), since he was judged for them in the person and cross of Christ (Isa. 53:5f.; 2 Cor. 5:21), and he will not again be called to account for them at the return of Christ. During this life, however, he is chastened for the sins he commits that he may not be condemned with the world (1 Cor. 5:5; 11:32; Heb. 12:7; cf. 2 Sam. 7:14f.; 12:13f.). But when Christ returns, the believer will be judged as to the use he has made of the talents (Matt. 25:14–30), the pounds (Luke 19:11–27), and the opportunities (Matt. 20:1–16) that have been entrusted to him. Salvation is a free gift of God (John 4:10; 10:28; Rom. 6:23). When James says that we are saved by works (James 2:24), he means by a faith that produces works (2:22, 26). Paul indicates that while we are saved by grace, we are yet saved unto good works (Eph. 2:8–10). In other words, the Lord has given his people an opportunity to lay up treasures in heaven, now that they are saved (Matt. 6:20), so that "the entrance into the eternal kingdom of our Lord and Savior Jesus Christ will be abundantly supplied" (2 Pet. 1:11).

It is with regard to these works that the believer will be judged when

Christ returns. Paul writes, "For we must all appear before the judgment seat of Christ, that each one may be recompensed for his deeds in the body, according to what he has done, whether good or bad" (2 Cor. 5:10). He also writes, "But you, why do you judge your brother? Or you again, why do you regard your brother with contempt? For we shall all stand before the judgment seat of God" (Rom. 14:10). And he continues, "So then each one of us shall give account of himself to God" (v. 12). When he comes, the fire will test our works; and if they are of wood, hay, or straw, they will be consumed, yet we will be saved so as by fire; if of gold, silver, or precious stone, we will receive a reward (1 Cor. 3:11–15). No doubt many will belong to the group that will be saved, but have little reward; others will have much. We are challenged to abide in Christ so that when he appears we will not be ashamed at his coming (1 John 2:28). Paul writes, "For who is our hope or joy or crown of exultation? Is it not even you, in the presence of our Lord Jesus at His coming?" (1 Thess. 2:19).

2. The believer's reward.   The Lord will keep his word as definitely as in the manner of salvation. Several items must be noted as they relate to the reward.

(1) First, what is the basis of the reward? Various things in the Scriptures are said to lead to a reward. As a steward of the mysteries of God (1 Cor. 4:1–5), the believer is to render an account of his stewardship. A definite reward is promised for those who are faithful (1 Cor. 4:2) in the use of the opportunities, the talents, and the pounds entrusted to them (Matt. 20:1–16; 25:14–30; Luke 19:11–27). As trustees of their material possessions, they will be rewarded according to the way in which they have used their possessions (Matt. 6:20; Gal. 6:7). He that sows sparingly will also reap sparingly (2 Cor. 9:6). Further, as one responsible for the souls of others, the believer will be rewarded according as he has led many to righteousness. The angel said to Daniel, "And those who have insight will shine brightly like the brightness of the expanse of heaven, and those who lead the many to righteousness, like the stars forever and ever" (Dan. 12:3). In similar manner Paul writes, "For who is our hope or joy or crown of exultation? Is it not even you, in the presence of our Lord Jesus at His coming?" (1 Thess. 2:19). As those who live in a needy world, we may do good to all men and reap a reward for so doing (Gal. 6:10). Hospitality will be rewarded (Matt. 10:40–42), as will the care of the sick and the persecuted (Matt. 25:35–40). Even a cup of cold water will not remain unnoticed in that day (Matt. 10:42). This is especially true of kindnesses done to the Jewish people. And finally, as sufferers in an evil world, Christians will be rewarded for endurance. Thus, we read that when they revile us, persecute us, say all manner of evil against us falsely, our reward will be great in heaven (Matt. 5:11f.; Luke 6:22f.). If we suffer, we shall reign with him (2 Tim. 2:12; cf. Rom. 8:17). As James

promises, "Blessed is a man who perseveres under trial; for once he has been approved, he will receive the crown of life, which the Lord has promised to those who love him" (James 1:12).

(2) What is the time of the reward? It is when he comes that the rewards will be given (Matt. 16:27; Rom. 2:5–10; 2 Tim. 4:8; Rev. 11:18; 22:12). In view of this, it is not altogether correct to say of a believer when he dies, that he has gone to his reward. Paul declared that it would be in that day when Christ appears that he would receive his reward, and not at death. Those who have fallen asleep in Jesus are now in his personal presence, but they still look forward to the day of reckoning and recompense.

(3) What is the nature of the reward? The Scriptures represent the rewards to be bestowed under the figure of a crown or trophy. We are told that it will be an imperishable wreath (1 Cor. 9:25), and we are warned against losing our crown (Rev. 3:11). Souls won to the Lord are going to be our crown of exultation (1 Thess. 2:19). Besides these, there are the crown of righteousness (2 Tim. 4:8), the crown of life (James 1:12; Rev. 2:10), and the crown of glory (1 Pet. 5:4). Whatever may be meant by the figure, we may be sure that it represents a glorious and eternal honor in the presence of the Lord. As a part of the reward there is also the promise of a place with Christ in his throne (Luke 19:11–27; 2 Tim. 2:11f.; Rev. 3:21).

C. To Remove the Restrainer

He will come to take the restrainer of the revelation of the man of lawlessness out of the way. Paul writes, "And you know what restrains him now, so that in his time he may be revealed. For the mystery of lawlessness is already at work; only he who now restrains will do so until he is taken out of the way. And then that lawless one will be revealed whom the Lord will slay with the breath of His mouth and bring to an end by the appearance of His coming" (2 Thess. 2:6–8). Two persons are here connected with Christ's return: the restraining one, who is to be taken out of the way, and the lawless one, who is to be slain with the breath of Christ's mouth. Paul tells us that the mystery of lawlessness was already working in his day, but "what restrains" and "he who now restrains" interfered with the full development of iniquity.

What or who is this restraint or restrainer? Some see it as the restraining power of law and order. Others see it as human government; still others identify it with Satan himself. It is certainly true that government does restrain evil, but can this be said of evil government? And, surely, Satan does not restrain evil.

In Gen. 6:3 the Holy Spirit is represented as striving with wicked mankind in the days of Noah, and it is said that he "shall not strive with man forever." When he ceased opposing the wickedness of man, the judgments of

God burst forth upon the world. It would seem that he is the restrainer also in the end time, when the days of Noah are to be repeated. He does the restraining of evil, often through the church; for, because of his presence in them, believers are the salt of the earth and the light of the world (Matt. 5:13–16). When the church will be caught up, the salt and the light will be withdrawn. For a brief time after the rapture, until individuals turn to the Lord, there will be no saved people on the earth. Evidently the Spirit will withdraw his special ministry of restraining evil. Then corruption and darkness will develop rapidly; then iniquity will abound, and the man of lawlessness will be revealed. The Holy Spirit will continue to be on earth as he was here during Old Testament times, but not in the special sense in which he is here during this age. Satan with his leaders is to have large authority on this earth before the final judgment. Christ's coming will remove the restrainer to the development of lawlessness and the program of the last days.

CHAPTER XLI

The Second Coming of Christ:
The Purpose of His Coming to Earth
and the Period Between the Rapture and the
Revelation

As already noted, the first phase of Christ's return will be his coming into the air, but it is clear that he will also come down to earth. Let us consider now the purpose of his coming to earth and the time that lies between the two.

I. THE PURPOSE OF HIS COMING TO EARTH

Christ's purpose in coming to the earth is very different from his purpose in coming into the air. This difference is in itself a proof that there are two phases to his coming. They must of necessity be separated from each other in point of time. What are these purposes?

A. To Reveal Himself and His Own

Christ has been hidden from the gaze of the natural eye for over nineteen centuries. He was among men once, and his own beheld him (John 1:14; 1 John 1:1-4), but he is now in the tabernacle above, ministering as High Priest in the Holy of Holies. And he will come again (Heb. 9:24-28), attended by a heavenly retinue of angels and by the hosts of redeemed men (Joel 3:11; Zech. 14:5; 1 Thess. 3:13; Jude 14). "Every eye will see Him, even those who pierced Him" (Rev. 1:7; cf. Zech. 12:10). Scripture declares that all the tribes of the earth "will see the Son of Man coming on the clouds of the sky with power and great glory" (Matt. 24:30). His feet will stand upon the Mount of Olives (Zech. 14:4). The angels told the disciples, "This Jesus, who has been taken up from you into heaven, will come in just the same way as you have watched Him go into heaven" (Acts 1:11). Christ's own will also be manifest at that time (Col. 3:4). It will be a glorious revelation of Christ with his people.

B. To Judge the Beast, the False Prophet, and Their Armies

As the years of unprecedented tribulation (Isa. 24:16-21; 26:20f.; Jer. 30:4-7; Ezek. 20:33-38; Matt. 24:21, 29; Luke 21:34-36) falling between the two phases of his coming draw to a close, the spirits emanating from the dragon, the beast, and the false prophet go forth and gather together to battle the kings of the earth (Rev. 16:12–16). Ostensibly, they gather to capture Jerusalem and the Jews in Palestine (Zech. 12:1–9; 13:8–14:2), but just at the moment when victory seems assured, Christ will descend from heaven with his armies (Rev. 19:11–16). Then these hordes will turn to fight the Son of God, but the conflict will be short and the outcome certain. The leaders will be taken and cast into the lake of fire (Ps. 2:3–9; 2 Thess. 2:8; Rev. 19:19f.), and their armies slain with the sword that proceeds out of Christ's mouth (2 Thess. 1:7–10; Rev. 19:21). Thus, the political opposition to Christ and his kingdom will be broken and the way prepared for the inauguration of a new regime.

C. To Bind Satan

When the beast and false prophet are cast into the lake of fire, Satan is bound for one thousand years (Rev. 20:1–3). Amillennialism and postmillennialism take the binding of Satan and the millennium to be figurative. Some teach that this binding took place on the cross when Christ overcame Satan. Satan's activities have been restricted (Heb. 2:14), and in that sense he is bound. Boettner, a postmillennialist, writes, "The usual amillennial interpretation of Revelation 20:2 is that the 'binding' of Satan took place at the first advent, and that it was accomplished when Christ triumphed over him at the cross."[1] On the other hand, some interpret the binding of Satan to be a continuing process through this dispensation. As the church advances, Satan's power is being restricted. We respond, however, that Satan is not bound. This can be observed from several Scriptures: he is the ruler of this world (John 16:11), the prince of the power of the air (Eph. 2:2), and the god of this age (2 Cor. 4:4). Peter told his readers, "Your adversary, the devil, prowls about like a roaring lion, seeking someone to devour" (1 Pet. 5:8). Surely, he is not chained at this time.

Some interpret the resurrection and the following millennium as life in the intermediate state between death and resurrection, when the believer in a disembodied state is living with Christ. Again, to quote Boettner, "For the Old Testament saints and for those who died in the early part of the Christian era this reign has already continued much longer than a literal one thousand years."[2] Others interpret it as spiritual resurrection which occurs at salvation. Feinberg, a premillennialist, writes, "It is the common interpretation of amillennialists that the first resurrection is the spiritual resurrection

---

[1]Boettner, *The Millennium*, p. 125.
[2]Boettner, *The Millennium*, p. 66.

that takes place at the regeneration of a sinner; the second resurrection is the general physical resurrection of all the dead of all time."[3] But the literal interpretation of this passage demands the literal binding of Satan and the literal resurrection.

If the figures used in Rev. 20:1–3 mean anything, they must signify the removal of Satan from the sphere of his previous operation and his deprivation of opportunity and ability to continue his work. No doubt the demons are included in this binding. In Matt. 8:29 demons intimate their knowledge of their impending doom; and Isa. 11:1–10 and 65:19–25 set forth the changes in nature, man, and animals following the return of Christ. The binding of Satan does not include the removal of the carnal nature from those who will still be in their mortal bodies. Inherited depravity will follow man into the millennium and be a source of sin during that period. Note that the binding of Satan is for a definite period of one thousand years. Some may interpret this to imply a long, indefinite period, but there is no reason why the Holy Spirit would not have used an indefinite term if he wanted to represent the time as indefinite.

D. To Save Israel

Paul declared that God has not rejected his people (Rom. 11:1); presently there is a "remnant according to God's gracious choice" (v. 5); and after "the fulness of the Gentiles has come in . . . all Israel will be saved" (vss. 25f.). When Christ returns, he will first deliver Israel from its earthly enemies (Jer. 30:7; Zech. 14:1–3). But he will not stop with this deliverance; he will regather all Israel, reuniting the house of Israel and the house of Judah (Isa. 11:11–14; 62:4; Jer. 31:35–37; 33:14–22; Ezek. 37:18–25); and further, he will save them and make a new covenant with them (Isa. 66:8; Jer. 31:31–34; Zech. 12:10–13:1; Heb. 8:8–12). The Old Testament saints will also be resurrected at this time to enter into the millennium (Dan. 12:2). These promises cannot mean that all Israel will be gradually gathered into the church, for Israel's conversion is specifically associated with her sight of Christ (Zech. 12:10; Rev. 1:7). This is also clear from the statement that Israel's hardening is to continue "until the fulness of the Gentiles has come in" (Rom. 11:25), that is, until God's present dealings with the Gentiles are completed. Nor do these promises mean that all Israelites that ever lived will be saved, for the Jew who dies without saving faith is lost as surely as the Gentile. They merely apply to those Israelites who will be left after the rebels have been purged out from among them (Ezek. 20:37f.). In that day Israel will repent and turn to the Lord (Zech. 12:10–13:1).

[3]Feinberg, *Premillennialism or Amillennialism?*, p. 188.

E. To Judge the Nations

We have seen that Christ will judge the beast, the false prophet, and their armies at his return, but kings, captains, and armies do not constitute the whole people. After Christ has dealt with these in the battle of Armageddon, he will have all nations gathered before him for judgment. This judgment is not to be confused with the judgment of Rev. 20:11–15 for the following reasons: (1) At the judgment of the nations (Joel 3:11–17; Matt. 25:31–46; cf. Acts 17:31; 2 Thess. 1:7–10), Christ is represented as sitting upon his glorious throne; at the judgment in Rev. 20:11–15, he sits upon a great white throne. (2) The former is on earth (Joel 3:17); the latter in the skies, for heaven and earth flee away. (3) The former takes place before the millennium, just as he comes to earth; the latter after the millennium. (4) Before the former, all nations are gathered; before the latter, only the dead. (5) In connection with the former there is no mention of a resurrection; in connection with the latter there is a resurrection. (6) Before the former, two classes are mentioned; before the latter, only one. (7) No books are mentioned before the former; the books are opened before the latter. (8) The issue of the former is twofold: for the sheep, eternal life and the kingdom, for the goats, eternal punishment; for the latter, it is simply the lake of fire. And (9) an important question before the former is the treatment of the Lord's brothers; the only question before the latter is their general conduct. While some of these statements are based on the argument from silence, so large a number of differences or omissions can only point to two different judgments. It seems clear, therefore, that here the nations will be judged as to their privilege to enter the millennial kingdom.

F. To Deliver and Bless Creation

Jesus spoke of a future regeneration during which the apostles would sit upon thrones and judge the twelve tribes of Israel (Matt. 19:28). The chief ruler of this kingdom is identified as "My servant David" (Ezek. 34:23; 37:24; cf. Isa. 55:3f.). Feinberg remarks, "The reference to God's servant David is to be understood as David's greater Son, the Lord Jesus Christ."[4] Isaiah speaks of this time as a time when the wolf shall dwell at peace with the lamb, and the leopard with the kid (Isa. 11:1–9), as a time when the wilderness shall blossom as the rose, and the glowing sand shall become a pool of water (35:1–10). Paul speaks of it as the deliverance of creation from its groaning and bondage (Rom. 8:19–22). Various physical changes are to take place on the earth (Isa. 2:2; Ezek. 47:1–12; Zech. 14:4–8), and the earth shall again yield her increase (Ezek. 34:25f.). It is to be noted that this regeneration is to

[4]Feinberg, *The Prophecy of Ezekiel*, p. 198.

take place "when the Son of Man will sit on His glorious throne" (Matt. 19:28). The entire 11th chapter of Isaiah likewise identifies this glorious future with the presence of the Son of Jesse among men. The same thing may also be included in the promise that Christ "shall appear a second time, not to bear sin, to those who eagerly await Him, for salvation" (Heb. 9:28). The ground was cursed for man's sake, and thorns and thistles are the result of his sin (Gen. 3:17–19; cf. Heb. 6:8), but when Christ comes back, he will remove the curse and restore even dumb creation to its former perfection and glory.

G. To Set Up His Kingdom

This subject is taken up more fully later on, but a few words must be said regarding it in this connection. The nobleman has gone into "a distant country to receive a kingdom for himself, and then return" (Luke 19:12). When he returns, he will set up his kingdom (vss. 15–19). God promised David that he would establish his kingdom forever (2 Sam. 7:8–16), and later confirmed his promise with an oath (Ps. 89:3f., 20–37). At the very time when Babylon was taking Jerusalem, God renewed this promise to his people (Jer. 33:19–22). The angel Gabriel declared that Jesus was the heir to that throne (Luke 1:31–33). He is the stone that was cut out of a mountain without hands, that will fill the whole earth, after he has demolished all the kingdoms of earth (Dan. 2:44f.). He will receive the kingdom at his Father's hands and set it up in the end (Dan. 7:13f.). Then and then only will the kingdom of this world become the kingdom of our God and his Christ (Rev. 11:15). The city of Jerusalem will become the capital of the renewed earth (Isa. 2:2–4; Mic. 4:1–3). All the nations will be obliged to come up to worship at Jerusalem at the feast of tabernacles (Zech. 14:16–19). Peace and righteousness will characterize the reign of Christ (Isa. 9:6f.).

II. THE PERIOD BETWEEN THE RAPTURE AND THE REVELATION

Having now discussed the events connected with Christ's coming into the air and his coming to the earth, we must next deal briefly with the period between these two events. This period is the tribulation. We know, of course, that believers must through many tribulations "enter the kingdom of God" (Acts 14:22); but there is, besides this common experience of Christians, a future period of tribulation. In Dan. 12:1 it is spoken of as "a time of distress such as never occurred since there was a nation"; in Matt. 24:21 it is described as "a great tribulation"; in Luke 21:34 it is referred to as "that day"; Rev. 3:10 speaks of it as "the hour of testing, that hour which is about to come upon the whole world, to test those who dwell upon the earth"; and

in Rev. 7:14 we read of those who had "come out of the great tribulation."
In the Old Testament it is referred to as the "time of Jacob's distress" (Jer.
30:7) and the time of God's indignation with the inhabitants of the earth
(Isa. 24:17–21; 26:20f.; 34:1–3). That the tribulation period will come between the two phases of Christ's coming appears from a study of the whole
program of the future. It will close with Christ's return in glory (Matt.
24:29f.).

A. THE DURATION OF THE PERIOD

We are nowhere told in so many words just how long the period will be,
though we are told that for the elect's sake the days will be shortened (Matt.
24:22). There are, however, some things that indicate that the time is seven
years. Whatever be the method of calculating the seventy weeks in Dan.
9:24–27, it is clear that they began with Nehemiah's return and the rebuilding of the walls and city of Jerusalem (Neh. 2:1–8; Dan. 9:25). It is clear also
that the sixty-ninth week ended with the crucifixion of the Messiah (Dan.
9:26) and that there is a break in the succession of weeks. The destruction of
the city and sanctuary in A.D. 70, and the repetition of wars and desolations
reaching to the end, come between the sixty-ninth and the seventieth weeks.
To many it seems perfectly clear that the seventieth week is still future and
that it is the tribulation period. It seems clear that a "week" in Daniel's
chronology is seven years. If, therefore, the seventieth week represents the
tribulation period, then we can assume that it will last for seven years. In
harmony with this, the latter half of the period is elsewhere referred to as "a
time, times, and half a time" (Dan. 7:25; 12:7; Rev. 12:14), as "forty-two
months" (Rev. 11:2; 13:5), and as 1,260 days (Rev. 11:3; 12:6; cf. Dan.
12:11f.). This is perhaps all that can be said about the duration of this period.

B. THE NATURE OF THE PERIOD

The Scriptures have a great deal to say about the nature of this period. Let us
briefly look at some of the aspects of the tribulation period.

1. *The political aspects.* The political aspects are indicated especially in
Daniel and Revelation. Dan. 2:31–43 pictures "the times of the Gentiles"
(Luke 21:24), and the following two verses (vss. 44f.), the millennial kingdom. After the Babylonian, Medo-Persian, Grecian, and Roman periods, the
final form of the Roman Empire appears with its ten cooperating kings. In
Dan. 7:1–28 this same prediction occurs under the figure of four beasts. The
last one, with its ten horns, represents the final form of the Roman Empire
with its ten kings. Rev. 13:1–10 gives this same prophecy, except that the
horns now have crowns, suggesting that the time of their power has come. In

Rev. 17:1–18 this same beast is dominated by the adulterous woman, evidently a religious system. Rev. 19:17–21 describes the end of this empire. From all this, one can conclude that during the tribulation period there will be a federated political world, developed chiefly from the Old Roman Empire, within which will be ten cooperating kingdoms. This rule will be autocratic and blasphemous. At first the religious system of those days will dominate the government, but after a time the ten kings will destroy it, and then great persecutions will be introduced against the believers of that time. But the emperor and his associates will be destroyed at the return of Christ, and their kingdom will give way to the kingdom which Christ will establish.

2. *The religious aspect.* The religious aspect may be ascertained from such Scriptures as Dan. 11:36–39; John 5:43; 2 Thess. 2:6–12; Rev. 13:11–18; and 17:1–17. Jesus predicted that another would come in his own name and that the Jews would accept him. This is one of the beasts in Rev. 13:1–18. The word "antichrist" occurs but five times in the New Testament (1 John 2:18, 22; 4:3; 2 John 7), and since the term is used of the personal antichrist only once or twice, it is better to use the more frequent terms used of the actors of the end-time. We have already indicated that in Rev. 17:1–6 the false religious system is seen riding the beast. This may be a federation of all the apostates who will pass into the tribulation. As noted earlier, at the beginning of this period, this false system, the harlot, will dominate the government. When in the midst of it the emperor breaks his covenant with the Jews and forbids the offering of sacrifices (Dan. 9:27), the ten kings will hate the harlot, cast her off, and destroy her (Rev. 17:16f.). From that time on, all will be required to worship the beast (Rev. 13:4–8), and the second beast will set out to force the world to do so (Rev. 13:11–17). He will use deception and lying wonders (2 Thess. 2:9–12; Rev. 13:13) and force (Rev. 13:7, 15; cf. 6:9–11; 20:4), persecuting those who will not worship the beast nor take his name (Rev. 13:16f.). He will require all to take the mark of the beast and will not allow any to buy or sell unless they take this mark. It is clear that in those days multitudes will be slain for the Word of God and the testimony which they hold. But with the coming of Christ and the destruction of the leaders and their armies, the whole religious system of the end-time will come to nought.

3. *The Israelitish aspect.* God has not cast away his people; even today there is a remnant according to the election of grace (Rom. 11:1–5). But what is more than that, God will once again take up Israel as a people, "for the gifts and the calling of God are irrevocable" (Rom. 11:29). It is impossible to go fully into this most interesting and important subject; we can only note the facts in outline form.

Israel is to return to Palestine, but it is clear that she will do so in unbelief.

It is after their return that the Israelites will be converted (Ezek. 37:1–14). In recent years there has been a determined effort on the part of many of the Jews to return to Palestine. This will go on until the emperor of the restored Roman Empire will make a covenant with them for seven years, allowing them to restore the sacrifices in their rebuilt temple in Jerusalem. But this prince will break his covenant in the midst of the week and cause the sacrifices and oblations to cease (Dan. 9:27). Somewhere in this period, perhaps just before the second half of it begins, God will have 144,000 Israelites sealed in their foreheads (Rev. 7:1–8). This, no doubt, indicates that they have now accepted Christ as their Messiah. This is but a remnant of Israel, and the sealing is for the purpose of their protection during the tribulation judgments that are yet to come. Then Satan will be cast out of heaven and will persecute Israel. But the earth will help the Israelites and swallow up the armies which Satan sends after them (Jer. 30:7; Dan. 12:1; Rev. 12). Following the abolition of the sacrifices, the beast will set up an image in the temple, spoken of as "the abomination of desolation" (Dan. 12:11; Matt. 24:15; Rev. 13:14f.; cf. 2 Thess. 2:4). Then will follow further persecution of the Jews. Probably this refers to the persecution of those who were converted under the ministry of the two witnesses (Rev. 11:1–7; 12:17). And finally, we have the persecution of all Israel in Palestine (Zech. 12:1–9; 13:8f.; 14:1–5). It is noteworthy that Israel's deliverance and salvation will take place in her darkest hour. Christ will come and the Jews will see him. Then they will mourn for him, plunge into the fountain for sin and uncleanness, and become a new nation (Zech. 12:10–13:2). God will save all Israel surviving these judgments (Rom. 11:25–27).

4. The economic aspect. The economic aspect of this period appears in Rev. 13:16–18 and 18:1–24. Buying and selling will be regulated on the basis of emperor-worship. Commerce will be glorified above everything else, and a great emporium city will be erected for that purpose. Babylon, the name given this city will be the great mercantile city of the world. But God will take note of all the oppressions of his people and will judge the great city in one hour. Heaven will rejoice when God judges this wicked woman and this wicked city (Rev. 19:1–5).

C. The Chief Actor of the Period

The person and work of Satan in general has already been considered; now it is in order to look at his part in the program of the future. He has something to do with the revival of the Roman Empire. In Dan. 7:2f. we are told that the winds stirred up the great sea and that, as a result, the four beasts emerged. Rev. 13:1 states that the dragon stood upon the sand of the seashore, and a beast came forth out of the sea. He it is who is back of all this movement for world federation, of which the unannounced purpose is the banishment of the faith from the earth. It is he who gives his power, throne, and great authority to the beast (Rev. 13:2–4). Thus, this monarch will be Satan-energized and Satan-empowered, and no one will be able to make war with him. Again, he will at first direct affairs from heaven, but in due time will be cast down to the earth (Rev. 12:7–13; cf. Luke 10:18). Knowing that his time is short, he will hate and persecute Israel with great fierceness (Rev. 12:13–17). His methods of operation will be deception, lying, signs, and fire from heaven (2 Thess. 2:9–11; Rev. 13:13–15). He will even institute devil and demon worship (Rev. 9:20; 13:4). It may be that this will take the form of idolatry. And finally, Satan will incite the kings of the whole earth to gather together for the battle of Armageddon (Rev. 16:12–16; 19:11–21). Thus, we see that the tribulation will be in a true sense the hour and power of darkness.

CHAPTER XLII

The Time of His Coming: Premillennial

Jesus said, "But of that day or hour no one knows, not even the angels in heaven, nor the Son, but the Father alone" (Mark 13:32) and, "It is not for you to know times or epochs which the Father has fixed by His own authority" (Acts 1:7). Yet he criticized the Pharisees and Sadducees because they knew how to discern the face of the heaven, but the signs of the times they could not discern (Matt. 16:3); and he asked them to learn from the fig tree that when it puts forth leaves, summer is nigh (Matt. 24:32f.). The men of Issachar are praised because they "understood the times, with knowledge of what Israel should do" (1 Chron. 12:32). Thus, the believer is to know in general as to the time, but not in particular. In general the answer is that his coming is imminent; he may come at any time (Matt. 24:36; 25:13; Mark 13:32; 1 Thess. 4:16f.; Titus 2:13). If the time had been definitely announced from the first, the church would have lost the incentive to watchfulness that is afforded it by the uncertainty of the time of this event.

We shall not enter into the question of the signs of his coming, since they deal more directly with his coming to earth than with his coming in the air. But we shall take up the two questions of outstanding importance: Will he come before the millennium? and will he come before the tribulation? To some extent the answers to both questions have already been anticipated, but it is necessary here to consider the questions in greater detail. In this chapter we shall consider the first question and show that his coming will be premillennial.

I. THE MEANING OF THE TERM

The term "millennium" is from the Latin and means a thousand years. It is not found in Scripture, but the term "a thousand years" occurs six times in Rev. 20:2-7. The Greek term "chiliasm" frequently occurs in theological literature and denotes the doctrine that Christ will come and set up an earthly kingdom for a thousand years. The fact of such a kingdom is firmly established in the teaching of the Old Testament, but the book of Revelation gives its duration.

Those who believe that the second coming of Christ will occur before the millennium are called "premillennialists" or "premillenarians." Postmillennialists teach that Christ will return visibly and personally after the millennium. Amillennialists do not accept a literal millennium; rather, they see the millennium as either the disembodied state of believers who are with the Lord awaiting the resurrection, or the present spiritual reign of Christ in the hearts of believers.

II. THE POSITION OF THE EARLY CHURCH

The early church was largely premillennial. Eschatology was not clearly systematized in the early centuries, but certain early writings can be drawn upon to support the fact that during the first three centuries of the church, premillennialism was widely held. Papias, who died c. A.D. 155, wrote that "there will be a millennium after the resurrection from the dead, when the personal reign of Christ will be established on this earth."[1] He also wrote, "The days will come in which vines shall grow, having each ten thousand branches, and in each branch ten thousand twigs, and in each true twig ten thousand shoots, and in every one of the shoots ten thousand clusters, and on every one of the clusters ten thousand grapes, and every grape when pressed will give five-and-twenty metretes of wine."[2] And though this is a gross exaggeration, nonetheless it does show a belief in the millennium. Barnabas, writing about A.D. 100, likened world history to the six creative days and the day of rest. After the six days, which he interpreted to be six thousand years, Christ would come again and "destroy the time of wicked man, and judge the ungodly, and change the sun, and the moon, and the stars, then shall He truly rest on the seventh day."[3] Barnabas continued by saying that the eighth day is the beginning of another world. Justin Martyr (c. A.D. 110–165) wrote, "I and others, who are right-minded Christians on all points, are assured that there will be a resurrection of the dead, and a thousand years in Jerusalem, which will then be built, adorned, and enlarged."[4] A later writer, Tertullian (c. A.D. 150–225), declared, "We do confess that a kingdom is promised to us upon the earth, although before heaven, only in another state of existence; inasmuch as it will be after the resurrection for a thousand years in the divinely-built city of Jerusalem." Further on he writes that after the thousand years are over "there will ensue the destruction of the world and the conflagration of all things at the judgment."[5] The eminent historian, Philip Schaff, observes, "The most striking point in the eschatology of the ante-Nicene age is the prominent chiliasm, or

---

[1]Papias, *Fragment VI.*
[2]Papias, *Fragment IV.*
[3]Barnabas, *The Epistle of Barnabas,* Chapter XV.
[4]Justin Martyr, *Dialogue with Trypho,* Chapter LXXX.
[5]Tertullian, *Against Marcion,* Book III, Chapter XXV.

millenarianism. . . . It was indeed not the doctrine of the church embodied in any creed or form of devotion, but a widely current opinion of distinguished teachers."[6]

From the 4th century on, the belief in the millennium declined. There were several reasons for this decline. (1) The persecutions against the church drew to an end with the conversion of Constantine, and the church saw a new day of peace dawning. (2) There was a change in biblical interpretation, from the literal hermeneutic to the allegorical method. The predictions of the millennial kingdom were spiritualized. (3) Many began to interpret the binding of Satan and the resurrection and reign of saints (Rev. 20:1–4) as the personal victory of believers over Satan. In that sense, believers are, in this present life, reigning with Christ.

But even with the decline of this doctrine, there were scattered voices of premillennialism heard throughout the centuries. The eschatological doctrines were neglected during the Dark Ages, but with the Reformation there was renewed interest. The Reformers, by and large, taught that the church was in some sense the predicted kingdom, but they did revive the doctrine of the Lord's return and the resurrection. By the seventeenth and eighteenth centuries, the voice of premillennialism was again being heard.

There has been a return to the position of the early church. Charles Wesley, Isaac Watts, Bengel, Lange, Godet, Ellicott, Trench, Alford, and many of the outstanding evangelists of past and present generations have espoused the premillennial position. During the last century there has been renewed emphasis upon this blessed hope.

III. THE PROOF OF THE DOCTRINE

A. The Manner and Time of the Setting Up of the Kingdom

Fully remembering that the term "kingdom" is often used of the spiritual reign of God in men's hearts, we yet find many references that speak of a future and earthly kingdom. The former "is not coming with signs to be observed" (Luke 17:20); but the latter will. In Dan. 2:44 we are told that "the God of heaven will set up a kingdom which will never be destroyed." That is, he will set up this kingdom when the ten kings have each received their kingdom with the beast "for one hour" (Rev. 17:12–18). Dan. 7:15–27 shows that these ten kings are followed by the kingdom that is "given to the people of the saints of the Highest One; His Kingdom will be an everlasting kingdom, and all the dominions will serve and obey Him." In other words, suddenly, in the days of those kings, this stone, Christ, will strike the image

[6]Schaff, *History of the Christian Church*, II, p. 614.

upon its feet and consume all these kingdoms (Dan. 2:34, 44). He will in judgment demolish the kingdoms of the earth, and demolition is not interpenetration. This is not the gospel converting the world. These metals are not converted into nobler ones, but are ground to powder and carried away by the wind like the chaff of the summer threshing-floor, so that their place is found no more. The stone does not interpenetrate them, but supersedes them.

B. The Blessings That are Associated with This Future Kingdom

This kingdom will stretch from sea to sea, from the river to the ends of the earth, from the desert regions to the islands (Ps. 72:6–11). The nations of the earth will ascend to the mountain of the Lord's house, that is, to Jerusalem, for worship (Isa. 2:2–4; Mic. 4:1–3). Those nations which do not come to Jerusalem to worship will be punished (Zech. 14:16–19). Christ will rule, sitting upon the throne of David; his rule will be with justice and righteousness (Isa. 9:6f.). Jer. 23:5f. says, " 'Behold the days are coming,' declares the Lord, 'when I shall raise up for David a righteous Branch; and He will reign as king and act wisely and do justice and righteousness in the land. In His days Judah will be saved, and Israel will dwell securely; and this is His name by which He will be called, the Lord our righteousness.' " God not only repeats this promise, but adds to it this assurance, "If you can break My covenant for the day, and My covenant for the night, so that day and night will not be at their appointed time, then My covenant may also be broken with David My servant that he shall not have a son to reign on his throne, and with the Levitical priests, My ministers" (Jer. 33:20f.). This promise goes back to God's covenant with David (2 Sam. 7:8–17), which was confirmed with an oath (Ps. 89:3f., 19–37). Both Judah and Israel are to be restored (Jer. 23:6f.), for God "will make them one nation in the land, on the mountains of Israel; and one king will be king for all of them" (Ezek. 37:22; cf. 24–28). Isa. 35 describes in glowing colors the restoration of nature in that period. These great blessings follow the return of Christ, and they speak of an earthly kingdom. In that day "the Lord will be king over all the earth" (Zech. 14:9).

C. The Distinction between Receiving the Kingdom and Inaugurating It

Under the figure of the nobleman, Christ is represented as going "to a distant country to receive a Kingdom for himself" (Luke 19:12). Just as Archaelaus, on the death of his father Herod, had to go to Rome to have the kingdom confirmed to him before he could actually rule as king, so Christ had to return to heaven to receive the kingdom from the Father (Dan. 7:13f.). The kingdom was pledged to him by the angel Gabriel (Luke 1:32f.), but it must not be overlooked that the Word says, "The Lord God will give Him the throne of His father David." For this purpose he went back to heaven. But as with Archaelaus, Christ did not establish his throne in the far country, but he will return to the scene from which he departed, and there set up his kingdom. Jesus is now seated, not upon David's throne, but upon his Father's throne (Rev. 3:21). The time will come when he shall sit upon his own throne (Matt. 19:28; 25:31). After he has thus come in glory, he will say to those on his right hand, "Come, you who are blessed of My Father, inherit the kingdom prepared for you from the foundation of the world" (Matt. 25:34).

D. The Promise to the Apostles of Rulership over the Twelve Tribes of Israel

Jesus said, "Truly I say to you, that you who have followed Me, in the regeneration when the Son of Man will sit on His glorious throne, you also shall sit upon twelve thrones, judging the twelve tribes of Israel" (Matt. 19:28). This promise is here clearly linked with the Lord's sitting upon his own throne, and Matt. 25:31 indicates that this will occur when he comes back in his glory. Perhaps this is what is meant in Isa. 1:26, "Then I will restore your judges as at the first, and your counselors as at the beginning; after that you will be called the city of righteousness, a faithful city." Perhaps the promise of the twelve thrones was behind the disciples' question, "Lord, is it at this time You are restoring the kingdom to Israel?" (Acts 1:6).

E. The Promise to Believers That They Will Reign with Christ

Not only will the twelve apostles reign with Christ when he comes, but to all believers it is said, "If we endure, we shall also reign with Him" (2 Tim. 2:12). In 1 Cor. 6:2f. Paul bluntly asks, "Do you not know that the saints will judge the world? And if the world is judged by you, are you not competent to constitute the smallest law courts? Do you not know that we shall judge angels?" In Rev. 5:10 we read, "And Thou hast made them to be a kingdom and priests to our God; and they will reign upon the earth." In Rev. 20:4–6 this reign is said to last for a thousand years.

F. The Conditions That are Predicted as Existing Just Prior to His Return

Far from showing that the world will be converted before his return, Scripture indicates the exact opposite. It will be as it was in the days of Noah and Lot when the Son of Man returns (Luke 17:26–30). Jesus asked, "When the Son of Man comes, will He find faith on the earth?" (Luke 18:8). Paul writes that in the latter times some will depart from the faith, "paying attention to deceitful spirits and doctrines of demons" (1 Tim. 4:1), and that "in the last days difficult times will come" (2 Tim. 3:1). He declares that Christ's coming will be unexpected (1 Thess. 5:2f.) and that it will be a coming for judgment upon the ungodly (2 Thess. 1:7–10; 2:1–12). Peter describes the men of that time as mocking at the thought of Christ's return (2 Pet. 3:3f.). Scripture further teaches that the conversion of Israel (Zech. 12:10–13:2; Acts 15:16) and of the Gentiles (Acts 15:17) will take place at his coming. During the present age, good and evil will grow side by side (Matt. 13:24–30, 36–43), but then the separation will take place. The bad will be destroyed and the good will enter the kingdom.

G. The Order of Events

The order, as given in Rev. 19:11–20:15, harmonizes with Ps. 2:3–8, and is as follows: the coming of Christ with his saints (Rev. 19:11–16), the battle of Armageddon (17–21), the binding of Satan (20:1–3), the enthronement of the saints of the first resurrection (4–6), the loosing of Satan after the thousand years (7–9), the judgment of Satan (v. 10), and the second resurrection and the great-white-throne judgment (11–15). Thus, if we follow the order of events in this passage, we must conclude that the Lord comes to earth before the millennium in order to establish it. This normal succession of events is credible and gives clear support to premillennialism.

CHAPTER XLIII

The Time of His Coming: Pretribulational

It has been shown that the Scriptures predict a period of tribulation, and thus far it has been assumed that it will come between the rapture and the revelation. We must now undertake to show that this is the case. Jewish teachers held that the period would come between the present age and the age to come. Westcott says, they were "commonly agreed that the passage from one age to the other would be through a period of intense sorrow and anguish, 'the travail-pains' of the new birth."[1] It has been shown that this period of intense sorrow and anguish will end with the coming of Christ to the earth. But will it begin with his coming into the air and the rapture of the saved, or will it begin before he thus comes, and will the church pass through the tribulation?

This question is variously answered. Some say that the church will pass through the tribulation and that the catching up of the redeemed will be immediately followed by their return with Christ. This is called post-tribulationalism. Others say that the church will pass through the first half of the period and that the rapture will take place in the middle of it. This is designated midtribulationalism. The partial-rapturists teach that the unspiritual part of the church will pass through the tribulation, but the mature and Spirit-filled will be caught up before the tribulation. And some say that Jesus will come for the church before the tribulation. In other words, his coming will be pretribulational, and the church as such will pass through no part of the tribulation. What are the facts? It is not necessary to examine each of the wrong conceptions listed; an investigation of the positive teaching of the Word will serve to establish the truth. The weight of the evidence seems to be that the church will not pass through the tribulation. Let us consider briefly some early Christian teaching and then examine the teaching of Scripture.

I. EARLY CHRISTIAN TEACHING

In view of the various teachings current today, the seriousness of the time in which we are living, and most of all, because of the bearing of this question on the belief in the imminence of the Lord's return, it is necessary to investigate this subject, though it can only be discussed briefly.

[1]Westcott, *Epistle to the Hebrews*, p. 6.

As noted earlier, the early church expected the premillennial coming of Christ. Was its teaching also pretribulational? In the testimony of the early Church Fathers, there is almost complete silence on the subject of the tribulation. They often speak of going through tribulations, but very seldom of a future period known as the tribulation. This is probably because during the first centuries of the church, the church was passing through many persecutions and it did not concern itself with the future tribulation. There are a couple intimations, however, of a belief in the pretribulational return of Christ. First, there is an interesting paragraph in the *Shepherd of Hermas* that gives some information on the subject. Hermas writes that he passed by a wild beast on the way, and that thereafter a maiden met him and saluted him, saying, "Hail, O Man!" He returned her salutation, and said, "Lady, hail!" Then she asked him, "Has nothing crossed your path?" To this, Hermas replied, "I was met by a beast of such a size that it could destroy peoples, but through the power of the Lord and His great mercy I escaped from it." Then the maiden said, "Well did you escape from it, because you cast your care on God, and opened your heart to the Lord, believing that you can be saved by no other than His great and glorious name. . . . You have escaped from great tribulation on account of your faith, and because you did not doubt in the presence of such a beast. Go, therefore, and tell the elect of the Lord His mighty deeds, and say to them this beast is a type of the great tribulation that is coming. If then ye prepare yourselves, and repent with all your heart, and turn to the Lord, it will be possible for you to escape it, if your heart be free and spotless, and ye spend the rest of your days in serving the Lord blamelessly."[2] This seems to show that there was teaching to the effect that the church would escape the great tribulation. The position, however, is somewhat confusing, for in another place he declares, "Happy ye who endure the great tribulation that is coming on."[3]

Irenaeus (c. 140–202) also seems to hold that the church will be caught up during the tribulation, for he says:

And therefore, when in the end the Church shall be suddenly caught up from this, it is said, "There shall be tribulation such as has not been since the beginning, neither shall be." For this is the last contest of the righteous, in which, when they overcome, they are crowned with incorruption.[4]

But, in another place, he also teaches that the church is present during the days of the antichrist.[5] Thus, while the belief among the Fathers concerning

[2]*Shepherd of Hermas*, Book I, Vision IV, Chapter ii.
[3]*Shepherd of Hermas*, Book I, Vision II, Chapter ii.
[4]Irenaeus, *Against Heresies*, Book V, Chapter xxix.
[5]Irenaeus, *Against Heresies*, Book V, Chapters xxvi, xxx.

the tribulation is not clear, and there seems to be some confusion, there is at least intimation of it. It is clear that the Fathers regarded the Lord's coming as imminent. The Lord had taught the church to expect his return at any moment, and the church looked for him to come in their day and taught his personal return as being imminent. The exception to this was the Alexandrian Fathers, who also rejected other fundamental doctrines. We may assume that the early church lived in the constant expectation of their Lord, and hence was not concerned with the possibility of a tribulation period in the future. This may be the reason for the silence concerning the tribulation in the Fathers.

Further, it is not strange that the leaders in the Middle Ages are silent concerning the pretribulational rapture. With the rise of Constantine and the state church, the church turned to an allegorizing of the Scriptures concerning the Lord's return. And with the denial of a literal millennium, the tribulation was allegorized or ignored.

The Reformers returned to the doctrine of the second coming, but their emphasis was on the doctrine of salvation rather than the development of the details of eschatology. Consequently, there was little, if any, development of this doctrine throughout the history of the Christian church. However, Christian doctrine is established on the basis of Scripture, and not on the basis of the development of doctrine, or the lack of it, in past generations. The Bible must be our sole authority in matters of doctrine, and it is to it that we must turn to establish biblical truth.

II. SCRIPTURAL TEACHING

Various arguments from Scripture can be presented which substantiate this doctrine of the Lord's pretribulational return for his church.

A. THE NATURE OF THE SEVENTIETH WEEK OF DANIEL

The seventieth week of Daniel is mentioned in Dan. 9:27. We have already pointed out that after the sixty-ninth week, the Messiah was to be cut off. These "weeks" began with the return and work of Nehemiah (Neh. 2:4-6; Dan. 9:25f.), and however we may reckon the time, we must perceive that the earthly life of Jesus was spent during the last four or five of the sixty-nine weeks. The church was not as yet in existence, but Jesus declared that he would build it (Matt. 16:18). Since the church was formed by the baptism of the Spirit (Acts 1:4f.; 11:16f.; 1 Cor. 12:13), we date the beginning of the church from Pentecost. It was, therefore, no part of the sixty-nine weeks. Nor will it be a part of the seventieth week. Daniel was told that the entire seventy weeks were decreed upon his people and his holy city (Dan. 9:24), and not merely sixty-nine. If that week is still future, and is in fact the future tribulation period, then there is no more likelihood that the church will be here during the last week, than there is evidence that it was in existence during the last part of the sixty-nine weeks. In other words, the church fills the parenthesis between the sixty-ninth and the seventieth weeks, and is no part of either period. This position argues against both the posttribulational and the midtribulational positions. These two positions have of necessity a certain overlap between Israel and the church in the last week.

B. The Nature and Purpose of the Tribulation

It is often said that since the church has not been exempted from persecutions throughout church history, there is no ground for supposing that it will escape the persecutions of the tribulation to come. But this is to misunderstand altogether the nature and purpose of the tribulation. "The hour of testing" is "to test those who dwell upon the earth" (Rev. 3:10). The phrase, "those who dwell upon the earth," is used over a dozen times in Revelation and has reference to the earth-dwellers. Mounce writes that when this "phrase occurs . . . the enemies of the church are always in mind."[6] These are the people who have identified themselves with this world, the unsaved. This period is also "the time of Jacob's distress" (Jer. 30:7). In Isa. 26:20f. the Lord speaks of this same period and discloses its true nature, "Come, my people, enter into your rooms, and close your doors behind you; hide for a little while, until indignation runs its course. For behold, the Lord is about to come out from His place to punish the inhabitants of the earth for their iniquity; and the earth shall reveal her bloodshed, and will no longer cover her slain." That is, the tribulation is the period in which God will go forth to punish a God-rejecting and Christ-rejecting world. The persecutions during that period are only incidentals. Futurist interpreters of the Revelation generally hold that Rev. 6–19 deals with the tribulation period. The main features of those chapters are the seals, trumpets, and bowls, but each of these is a judgment that emanates from heaven. It is God's visitation of wrath upon this sin-cursed world.

When God got ready to punish Sodom and Gomorrah, he first took Lot and his family out of the city. Abraham had induced God to promise to save the city if he found ten righteous in it; he did not seem to think it necessary to argue that God should take Lot out of the city in case he did not find ten. But God would not "sweep away the righteous with the wicked" (Gen. 18:23), and so he took Lot out before he rained brimstone and fire on the cities of the plain (Gen. 19:12-25). Peter uses this incident to prove that "the Lord knows how to rescue the godly from temptation [lit. 'trial'; same term

[6]Mounce, *The Book of Revelation*, p. 120.

as in Rev. 3:10], and to keep the unrighteous under punishment for the day
of judgment" (2 Pet. 2:9). So with the case of Noah: when God got ready to
destroy the world with a flood, he delivered Noah and his family from it.

C. THE DISTINCTION BETWEEN ISRAEL AND THE CHURCH

Without going into a lengthy study of this aspect of biblical revelation, we do
observe that the church and Israel are two distinct entities. This can be seen
in several ways. (1) In the past God dealt primarily with Israel; now he is
dealing with the church. In the future he will again deal with Israel. Rom. 11
teaches that Israel as a nation has been cut off so that the Gentiles could be
grafted in. In the future Israel will again be grafted in (cf. Acts 15:16–18;
Rom. 15:8–12). (2) Israel is a nation; the church is a body of individuals
called out from the nations. (3) Daniel's seventy weeks deal with Israel (Dan.
9:24); the church fits into the time between the sixty-ninth and the seventieth week. (4) Christ is to return to Israel to establish the kingdom; his
return for the church is to take the church to be with him. And (5) the great
Old Testament covenants were made with Abraham and his seed, Israel
(Gen. 12:1–3; 2 Sam. 7:11–16; Jer. 31:31–34); the church shares in the
spiritual benefits of these covenants, but not yet the physical (Rom. 4:11;
1 Cor. 11:25; 2 Cor. 3:6; Heb. 10:16f.). The literal physical fulfillment of
these covenants is yet future and will take place in the kingdom age. These
and other distinctions made between the church and Israel demonstrate that
God has a different program for each. God's program on earth for the church
will come to an end when we are caught up to be with him in the air. This
will signal the beginning of God's renewed dealings with Israel, just as
Israel's rejection in New Testament times signaled the beginning of a new
people of God called the church, the body of Christ.

D. THE MISSION OF THE HOLY SPIRIT AS A RESTRAINER

Paul wrote that the mystery of lawlessness was already at work in his day,
but that because of "what restrains him now" and "he who now restrains,"
the lawless one had not yet been revealed (2 Thess. 2:3–7). He added,
however, that this one would be taken out of the way, and that then the
lawless one would be revealed (vss. 7f.). As the Holy Spirit strove with men
in the antediluvian age (Gen. 6:3), so he strives now against the full development of lawlessness. But as he then ceased striving with men, so he will
again cease striving with them. This he will do when he is taken out of the
way. The Holy Spirit has the distinct mission of forming and indwelling the
church of Christ. He came for that purpose on the day of Pentecost and will
perform that work until the church is completed. Then he will be, in a certain
sense, withdrawn with the church. Because the Holy Spirit is omnipresent,

the withdrawal will involve a withdrawal of ministry, rather than of person. It is easy to see that when his interference is withdrawn, wickedness will develop rapidly and the lawless one will appear among men. The church is an instrument used by the Spirit in the restraining of evil. With the rapture, not a single believer will be left, and the Spirit's ministry of restraining will cease.

E. The Necessity for an Interval between the Rapture and the Revelation

Posttribulationalists generally hold that the saved will be caught up to meet Christ as he descends from heaven, but that they will immediately return to earth with him. They deny that there will be an interval between the two events.[7] But a careful study of the Scriptures discloses that there will be an interval between Christ's coming into the air and his coming down to the earth. It reveals that there are two things at least that must take place between these two events: the judgment of the believers and the marriage supper of the Lamb. Paul writes, "For we must all appear before the judgment seat of Christ, that each one may be recompensed for his deeds in the body, according to what he has done, whether good or bad" (2 Cor. 5:10; cf. John 5:22; Rom. 14:10). The believer will be judged to ascertain whether he is eligible for a reward or not, and if so, how large that reward is to be (1 Cor. 3:12–15). It is clear that the Lord will call his servants to himself for a private judgment of their works (Luke 19:15; 2 Cor. 5:10). This is made necessary also by the fact that when they come back with him, they immediately enter upon their part of the rule over the earthly kingdom (Rev. 2:26; 19:14, 19; 20:4). This much seems to be clear. In addition to the judgment seat of Christ, there is also the marriage supper of the Lamb. In Rev. 19:1–10 the scene is set in heaven; in v. 11 heaven is opened and Christ with his saints is seen coming down to earth. The marriage supper is brought before us in vss. 7–9, and is therefore in heaven. When the Lord Jesus returns to the earth with his bride, there will, no doubt, be certain celebrations on earth as well with redeemed of all ages. These two events, the judgment of Christ and the marriage supper of the Lamb, must take place before the coming of Christ to establish his kingdom. Obviously, these events would not necessarily demand the full seven years, but they do require a measure of time.

In addition to the events in heaven, there are also developments on earth in preparation for the kingdom. God will be preparing a company of redeemed to enter into the millennial kingdom. This will include believing Jew and Gentile alike. At the return of Christ, believers will enter the kingdom,

---

[7]For an excellent study of posttribulationalism, see *The Church and the Tribulation* by Robert Gundry, a leading posttribulationalist.

and unbelievers will be taken away in judgment (Matt. 13:37–43, 47–50; 24:40f.; 25:1–12). Just as our Lord worked for over three years with those who were to form the nucleus of the coming church, so it seems proper that those saved during the tribulation period will be those with whom the Lord will establish his kingdom when he returns. This gathering of the remnant of Israel and the saved from among the Gentiles will take a measure of time. With the return of Christ in glory, there will be a major turning to the Lord (Zech. 12:10–14), just as on the day of Pentecost with the coming of the Spirit and the preaching of Peter (Acts 2:14–41; cf. Joel 2:28–32; Rom. 11:25–27).

F. The Exhortations to Constant Expectation of the Lord's Return

Again and again we are admonished to watch: "Therefore be on the alert, for you do not know which day your Lord is coming" (Matt. 24:42); "Be on the alert then, for you do not know the day nor the hour" (Matt. 25:13); and "Therefore, be on the alert—for you do not know when the master of the house is coming, whether in the evening, at midnight, at cockcrowing, or in the morning—lest he come suddenly and find you asleep" (Mark 13:35f.; cf. 1 Thess. 5:6; Rev. 3:3). We are also asked to look for that blessed hope (Titus 2:13; cf. Heb. 9:28). How can we watch and look for his return if there is even a single event that is predicted to precede Christ's return? If the tribulation precedes the second coming, then we are obliged to look for it as the first thing on the program. Then we cannot expect the Lord to return at any time; then the truth of the Lord's return cannot be the incentive to holiness, service, and watchfulness that the Scriptures represent it to be. Scripture, however, teaches the imminency of the return of the Lord.

Those who take a different view of this subject recognize the force of this argument. They therefore endeavor to show that the apostles did not believe that Christ would come at any time. A number of things are cited to prove this. Most of these are but legitimate plans of persons concerned for the future, dependent upon the Lord's opening the way, as when Paul announced his plan to go to Rome and Spain (Rom. 15:22–25, 30–32). It is claimed that Paul could not have expected Christ to return at any time when he made this plan. But that is to forget that in the same Epistle he declared that his coming was dependent upon God's will (1:10). The same can no doubt be said about all his plans (1 Cor. 4:19; 16:5–8), as also about the plans of all the other writers of the New Testament (James 4:13–16; cf. John 21:18–23). It is further maintained that the parables in Matt. 13 imply a long interval, that the parable of the Nobleman was expressly spoken because the Lord's followers "supposed that the kingdom of God was going to appear immediately" (Luke 19:11), and that the parable of the Talents states, "Now after a long time the master of those slaves came and settled accounts with them" (Matt. 25:19).

But it is improbable that the disciples held that a long time was necessary to fulfill the parables in Matt. 13. God knew that there would be a long interval, but there is nothing to indicate that the disciples knew. In the parable of the Nobleman the point is merely that the disciples thought that Christ would set up his kingdom now as he approached Jerusalem. Christ told them that he would have to return to heaven to receive the kingdom, but there is nothing to indicate that it would take a long time to receive it. And the long time in Matt. 25:19 does not need to mean more than the lifetime of the generation that existed when he went into another country. So soon did the disciples expect Christ's return that our Lord had occasionally to warn them not to give up all work in the light of it. In harmony with this is the admonition by James, "Be patient, therefore, brethren, until the coming of the Lord" (5:7). Paul had to admonish the Thessalonians to return to their daily occupations, while at the same time he spoke of himself and that generation of believers as remaining until the coming of the Lord (1 Thess. 4:11f., 15f.; 2 Thess. 3:10–12).

G. THE PROMISE TO THE CHURCH IN PHILADELPHIA

The promise in Rev. 3:10 points to a pretribulational rapture: "Because you have kept the word of My perseverance, I also will keep you from the hour of testing, that hour which is about to come upon the whole world, to test those who dwell upon the earth." Four things are to be noted in this verse.

1. The word "hour." This is used to designate the time of the coming trial and indicates a period of time. The article before "hour" makes the time a specific time. As Walvoord states, "The point is not that the church will escape the wrath of God, but that it will escape the *time* of the wrath of God."[8]

2. The extent of the trial. It is clear that this is no local tribulation, for the hour is to come "upon the whole world." Thus, it is to embrace the entire world. Mounce observes, "The hour of trial is that period of testing and tribulation that precedes the establishment of the eternal kingdom. It is mentioned in such passages as Daniel 12:2, Mark 13:14, and II Thessalonians 2:1–12."[9]

---

[8]Walvoord, *The Blessed Hope and the Tribulation,* p. 54.
[9]Mounce, *The Book of Revelation,* p. 119.

3. The purpose of this hour of trial.   It is directed at those who "dwell upon the earth." It is significant to note that the word for "dwell" is not the ordinary *oikeo*, but the strengthened form of the word, *katoikeo*, meaning those who have settled down upon the earth, who have identified themselves with it. This phrase is used over a dozen times in Revelation, and it has reference to the earth-dwellers. Alford states that in these references "the expression applies to those who are not of the church of Christ."[10] The trial is not for the church; the church will be delivered from it.

4. Who will be kept from the hour of trial.   It is said that the faithful will be kept from this hour of trial. Moffatt says:

> It is impossible from the grammar and difficult from the sense, to decide whether *terein ek* means successful endurance (pregnant sense as in John xvii.15) or absolute immunity (cf. 2 Peter ii.9), safe emergence from the trial or escape from it entirely (thanks to the timely advent of Christ, v. 11).[11]

The promise in Rev. 3:10 seems to be not merely that God will keep the faithful from temptation, as if to shield them against it, but that he will keep them from the hour of trial, the period as a whole. This seems to indicate that the believers will be taken away before the tribulation begins.

H. Certain Other Considerations

There are three other arguments which are frequently used to support the pretribulational rapture of the church. (1) There are the scattered verses in the New Testament indicating that the church will not come under God's wrath. Paul comforts the Thessalonians, "For God has not destined us for wrath, but for obtaining salvation through our Lord Jesus Christ" (1 Thess. 5:9), and again, "Jesus . . . delivers us from the wrath to come" (1 Thess. 1:10). To be sure, the church has been promised persecution and tribulation (John 16:33; Acts 5:41; 14:22; 2 Cor. 1:7; Phil. 1:29; 2 Tim. 3:12; 1 Pet. 4:13), but this persecution is not the wrath of God (Rev. 6:16f.; 14:7). The believer is looking for the "blessed hope" (Titus 2:13; cf. 1 Thess. 1:10; 4:18; 5:11; 1 John 2:28). (2) There is no mention of the church in Rev. 4–19. The term never occurs in this section. This is worthy of note because of its frequent occurrence in the first chapters and its appearance again in 22:16. If the church were on the earth, we would expect it to be mentioned frequently. And (3) many feel that the twenty-four elders of Revelation (4:4, 10; 5:5;

[10]Alford, *The Greek New Testament,* IV, p. 586.
[11]Moffatt, "The Revelation of St. John the Divine," in *Expositor's Greek Testament,* V, p. 368.

etc.) represent the church in heaven. There is, however, not sufficient evidence to be certain as to this identification. It is probably as accurate to identify them as some type of heavenly beings such as the seraphim (Isa. 6:2), cherubim (Ezek. 10:8), or living creatures (Rev. 4:6), or as some other type of angelic being around the throne of God.

In conclusion, we would call attention to a difficulty that has been pointed out about this view. Paul writes, "Behold, I tell you a mystery; we shall not all sleep, but we shall all be changed, in a moment, in the twinkling of an eye, at the last trumpet; for the trumpet will sound, and the dead will be raised imperishable, and we shall be changed" (1 Cor. 15:51f.). By common consent it is agreed that this last trumpet in 1 Cor. 15 and that of 1 Thess. 4:16 are one and the same. Some also seek to identify this trumpet with the seventh trumpet of Rev. 11:15. This view is espoused by midtribulationalists. But these two trumpets are not to be equated. The word "last" may mean last in a series, but it may also mean last in the sense of end of the age. In the Old Testament, trumpets were used for several purposes and at various times (Lev. 23:24; Num. 10:1–10), and there could be any number of "last" trumpets. So here also, there is no need to equate the two as the same. The trumpet of 1 Cor. 15:52 and 1 Thess. 4:16 cannot be the same as the seventh trumpet in the Revelation, if we remember the whole scope of the teaching concerning Christ's return.

CHAPTER XLIV

The Resurrections

There is of necessity a good bit of overlapping in the treatment of the doctrine of eschatology. Much already said about the resurrections will be repeated here, in order to treat the subject more fully. And there is much reason for such a closer examination of the Scriptures, for from the earliest dawn of history men have been asking the question, "If a man dies, will he live again?" (Job 14:14). There have always been those who have denied the resurrection (Matt. 22:23; Acts 23:8; 1 Cor. 15:12). There have perhaps also always been those who have professed to believe in a resurrection, but who have denied that it will be a bodily resurrection. It is, therefore, important that we search the Scriptures in order to ascertain just what they do teach on the subject.

I. THE CERTAINTY OF THE RESURRECTION

Whether as a matter of hope or of fear and dread, man has generally felt that there is a life after death. The early Egyptians reveal this belief in their care of the dead; the Babylonians in their dread of it as a sad and doleful existence. Socrates held that life continued after death; the American Indians looked for a future hunting ground. Brahmanism, Hinduism, Buddhism, Confucianism, and Mohammedanism all hold that man continues to exist after death. Whence this universal belief? Is this fundamental premonition of human nature a lie? No, that the mind cannot rest in the prospect of extinction affords ground for the hope that there is a life after death. But we are here concerned with more than the mere fact of existence after death; we would like to know whether that existence is conscious and whether there will be a resurrection of the body as well.

A. Existence after Death

Science, with its belief in the indestructibility of matter and the conservation of energy, cannot say that the Christian belief is unreasonable; and philosophy, with its recognition of the inequities of life, cannot well avoid postulating a life after death, when the wrongs of this life will be righted. This possibility and necessity is converted into certainty in the Scriptures. The Old Testament teaches that there is a life after death. It represents all men as going down to Sheol (the Hades of the New Testament). The wicked, of course, go there (Ps. 9:17; 31:17; 49:14; Isa. 5:14). Korah, Dathan, and Abiram are said to have gone down alive into Sheol (Num. 16:33). But the righteous also go there (Job 14:13; 17:16; Ps. 6:5; 16:10; 88:3). Jacob looked forward to going to his son Joseph in Sheol (Gen. 37:35; cf. 42:38; 44:29). Hezekiah looked upon death as an entering "the gates of Sheol" (Isa. 38:10). The idea of going into Sheol is probably also present in the oft-recurring phrase, "he was gathered to his people" (Gen. 25:8, 17; 35:29; 49:33; Num. 20:24; 27:13; Deut. 32:50; Judg. 2:10).

In the New Testament also, both the wicked and the righteous are represented as going down to Hades before the resurrection of the Lord. The rich man, we are told, went to Hades, and he and Lazarus were within speaking distance of each other in that region (Luke 16:19–31). Jesus himself went down to Hades (Acts 2:27, 31). Christ now has the keys of death and Hades (Rev. 1:18), and some day both of these will deliver up the dead in them (Rev. 20:13f.). The word "Hades" occurs ten times in the New Testament (Matt. 11:23; 16:18; Luke 10:15; 16:23; Acts 2:27, 31; Rev. 1:18; 6:8; 20:13f.). The two words, Sheol in the Old Testament, and Hades in the New Testament, are by common consent held to be exact equivalents.

If, then, the Scriptures teach that there is an existence after death, is it a conscious existence? The Old Testament is not explicit on this point. To be gathered to one's people, to go down to one's son, and similar expressions, imply such an existence, though they do not state it. Eccl. 9:5f., 10 seems to deny that it is a conscious existence, for it declares that "there is no activity or planning or wisdom in Sheol where you are going." But we must remember that this book is written from the standpoint of knowledge under the sun, that is, from the viewpoint of the natural man. Divine revelation alone can tell us of the true nature of life after death. Isa. 14:9–11, 15–17 definitely teaches that it is a conscious existence. And that which is hinted at in the Old Testament is clearly taught in the New Testament. Jesus taught it in Matt. 22:31f. and in the story of the rich man and Lazarus (Luke 16:19–31). The rich man and Lazarus could talk, think, remember, feel, and care. The same things are implied in Jesus' statement to the penitent thief that today he should be with Christ in Paradise (Luke 23:43). Incidentally, the New Testament seems to teach that there were two compartments in Hades, one for the wicked and one for the righteous. The one for the righteous was called Paradise; the one for the wicked is not named, but it is described as a place of torment. Thus, it is clear that the term "sleep," when applied to death, refers to the body only (Matt. 27:52; John 11:11–13; 1 Cor. 11:30; 15:20, 51; 1 Thess. 4:14; 5:10).

After the resurrection of Christ there seems to have come a change. From that time on, believers are represented as going into the presence of Christ at death. Thus, Paul represented his embodied condition as one in which he was "absent from the Lord," and his disembodied condition as one in which he would be "at home with the Lord" (2 Cor. 5:6–9). He expressed his desire to "depart and be with Christ, for that is very much better" (Phil. 1:23). We also see the "souls of those who had been slain" under the altar and conscious (Rev. 6:9–11). They still go to Paradise, but Paradise is now above (2 Cor. 12:2–4). It is possible that when Christ arose, he took with him not only a first-fruit of men whom he raised bodily (Matt. 27:52f.), but also the souls of all the righteous in Hades. Now all believers go into Christ's presence at death, while unbelievers continue to go to Hades, as in Old Testament times.

B. The Old Testament Teaching as to the Bodily Resurrection

To begin with, the Old Testament records the bodily raising of at least three persons: the widow's son (1 Kings 17:21f.), the Shunammite's son (2 Kings 4:32–36), and the man who revived when he touched the bones of Elisha (2 Kings 13:21). From this time on, at any rate, Israel had proof of the possibility of a bodily resurrection. But the belief in such a resurrection goes back further than that. Abraham expected that God would raise Isaac from the dead on Mt. Moriah (Gen. 22:5; Heb. 11:19).

The Psalmist was confident that he would not be left in Sheol (Ps. 16:10; cf. 17:15). That this includes a prophecy of Christ's resurrection, does not affect the argument (Acts 2:24–28). Further, we note Isaiah's expectation of a bodily resurrection (Isa. 26:19), the Lord's promise in Hosea (13:14), and his promise in Daniel (12:1–3, 13). This is not a great amount of teaching, but it begins at the time of Abraham and continues to the time of the return from Babylon. It is clear and sufficient to prove that the doctrine was taught and believed during that period.

C. The New Testament Teaching as to a Bodily Resurrection

The New Testament records the raising of five persons: Jairus' daughter (Matt. 9:24f.), the young man of Nain (Luke 7:14f.), Lazarus (John 11:43f.), Dorcas (Acts 9:40f.), and Eutychus (Acts 20:9–12). In addition, we read of the raising of many saints after the resurrection of Christ (Matt. 27:52f.). As to the teaching of a future resurrection, Christ taught it (John 5:28f.; 6:39f., 44, 54; Luke 14:14; 20:35f.) and the apostles taught it (Acts 24:15; 1 Cor. 15; Phil. 3:11; 1 Thess. 4:14–16; Rev. 20:4–6, 12f.). And finally, the resurrection of Christ is the guarantee of our own bodily resurrection (Rom. 8:11; 1 Cor. 6:14; 1 Cor. 15:20–22; 2 Cor. 4:14). He "abolished death, and brought life and immortality to light through the gospel" (2 Tim. 1:10). There is, therefore, abundant evidence that the New Testament teaches a bodily resurrection.

II. THE NATURE OF THE RESURRECTION

"But some one will say, 'How are the dead raised? And with what kind of body do they come?'" (1 Cor. 15:35). This is now our subject for investigation. We note first that the Scriptures speak of three kinds of resurrections: a judicial resurrection in which the believer has been raised with Christ (Rom. 6:4f.; Eph. 2:5f.; Col. 2:12f.), a spiritual resurrection, equivalent to regeneration (John 5:25f.), and a physical resurrection (John 5:28f.). We are concerned just now with the physical resurrection.

A. THE FACT OF THE BODILY RESURRECTION

In at least four ways the Scriptures indicate that the body is to be raised. (1) In clear statements to that effect (Ps. 16:9f.; Dan. 12:2; John 5:28f.). Paul writes of the burial and resurrection of the body, "It is sown a natural body, it is raised a spiritual body. If there is a natural body, there is also a spiritual body" (1 Cor. 15:44). A natural body is that body which consists of flesh and blood; needs food, air, and rest; and is subject to decay and pain. It is the body which is adapted to existence on this planet. The spiritual body is the body which is adapted to heavenly existence, a powerful, glorious body. It is a body like the resurrected body of our Lord. Paul states, further, that Christ will transform "the body of our humble state into conformity with the body of His glory" (Phil. 3:21). (2) In the declaration that the body is included in our redemption (Rom. 8:23; 1 Cor. 6:13–15, 19f.). When Christ died for us, he died for the whole man. The full benefits of his atonement are not realized until the body has been made immortal, an event which will take place at the resurrection. (3) In the kind of body with which Christ was raised. He was raised in a physical body (Luke 24:39; John 20:27). To deny the physical resurrection is to deny the physical resurrection of Christ (1 Cor. 15:13). (4) In the literalness of the Lord's return and the judgments. The man Christ Jesus will return to judge not disembodied spirits, but embodied men (1 Thess. 4:16f.; Rev. 20:11–13).

B. THE NATURE OF THE RESURRECTION BODY

In general it may be said that the resurrection body will not be an entirely new creation. If that were the case, it would not be the present body, but another body. But the body which is sown will be raised (1 Cor. 15:43f., 53f.). Nor, on the other hand, will the resurrection body necessarily be in every detail composed of the identical particles contained in this body (1 Cor. 15:37f.). All that Scripture warrants us in saying, is that the resurrection body will sustain a similar relation to the present body as the wheat in the stalk sustains to the wheat in the ground out of which it grew. An adult has the same body with which he was born, though it has undergone continual change and does not contain the same cells with which it was born. So the resurrection body will be the same body, though its make-up will be changed.

1. The bodies of believers. Several Scriptures state or imply that the resurrection body of believers will be like Christ's glorified body (1 Cor. 15:49; Phil. 3:21; 1 John 3:2). Some details may be mentioned from 1 Cor. 15. (1) It will not be composed of flesh and blood (vss. 50f.). Christ took on him flesh and blood (Heb. 2:14), but after his resurrection he speaks of his body as composed of flesh and bones (Luke 24:39). Thus, he was not pure spirit, and neither shall we be pure spirit at the resurrection. (2) It will be incorruptible, or imperishable (vss. 42, 53f.). It is, therefore, not subject to sickness, death, or decay. It is an enduring body. (3) It will be a glorious body (v. 43). We may get some idea of what that means by thinking of the transfiguration of Christ (Matt. 17:2), and of the description of the glorified Christ in heaven (Rev. 1:13–16). (4) It will be powerful (v. 43). That is, it will not become weary, but will be able to perform mighty feats in the service of Christ (Rev. 22:3–5). (5) It will be a spiritual body (v. 44). By that, probably is meant that its life is that of the spirit. And finally, (6) it will be a heavenly body (vss. 47–49). In 2 Cor. 5:1f. Paul speaks of a "building from God" and "our dwelling from heaven." It will be heavenly as contrasted with the present, which is earthly. These details may not fully satisfy the Christian's curiosity as to the nature of the resurrection body, but they tell us a great deal more about it than can any prognostication of man worthy of credence.

2. The bodies of unbelievers. Though the Scriptures have less to say about the resurrection of the unsaved than about the saved, the evidence for it is by no means weak or unsatisfactory. Jesus declared that the hour is coming when all that are in the tombs shall come forth, some unto the resurrection of life and some to the resurrection of judgment (John 5:28f.). He warned his disciples not to "fear those who kill the body, but are unable to kill the soul; but rather fear Him who is able to destroy both soul and body in hell" (Matt. 10:28). Before Felix, Paul declared that Israel had hope toward God, "that there shall certainly be a resurrection of both the righteous and the wicked" (Acts 24:15). Dan. 12:2 indicates that many who sleep in the dust will awake "to disgrace and everlasting contempt," and Rev. 20:12f. clearly teaches that the unsaved will be raised, judged, and cast into the lake of fire. Thus, it is clear that the unsaved too will be raised bodily. Curiosity would indeed pry into the nature of this resurrection body, but the silence of Scripture on this point indicates that we should be content with such things as have been revealed, and leave the question where Scripture leaves it—unanswered.

III. THE TIME OF THE RESURRECTIONS

Various things have already been said to prove that there is no general resurrection in which all men will arise at the same time, but they must here be gathered together to show their full force. 1 Thess. 4:16 shows that when our Lord comes into the air, only the dead in Christ will be raised. The phrase "in Christ" used here can have no other meaning than belongs to it elsewhere. It describes the fundamental, mystical union between the believer and Christ, here between the dead in Christ and Christ. Paul also limits the first resurrection to Christians when he says, "those who are Christ's at His coming" (1 Cor. 15:23). Paul believed in the resurrection of saved and unsaved, but he did not teach that they rise at the same time. John 5:28f. does not simply refer to two issues following the resurrection, but to two resurrections, the one unto life and the one unto judgment. Dan. 12:2 likewise teaches two resurrections, and not merely two issues following the one resurrection. Perhaps the clearest reference to two resurrections is found in Rev. 20:4–6. Additionally, Heb. 11:35, speaking of those who refused deliverance "in order that they might obtain a better resurrection," also points to that same expectation.

Objection has been raised to this view on the ground of certain terms. One is the repeated phrase, "on the last day" (John 6:39f., 44, 54; 11:24; cf. 12:48). But it is perfectly evident that the term "day" is sometimes used in the sense of a long period. Abraham rejoiced to see Christ's day (John 8:56). The period of the Exodus is spoken of as "the day when I took them by the hand" (Heb. 8:9) and "the day of trial in the wilderness" (Heb. 3:8). The long period of Israel's disobedience is described as "all day long" (Rom. 10:21). Jesus lamented over Jerusalem because it did not know in "this day" the things which belong unto peace (Luke 19:42). And Paul says this whole age is "the day of salvation" (2 Cor. 6:2). Peter indicates that God reckons time differently than we do when he writes, "With the Lord one day is as a thousand years, and a thousand years as one day" (2 Pet. 3:8). The hour in John 5:25, in which the spiritually dead hear Christ's voice and live, has already lasted nineteen centuries. Therefore, it seems reasonable that the hour in John 5:28, in which the dead in the tombs hear his voice and come forth, could span a period of time sufficient to include two distinct and specific resurrections.

It is clear that the first resurrection will take place when Christ comes in the air (1 Cor. 15:23; 1 Thess. 4:16). All the saved of this age will then be raised. The Old Testament saints and those tribulation saints killed during the tribulation will be raised at the moment of Christ's coming to earth (Dan. 12:1f.; Rev. 20:4). Thus, the first resurrection will be completed. The second resurrection will take place a thousand years later (Rev. 20:5, 11–13). It seems as if God is as longsuffering as possible with the unsaved dead. They are in torments in the intermediate state, but they are not in the final place of punishment as yet. Thus, the goodness of God puts off the day of final reckoning until after the millennium. But though it tarry, it will surely come. The unsaved might well wish to remain disembodied, but their wishes will have nothing to do with the facts. They too will come forth in their bodies and will suffer the eternal punishment of God in their bodies.

CHAPTER XLV

The Judgments

Although the two resurrections do already indicate man's future estate, they will not obviate the judgments. The whole philosophy of the future judgments rests upon the sovereign right of God to punish disobedience and the personal right of the individual to plead his case in court. Though God is sovereign, as judge of all the earth, he will do right (Gen. 18:25). He will do this not in order to submit to an external law, but as the expression of his own character. The individual will have the opportunity to show why he acted as he did and to know the reasons for his sentence. These are fundamental factors in every righteous government. Insofar as human governments follow this order, they are imitating God's methods of government. What does the Bible say of these judgments?

I. THE CERTAINTY OF THE JUDGMENTS

That there will be a judgment both of the righteous and of the unrighteous, is intimated by men's consciences. The author of Ecclesiastes, speaking from the standpoint of the natural man, encourages young men to live after the desires of their heart, but adds by way of warning, that for all these things God will bring them into judgment (11:9). In the next chapter he writes, "God will bring every act to judgment, everything which is hidden, whether it is good or evil" (12:14). Paul speaks of the conscience as either excusing or else defending men, in view of "the day when, according to my gospel, God will judge the secrets of men through Christ Jesus" (Rom. 2:16). And Heb. 10:27 declares that those who sin willfully have "a certain terrifying expectation of judgment." It is impossible to think of the depths of depravity to which man would descend if the fear of a future judgment were taken away from him. In other words, conscience seems to say that if there is no judgment, there ought to be one.

This spontaneous feeling of the human heart is corroborated by Scripture. In Genesis, Abraham recognized God as the judge of all the earth (18:25), and Hannah said that "the Lord will judge the ends of the earth" (1 Sam. 2:10). David spoke of the Lord "coming to judge the earth" (1 Chron. 16:33; cf. Ps. 96:13; 98:9), and said that he had "established His throne for judgment" (Ps. 9:7). In Joel, God says, "Let the nations be aroused and come up to the valley of Jehoshaphat, for there I will sit to judge all the surrounding nations" (3:12; cf. Isa. 2:4). In the New Testament this fact is more frequently asserted. Jesus said, "For the Son of Man is going to come in the glory of His Father with His angels; and will then recompense every man according to his deeds" (Matt. 16:27). At Athens Paul declared that God had "fixed a day in which He will judge the world in righteousness through a Man whom He has appointed" (Acts 17:31; cf. Rom. 2:16; 2 Thess. 1:7-9). He further declared that "we must all appear before the judgment seat of Christ, that each one may be recompensed for his deeds in the body, according to what he has done, whether good or bad" (2 Cor. 5:10; cf. Rom. 14:10). The writer to the Hebrews says that after death comes the judgment (9:27). It was John who "saw the dead, the great and the small, standing before the throne" to be judged (Rev. 20:12). God has given assurance of the fact of judgment by raising Christ, the judge, from the dead (Acts 17:31).

II. THE OBJECT OF THE JUDGMENTS

Why will it be necessary for God to conduct these judgments? Strong says, "The object of the final judgment is not the ascertainment but the manifestation, of character, and the assignment of outward conditions corresponding to it."[1] God already knows the conditions of all moral creatures, and the last day will only be a revelation of the righteous judgment of God. Our memory, conscience, and character are preparations and will be evidences for this final exposure (Luke 16:25; Rom. 2:15f.; Eph. 4:19; Heb. 3:8; 10:27). The judgments will take place in order to show God's righteousness in treating men as he treats them. Before God's tribunals, every mouth will be closed (cf. Rom. 3:19). It is not necessary to suppose that everyone will acknowledge that he receives the just reward for his deeds, but it is implied that no one will have any just cause for complaint, and so will not make a complaint.

III. THE JUDGE

God is the judge of all (Heb. 12:23), but he will perform his work through Jesus Christ. "He has given all judgment to the Son" (John 5:22), and has done so "because He is the Son of Man" (John 5:27). Of this fact, he has "furnished proof to all men by raising Him from the dead" (Acts 17:31). Christ will judge "the living and the dead" (Acts 10:42; 2 Tim. 4:1). He will judge the believers for their works (2 Cor. 5:10; cf. Rom. 14:10); the beast,

---

[1]Strong, *Systematic Theology*, p. 1025.

false prophet, and their armies (Rev. 19:19–21); the nations gathered before him (Matt. 25:31f.); Satan (Rev. 20:1–3, 10; cf. Gen. 3:15; Heb. 2:14); the nations of the millennial earth (Isa. 2:4; Ezek. 37:24f.; Dan. 7:13f.; Rev. 11:15); and the impenitent dead (Rev. 20:11–15). This function has been assigned to him as a reward for his humiliation (Phil. 2:9–11), and because he alone is qualified for the task. As God, he has the insight (Isa. 11:3) and the authority to judge men; as man, he understands and sympathizes with man. In his person, justice and mercy meet, and as judge of all the earth, he will do right (Gen. 18:25).

IV. THE VARIOUS JUDGMENTS

In a comprehensive survey of the subject we must begin with the judgment already past. In Christ our sins were judged once and for all (Isa. 53:4–6; John 1:29; 2 Cor. 5:21; Gal. 3:13; Heb. 10:10–14; 1 Pet. 2:24; 1 John 2:2). The believer in Christ is accordingly freed from the guilt and penalty of sin, because Christ has accepted the guilt and paid the penalty for him. No believer will be judged for his sins, since he has been judged for them already in Christ (John 5:24). There is, however, a present judgment for believers. It is the judgment of sin in their own life. Paul admonishes believers to judge themselves in private (1 Cor. 11:31f.) and in church life (1 Cor. 5:5; 1 Tim. 1:20; 5:19f.). The Lord chastens his disobedient children in order to induce them to judge and put away sin out of their lives (2 Sam. 7:14f.; 12:13f.; Heb. 12:5–13). But we are here concerned with the judgments still future. We say judgments, for there is no more a general judgment than a general resurrection. The time elements, the subjects, and the issues indicate that there are at least seven future judgments.

A. The Judgment of Believers

As we have seen, when the Lord returns, he will judge believers for their works (Rom. 14:10; 1 Cor. 3:11–15; 4:5; 2 Cor. 5:10). Everyone will be asked to give an account of the use he has made of the talents (Matt. 25:14–30), the pounds or minas (Luke 19:11–27), and the opportunities (Matt. 20:1–16) that have been entrusted to him. The day will declare whether a man has built of wood, hay, and straw or of gold, silver, and precious stones (1 Cor. 3:12). If of the former, his works will be burnt up, and yet he will be saved so as through fire (v. 15); if of the latter, he will receive a reward (v. 14). Scripture lists several crowns or trophies: the incorruptible or imperishable crown (1 Cor. 9:25), the crown of righteousness (2 Tim. 4:8), the crown of life (James 1:12; Rev. 2:10), the crown of glory (1 Pet. 5:4), and the crown of rejoicing or exultation (1 Thess. 2:19; cf. Phil. 4:1).

B. The Judgments of Israel

In a peculiar sense, the tribulation will be the day of Jacob's trouble, but we are told, "he will be saved from it" (Jer. 30:7). We note the persecutions of Israel during that period in the Revelation (12:6, 13–17); only the remnant sealed in their foreheads will be spared (Rev. 7:1–8). But it appears that there will be a further judgment issuing from God himself in connection with the regathering of the dispersed of Israel. Ezekiel, speaking of this judgment, describes it as a purging out of the rebels from among Israel on their way back to the holy land. They will be brought out of the land of their sojourn, but they will perish in the wilderness and not enter into the land of Israel (Ezek. 20:33–38). Malachi seems to have this same judgment in mind when he represents the Lord as sitting as a refiner, purifying the sons of Levi (Mal. 3:2–5). These judgments are on the earth and take place in connection with the Lord's return. They decide the question as to which of the Israelites shall get back into the holy land and constitute the Israel of the coming age.

C. The Judgment of Babylon

Under the figure of a woman, the Revelation pictures for us a federated religious system (17:1–19:4). At first the woman rides the beast. This shows that the ecclesiastical system will for a time dominate the political system. But the ten horns (kings) will turn and hate the woman, make her desolate, and destroy her. Then the beast will advance himself to the place of supreme religious authority. There seems to be a definite coalition between the religious and commercial unions as well. When Babylon, as a religious system, is destroyed, she will raise up her head in a great world-wide commercial organization. But her prosperity will be short-lived. In one day the Lord God will judge and completely destroy her. The merchants of the earth will bewail her destruction, but the inhabitants of heaven will rejoice and sing "Hallelujah!" when she is overthrown. Her judgment takes place before the Lord's return to earth (Rev. 19:1–4, 11–21), and her judgment is an eternal punishment (Rev. 19:19–21).

D. The Judgment of the Beast, the False Prophet, and Their Armies

The evil spirits emanating from the dragon, the beast, and the false prophet will, near the end of the tribulation, go forth and gather the nations of the earth for the battle of the great day of God (Rev. 16:12–16). Ostensibly, they gather to capture Jerusalem and the Jews in Palestine (Zech. 12:1–9; 13:8–14:2); but just when victory seems assured, Christ will descend from heaven with his armies (Rev. 19:11–16) and intervene in behalf of Israel. Then these hordes will turn to fight the Son of God, but the conflict will be short and decisive. The beast and the false prophet will be taken and cast alive into the lake of fire (Rev. 19:19f.), and their armies slain with the sword that proceeds out of Christ's mouth (2 Thess. 1:7–10; 2:8; Rev. 19:21). Thus, the political opposition will be broken and the way be opened for the ushering in of the reign of Christ. It should be noted that this judgment will take place at the return of Christ to earth. It will involve only the armies with their leaders who have come out in opposition to Christ. The issue is the lake of fire and eternal condemnation.

E. The Judgment of the Nations

Passages such as Joel 3:11–17; Matt. 25:31–46; and 2 Thess. 1:7–10 seem to deal with this judgment. This judgment must be distinguished from the one before the great white throne, for this one precedes the millennium. It must also be distinguished from the judgment of the beast, the false prophet, and their armies. The nations send the armies, but are distinct from them. After Christ has dealt with the armies, he will gather together the nations for judgment. It should be noted that the sheep go into the kingdom, and the goats into eternal punishment. But it should also be noted that though the treatment of the Lord's brethren, probably Israel, is mentioned in connection with the judgment, the deeper reasons for the judgment lie in the fact that the sheep have eternal life, and the goats do not have it.

F. The Judgment of Satan and His Angels

During the tribulation, Satan will be cast down to the earth (Rev. 12:7–9, 12). When Christ comes to the earth, Satan will be bound and cast into the abyss for a thousand years (Rev. 20:1–3). After the thousand years, he will be loosed for a little season. During this time, he will go forth once again to deceive the nations of the earth and will succeed in gathering together a great multitude to war against the camp of the saints and the beloved city (Rev. 20:7–9; cf. Ezek. 38, 39). But fire will come down out of heaven and devour them all. No doubt they will come up for judgment before the great white throne a little later and be cast into the lake of fire with the rest of the unsaved. After that, Satan himself will be judged and cast into the lake of fire (Rev. 20:9f.). Probably at this time also the fallen angels will be judged (2 Pet. 2:4; Jude 6). We are told that the eternal fire is prepared for "the devil and his angels" (Matt. 25:41), and this may be the time when they will be consigned to their doom (cf. Matt. 8:29; Luke 8:31).

G. The Judgment of the Unsaved Dead

This judgment takes place after the millennium (Rev. 20:11–15; 21:8). At the end of the millennium the second resurrection takes place (Rev. 20:5); a blessing is pronounced upon those who have a part in the first resurrection, but not upon those who rise at the time of the second resurrection. It is implied that their lot is not a happy one. They are the unsaved of all past history. They arise and appear before the great white throne. This group will include rich and beggar, free and slave, king and subject, educated and uneducated, employer and employee; all will stand equally guilty before the judge.

1. The basis of this judgment.   Two things may be said as to the basis of this judgment. (1) These people will be judged "from the things which were written in the books" (Rev. 20:12). These are evidently the books in which the names of the unbelievers are recorded. But besides the books, we read of "another book . . . which is the book of life" (Rev. 20:12). This is the book of divine grace in which the names of the heirs of grace are recorded (Luke 10:20; Rev. 3:5; 13:8; 17:8; 20:12, 15; 21:27). Further, (2) these will be judged according to their works. "Judgment proceeds on the evidence supplied both by the record of deeds and the book of life."[2] The believer will be rewarded according to his works, but the unbeliever will be judged according to them (cf. Rom. 2:5–11). Ignorance of the Lord's will will not excuse anyone, but it will ameliorate the punishment (Luke 12:47f.).

2. The duration of the punishment.   All those whose names are not found written in the book of life will be cast into the lake of fire (Rev. 20:15). The lake of fire is said to be the second death (Rev. 21:8). This brings with it the question, will the future punishment be eternal? It will be, according to the clear and awful revelation of the Word of God. Between the rich man and Lazarus there was a great gulf fixed, so that passage from the one realm to the other was impossible (Luke 16:26). In Gehenna "their worm does not die, and the fire is not quenched" (Mark 9:48). This seems to be a quotation from Isa. 66:24, and it implies that there will always be something for the worm to feed on and for the fire to consume. The smoke of the torment of the worshippers of the beast is said to go up "forever and ever" (Rev. 14:11). Surely, they are not singled out from among the earth's wicked to receive a severer punishment than the other equally wicked men! The beast and the false prophet seem to be alive after the one thousand years of punishment in the lake of fire (Rev. 19:20; 20:10). And the wicked are cast into this same lake of fire (Rev. 20:12–15; 21:8). It would have been good for Judas not to have been born (Matt. 26:24). This could hardly be said of a man that would after centuries and millenniums be finally restored to blissful life.

But perhaps the most important item is the meaning of the Greek words

---

[2]Mounce, *The Book of Revelation*, p. 366.

aion and *aionios*. The former occurs over 120 times in the New Testament and is translated by such words as "world" (2 Cor. 4:4), "age" (1 Cor. 1:20), "never" (John 4:14), and "forever" (John 6:51). With the preposition *eis*, it always implies duration without end. The adjective *aionios* occurs some 70 times in the New Testament. It is used in reference to God (Rom. 16:26), Christ (2 Tim. 1:9), the Holy Spirit (Heb. 9:14), the blessings for believers (2 Thess. 2:16; Heb. 9:12), the punishment of the wicked (2 Thess. 1:9), etc. Sometimes the term occurs twice in a phrase, "forever and ever" (lit., "the age of the age," Heb. 1:8), and often in the plural, "forevermore" (lit., "the ages of the ages," Gal. 1:5). Notice also another type of references: Ps. 52:5; Matt. 12:31f.; Mark 3:29; Heb. 6:4–6; 10:26–29; 2 Pet. 2:17; Jude 13. Perhaps the strongest single reference is Matt. 25:46, where the eternity of the punishment of the wicked is set over against the eternity of the bliss of the saved. If the believer will live eternally in the presence of God and in his favor, the unbeliever will exist eternally away from the beneficial presence of God.

3. Objections to this doctrine. Various objections to this doctrine have been offered. (1) The wicked will be destroyed (Ps. 9:5; 92:7; 2 Thess. 1:8f.). To this we reply that Noah's generation was destroyed (Luke 17:27), and so were the cities of Sodom and Gomorrah (Luke 17:29), but they shall yet come up for judgment (Matt. 11:24). Destruction does not mean annihilation; rather, whatever has been destroyed can no longer serve the use for which it was designed. (2) The wicked will perish (Ps. 37:20; Prov. 10:28; Luke 13:1–3). But to perish is not to cease to exist. The disciples cried out, "Save us, Lord; we are perishing!" (Matt. 8:25), but they did not mean that they were in danger of annihilation. Caiaphas said, "That the whole nation should not perish" (John 11:50), but he merely meant to express his fear that the Romans would come and take away their place and nation. Paul uses the same word of the physical weakening of the body. He says, "Though our outer man is decaying (perish), yet our inner man is being renewed day by day" (2 Cor. 4:16). (3) For the wicked the day that shall come will "leave them neither root nor branch" (Mal. 4:1). But that reference has to do with the body only. Physically they will be consumed, but spiritually they will continue to exist (cf. also Prov. 2:22). (4) The wicked are said to die in their sins (Ezek. 18:4; John 8:21; Rom. 6:23). But death is separation, not extinction. Witness the rich man and Lazarus (Luke 16:19–31) and the souls under the altar (Rev. 6:9–11). If the first death does not mean extinction, how can we hold that the second does (Rev. 20:15; 21:8; cf. 19:20; 20:10)? (5) All things are to be restored. This is a partial statement of Acts 3:21; the full statement is limited by the words, "about which God spoke by the mouth of His holy prophets from ancient time." It speaks of the coming kingdom of God on earth. (6) The strongest objection is thought to be the idea that a God of love could not punish his creatures eternally. But this is to forget that at death character is fixed, and that the law of congruity requires that the living be separated from the dead. It is not a question of God's love, but of the soul's life. But having said all this, we repeat that there will be degrees of punishment (Luke 12:47f.; Rom. 2:5f.; Rev. 20:12f.), according to God's justice.

CHAPTER XLVI

The Millennium

The word "millennium" comes from the Latin *mille* and *annus*, meaning a thousand years. The doctrine of the millennium is often spoken of as *chiliasm* (from *chilioi*, meaning a thousand). It holds that Christ will reign over an earthly kingdom for a thousand years. It implies that Christ will come back before the millennium. This is known as the doctrine of premillennialism. Those who hold that Christ will come back after a period of universal peace and righteousness, hold the doctrine of postmillennialism. Those who deny that there will be a millennium hold what is known as the doctrine of amillennialism. The word "millennium" does not occur in the Bible, but the thousand years are mentioned some six times in Rev. 20:2–7. We have already shown that Christ's coming will be premillennial; now we look at the millennium itself, examining its scriptural basis and its character.

I. THE SCRIPTURAL BASIS OF THE MILLENNIUM

Man's hope and expectation has value only insofar as it is based on Scripture. What is the scriptural support for the millennium?

A. THE DAY OF THE LORD

The day of the Lord is referred to in 2 Thess. 2:2, and in many Old Testament passages (Joel 2:11; Amos 5:18; Zeph. 1:14–16; Mal. 4:2; cf. Isa. 10:20; 27:1–6). At his first advent, Christ came as the sunrise from on high (Luke 1:78). While he was in the world, he was the light of the world (John 9:5). But men loved darkness rather than light (John 3:19), and so they rejected him (John 1:11). Now the church is the light of the world (Matt. 5:14; Phil. 2:15), reflecting the light of the invisible sun (2 Cor. 4:6). Already "the night is almost gone, and the day is at hand" (Rom. 13:12). The morning star will herald the breaking of a new day (Rev. 2:28; cf. 2 Pet. 1:19), and the sun of righteousness will fully usher it in shortly thereafter (Mal. 4:2). This is the period of which prophets, poets, and sages have spoken; it is earth's coming jubilee or sabbath.

B. The Promised Kingdom

Furthermore, the God of heaven will set up a kingdom that is never to be destroyed (Dan. 2:44; 7:13f., 26f.; Rev. 11:15). This is not the present spiritual kingdom, for it will be set up only after the ten-kingdom empire has come and passed out of existence. It is evident that this kingdom will not interpenetrate the kingdoms of this world, but replace them. Demolition is not conversion. In order to keep his covenant with David (2 Sam. 7:11–16), sealed with an oath (Ps. 89:3f., 20–37), God must restore the earthly kingdom. When the realization of this hope seemed to sink forever at the capture of Jerusalem by the Babylonians, God reaffirmed the promise he had given to David (Jer. 33:19–22). The angel Gabriel declared to Mary that the Lord God would give to Christ "the throne of His father David" (Luke 1:32). To show his qualification for this position Matthew traces his descent from Abraham, through David, to his adopted father, Joseph (Matt. 1:1–16); and Luke traces his descent from Adam, through David, to his mother Mary (Luke 3:23–38).

C. The Revealed Purpose of Christ

The revealed purpose of Christ in his coming back to earth is to set up his kingdom (Matt. 25:31–46; Luke 19:12–15; Rev. 19:11–20:6). Jesus has ascended into heaven and is now seated with his Father in his throne, but the time is coming when he will sit upon his own throne (Matt. 19:28; 25:31; Rev. 3:21). The disciples looked forward to the setting up of such a kingdom. Jesus refused to reveal to them the time of its setting up, but he never rebuked nor corrected them for holding such a belief (Acts 1:6f.). The sons of Zebedee were selfish in their request that they might sit the one on his right hand and the other on his left, but the Lord did not rebuke them for expecting such a kingdom. More than that, he implied that their hope was well founded when he declared that these places would be assigned to those for whom they had been prepared by the Father (Matt. 20:20–24). Peter referred to the day of restitution as the time when Jesus would return (Acts 3:19–21). Paul must have taught that Christ would be an earthly king, at Thessalonica, for the populace could hardly have become enraged at the thought of a king who ruled in the realm of the spirit (Acts 17:7). And John predicted and portrayed the coming of Christ to set up this kingdom (Rev. 19:11–20:6).

From this it would seem to be clear that the Scriptures teach that there will be a period during which peace and righteousness will reign upon the earth, and that, therefore, the amillennial view is untenable. The postmillennial view is also untenable because Christ will be reigning physically and literally here upon the earth. The view that things are getting better and better upon the earth, and that righteousness is increasing, has met with resounding defeat with the advent of the two world wars and the events of history since the second world war.

II. THE CHARACTER OF THE MILLENNIUM

It is difficult in a few words to set forth the teaching of the Bible on this point; we find ourselves overwhelmed with material concerning the future. Without attempting to be exhaustive, we shall gather together the main ideas under seven appropriate heads.

A. As Regards Christ

Christ will be personally present on earth and sit on the throne of his father David. He will reign over all the earth (Ps. 72:6–11; Isa. 2:2–4; 11:1–5; Jer. 23:5f.; Zech. 14:9). Two things will characterize his kingdom: universal peace (Ps. 72:7; Isa. 2:4) and universal righteousness (Isa. 11:4f.; Jer. 23:5f.; cf. Heb. 7:2). But before this universal peace will set in, there will first be worldwide war (Joel 3:9f.; Rev. 16:14). The rider on the white horse in Rev. 6:1–4 is not the same as the one in Rev. 19:11. The former is probably the prince of the revived Roman Empire, and his rule of peace will be of but short duration (1 Thess. 5:3). Righteousness will be maintained in the earth by the speedy judgment of sin (Zech. 14:17–19). Jesus will rule with a rod of iron (Ps. 2:8f.; Rev. 2:27; 19:15). Satan will be removed from the earth, and he will not be deceiving the nations any longer (Rev. 20:2f.).

B. As Regards the Church

The church will reign with Christ (Luke 19:16–19; 1 Cor. 6:2; 2 Tim. 2:12; Rev. 2:27; 5:9f.; 20:4–6). The church-state nation of early medieval and medieval times was premature, but it will yet find realization. Old Testament saints will also reign with Christ, and the church will sit with Christ in his throne (Rev. 3:21). It would seem that the believers will have individual rather than collective responsibility in the kingdom (Luke 19:16–19), but for the most part the details connected with that reign must be left unsettled.

C. As Regards Israel

Most of the teaching concerning this period affects Israel, especially insofar as the Old Testament is concerned. We note that Israel is to be regathered (Isa. 11:10–13; Jer. 16:14f.; 23:5–8; 30:6–11; Ezek. 37:1–4; Matt. 24:20–33). The establishment of the state of Israel in Palestine is surely a forerunner of the ultimate regathering. A good many Israelites will be brought out of the land of their sojourn, but because of a rebellious spirit will not be permitted to enter the land (Ezek. 20:33–38). Then Israel will repent and be converted (Isa. 66:8; Jer. 31:31–37; Ezek. 36:24–29; 37:1–14; Zech. 12:10–13:2; Rom. 11:25f.). Finally, they will receive him who came to be their Savior long ago, and their acceptance of the Lord will be life from the dead (Rom. 11:15). Next we find that Ephraim and Judah are to be reunited (Isa. 11:13; Jer. 3:18; Ezek. 37:16–22; Hos. 1:11). Further, we note that the temple and its worship are to be restored (Ezek. 37:26–28; 40–46; Zech. 14:16f.). When we remember that sacrifices can be memorial as well as typical, we see no reason why this prophecy too should not be interpreted literally. Again, Palestine is to be divided among the tribes (Ezek. 47, 48) and to be Israel's possession forever (Ezek. 34:28; 37:25). Further, Israel is to have her judges restored to her (Isa. 1:26; Matt. 19:28). And finally, Israel is to evangelize the Gentiles (Isa. 66:19; Zech. 8:13, 20–23). No doubt, this refers to the nations that will be born during the millennium, for at the outset the millennium will consist of converted people only.

D. As Regards the Nations

Following the judgment of the nations, the sheep will enter the kingdom (Matt. 25:34–40). They will form the nucleus of the kingdom, together with restored and converted Israel. But it is evident that multitudes will be born during that age (Isa. 65:20; Jer. 30:20; Mic. 4:1–5; Zech. 8:4–6), and these will need to be evangelized. Israel will be the evangelists, perhaps, to these Gentiles (Isa. 66:19; Zech. 8:13, 20–23; Acts 15:16f.). Finally, we note that the Gentiles will go up to worship at Jerusalem, especially at the annual feast of tabernacles (Isa. 2:2–4; Zech. 14:16–19). Then we will have a united people of God and a united worship (Isa. 19:23–25).

E. As Regards Satan

At the beginning of this period, Satan will be bound and cast into the abyss for a thousand years (Rev. 20:1–3). No doubt the evil spirits will be incarcerated with him. For this time he will not deceive the nations, as he has been doing. He will not only be made powerless by the binding with a chain, but also be removed from the scene of the action. We can scarcely realize what a change that will bring into human life. Of course, man will still have a carnal nature, and all manner of mischief can spring from this source alone. But, undoubtedly, when Satan is removed to the abyss, the temptations to sin will be greatly reduced. The difference will be especially noticeable because of the freedom he has exercised during the tribulation period just preceding. The demons indicated in the day of Christ that they knew that they were destined for the abyss (Matt. 8:29; Luke 8:31). No doubt, Satan, too, knows that he is to be thrust into this place. Some think that the angel who binds Satan is Christ; others think that some other angel will perform this work. We need not think of a material chain; it is sufficient to see in the language an assurance that he will be made powerless and be removed from the earth.

F. As Regards Nature

This is the time which Jesus calls "the regeneration" (Matt. 19:28). It is creation's rebirth. Creation is now groaning and travailing in pain, but it will be delivered from the bondage of corruption when Christ returns (Rom. 8:19–22). Great topographical changes will take place (Isa. 35:1f.; 55:13; Zech. 14:4–10). The nature of ferocious animals will be changed (Isa. 11:6–9; 35:9; 65:25; Ezek. 34:25). Rain and soil-fertility will be restored (Isa. 35:2, 6f.; Ezek. 34:6f.; Joel 2:22–26); crop failure will occur only for those who fail to come to worship at Jerusalem (Zech. 14:17–19). Human life will be prolonged, but there will be deaths during that period (Isa. 65:20). Sickness will decrease with the decrease of sin, but it will not be entirely removed.

G. As Regards Conditions in General

The Scriptures represent this period as one of great joy and happiness. Physical healing will be granted to many (Isa. 35:5f.); the ransomed of the Lord will return and come with singing to Zion, and everlasting joy will be upon their heads; they shall obtain gladness and joy, and sorrow and sighing will be done away with (Isa. 35:10; 51:11). It will be a time of great material prosperity and security (Mic. 4:2–5). It will be a time when "the earth will be full of the knowledge of the Lord as the waters cover the sea" (Isa. 11:9). Friendly relations will exist, not only between individuals, but also between nations, and men will no longer learn war (Isa. 2:4). Man's headship in creation, lost through the fall and regained through the death of Christ, will be restored (Gen. 1:28; 3:17–19; Heb. 2:5–10).

CHAPTER XLVII

The Final State

It is evident that the millennium is not the final state, for the very word "millennium" indicates its temporary character. What are some of the final events of history?

I. THE FINAL STATE OF SATAN

This was mentioned when the destiny of angels was considered, but a few details need to be added.

A. HE WILL BE LOOSED FROM HIS PRISON

The Scriptures teach that at the close of the thousand years Satan will be loosed for a little time (Rev. 20:3, 7–10). Why he is loosed is not stated, but some purpose in the divine plan must call for it. Perhaps it is to show the insincerity of many who have submitted to Christ during the millennium; perhaps it is also to prove that a thousand years in the abyss have not served to change Satan. During this interim, Satan will gather together the nations, Gog and Magog, the number of whom is as the sand of the sea. Under his leadership, these armies will proceed to compass the camp of the saints about, and the beloved city. This city is, no doubt, the city of Jerusalem. But the contest is short-lived and the issue decisive. Fire will fall down out of heaven and devour those armies (cf. Ezek. 38, 39).

B. HE WILL BE FINALLY JUDGED AND SENTENCED

Thus, the career of Satan and his followers will come to an end, but they must yet appear before the great white throne for judgment with the rest of the lost. At this time Satan will be judged and consigned to his final place of punishment, the lake of fire.

II. THE FINAL JUDGMENT

The next thing mentioned is the judgment before the great white throne of the resurrected unbelievers (Rev. 20:11–15; 21:8). The nature of this judgment has already been considered; here a few additional details can be mentioned. It appears that this judgment will take place somewhere in the skies, for we are told that "earth and heaven fled away" (Rev. 20:11). The language leads us to suppose that the appearance of the throne, with the Lord sitting on it, is the cause of this. Seemingly, this judgment deals only with the unsaved, though perhaps those believers who died during the millennium are judged at this time as well. Here we have the second resurrection, and it takes place after the thousand years. It is interesting to note that the sea will give up its dead, as will also death and Hades. After all whose names are not found written in the book of life have been cast into the lake of fire, death and Hades themselves will be cast into this place of punishment. This judgment is to be distinguished from that of the nations (Matt. 25:31–46). Further, the second death is not to be considered annihilation, but eternal punishment.

III. THE FINAL KINGDOM

It is, apparently, at this time that Christ will deliver "up the kingdom to the God and Father, when He has abolished all rule and all authority and power" (1 Cor. 15:24). Death is the last enemy that will be abolished, and so this seems to be the time when Christ will deliver the kingdom to God (1 Cor. 15:26). There is no break between the millennium and the eternal state, except for the great-white-throne judgment. Satan's hosts do not succeed in their attack; in fact, it is not even certain that they actually make an attack upon the camp of the saints and the beloved city. All they will do is to come up against it, when the fire will fall from heaven and consume them. The temporal phase of the kingdom having thus come to an end, Christ will turn it over to the Father. "And when all things are subjected to Him, then the Son Himself also will be subjected to the One who subjected all things to Him, that God may be all in all" (1 Cor. 15:28). This probably means that the Son, who during the millennium was the supreme ruler on earth, will again take his eternal place, and the Father, Son, and Holy Spirit, one God, will then be all in all. Thus, the eternal state will be ushered in.

IV. THE NEW CREATION

There will be a new heaven, a new earth, and a new Jerusalem.

A. THE NEW HEAVEN AND THE NEW EARTH

Several passages of Scripture bring them to our attention (Isa. 65:17; 66:22; 2 Pet. 3:10–13; Rev. 21:1f.). They are called "new," but this does not mean new in the absolute sense, for the earth abideth forever (Ps. 104:5; 119:90; Eccl. 1:4). The passages of Scripture which speak of the earth passing away (Matt. 5:18; Mark 13:31; Heb. 1:10–13; Rev. 21:1) do not signify a passing into nonexistence, but rather they suggest the idea of transition. Neither heaven nor earth will be annihilated. As during the millennium, these will be regenerated (Matt. 19:28), so in the new creation, they will be sanctified (2 Pet. 3:10–13). Why should it be thought a strange thing that matter is to exist forever? If God desires it to continue, then all human opinion to the contrary does not count. We note that as righteousness reigned on earth during the millennium, so it will dwell on the new earth (2 Pet. 3:13). Some of the redeemed will, no doubt, be at home in the new heaven, but even those who dwell on the new earth will have contact with the new heaven.

B. The New Jerusalem

The final subject of prophecy is the New Jerusalem (Rev. 21:2–22:5). Needless to say, the New Jerusalem must be distinguished from both the new heaven and the new earth, for it is represented as coming down out of heaven, and the kings of the earth are said to bring their glory to it (Rev. 21:2, 24). Some hold that this city appears over the earth during the millennium and is the home of the saints who are already with Christ, but the mention of the appearing of the new heaven and the new earth in the preceding verse makes it seem improbable that the writer is here going back to the beginning of the millennium. We take it, therefore, that the New Jerusalem will appear only after the new heaven and the new earth have appeared. Note briefly the description of this city.

1. Its character. There is abundant reason for holding that this is a literal city. It has foundations, gates, walls, and streets. It has the measurements of a cube (Rev. 21:16), which may signify either a geometric cube or a pyramid. Its foundations are garnished with "every kind of precious stone" (Rev. 21:19f.), twelve of which are mentioned. It has twelve gates, bearing the names of the twelve tribes of Israel (Rev. 21:12f.); and the twelve foundations bear the names of the twelve apostles (Rev. 21:14). The wall is of jasper and the city is of pure gold (Rev. 21:18). Every gate is a pearl (Rev. 21:21), and the gates are never closed (Rev. 21:25), though twelve angels stand before them (Rev. 21:12). Its street is of pure gold (Rev. 21:21), and there is a river of life and the tree of life (Rev. 22:1f.). The city has "no need of the sun or of the moon to shine upon it, for the glory of God has illumined it, and its lamp is the Lamb" (Rev. 21:23). Truly it is a city of perfect security and beauty!

2. Its inhabitants. The New Jerusalem is said to be the bride, the Lamb's wife (Rev. 21:9f.; cf. John 14:2). And yet it is evident that this is a figure of speech, a metonymy, for people live in it (Rev. 21:27; 22:3-5). Mystery Babylon had a city; so the true church has a city. Perhaps this is the city for which Abraham looked (Heb. 11:10; cf. vss. 15f.); it is the one that believers today seek (Heb. 13:14). The city has no need of a temple, "for the Lord God, the Almighty, and the Lamb, are its temple" (Rev. 21:22). While it would seem to be the home of the redeemed, it is clear that both the Father and the Son will dwell in it also. This may not be their constant abiding place, for heaven is that; but it certainly will be a place frequented by them, if we may use such language of those who are omnipresent. But surely God will dwell with his people.

3. Its blessedness. The saved nations are said to walk by its light (Rev. 21:24). Does this suggest, perhaps, that the city will be suspended over the new earth? There is no night there, for the glory of the Lord illumines it (Rev. 21:23, 25). The kings of the earth will bring their glory to it (Rev. 21:24, 26); this means their praise and worship. Apparently, they do not reside in the city, but make visits to it. We are told that there will be no more curse; that the throne of God and of the Lamb will be there (Rev. 22:3; cf. 1 Cor. 15:24); that his servants will serve him, having his name in their foreheads; that they will see his face; and that they will reign with him forever and ever (Rev. 22:3-5).

When we consider God's plan and provision for man, we may well exclaim with Paul, "Oh, the depth of the riches both of the wisdom and knowledge of God! How unsearchable are His judgments and unfathomable His ways!" (Rom. 11:33). We must praise him as we think of his grace toward us who by grace "have been saved through faith" (Eph. 2:8). God has "raised us up with Him, and seated us with Him in the heavenly places, in Christ Jesus, in order that in the ages to come He might show the surpassing riches of His grace in kindness toward us in Christ Jesus" (Eph. 2:6f.).

Bibliography*

Alford, Henry. *The Greek Testament.* Chicago: Moody Press, 1968. 4 vols.

Allis, Oswald T. *The Five Books of Moses.* Philadelphia: The Presbyterian and Reformed Publishing Company, 1949.

Archer, Gleason L. *A Survey of Old Testament Introduction.* Chicago: Moody Press, 1964.

Baker, Charles F. *A Dispensational Theology.* Grand Rapids: Grace Bible College Publications, 1971.

Bancroft, Emery H. *Christian Theology.* Grand Rapids: Zondervan Publishing House, rev. and ed., 1949.

Barnhouse, Donald Grey. "Adam and Modern Science," *Eternity Magazine,* Vol. 11, No. 5 (May, 1960).

Bavinck, Herman. *The Doctrine of God.* William Hendriksen, trans. Grand Rapids: Baker Book House, 1977.

———. *Our Reasonable Faith.* Henry Zylstra, trans. Grand Rapids: Baker Book House, 1978.

———. *The Philosophy of Revelation.* Grand Rapids: Wm. B. Eerdmans Publishing Co., 1953.

Berkhof, Louis. *The Assurance of Faith.* Grand Rapids: Wm. B. Eerdmans Publishing Co., 2nd ed., 1939.

———. *The History of Christian Doctrines.* Grand Rapids: Baker Book House, 1976.

———. *Systematic Theology.* Grand Rapids: Wm. B. Eerdmans Publishing Co., 4th rev. and enlarged ed., 1965.

Berkouwer, Gerrit Cornelis. *Studies in Dogmatics.* Grand Rapids: Wm. B. Eerdmans Publishing Co., 1952–76. 14 vols.

Bloesch, Donald G. *Essentials of Evangelical Theology.* San Francisco: Harper and Row, 1978. 2 vols.

Boettner, Loraine. *Immortality.* Philadelphia: The Presbyterian and Reformed Publishing Co., 1962.

———. *The Millennium.* Philadelphia: The Presbyterian and Reformed Publishing Co., 1964.

———. *The Reformed Doctrine of Predestination.* Philadelphia: The Presbyterian and Reformed Publishing Co., 1963.

———. *Studies in Theology.* Philadelphia: The Presbyterian and Reformed Publishing Co., 1964.

*This is a select bibliography containing all the works cited in this volume as well as other selected theology books. It is not meant to be exhaustive. The publication date given is the printing date, not necessarily the date of the copyright.

405

Boice, James Montgomery. *The Sovereign God*. Downers Grove, Ill.: InterVarsity Press, 1978.

Bruce, Frederick Fyvie. *Commentary on the Book of the Acts* in New International Commentary on the New Testament. Grand Rapids: Wm. B. Eerdmans Publishing Co., 1954.

————. *The Epistle to the Hebrews* in New International Commentary on the New Testament. Grand Rapids: Wm. B. Eerdmans Publishing Co., 1967.

Bruner, Frederick Dale. *A Theology of the Holy Spirit*. Grand Rapids: Wm. B. Eerdmans Publishing Co., 1970.

Buswell, James Oliver. *A Systematic Theology of the Christian Religion*. Grand Rapids: Zondervan Publishing House, 1978. 2 vols. in 1.

Cambron, Mark G. *Bible Doctrines: Beliefs that Matter*. Grand Rapids: Zondervan Publishing House, 1977.

Carnell, Edward John. *An Introduction to Christian Apologetics*. Grand Rapids: Wm. B. Eerdmans Publishing Co., 1964.

Chafer, Lewis Sperry. *Systematic Theology*. Dallas: Dallas Theological Seminary Press, 1948. 8 vols.

Clarkson, John F., et al., eds. *The Church Teaches*. St. Louis: B. Herder Book Co., 1955.

Culp, G. Richard. *Remember Thy Creator*. Grand Rapids: Baker Book House, 1975.

Culver, Robert Duncan. *The Living God*. Wheaton, Ill.: Victor Books, 1978.

Custance, Arthur C. *The Nature of the Forbidden Fruit* in Doorway Papers. Ottawa: Author, 1958.

————. *Without Form and Void*. Brockville, Ontario: Doorway Papers, 1970.

Davidheiser, Bolton. *Evolution and Christian Faith*. Grand Rapids: Baker Book House, 1969.

Davis, John J. *Conquest and Crisis*. Grand Rapids: Baker Book House, 1977.

————. *Paradise to Prison*. Grand Rapids: Baker Book House, 1975.

Deissmann, Gustav Adolf. *Light from the Ancient East*. Grand Rapids: Baker Book House, 1965.

Dickason, C. Fred. *Angels, Elect and Evil*. Chicago: Moody Press, 1976.

Dodd, C. H. *The Epistle of Paul to the Romans* in Moffatt New Testament Commentary. London: Hodder and Stoughton, 1934.

Driver, Samuel Rolles. *The Book of Exodus* in The Cambridge Bible. Cambridge: The University Press, 1911.

Eusebius, Pamphilus. *Ecclesiastical History*. Isaac Boyle, trans. Grand Rapids: Baker Book House, 1962.

Evans, William. *The Great Doctrines of the Bible*. Chicago: Moody Press, rev., 1949.

Feinberg, Charles L. *Premillennialism or Amillennialism?* New York: American Board of Missions to the Jews, 2nd and enlarged ed., 1961.

————. *The Prophecy of Ezekiel*. Chicago: Moody Press, 1975.

Fitch, William. *The Ministry of the Holy Spirit*. Grand Rapids: Zondervan Publishing House, 1974.

Fitzwater, P. B. *Christian Theology*. Grand Rapids: Wm. B. Eerdmans Publishing Co., 1948.

Flannery, Austin P., ed. *Documents of Vatican II*. Grand Rapids: Wm. B. Eerdmans Publishing Co., 1975.

Fortman, Edmund J. *The Triune God.* Philadelphia: Westminster Press, 1972.

Freeman, Hobart E. *An Introduction to the Old Testament Prophets.* Chicago: Moody Press, 1968.

Geisler, Norman L. *A Popular Survey of the Old Testament.* Grand Rapids: Baker Book House, 1977.

Gilluly, James, et al., *Principles of Geology.* San Francisco: W. H. Freeman and Company, 1968.

Gundry, Robert H. *The Church and the Tribulation.* Grand Rapids: Zondervan Publishing House, 1973.

Hammond, T. C. *In Understanding Be Men.* London: InterVarsity Fellowship, 4th ed., 1952.

Harris, R. Laird. *Inspiration and Canonicity of the Bible.* Grand Rapids: Zondervan Publishing House, enlarged and rev., 1969.

Harrison, Everett F., ed. *Baker's Dictionary of Theology.* Grand Rapids: Baker Book House, 1978.

Harrison, Roland Kenneth. *Introduction to the Old Testament.* Grand Rapids: Wm. B. Eerdmans Publishing Co., 1969.

Hendriksen, William. *Exposition of Philippians* in New Testament Commentary. Grand Rapids: Baker Book House, 1974.

_____. *Exposition of the Gospel According to Matthew* in New Testament Commentary. Grand Rapids: Baker Book House, 1973.

Henry, Carl F. H., ed. *Basic Christian Doctrines.* Grand Rapids: Baker Book House, 1979.

Herskovits, Melville F. *Cultural Anthropology.* New York: Alfred A. Knopf, 1955.

Hiebert, D. Edmond. *An Introduction to the New Testament.* Chicago: Moody Press, 1977. 3 vols.

_____. *The Thessalonian Epistles.* Chicago: Moody Press, 1971.

Hodge, Charles. *Commentary on the Epistle to the Romans.* Grand Rapids: Wm. B. Eerdmans Publishing Co., 1972.

_____. *Systematic Theology.* Grand Rapids: Wm. B. Eerdmans Publishing Co., 1952. 3 vols.

Hoekema, Anthony A. *The Bible and the Future.* Grand Rapids: Wm. B. Eerdmans Publishing Co., 1979.

_____. *Holy Spirit Baptism.* Grand Rapids: Wm. B. Eerdmans Publishing Co., 1972.

Hoeksema, Herman. *Reformed Dogmatics.* Grand Rapids: Reformed Free Publishing Association, 1966.

Howard, David M. *By the Power of the Holy Spirit.* Downers Grove, Ill.: InterVarsity Press, 1973.

Hoyt, Herman A. *An Exposition of the Book of Revelation.* Winona Lake, Ind.: Brethren Missionary Herald Co., 1966.

Josephus, Flavius. *The Works of Flavius Josephus.* William Whiston, trans. Edinburgh: William P. Nimmo and Co., n.d.

Keil, Carl Friedrich. *The Twelve Minor Prophets* in Biblical Commentary on the Old Testament. James Martin, trans. Grand Rapids: Wm. B. Eerdmans Publishing Co., 1971. 2 vols.

Kent, Homer A. *The Freedom of God's Sons.* Grand Rapids: Baker Book House, 1976.

Kepler, Thomas S., comp. *Contemporary Religious Thought*. New York: Abingdon Press, 1941.

Kidner, Derek. *Genesis* in Tyndale Old Testament Commentaries. Downers Grove, Ill.: InterVarsity Press, 1972.

Kittel, Gerhard, and Gerhard Friedrich, eds. *Theological Dictionary of the New Testament*. Geoffrey W. Bromiley, trans. Grand Rapids: Wm. B. Eerdmans Publishing Co., 1964–76. 10 vols.

Kromminga, John H. *All One Body We*. Grand Rapids: Wm. B. Eerdmans Publishing Co., 1970.

Kuen, Alfred. *I Will Build My Church*. Ruby Lindblad, trans. Chicago: Moody Press, 1971.

Kuyper, Abraham, *The Work of the Holy Spirit*. Grand Rapids: Wm. B. Eerdmans Publishing Co., 1956.

Ladd, George Eldon. *A Theology of the New Testament*. Grand Rapids: Wm. B. Eerdmans Publishing Co., 1974.

Leith, John H., ed. *Creeds of the Churches*. Chicago: Aldine Publishing Co., 1963.

Leupold, Herbert Carl. *Exposition of Genesis*. Grand Rapids: Baker Book House, 1974. 2 vols.

Marshall, I. Howard. *Christian Beliefs*. Chicago: InterVarsity Press, 1963.

McClain, Alva J. *The Greatness of the Kingdom*. Chicago: Moody Press, 1968.

McDowell, Joslin, comp. *Evidence That Demands a Verdict*. San Bernardino: Campus Crusade for Christ, 1972.

———, comp. *More Evidence That Demands a Verdict*. San Bernardino: Campus Crusade for Christ, 1975.

Metzger, Bruce M. *The Text of the New Testament*. New York: Oxford University Press, 1968.

Moffatt, James. "The Revelation of St. John the Divine" in Vol. V of *The Expositor's Greek Testament*. W. Robertson Nicoll, ed. Grand Rapids: Wm. B. Eerdmans Publishing Co., 1951.

Morris, Henry M. *The Genesis Record*. San Diego: Creation-Life Publishers, 1976.

Morris, Leon. *The Apostolic Preaching of the Cross*. Grand Rapids: Wm. B. Eerdmans Publishing Co., 1956.

———. *Glory in the Cross*. Grand Rapids: Baker Book House, 1979.

———. *The Gospel According to John* in New International Commentary on the New Testament. Grand Rapids: Wm. B. Eerdmans Publishing Co., 1973.

———. *Spirit of the Living God*. Chicago: InterVarsity Press, 1960.

Mounce, Robert H. *The Book of Revelation* in New International Commentary on the New Testament. Grand Rapids: Wm. B. Eerdmans Publishing Co., 1977.

Müller, Jacobus J. *The Epistles of Paul to the Philippians and to Philemon* in New International Commentary on the New Testament. Grand Rapids: Wm. B. Eerdmans Publishing Co., 1974.

Mullins, Edgar Young. *The Christian Religion in Its Doctrinal Expression*. Philadelphia: The Judson Press, 1954.

Murray, John. *The Epistle to the Romans* in New International Commentary on the New Testament. Grand Rapids: Wm. B. Eerdmans Publishing Co., 1971.

Pache, René. *The Inspiration and Authority of Scripture*. Helen I. Needham, trans. Chicago: Moody Press, 1969.

_____. *The Person and Work of the Holy Spirit.* J. D. Emerson, trans. Chicago: Moody Press, 1977.

_____. *The Return of Jesus Christ.* William Sanford LaSor, trans. Chicago: Moody Press, 1955.

Packer, James Innell. *Evangelism and the Sovereignty of God.* Chicago: InterVarsity Press, 1967.

_____. *Knowing God.* Downers Grove, Ill.: InterVarsity Press, 1973.

Pentecost, J. Dwight. *The Divine Comforter.* Chicago: Moody Press, 1975.

_____. *Things to Come.* Grand Rapids: Dunham Publishing Co., 1966.

_____. *Your Adversary the Devil.* Grand Rapids: Zondervan Publishing House, 1973.

Pieper, Franz August Otto. *Christian Dogmatics.* St. Louis: Concordia Publishing House, 1950–57. 4 vols.

Pinnock, Clark H. *Biblical Revelation.* Chicago: Moody Press, 1976.

_____, ed. *Grace Unlimited.* Minneapolis: Bethany Fellowship, 1975.

Purkiser, W. T., et al. *God, Man, and Salvation.* Kansas City, Mo.: Beacon Hill Press of Kansas City, 1977.

Radmacher, Earl D. *What the Church Is All About.* Chicago: Moody Press, 1978.

Ramm, Bernard. *The Christian View of Science and Scripture.* Grand Rapids: Wm. B. Eerdmans Publishing Co., 1954.

Ridderbos, Herman. *The Coming of the Kingdom.* Raymond O. Zorn, ed. H. de Jongste, trans. Philadelphia: The Presbyterian and Reformed Publishing Co., 1962.

_____. *Paul: An Outline of His Theology.* John De Witt, trans. Grand Rapids: Wm. B. Eerdmans Publishing Co., 1977.

Roberts, Alexander, and James Donaldson, eds. *The Ante-Nicene Fathers.* Buffalo: The Christian Literature Publishing Co., 1885. 9 vols.

Roucek, Joseph S. *The Study of Foreign Languages.* New York: Philosophical Library, 1968.

Ryrie, Charles Caldwell. *The Basis of the Premillennial Faith.* New York: Loizeaux Brothers, 1958.

_____. *The Holy Spirit.* Chicago: Moody Press, 1965.

_____. *The Grace of God.* Chicago: Moody Press, 1966.

Saucy, Robert L. *The Bible: Breathed from God.* Wheaton, Ill.: Victor Books, 1978.

_____. *The Church in God's Program.* Chicago: Moody Press, 1977.

Schaeffer, Francis A. *Death in the City.* Downers Grove, Ill.: InterVarsity Press, 1972.

Schaff, Philip. *History of the Christian Church.* Grand Rapids: Wm. B. Eerdmans Publishing Co., 3rd ed., 1950. 8 vols.

Shedd, William G. T. *Dogmatic Theology.* Grand Rapids: Zondervan Publishing House, n.d. 3 vols.

Simpson, E. K., and F. F. Bruce. *Commentary on the Epistles to the Ephesians and the Colossians* in New International Commentary on the New Testament. Grand Rapids: Wm. B. Eerdmans Publishing Co., 1975.

Smeaton, George. *The Apostles' Doctrine of the Atonement.* Grand Rapids: Zondervan Publishing House, 1957.

Stanton, Gerald B. *Kept From the Hour.* Grand Rapids: Zondervan Publishing House, 1956.

Stott, J. R. W. *The Epistles of John* in Tyndale New Testament Commentaries. Grand Rapids: Wm. B. Eerdmans Publishing Co., 1969.

Strauss, Lehman. *The Third Person.* New York: Loizeaux Brothers, 1954.

Strong, Augustus Hopkins. *Systematic Theology.* Old Tappan, N.J.: Fleming H. Revell Co., 1969. 3 vols. in 1.

Swadesh, Morris. *The Origin and Diversification of Language.* Chicago: Aldine-Atherton, Inc., 1971.

Swete, Henry Barclay. *The Holy Spirit in the New Testament.* Grand Rapids: Baker Book House, 1964.

Tan, Paul Lee. *The Interpretation of Prophecy.* Winona Lake, Ind.: BMH Books, Inc., 1974.

Taylor, Vincent. *The Atonement in New Testament Teaching.* London: The Epworth Press, 1941.

Thomas, Robert L. *Understanding Spiritual Gifts.* Chicago: Moody Press, 1978.

Unger, Merrill F. *The Baptizing Work of the Holy Spirit.* Wheaton, Ill.: Van Kampen Press, 1953.

————. *Biblical Demonology.* Wheaton, Ill.: Scripture Press Publications, 1972.

Van Til, Cornelius. *The Defense of the Faith.* Philadelphia: The Presbyterian and Reformed Publishing Co., rev. and abridged, 1963.

Vos, Geerhardus, *Biblical Theology.* Grand Rapids: Wm. B. Eerdmans Publishing Co., 1977.

Waltke, Bruce K. *Creation and Chaos.* Portland, Ore.: Western Conservative Baptist Seminary, 1974.

Walvoord, John F. *The Blessed Hope and the Tribulation.* Grand Rapids: Zondervan Publishing House, 1976.

————, ed. *Inspiration and Interpretation.* Grand Rapids: Wm. B. Eerdmans Publishing Co., 1957.

————. *Jesus Christ Our Lord.* Chicago: Moody Press, 1971.

————. *The Millennial Kingdom.* Grand Rapids: Zondervan Publishing House, 1978.

Warfield, Benjamin Breckinridge. *The Inspiration and Authority of the Bible.* Samuel G. Craig, ed. Grand Rapids: Baker Book House, 1964.

Webb, Robert Alexander. *The Reformed Doctrine of Adoption.* Grand Rapids: Wm. B. Eerdmans Publishing Co., 1947.

Westcott, Brooke Foss. *The Epistles to the Hebrews.* Grand Rapids: Wm. B. Eerdmans Publishing Co., 1973.

Whipple, Fred L. "The History of the Solar System," *Adventures in Earth History.* Preston Cloud, ed. San Francisco: W. H. Freeman, 1970.

Whitcomb, John C. "Esther," *The Wycliffe Bible Commentary.* Charles F. Pfeiffer and Everett F. Harrison, eds. Chicago: Moody Press, 1976.

Wood, Leon. *A Commentary on Daniel.* Grand Rapids: Zondervan Publishing House, 1976.

————. *The Holy Spirit in the Old Testament.* Grand Rapids: Zondervan Publishing House, 1976.

Young, Davis A. *Creation and the Flood.* Grand Rapids: Baker Book House, 1977.

Young, Edward J. *The Book of Isaiah.* Grand Rapids: Wm. B. Eerdmans Publishing Co., 1969–72. 3 vols.

———. *An Introduction to the Old Testament.* Grand Rapids: Wm. B. Eerdmans Publishing Co., 1956.

———.. *My Servants the Prophets.* Grand Rapids: Wm. B. Eerdmans Publishing Co., 1955.

———. *The Prophecy of Daniel.* Grand Rapids: Wm. B. Eerdmans Publishing Co., 1975.

Index of Subjects

Abraham's bosom, 339

Abyss: Satan's temporary prison, 148, 356f.

Accident theory of the death of Christ, 232

Adoption, doctrine of, 285f.

Advent of Christ: first, see Incarnation; second, 335ff.; relation of first to second, 215

Agnosticism: opposed to theism, 33f.; unsatisfactory position, 34

Amillennial view of the future, 395

Analogy: argument for revelation from, 44

Angel of the Lord, and the trinity in the OT, 91; preincarnate Christ, 209f.

Angelology, 131ff.; see also Angels

Angels, doctrine of, 131ff.; origin of, 133; nature of, 133ff.; classification of, 137ff.; good angels, 137ff.; their works, 144f.; evil angels, 140ff.; their works, 145ff.; destiny of angels, 147f.

Annihilationists: on death, 340; on eternal punishment, 393f.

Anthropology, 149ff.; see also Man; definition of, 149

Anthropomorphisms: used of the substance of God, 76

Antichrist, 361

Apollinarians: on the person of Christ, 207

Apologetics: involved in systematic theology, 20

A Priori argument for revelation, 43f.

Archangels: description of, 139

Archeology: involved in exegetical theology, 19f.; proves OT records, 57, 70

Arians: on the person of Christ, 207

Armageddon: Christ's coming to, 358

Arminian: view of imputed sin, 187; theory of atonement, 233f.

Ascension of Christ, 248f.

Assurance: result of faith, 274

Athanasian Creed on trinity, 90

Atheism: practical, dogmatic, and virtual, 32f.; unnatural and unsatisfactory, 33; opposed to creation record, 115ff.

Atonement: various theories of, 231ff.; idea of satisfaction present in, 237ff.; limited or unlimited?, 240ff., 260; and Christ's resurrection, 248

Attributes of God: non-moral, 80ff.; moral, 83ff.; see also God, attributes of; not surrendered by the incarnate Christ, 215ff.

Authority: Scriptures only true source, 41; contrasted with inspiration, 63, 66

Babylon: judgment of, 390

Babylonian legends, and the history of the OT, 57

Baptism: of Spirit, 255; of water and regeneration, 280; an ordinance of the church, 323ff.; its significance, 324f.; its mode and subjects, 325f.

Beast: judgment of, 355f., 386f.; activities of, 360f.

Belief: see Faith

Believers: judgment of, 389

Benevolence: an attribute of God, 86

Bible: an embodiment of the divine revelation, 43ff.; its indestructibility, 45f.; its character, 46f.; its claim to revelation, 48f.; its

413

Index of Scripture References

425